Working with Vulnerable Families

A Partnership Approach

Second Edition

Poverty, domestic violence, marginalisation and drug and alcohol dependence are just some of the issues faced by many Australian families. Now in its second edition, *Working with Vulnerable Families* provides a comprehensive and evidence-based introduction to family-centred practice in Australia. It explores the ways in which health, education and social welfare professionals can support and protect children and their families.

Fully revised and updated, with 8 new chapters, the book examines recent research and programs on relationship-based family support, parental substance misuse, working with Aboriginal and Torres Strait Islander families, and children and family violence. It encourages readers to 'think child, think family, think community' in order to promote the development, wellbeing and safety of young children and future generations.

Each chapter features learning goals, local case studies, reflective questions and links to online resources to help reinforce and extend the reader's understanding. Written by a diverse team of experts from around Australia, this is an indispensable resource for students and practitioners alike.

Fiona Arney is Professor and Chair of Child Protection and Director of the Australian Centre for Child Protection at the University of South Australia.

Dorothy Scott is Emeritus Professor and has an adjunct academic position at the Australian Centre for Child Protection at the University of South Australia, and is also an honorary Professorial Fellow at the University of Melbourne.

WITHDRAWN

LIVERPOOL JMU LIBRARY

3 1111 01440 2836

Working with Vulnerable Families

A Partnership Approach

Second Edition

Edited by
Fiona Arney and Dorothy Scott

CAMBRIDGE
UNIVERSITY PRESS

477 Williamstown Road, Port Melbourne, VIC 3207, Australia

Published in the United States of America by Cambridge University Press, New York

Cambridge University Press is part of the University of Cambridge.

It furthers the University's mission by disseminating knowledge in the pursuit of education, learning, and research at the highest international levels of excellence.

www.cambridge.org
Information on this title: www.cambridge.org/9781107610668

© Cambridge University Press 2013

This publication is in copyright. Subject to statutory exception and to the provisions of relevant collective licensing agreements, no reproduction of any part may take place without the written permission of Cambridge University Press.

First published 2010
Reprinted 2011, 2012
Second edition 2013

Cover designed by Leigh Ashforth (Watershed Design)
Typeset by Integra Software Services Pvt. Ltd
Printed in China by C & C Offset Printing Co. Ltd

A catalogue record for this publication is available from the British Library

A Cataloguing-in-Publication entry is available from the catalogue of the National Library of Australia at www.nla.gov.au

ISBN 978-1-107-61066-8 Paperback

Reproduction and communication for educational purposes
The Australian *Copyright Act 1968* (the Act) allows a maximum of one chapter or 10% of the pages of this work, whichever is the greater, to be reproduced and/or communicated by any educational institution for its educational purposes provided that the educational institution (or the body that administers it) has given a remuneration notice to Copyright Agency Limited (CAL) under the Act.

For details of the CAL licence for educational institutions contact:

Copyright Agency Limited
Level 15, 233 Castlereagh Street
Sydney NSW 2000
Facsimile: (02) 9394 7601
E-mail: info@copyright.com.au

Cambridge University Press has no responsibility for the persistence or accuracy of URLs for external or third-party internet websites referred to in this publication, and does not guarantee that any content on such websites is, or will remain, accurate or appropriate.

This book is dedicated to our partners,
Alwin Chong and Alan Clayton

Foreword

Nelson Mandela suggested that the soul of a nation was reflected in how well it treated its most vulnerable; Hilary Clinton used an old African saying, 'it takes a village to raise a child' for the title of a book. Both quotations are pertinent to this book.

We live in a world of pressures – to earn lots of money, to be smart, to be successful, to look like a film star, to have a big house, to cook like a TV hostess, to eat like a king, to work long hours, to have lots of stuff. Where are our children in all of this frenetic activity? How can we be parents as well as workers? Where are our role models? How valued are the carers of our children? How much do we value children for themselves? What if my child does not look or behave like the one on the back of the Farex packet smiling sweetly at dinnertime? Does anyone care? The authors of this book do, and they have taken a determined and well-researched path to help us understand and help vulnerable families in today's challenging society.

I feel honoured to have been asked to write the foreword for this wonderful book, which is so very timely for Australian parents, children and those who work in the range of services aimed at helping them grow through the most vulnerable times of their lives. The book has emerged from the Australian Centre for Child Protection at the University of South Australia under the leadership of its current Director, Professor Fiona Arney and its foundation Director, Emeritus Professor Dorothy Scott. The Centre showcases a wonderful blend of research, advocacy, practitioner training and support.

The public health approach to child abuse and neglect suggested here is a sensible and urgent one. To continue to observe the increases in child abuse substantiations and to only respond to the crisis end in punitive ways is both illogical and inhumane. Approaches that attempt to prevent families reaching such crisis situations and that harness all possible ways to enhance family functioning in this challenging 21st century are clearly the way in which child abuse and neglect will be reduced. A public health approach to child maltreatment means that we need to know the causes, to intervene in effective ways along the various pathways and to build the capacity of practitioners to do so.

I appreciate the ways in which the book relates the understandings of how children and parents interact and develop and how, for so many families, the challenges of parenting make the family vulnerable due to a variety of different scenarios. Understanding these contexts is essential if we are to deliver the services that will really help. I have just become a grandmother, which is a joy beyond imagination, and this little one is surrounded by love and care, with easy access to his child health nurse and a good GP and his nursery placement is already being planned. I often imagine the circumstances of other children not so blessed and feel anguish for them and their families.

From the various chapters emerge a holistic, sensible, caring and evidence-based set of approaches to help vulnerable families, with many real-life examples of what works best. Although this has an Australian focus (good for us that we have at last some great home-grown examples!) this book is relevant for all children, all families and communities everywhere. The principles apply wherever children are being born and nurtured.

Fiona J. Stanley

AC Patron, Telethon Institute for Child Health Research

Distinguished Research Professor, University of Western Australia

Vice-Chancellor's Fellow, University of Melbourne

FFA, FASSA, MSc, MD, FFPHM, FAFPHM, FRACP, FRANZCOG, Hon DSc, Hon DUniv,

Hon MD, Hon FRACGP, Hon FRCPCH, Hon MD, Hon DSc, Hon LLB (*honoris causa*)

Contents

Foreword – Fiona Stanley   *page* vii
List of figures   xiv
List of tables   xv
List of text boxes   xvi
Contributors   xvii
Acknowledgements   xxiv

Introduction   **1**
Fiona Arney and Dorothy Scott

1 Think child, think family, think community   **6**
Dorothy Scott, Fiona Arney and Graham Vimpani
   Introduction   6
   Descriptive knowledge   7
   Genetic influences   8
   Parent–child attachment   8
   Experience-based brain development   10
   Parenting adaptability   11
   Family theory   12
   An ecological perspective   13
   Social networks   14
   Communities and social capital   16
   Prescriptive knowledge   17
   Family-centred practice   18
   Relationship-based practice   20
   Conclusion   22

2 Working within and between organisations   **24**
Dorothy Scott
   Introduction   24
   Contemporary policy context   25
   How we play our roles   28
   Working together   31
   Conclusion   40

3 Family-centred practice in early childhood settings   42
Dorothy Scott
   Introduction   42
   Looking back to see ahead   43
   Contemporary policy context   46
   Innovative exemplars   47
   Common principles   53
   Conclusion   55

4 Including fathers in work with vulnerable families   57
Richard Fletcher
   Introduction   57
   Has fathering changed?   58
   Fatherhood in the law   59
   The task for child and family workers   60
   Barriers for fathers: internal constraints   60
   Barriers for fathers: opportunity constraints   61
   Barriers for fathers: service constraints   62
   Interaction of barriers   63
   Implications for services   63
   Evidence of fathers' impact   66
   What about 'bad' dads?   68
   Strengths-based practice with fathers   70
   A pilot home visiting service for fathers whose
       partners have postnatal depression   72
   A group program for men to end violent and abusive behaviour   73
   Conclusion   75

**5 Parenting in a new culture: working with
   refugee families**   77
Kerry Lewig, Fiona Arney, Mary Salveron and Maria Barredo
   Introduction   77
   Who are refugees?   78
   Australia's Refugee and Humanitarian Program   79
   Resettlement in Australia   80
   The refugee experience   81
   Working with refugee families   86
   The challenges of parenting in a new culture   87
   Challenges in working with families from refugee backgrounds   94
   What helps practitioners in their work with refugee families?   96
   Conclusion   101

6 Working with Aboriginal families   103
Gary Robinson and Sarah Mares
   Introduction   103
   Demography   104

Policy context   105
Parenting and family functioning   108
Parenting interventions   108
Culture and parenting   109
Adaptation of mainstream and evidence-based programs
    for Aboriginal families   110
Identifying and responding to vulnerability in remote and
    urban contexts   113
Conclusion   121

**7 Family decision-making approaches for Aboriginal
and Torres Strait Islander families**   **123**
Fiona Arney, Alwin Chong and Kate McGuinness
Introduction   123
What can we learn from the past?   124
The Stolen Generations   125
Intergenerational/transgenerational issues   126
The involvement of Aboriginal families and communities in
    contemporary child protection systems   128
The role of family decision-making   130
Family Group Conferencing in Alice Springs: a case study   133
Conclusion   140

**8 The relationship between family support workers
and families where child neglect is a concern**   **142**
Elizabeth Reimer
Introduction   143
Parent characteristics   146
The key is trust   148
Being 'real in role'   148
Achieving a collaborative approach   151
Important worker characteristics   153
Conclusion   159

9 Working with parents with substance misuse problems   **160**
Sharon Dawe and Paul Harnett
Introduction   160
Outcomes for children in families with parental
    substance misuse   161
The intervention context: a brief overview of interventions
    that help families with parental substance misuse 162
The PuP Integrated Framework: a model of assessment to
    guide clinical practice   165
The importance of setting goals   172
Conclusion   175

10 Children in the midst of family and domestic violence   **176**
Cathy Humphreys and Menka Tsantefski
Introduction   176
Understanding the knowledge base   177
Prevalence and gendered issues   178
Issues of diversity   179
Adult and child victims   181
Poly-victimisation for children   183
Issues for men as fathers   183
Further adult problems: drugs and alcohol and mental health   184
Practice responses   185
Understanding the policy and legal contexts   189
Multi-agency advocacy at a strategic and operational level   190
Conclusion   192

11 Attachment theory: from concept to supporting
children in out-of-home care   **194**
Sara McLean
Introduction   194
What is attachment theory?   195
Early experimental studies of attachment   195
Overview of attachment theory and child development   197
The importance of theory and evidence in child
     protection practice   199
Limitations to our knowledge about the role of attachment
     for children in out-of-home care   200
What examples of conceptual blurring are there in child
     protection practice?   202
Attachment can be misunderstood in practice   204
Practice example 1: some children don't need attachment   205
Practice example 2: attachment is a close and trusting relationship   207
Practice example 3: a child should have one primary attachment   209
Enhancing practice in out-of-home care   211
Conclusion   212

12 Understanding the journey of parents whose children
are in out-of-home care   **213**
Mary Salveron and Fiona Arney
Introduction   213
Characteristics of parents of children in out-of-home care   215
Involving parents and families in care and protection practice   216
Maintaining connections between children in out-of-home
     care and their parents   217
Negotiation and reconstruction of parent identities after child removal   218

The impact of child removal on parental emotions and sense of self 218
Fighting internal and external battles 220
Reconstructing parental identity and recovery after child removal 224
The role of parents 225
The role of workers 228
The role of social support and respectful relationships 230
The Parents Plus Playgroups: an innovative program for parents
who have had their children removed from their care 231
Conclusion 233

**13 Spreading and implementing promising approaches
in child and family services** **235**
*Fiona Arney, Kerry Lewig, Robyn Mildon, Aron Shlonsky,
Christine Gibson and Leah Bromfield*
Introduction 235
The role of implementation in improving outcomes for families 236
Developing a theory of change 238
Factors that influence program adoption and implementation 239
The new program or practice 240
The practitioner 240
The organisation 241
The wider service environment 241
Types of implementation frameworks 242
Conclusion 245

References 247
Index 291

List of figures

Figure 2.1   Levels of analysis for breadth of service provider role
              performance (based on Scott, 2009)   *page* 30
Figure 6.1   Potential contributors to vulnerability   115
Figure 9.1   The Integrated Framework   167
Figure 12.1   Parental emotions surrounding removal of their child or children
              and after removal   219
Figure 12.2   Aspects of parents fighting for and fighting against (with internal
              and external dimensions)   221
Figure 12.3   Negotiating and reconstructing parental identity after removal 225
Figure 12.4   Characteristics of a positive parent–worker relationship   229

List of tables

Table 5.1   Major source countries of refugees at the end of 2011
            (UNHCR, 2011)   *page* 79
Table 9.1   The Integrated Framework: considerations for assessment
            and intervention   173
Table 12.1 Processes, cognitive and emotional tasks and individual strategies
            and behaviours associated with self-recovery and negotiating and
            reconstructing parental identity after child removal   226

List of text boxes

Box 5.1   Australian Humanitarian Program visa categories   *page* 80
Box 6.1   Practice points: working with communities   120
Box 6.2   Practice points: working with individuals   120
Box 9.1   The case of Julie and Beckie   164
Box 9.2   Julie's first goal   174
Box 13.1   Scared Straight   237

Contributors

Professor **FIONA ARNEY** is the Chair of Child Protection and Director of the Australian Centre for Child Protection at the University of South Australia. Fiona was Deputy Director of the Centre until she moved to the Menzies School of Health Research in early 2010 to establish and lead their Child Protection Research Program. With 16 years' research experience with children, parents, families and practitioners, she has a strong body of research, especially in relation to Aboriginal children and families. Fiona is a member of research teams examining the factors affecting the use of research in policy and practice and the organisational and individual preconditions required for the adoption and adaptation of promising practices.

MARIA BARREDO is a cross-cultural facilitator and cultural competency trainer with over 20 years of experience working with migrant and refugee communities. She is working in Central Australian Aboriginal Congress in Alice Springs managing a primary health care clinic servicing the Aboriginal population in Central Australia. Maria was a Board Director in the Australia Refugee Association from 2003 to 2009; a member of the South Australian Multicultural and Ethnic Affairs Commission (from 2003 to 2008), and a National Chair of Women's Policy with the Federation of Ethnic Communities Council of Australia for four years. Maria was the senior adviser to the Archbishop of Adelaide as well as Director of Multicultural Affairs of the Catholic Archdiocese of Adelaide for seven years. Prior to that she was a regional coordinator of the Migrant and Refugee Settlement Program under the Migrant Resource Centre in SA.

Associate Professor **LEAH BROMFIELD** is the Deputy Director of the Australian Centre for Child Protection at the University of South Australia. Prior to her appointment to UniSA in 2010, she was a Senior Research Fellow at the Australian Institute of Family Studies and managed the National Child Protection Clearinghouse. She has completed a PhD on the topic of chronic maltreatment and cumulative harm in a child protection sample. She has broad research interests and experience in the fields of child abuse prevention, child protection and out-of-home care. Her areas of specialty are child protection systems, chronic maltreatment and cumulative harm, and research into policy/practice.

ALWIN CHONG is a Wakamin man from Far North Queensland and is currently the Transition Manager with the Aboriginal Health Council of South Australia Inc. (AHCSA). He previously worked with the Menzies School of Health Research as the Indigenous Strategy and Development Coordinator in Darwin. Prior to relocating to Darwin, Alwin worked with the Aboriginal Health Council of SA (AHCSA) as the Senior Research and Ethics Officer for 11 years. An essential component of the position was the management of the Aboriginal Health Research Ethics Committee (AHCSA), a subcommittee of the Council and the peak ethics body for Aboriginal Health in South Australia, which involves working with researchers. Alwin has undertaken extensive research into and promoted Indigenous Management practices, conducted an exclusive literature review, delivered seminar papers and collaborated with several academic colleagues who have incorporated Indigenous Management practices into their teaching modules

SHARON DAWE is a Professor in Clinical Psychology at Griffith University. She has been working as a researcher and clinician in the field of substance misuse and mental health for over 20 years, beginning her clinical career at Odyssey House, Auckland, New Zealand. She then moved to the United Kingdom, where she worked at the Maudsley Hospital, London, as a clinical psychologist in the drug dependence unit. Her PhD, completed at the Institute of Psychiatry, University of London, investigated the neural mechanisms involved in drug reward. Her current work focuses on reducing child maltreatment in high-risk families with parental substance abuse and mental illness. She has developed the Parents Under Pressure program in collaboration with Paul H. Harnett of the University of Queensland. She holds an adjunct position with the Australian Centre for Child Protection.

Dr **RICHARD FLETCHER**, PhD, taught science in NSW, Kenya and the United States before returning to Australia to pioneer domestic violence prevention within Health Promotion. He subsequently initiated Men's and Boys' Health as areas of study and is currently Leader of the Fathers and Families Research Program at the Family Action Centre, Faculty of Health, University of Newcastle, NSW.

CHRISTINE GIBSON is the Community Research Liaison Coordinator at the Australian Centre for Child Protection at the University of South Australia. Previously she was Manager of Research and Quality Assurance for UnitingCare Burnside (a respected

NSW child welfare agency) and, prior to that, a Lecturer in the School of Social Work at the University of New South Wales and a consultant. Her practice has been in the fields of child and family welfare, out-of-home care, domestic violence, tenancy and immigration. As well as having substantial experience with both the conduct and the oversight of studies evaluating service interventions, she has conducted research on out-of-home care, homeless children and the application of diffusion of innovation theory to child welfare. Christine has contributed to policy debate and law reform at national and state levels. She holds a Bachelor degree in Social Work and a Masters degree in Policy Studies.

PAUL HARNETT is a Senior Lecturer in Clinical Psychology at the University of Queensland. He has worked clinically and conducted research in the area of child protection since 1987. He spent many years working as a Clinical Psychologist in a specialist child protection team at the Maudsley Hospital in London. In Australia, he has worked as a Clinical Psychologist in care and protection for the NSW Department of Community Services. Over the past 12 years his work has focused on developing an evidence-based assessment model for child protection (Capacity to Change, C2C) and the Parents Under Pressure (PuP) program, an internationally recognised training program for clinicians working with families in which there are many difficult life circumstances such as anxiety, substance misuse and family conflict and helping parents facing such adversities to develop positive and secure relationships with their children. A major motivating force for his work are the memories of the young children he cared for while working as a residential care worker in a South London children's home in the late 1980s.

CATHY HUMPHREYS is Professor of Social Work at the University of Melbourne. For five years she held the Alfred Felton Chair of Child and Family Welfare, a professorship established in collaboration with the Alfred Felton Trust, the Department of Social Work at the University of Melbourne and the Centre for Excellence for Child and Family Welfare in Victoria, the peak body for more than 95 child and family welfare agencies in Victoria. The Chair is now supported by the University of Melbourne-Sector Research Partnership, a consortium of 14 Victorian community sector organisations that are driving research in the children, youth and families area. A sustained program of research in the areas of domestic and family violence, out of home care and research utilization has now been established. Cathy Humphreys has extensive practice experience, having worked as a social work practitioner in the mental health, domestic violence, and children, youth and families sector for 16 years before becoming a social work academic.

KERRY LEWIG is a project manager at the Australian Centre for Child Protection, University of South Australia. Her research interests prior to joining the Australian Centre for Child Protection have been in the areas of work satisfaction, engagement, work stress and burnout in the human services and volunteer sectors. Kerry's work at the Centre has included projects that have sought to understand the role that research plays in child protection practice and policy-making, the factors influencing the implementation and dissemination of promising child and family welfare programs, and the reasons why newly arrived refugee families come into contact with the child protection system and how these families may be best supported to adjust to the challenges of parenting in a new culture. Her current research interest is in the field of child protection workforce retention and wellbeing. Kerry is a registered psychologist and holds a Masters degree in Organisational Psychology.

Dr **SARAH MARES** is a child and family psychiatrist with an established clinical and academic interest in the peri-natal and early childhood periods and in prevention and intervention with highly disadvantaged populations, including those involved with child protection services, Indigenous families in remote communities and refugee and asylum-seeking families. She is currently Senior Research Fellow at the Centre for Child Development and Education, Menzies School of Health Research in Darwin and prior to this was Senior Staff Specialist in the Alternate Care Clinic for children in out-of-home care at Redbank House in Western Sydney. She is an experienced multidisciplinary educator, supervisor and consultant. Her publications include Mares, Newman & Warren (2005/2011), *An Introduction to Clinical Skills in Infant Mental Health: The First Three Years*, ACER Press, and Newman & Mares (eds) (2012), *Contemporary Approaches to Infant and Child Mental Health*, IP Press.

KATE MCGUINNESS is a Research Fellow in the Centre for Child Development and Education at the Menzies School of Health Research, based in Darwin, Northern Territory. Kate has over 17 years' experience working with children and families as a practitioner, policy adviser and researcher. Kate has worked for a range of government and non-government organisations in Australia, Ireland and the UK including as a paediatic social worker and child protection practitioner. Kate's current research interests focus on the prevention of child abuse and neglect in the Northern Territory, social work practice in culturally diverse contexts and, more broadly, how research can be effectively translated into evidence-informed practice in the human services.

SARA MCLEAN is a registered Psychologist who has been working in child and adolescent mental health since 1997. Her experience includes clinical work in both community teams and in interagency multidisciplinary teams that support children and adolescents with significant and serious mental health and behavioural concerns. Her PhD research focused on challenging and aggressive behaviour among children who have been removed from their family of origin due to abuse or neglect (children living in out-of-home care). This research critically analysed the models and approaches that guide workers' practice in the management of children exhibiting problem behaviours. As a Research Fellow at the Australian Centre for Child Protection, she combines her clinical and research skills to examine the support needs of children in out-of-home care.

Dr **ROBYN MILDON** is the Director of Knowledge Exchange and Implementation at the Parenting Research Centre. Robyn's work focuses on two main areas: the use of effective implementation strategies to improve the utilisation of evidence-informed information and practice and closing the gap between 'what we know' and 'what we do' by improving the science and practice of implementation. Robyn and her team work in partnership with agencies and services to develop, implement and evaluate evidence-based programs and practice approaches to working with families. Robyn has authored and co-authored numerous papers published in peer-reviewed journals and edited book chapters and presented at several national and international conferences, including invited keynote presentations and invited workshops.

ELIZABETH REIMER is an Associate Researcher at the Centre for Children and Young People and Lecturer in the School of Arts and Social Sciences at Southern Cross University. She has previously worked as a PhD candidate at the Australian Centre for Child Protection (University of South Australia), as Senior Policy and Research Officer for the Inquiry into the Child Protection System in the Northern Territory 2010, and as a Policy Officer at NSW Family Services Inc. Elizabeth's research focus includes family support, youth work, prevention and early intervention dimensions of the child wellbeing continuum, child neglect, and personalised ways of working in professional family work relationships.

Associate Professor **GARY ROBINSON** heads the Indigenous Parenting and Family Research Unit within the Centre for Child Development and Education, which is funded to implement innovative programs to improve educational outcomes for Indigenous children. Formerly Principal Research Fellow in Childhood Intervention, Development and Wellbeing at the Charles Darwin University, Gary's ethnographic publications remain influential in approaches to Aboriginal youth suicide and conflict. His publications arising out of the Coordinated Care Trial evaluation reports, the ABCD projects, and the report of the Accelerated Literacy Evaluation have been highly influential. Associate Professor Robinson's recent publications have focused on health service development, mental health services, Indigenous child development and social–emotional wellbeing. The increasing impact of his published research is reflected in the invitation to develop a number of discussion papers to inform the Northern Territory Early Childhood Planning process.

Dr **MARY SALVERON**, one of the founding staff at the Australian Centre for Child Protection in 2005, recently returned to the Centre as Postdoctoral Research Fellow investigating the Signs of Safety approach in Western Australia. Funded by the Department for Child Protection (WA), the research collaboration aims to examine the implementation, delivery and uptake of the Signs of Safety approach and its impact on children, parents, carers, practitioners and other partner organisations/ agencies. Mary has over seven years' experience in the fields of child protection and early childhood and has undertaken research into the factors that help and hinder the spread of innovations in child protection, as well as research and evaluations with diverse populations. Her practice experience also extends to managing the health programs and promotions delivered by a community-controlled Aboriginal organisation in country South Australia.

Emeritus Professor **DOROTHY SCOTT** has an adjunct academic position at the Australian Centre for Child Protection at the University of South Australia, and is also a Professorial Fellow at the University of Melbourne. Dorothy was the Foundation Chair of Child Protection and the inaugural Director of the Australian Centre for Child Protection at the University of South Australia. Previously she was Head of the School of Social Work at the University of Melbourne and, prior to that, the Executive Director of the Ian Potter Foundation. Her clinical practice has been in the fields of child welfare, sexual assault and mental health. Her research has also been in these areas as well as in the fields of maternal and child health, and child protection policy reform. She has been an adviser to national and state governments, and for her services to the community she was awarded the Medal of the Order of Australia and the Centenary Medal.

ARON SHLONSKY is Professor of Evidence Informed Practice at the University of Melbourne Department of Social Work, Associate Professor at the University of Toronto Faculty of Social Work, Scientific Director of the Ontario Child Abuse and Neglect Data System (OCANDS) and Co-Chair of the Campbell Collaboration Social Welfare Coordinating Group. After graduating from UC Berkeley with a doctorate in Social Welfare and a Masters degree in Public Health, Shlonsky was an Assistant Professor at Columbia University School of Social Work. His professional interests include child welfare, the assessment of risk, administrative data analytics, and the use of evidence in practice.

Dr **MENKA TSANTEFSKI** is a Lecturer in Social Work specializing in child and family related subjects. Prior to joining the University of Melbourne, Menka designed and managed programs for families affected by parental substance use and, for over 15 years, provided home-based services to vulnerable children, their parents and extended families in a range of roles and settings. She has also delivered training and secondary consultations to adult-focused services to improve responsiveness to children's needs.

GRAHAM VIMPANI AM is Professor and Head of the Discipline of Paediatrics and Child Health at the University of Newcastle; Clinical Chair of Kaleidoscope: Hunter Children's Health Network within the Hunter New England Area Health Service; and Medical Director of the Child Protection Team of the John Hunter Children's Hospital in Newcastle. He is a community paediatrician with a long-standing interest in promoting child health and development through a range of early intervention strategies that address the support needs of families with infants and young children. He is Co-Chair of the Children's and Young People's Health Priority Task Force in NSW and a member of the Health Care Advisory Council. He is Chair of the Board of NIFTeY Australia (the National Investment for the Early Years), a cross-sectoral advocacy body established in 1999 to promote greater awareness of the importance of the early years of life.

Acknowledgements

We would like to thank the following for their contributions to the book:

- the families, practitioners, policy-makers and researchers who have given so much towards our efforts. By participating in our research, by sharing your wisdom and knowledge, and by collaborating with us in our endeavours, you have made a great contribution to the lives of vulnerable children and their families

- our colleagues at the Australian Centre for Child Protection for their assistance in preparing the manuscript, and particularly to Kate Greenfield for coordinating our efforts and compiling the final draft, and

- our friends and families for their valuable support and patience during our writing efforts.

We would also like to acknowledge the following funding sources for their contributions to the research presented in specific chapters of this book:

- the South Australian Department for Families and Communities for their funding of the Working with Refugee Families project described in Chapter 5

- the Alice Springs Transformation Plan for funding the study of the implementation of Family Group Conferencing in Alice Springs, described in Chapter 7

- Good Beginnings Australia for funding the evaluation of the Parents Plus Program presented in Chapter 12

- the Australian Research Council for supporting the research examining the diffusion of innovations across Australia reported in Chapter 13. This research was supported under the Australian Research Council's Linkage Projects funding scheme (project number LP0669297).

Fiona Arney and Dorothy Scott

Introduction

Fiona Arney and Dorothy Sc[...]

The challenge of ending child abuse is the challenge of break[...]
problems and children's pain.

(UNICEF, A League Table of Child Maltreatment Deaths in Rich Nations, September 2003)

This book is about working with vulnerable parents so that we may prevent child abuse and neglect and enhance the wellbeing of our children.

Who are 'vulnerable families'? In this book, when we refer to families we are talking about children and the adults who care for them, be they mothers, fathers, grandmothers, grandfathers or other extended family members. If we are honest, all parents will acknowledge times when they have felt very vulnerable and when their feelings of vulnerability have impacted upon family life. The birth of a child is a joyous event but brings with it a time of significant change and disruption to families as well as the need for adjustment, which some parents may find overwhelming. Parents can also experience vulnerability when facing natural disasters such as fire or flood; stressful life events such as marital breakdown; the illness or death of a family member or friend; the loss of a job; or eviction. Life challenges such as these can overwhelm a family's ability to cope, but for some it may also provide opportunities for growth and positive change.

All families differ in their ability to manage difficult challenges and have different internal and external resources to draw upon. Internal resources (such as good family attachments, cohesion and communication) and external resources (such as good social support and financial security) have all been shown to help families manage difficult times. Some parents are doubly blessed. Those who have grown up in stable and nurturing families are more likely to have a supportive extended family to help them as they embark on raising their own children. Other parents are not so lucky. Many have not had a childhood grounded in a stable and nurturing family and this disadvantage may be compounded if they have to raise their own children without the support of an extended family. However, history, as we know, is not destiny and many parents who have suffered deprivation in their childhood do make strong supportive 'kin-like' relationships with friends and neighbours who provide support to both them and their children.

...ome situations in which a family's needs cannot be met from within ...sources or their kith and kinship networks, where services can make a ...ontribution to child and family wellbeing. In this new edition we revisit and ... explore some of the knowledge, skills and strategies that service providers ...d in order to work successfully with parents and families, including those with ...ultiple and complex needs who are trying to nurture young children in the face of adversity.

The knowledge and skills required for this work rest on a foundation of values. The values we bring to our work and those of the wider society are fundamental in determining the level of respect and compassion we show to families. In many of the interventions we look at in this book, you will find embedded the principles of 'relationship-based practice', which are founded on empathy, respect, genuineness and optimism.

The chapters in this volume are presented in such a way that those that are more preventive in their orientation and based in universal services come first and those that are more specialist and remedial in their orientation follow. The range of interventions examined in the book covers the spectrum of primary, secondary and tertiary prevention. These terms come from the field of public health. Primary prevention services are usually 'universal' or accessible to all families. For example, local child and family health services, preschools and primary schools are ideal settings for reaching all families. Secondary prevention services are offered to families who may be at greater risk or who already show signs of struggling in the hope that, with early intervention, a service may help to prevent the situation deteriorating. These can be offered from the 'platform' of universal services or from a more specialised service setting. Tertiary prevention services respond to the needs of families once there is already an established problem. These typically involve specialist or statutory services, with the objective to reduce the harm the problem has caused and to prevent its recurrence.

While we do not want to suggest that social problems such as child neglect should be thought of as diseases, we think that a public health approach is useful for three reasons. One, it draws our attention to the environment as well as to the individual. Two, it emphasises prevention as well as remediation. And three, wherever possible, it is based on evidence.

The opening chapters of the book are updated chapters from the first edition of this volume and provide broad concepts of working with vulnerable families generally, including within organisational settings and between different services, and with early intervention, such as in early childhood health and education settings. Some readers will already be familiar with some of this content, while for others it may be new.

In Chapter 1, Dorothy Scott, Fiona Arney and Graham Vimpani investigate the importance of considering the child, their family and community strengths and supports in working with vulnerable families. They explore the bio-psychosocial impacts upon children's development and wellbeing and describe the relevance of ecological and family-centred frameworks to practice with children and their families.

In Chapter 2, Dorothy Scott describes the way in which the 'think child, think family, think community' approach to working with families with complex needs requires enhanced practitioner skills and knowledge, as well as mechanisms for building bridges between services. In the latter half of the chapter, she identifies the potential conflicts (and suggested strategies) that can occur between and within organisations, between professions, and between and within individuals when working with families with multiple and complex needs.

In Chapter 3, Dorothy Scott describes the important role of early childhood services in working with vulnerable families to give children the best start to life. This chapter presents a range of innovative exemplars of working with families in early childhood settings.

Building on the concepts and ideas introduced in the first three chapters, we then examine the specific needs of population groups such as fathers, refugee families and Aboriginal and Torres Strait Islander families. These population groups have been selected because of their need for approaches that differ from those typically developed in child and family services, which may be geared more towards working with mothers or with children, parents and carers of white Australian descent.

Richard Fletcher presents the rationale for working with fathers in vulnerable families in Chapter 4, including the unique contribution they can make to their children's development and wellbeing. In this chapter he describes strategies and programs for working with fathers in a range of settings, including home-based programs for fathers whose partners have postnatal depression, and a program to end violent and abusive behaviours.

In Chapter 5, Kerry Lewig, Fiona Arney, Mary Salveron and Maria Barredo describe the contextual and cultural challenges in relation to parenting in a new culture for families from refugee backgrounds. They describe the results of qualitative research with child protection practitioners and members of eight community groups with refugee experiences, examining the role of the Government in parenting, the need for culturally sensitive and family-inclusive practice in child and family services and strategies to support parents from refugee and migrant backgrounds in Australia.

The focus on early intervention in early childhood is continued in Chapter 6, with a specific focus on culturally appropriate ways of working with Aboriginal and Torres

Strait Islander children and their families. In this chapter, Gary Robinson and Sarah Mares describe a group-based approach developed and delivered in the Northern Territory to promote the development of young Aboriginal children.

In Chapter 7, Fiona Arney, Alwin Chong and Kate McGuinness describe the impact of past child protection policies on Aboriginal Australians today, and examine an approach for incorporating family members in decision-making about Aboriginal and Torres Strait Islander children involved with the child protection system.

The next three chapters focus on aspects of working with families where children remain in the care of their parents but face serious risks from child neglect, alcohol and drug misuse and family violence.

In Chapter 8, Elizabeth Reimer describes practices and approaches that can build family strengths and momentum for change through relationship-based practice. Drawing upon a significant piece of new research, this chapter focuses on the characteristics of the practitioner, and the role of supervision and support, in working with families where child neglect has been identified as a concern.

In Chapter 9, Sharon Dawe and Paul Harnett describe an integrated approach to working with families where there are concerns about the welfare of children and where parents have a history of problematic drug and alcohol use. Examples from the Parents Under Pressure program are used in this chapter to highlight the relevance and applicability of the integrated approach to assessment and intervention with families.

Cathy Humphreys and Menka Tsantefski also explore working with families with complex needs in Chapter 10 by focusing on parenting in the context of family violence. In this chapter, they describe the impact of family violence on children and on the mother–child relationship, and explore practices for supporting women and children in these contexts.

Later chapters in the book focus on two issues relating to children who have been placed in out-of-home care (foster and kinship care) and apply concepts relating to attachment to understanding the needs and behaviour of these children, and the experience of parents who have had their children removed from their care.

Chapter 11 examines the application of attachment theory to children who have experienced frightening or stressful caregiving relationships. In this chapter, Sara McLean describes how children's behaviour with caregivers may be interpreted and how the concepts of attachment and trauma are understood and applied with children who have experienced abuse or neglect.

Chapter 12 focuses on the experiences of parents who have had their children removed from their care. Drawing upon research undertaken by Mary Salveron as part of her postgraduate studies, she and Fiona Arney explore the destruction and reconstruction of parental identity and the role of practitioners in supporting this transformational process in child protection services.

The final chapter of the book considers the role of research and other forms of evidence in influencing child protection policy and practice development and implementation. Using insights from Australian policies and programs, Fiona Arney, Kerry Lewig, Robyn Mildon, Aron Shlonsky, Christine Gibson and Leah Bromfield describe the factors that enhance and inhibit service development and delivery in this field.

This book has been written with a diverse range of readers in mind – for students and practitioners from different disciplines and fields of service, including the health, education and social services, and encompassing both traditionally 'child-focused' and 'adult-focused' sectors, who are interested in family-focused, child-sensitive practice. We also hope that the book will be of interest to supervisors, team leaders and managers of services, as well as policy-makers and professional educators.

All contributors to this book bring research to bear on the challenges of working with vulnerable families while appreciating that working with families requires a special synthesis of head, heart and hands. We hope we have captured something of our deep respect for this complex and creative work, and for the compassion and commitment of those who work with, and walk alongside, parents who struggle in the face of adversity to nurture their children

1

Think child, think family, think community

Dorothy Scott, Fiona Arney and Graham Vimpani

▇ Learning goals

This chapter will enable you to:

- **BE AWARE** of some of the bio-psychosocial factors and conceptual frameworks that affect child wellbeing and the capacity of families to nurture young children

- 'THINK child, think family and think community' in the way you might work

- **APPRECIATE** the centrality of 'relationship-based practice'

- **IDENTIFY** the values, knowledge and skills you bring to working with vulnerable families, and reflect on areas in which you may have gaps.

▇ Introduction

PROMOTING CHILD DEVELOPMENT, wellbeing and safety relies upon the ability to 'think child, think family and think community'. Our knowledge about how biological, psychological and social factors interact to influence the development and wellbeing of children has never been greater. In a growing number of countries, this knowledge has led to an intense interest in early childhood, motivated by social justice concerns as well as by an increasing awareness that the economic future of a society depends on the degree to which its children are healthy, educated and well adjusted.

Some children are exposed to a volatile mix of poverty, violence, parental mental illness and substance dependence that can erode the capacity of families to nurture their children, causing intense suffering and long-term harm. There are a number of conceptual frameworks and ideas that enable us to understand this, including an ecological model of human development.

Family-centred practice is based on four elements: the centrality of the family as the unit of attention; maximisation of families' choices; a strengths rather than a deficits perspective; and cultural sensitivity. The quality of the worker–family relationship is the cornerstone of family-centred practice. The key practitioner qualities of empathy, respect, genuineness and optimism are vital to working with vulnerable families.

We each bring a unique combination of personal qualities and values, knowledge and skills to our work. It is important for us to identify our strengths as well as the areas in which further professional development or the expertise of others may be required if we are to serve families and their children well.

■ Descriptive knowledge

We now know a lot about the long-term consequences of different forms of childhood adversity (including child abuse and neglect, children's witnessing of domestic violence, parental mental illness and parental substance dependence) on adult physical and mental health (Middlebrooks & Audage, 2007). It takes only a little imagination and the willingness to listen to those who were, or are still, exposed to such adversity, to understand the intensity of suffering that children in such situations can experience.

We also know quite a lot about the factors associated with the resilience of some children to such adversity. In particular, there is a strong understanding of the vital role a concerned, caring and committed adult plays in the life of a vulnerable child in helping the child to survive, recover and thrive, despite adversity.

The breadth of the knowledge that helps us to understand the many influences on children's development and wellbeing is nicely captured in the title of the book *From Neurons to Neighborhoods* (Shonkoff & Phillips, 2000), auspiced by the US National Research Council and Institute of Medicine of the National Academies. Based on the work of 17 experts from a broad range of disciplines, the key conclusions of this publication are worth stating:

- The nature–nurture debate is obsolete.
- Early intervention can improve the odds for vulnerable children.
- How young children feel is as important as how they think.
- Nurturing and dependable relationships are crucial.
- Culture influences development via child-rearing beliefs and practices.
- There is little evidence that 'special stimulation' leads to 'advanced brain development' in infancy.

REFLECTIVE QUESTIONS

Do you know more about the biological, psychological or social factors influencing child and family wellbeing? What might be the advantages and disadvantages of your particular knowledge base? How might you address any major knowledge gaps you can identify?

■ Genetic influences

There is growing evidence that many of the long-term consequences of childhood adversity are, at least in part, a result of interactions between environmental experience and our genetic make-up. For example, Caspi et al. (2003) found that the risks of later depression in children who had been abused were greater in those who had two copies of the short variant of a gene involved in serotonin transmission (5-HTT). Those with two copies of the long variant of the gene had no increased risk of depression, while those with one of each had intermediate risks.

More recently, McGowan and colleagues (2009) found that individuals who suicided as adults following a history of childhood abuse had differences in a neuron-specific glucocorticoid receptor promoter that is associated with the functioning of one of the major stress response systems (HPA), compared with those who suicided without a history of childhood abuse or who died from accidental causes. Specifically, they found that hippocampal NR3C1 gene expression was reduced in suicide victims who had been abused as children compared with victims who had not been abused, or those who had died from accidental causes. The effect of this is to increase activation of the HPA stress response system.

■ Parent–child attachment

Innately, children behave in ways that enable them to stay close to adult caregivers who can provide a secure base from which to explore the world. Children are said to build 'internal working models' of their own self-worth from the way they experience and see their caregivers' abilities and readiness to provide security and protection. In this way, children can build different types of attachment relationships with different caregivers. Children who are not provided with sensitive and responsive caregiving are unable to build working models that will result in secure attachment behaviours and will experience less adaptive forms of attachment to their caregiver/s. This is likely to influence not only their relationships with their caregivers but also subsequent relationships with significant others. However, attachment patterns in the early years, while associated with later outcomes, are not necessarily deterministic. Research has shown that children can still develop positively, despite receiving early caregiving that

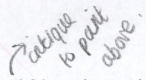
Critique to part above

was deficient, as long as subsequent caregiving experiences are warm and loving and provide a secure base (Bacon & Richardson, 2001).

For a long time there has been abundant evidence about the importance of parent–child attachment, which is itself influenced by complex biological, psychological and social factors. From the early work of John Bowlby in the 1950s on attachment and separation anxiety in infants and young children (Bowlby, 1953) to recent work on breastfeeding as a protective factor in relation to maternal neglect (Strathearn et al., 2009), researchers have helped to identify the factors that enhance or impair parent–child attachment. As Daniel Siegel says:

> Human infants have an inborn, genetically determined motivational system that drives them to become attached to their caregivers. Although infants become attached to their caregivers whether or not those caregivers are sensitive and responsive, attachment thrives especially on predictable, sensitive, attuned communication in which a parent shows an interest in, and aligns states of mind with those of a child … Early attachment experiences directly affect the development of the brain (Kraemer, 1992) … Human connections create neuronal connections … Caregivers are the architects of the way in which experience influences the unfolding of genetically pre-programmed but experience-dependent brain development … These salient emotional relationships have a direct effect on the development of the domains of mental functioning that serve as our conceptual anchor points: memory, narrative, emotion, representations and states of mind. In this way, attachment relationships may serve to create the central foundation from which the mind develops. Insecure attachment may serve as a significant risk factor in the development of psychopathology (Jones, Main & del Carmen, 1996). Secure attachment, in contrast, appears to confer a form of emotional resilience (Rutter, 1997).

→ two different types of attachment.

(Siegel, 1999, pp. 93–4)

Some of the implications of attachment theory and research for working with vulnerable families and children where there is impaired attachment have been identified (Howe et al., 1999). The preventive implications of this knowledge are also gaining greater interest. For example, Boukydis (2006) has outlined how health professionals can use ultrasound consultation to enhance the attachment of mothers to their unborn babies, decrease maternal anxiety and increase positive attitudes towards health during pregnancy.

Following birth, the Circle of Security Model, a video-based intervention aimed at strengthening parental capacity to observe and respond to their infants (http://circleofsecurity.net), is gaining currency. The Circle of Security Model is an early intervention approach that can be taught to a broad range of practitioners in health, early childhood education and social service settings. Chapter 11 further explores the application of attachment concepts to practice with vulnerable children.

■ Experience-based brain development

There have been great advances in our understanding of the way in which children's early experiences of their world continuously interact with genetic predispositions to shape the architecture and function of the brain. These experiences begin before birth and, if healthy and stimulating, can help establish brain architecture that 'operates at full genetic potential'. Conversely, adverse experience leads to 'weak brain architecture with impaired capabilities' (National Scientific Council on the Developing Child, 2007, p. 3).

Brain growth following birth is rapid and is made up of the establishment of myriads of connections between brain cells and supportive tissue. With the exception of brain cells in the hippocampus, a part of the brain involved in memory, new cells are not added after birth. As young children get older, the pathways between cells are pruned down on a 'use it or lose it' principle.

It is important to recognise that the parts of our brain that are responsible for different sets of functions (such as language, memory of recent events, memory of facial expressions, planning and emotional responsiveness) mature at different times. Sensitive periods in which different parts of the brain develop particular functions occur at different ages (Gogtay et al., 2004). Further, the pathways involved in processing lower levels of information mature earlier than those processing higher-level information (Burkhalter, Bernardo & Charles, 1993). The performance of higher-level pathways in turn builds on the functionality of lower-level pathways. Experiences encountered by young children need to be age appropriate, because children's abilities to interpret what they experience change over time as their pathways are built. For example, looking at pictures and not focusing on written words is important for a toddler.

The nature of the relationships in the child's world and the level of stress experienced have important roles in fine-tuning brain architecture. Adverse early experiences can have damaging effects on the way the brain develops (Nelson, 2007; Rice & Barone Jr, 2000; Siegel, 1999). Too much unpredictable and uncontrollable stress during the sensitive period when the stress response system (that is, the body's physical, emotional and cognitive responses to stress) is maturing in early life is likely to lead to the development of a dysregulated stress response system (Perry, 1997). This in turn affects the way children are able to self-regulate their impulses and behaviour and their ability to learn.

Excessive stress experienced by children recalibrates the stress response system, such that children's feelings may progress rapidly from calmness to anxiety and terror when confronted with a threat – moods that affect learning capacity and interpersonal behaviour. This is one of the reasons why abuse may affect young children so profoundly, well before they are able to verbally express their feelings about the abuse, increasing their risks of behavioural, health and learning problems and the early onset of health problems in adult life (Anda et al., 2006). This is one reason why studies of children entering out-of-home care show that these children as a group are among the least healthy in our community (American Academy of Pediatrics, 2002).

Nevertheless, it is important to recognise that brain plasticity (the ability of the brain to develop new neural pathways) continues throughout life, even though the degree of adaptability diminishes with age (Karmarkar & Dan, 2006). For example, while the best time to become fluent in hearing, understanding and speaking multiple languages is early in life, people can still learn foreign languages across their life span. However, it does need to be recognised that, while 'the residual capacity for plasticity in mature neural circuits allows for some recovery of brain capabilities' when subjected to new experiences, these must be 'tailored to activate the relevant neural circuits and the individual's attention engaged in the task'. The task will inevitably be 'harder, more expensive in terms of societal and individual effort and potentially less extensive and durable' (National Scientific Council on the Developing Child, 2007, p. 8).

REFLECTIVE QUESTION

Imagine you are a teacher in a primary school and one of your students repeatedly hits out at other children when they get too close to him physically. You know this child is in foster care because of earlier emotional and physical abuse. How might an understanding of the influence of earlier experiences in a stressful environment on brain development and stress response systems help to explain this boy's behaviour?

■ Parenting adaptability

Parent–child attachment and positive child development depend upon a parent's ability to meet their child's needs in a consistent and effective way. Parents do this by demonstrating adaptability in their parenting – being able to constantly adjust their responses to meet the child's changing needs. Parenting that shows adaptability has three components:

- perceptiveness: being 'tuned in' to the child, the situation and the parent's own responses; picking up and accurately interpreting the child's signals
- responsiveness: having the capacity to stay 'in sync' with the child; being able to continually change and adjust, responding in light of cues being given by the child or by the context

- flexibility: the behavioural capacity of the parent; having a broad behavioural repertoire (Centre for Community Child Health, 2004a, pp. 80–1).

Children's needs for parental adaptability will vary over the child's development (for example, the needs of an infant are different from those of a preschooler), in different contexts (for example, a child living in a high-risk neighbourhood will have needs different from those of a child living in a low-risk neighbourhood with high social capital), in response to characteristics of the child (for example, whether the child has an easygoing or a more active temperament; whether the child has a disability) and as a result of day-to-day variation (for example, the needs of a child when tired or sick are likely to be higher than when the child is alert or healthy).

In the same way as children's needs for adaptable parenting are variable and determined by many factors, so too are levels of parenting adaptability multiply influenced. How effectively a parent can respond to their child's needs may be determined by their own experiences of being parented, their mental health and use of drugs and alcohol, their financial resources, their experiences of parenting other children and whether they are adequately supported by friends, families and, where needed, services (Centre for Community Child Health, 2004a). The chapters of this book explore many features that relate to supporting parents in meeting the needs of their children in adaptable ways. The following sections of this chapter describe a range of frameworks that can be used to support parents and communities in raising children in effective and adaptable ways.

■ Family theory

There are many conceptual frameworks relating to family structure and interaction (Handel & Whitchurch, 1994), derived mainly from the disciplines of anthropology and sociology. Family systems theory, which forms the main conceptual underpinning of family therapy, incorporates individual, family and social perspectives, and has been applied in general ways to understand families across the family life cycle, as well as in counselling and therapy settings (Carter & McGoldrick, 1999).

Synthesising psychodynamic and family systems concepts and drawing on the ideas of British social worker and psychoanalyst Clare Winnicott, Gillian Schofield (1998) offers three guiding principles for understanding the worlds of the family – inner, outer, past and present.

- Inner worlds express themselves and have an impact on outer worlds. (For example, chronic maternal depression often exhibits itself in self-neglect and the neglect of children.)
- Outer worlds affect inner worlds. (For example, depressing environments induce despair and violent environments induce fear.)

- Past worlds affect present worlds. (For example, experiences in the parent's childhood may affect the way they parent their own children, and the way they perceive and give meaning to events.)

Practitioners in child and family services, especially those in socially disadvantaged communities, often encounter parents who carry within them the pain of past worlds that can greatly impair their capacity to nurture their child. When this coexists with an outer world that is characterised by the fear of violence or the despair of poverty, then there is a double layer of difficulty in nurturing their children.

REFLECTIVE QUESTIONS

Apply ideas about inner, outer, past and present worlds to a parent you know who may be struggling to nurture their child or children. What insight does this give you into why patterns of behaviour may be resistant to change? How do such insights affect your attitudes and feelings towards the parent?

■ An ecological perspective

In the 1970s Urie Bronfenbrenner, Director of the College of Human Ecology at Cornell University, began to emphasise the importance of understanding the development of children in terms of their time and place; that is, the wider context of the family, social network, community and wider society in which they are born and develop. His highly influential ecological model of human development highlights the importance of different contexts in which the child is embedded:

- the various 'microsystems' of which a child is a part, such as the family, the immediate neighbourhood, the early childhood centre or the classroom
- the mesosystem – a system of microsystems and the interrelationships between them, including the extent to which experiences are reinforcing or conflictual based on their similar or different norms and values
- the exosystem, comprising settings of which the child is not a member, but of which others who influence the child – such as parents or siblings – are significant members; for example, the parents' workplaces or siblings' peer groups, or health and educational services
- the macrosystem or the overarching cultural blueprint of a society (individualist or collectivist; secular or religious; patriarchal or matriarchal; violent or peaceful).

Bronfenbrenner (1979) has likened these systems to 'a nest of Russian dolls'. Those who work in child and family services may, under some circumstances, become important figures in the lives of children and their parents, and thus become one of the family's microsystems, or more remotely influence the child as part of the mesosystem. The organisations through which such services are delivered are part of the exosystem, and the values transmitted through social policies and services reflect core macrosystem values such as the status of children and families or the importance of social equality.

James Garbarino extended the work of Urie Bronfenbrenner, describing the family as the 'headquarters of human development' and applying an ecological model to the specific problem of child abuse and neglect (Garbarino, 1982). He later coined the evocative phrase 'socially toxic societies' to describe social environments of low social cohesion, adversity and violence, which are strongly correlated with child abuse, juvenile crime and adolescent substance dependence (Garbarino, 1999).

These problems all have very similar 'causal pathways' to other closely associated problems such as low birth weight, conduct disorders, teenage pregnancy, poor academic achievement and adolescent mental health problems. This means these problems all share similar risk and protective factors (Durlak, 1998). Preventive strategies that are broadly based and tackle the common risk and protective factors, rather than target a specific problem in isolation such as low birth weight, have been found to be most effective (Durlak, 1998). Common risk factors include poor parent–child attachment, low peer connectedness, social isolation and poverty.

REFLECTIVE QUESTIONS
Think about the possible effects of a situation in which a young child experiences very different values and norms in their family of origin, and another microsystem such as a child care centre or the classroom.

How might living in poverty affect the life chances of children growing up in Australia?

Using at least three different generations in your own family, think about how the wider social and historical context has influenced parenting in each of these generations, and how the roles of children (such as that of contributor to the family as an economic and social unit, and that of consumer) may also have changed across time and place in the intergenerational experiences of your family.

■ Social networks

It has been long known that social support is a major protective factor in relation to individual wellbeing (Brown & Harris, 1978; d'Abbs, 1982; Gottlieb, 1981; Henderson, Byrne & Duncan-Jones, 1981). The social networks, or webs of kith and kin relationships into which we are born, and which we build across the life span, can buffer us from stressful life events and provide access to a broad range of resources. Social networks also make demands on us, exerting pressures on individuals to conform to their norms and creating a system of mutual obligations.

At times of key transitions in the life course, social support is especially important. For example, social support is a protective factor in relation to maternal depression (Brown et al., 1994). Social networks may change markedly during transitions such as marital separation, and the impact of such stressful life events on relationships with family and friends may lead to diminished rather than greater social support at the time when it is most needed (Webber & Boromeo, 2005).

There is a significant body of research on the relationship between a lack of social support and poor-quality child-rearing, and child abuse and neglect (Crittenden, 1985; Quittner, Glueckouff & Jackson, 1990) although this is not a simple one-way relationship. An understanding of the 'natural helping networks' in a neighbourhood is vital in both community development work and in working with individual families (Collins & Pancoast, 1976). For 'socially excluded families', such as those families with an intergenerational history of child neglect and who have very truncated social networks, carefully matched and very well supported volunteer families can be an important element in assisting them to fulfil parental and other social roles (Mitchell, 1995; Mitchell & Campbell, 2011).

Another approach in using social network ideas to assist vulnerable families has been recently developed by the Australian Centre for Social Innovation (www.tacsi. org.au). The award-winning 'Family by Family' program (www.familybyfamily.org.au) reaches out to families living in very socially disadvantaged neighbourhoods through 'family friendly' activities in places such as supermarket carparks and parks. Both 'seeking families', those wishing to improve some aspect of their family life, and 'sharing families', families who may have gone through tough times and who are willing to spend time with and support another family, are 'linked up'. Designed to avoid the stigma, coercion and psychological costs of 'clienthood' often associated with using formal services, Family by Family has been very successful in recruiting families with children who are experiencing serious vulnerability, many of whom have a history of child protection involvement. It is a promising program, with encouraging results from its initial evaluation (www.familybyfamily.org.au).

ACTIVITY
Draw a map of your own social network, placing yourself as a circle in the centre and then representing each family member, friend, neighbour, colleague etc. with whom you are in contact as separate circles around you. Draw a line between all individuals and others in your social network with whom they have contact. Can you see separate clusters in the pattern (for example, indicating the different subgroups to which you belong)? To what degree are the people in your social network directly connected with others? What are the implications of this for you in relation to the flow of information, obligations, practical assistance and personal autonomy?

REFLECTIVE QUESTIONS

Think about the factors that might shape an individual's ability to receive assistance from family and friends if they urgently needed someone to take care of their child if they were hospitalised.

To whom would you first turn if you needed practical support such as money or accommodation? To whom would you first turn if you needed emotional support? Are they the same people? Who might turn to you for such support? What would happen if the support you needed was not available from family and friends? What would make it easier or harder for you to approach a government or non-government service for assistance?

■ Communities and social capital

Old wisdom supports much of our new knowledge, as indicated by the proverb 'It takes a village to raise a child.' The next question therefore is 'And what might it take to rebuild the village?'. The work of Robert Putnam, popularised in books such as *Bowling Alone* (Putnam, 2000), has highlighted the importance of 'social capital', or the trust and reciprocity that transcend kith, kin and clan and form the social glue that holds communities, and ultimately societies, together.

Putnam differentiates 'bonding social capital' based on the affiliations that exist within homogeneous groupings (people of a similar religion, age group, ethnicity, social class and so on) and 'bridging social capital', those webs of relationships that create linkages between such different groups in a society. Services for children and families can be delivered in ways that enhance both bonding and bridging social capital in the communities they serve. For example, maternal and child health centres, playgroups, kindergartens and schools can serve as 'the village well', or the nucleus in social networks for families with young children.

Alternatively, services can militate against the establishment of bridging social capital; for example, where schools that reflect the values of the dominant culture may be antithetical to the values of the subculture of the child and make some families feel unwelcome.

There is an impressive history of community work that long precedes the recent literature on social capital. Some child and family welfare services have embraced community development as part of their mission and have pioneered new approaches to rebuilding community. This approach is very different from that of traditional service provision; rather than being in the role of consumers or clients, parents are engaged as citizens and as potential contributors in their communities (Beilharz, 2002). For example, in the Shared Action initiative in the Long Gully community in central Victoria, parents were keen to establish a children's football club and were supported to take on the leadership roles this required (Beilharz, 2002).

ACTIVITY

Observe the neighbourhood in which you live over a period of one week and note the indicators of 'social capital' (trust and reciprocity). Compare this with another neighbourhood where you may have lived, or with which you are familiar. How might you explain the similarities or differences? What might it be like to live in a community that is low in social capital?

Consider the degree to which organisations in your local community, such as playgroups, schools, children's sporting clubs, churches and resident associations might strengthen bonding social capital. How welcome do you think a family with same-sex parents, or a recently arrived refugee family, might be in such settings? What potential might such settings have to strengthen bridging social capital by bringing together families from diverse backgrounds?

■ Prescriptive knowledge

It is one thing to know about a phenomenon (descriptive knowledge) and another thing to know how to intervene in relation to the phenomenon (prescriptive knowledge). Knowing about anatomy is different from knowing how to do surgery; just as knowing how children learn is different from knowing how to teach them. In relation to working with vulnerable families, some would say that it is more of a craft than a science. Nevertheless, there is a growing research base to guide practitioners working with troubled families and the potential for 'evidence-informed practice' is continually increasing (see Chapter 13).

Our descriptive knowledge is still much greater than our prescriptive knowledge. For example, while quite a lot is now known about the effects on a child of exposure to alcohol *in utero*, as well as the effects on the mother and the child of exposure to domestic violence, a practitioner needs to know more than this. 'How should I respond to a depressed pregnant woman with a drinking problem who shows signs of being physically assaulted by her partner?' is a very different type of question from 'What are the effects of exposure to alcohol and domestic violence?'

Similarly, we know about the effects of 'low warmth–high criticism' parenting styles, but this does not give a practitioner an answer to the question 'How do I respond when I see a stressed single father with a childhood history of physical abuse, who is facing eviction and serious financial pressures, speaking to his four-year-old son in a harsh and punitive way?'

In relation to such practice questions, 'evidence-informed' rather than 'evidence-based' practice is a more realistic goal, as evidence is often not available or, if it is, it is not applicable to a specific situation. There may be no 'right answer' to such practice questions, as what may be appropriate and effective will depend on the context. Practitioner judgement and 'practice wisdom' thus need to complement research as sources of 'knowledge for practice'.

The 'how to' questions in practice are very dependent not only on a practitioner's values, knowledge and skills, but also on the nature of the practitioner's relationship with the family, the professional role, the organisational setting, and the policy and legal context in which practitioners work.

ACTIVITY

Think of a 'knowledge about' question that relates to risk and protective factors for child development and wellbeing. Using appropriate 'key words', search the internet to explore this question and critically assess the quality of the information you can find.

Now consider a 'knowledge how' question that might face a practitioner trying to reduce these risk factors and strengthen the protective factors. How would you go about finding answers to this question?

■ Family-centred practice

Just as an ecological perspective can give an overarching conceptual framework for understanding human development, so a family-centred perspective can give an overarching conceptual framework for working with vulnerable families, regardless of specific practitioner roles, settings and services.

The term 'family-centred practice' encompasses many approaches to working with families. Allen and Petr (1998) have argued that there are four core elements of family-centred practice:

- the centrality of the family as the unit of attention
- an emphasis on maximising families' choices
- a strengths rather than a deficits perspective
- cultural sensitivity.

Family-centred practice with vulnerable families requires a practitioner to have not only the appropriate knowledge and skills, but also appropriate values and personal qualities. Values based on compassion, respect, integrity and self-determination are the foundation, while personal qualities include a high level of emotional intelligence, interpersonal skills and self-awareness.

There are many challenges in family-centred practice. Sometimes what is described as family-centred practice is really mother-centred practice. This can ignore the significance of fathers and place an undue burden of responsibility on mothers. In Chapter 4 we explore father-inclusive practice. Sometimes what is described as family-centred practice is nuclear family-centred practice, ignoring the role of extended family members, especially relatives such as grandparents who may be very significant in the lives of children.

Sometimes what is described as family-centred practice is really parent-centred practice. This renders children invisible and inaudible. Sometimes what is described as family-centred practice is really child-centred practice, and this may reinforce parental feelings of failure and shame, exacerbating problems such as depression or substance use and posing greater risk to children. There will therefore be many dilemmas for practitioners committed to family-centred practice.

Similarly, while family-centred practice is 'strengths based', in some situations deficits will need to be clearly identified if children are to be safe and to have their needs met. In these situations, the challenge is to find ways of engaging with and advocating for children while working collaboratively with parents and the extended family.

A commitment to the self-determination of families underpins efforts to maximise their choices. The ethos is one of 'power with', not 'power over'. Even when the scope for choice is very circumscribed, there is usually still some room to give children and parents some control. For example, even when a child in care is separated from his or her parents, and the level of access is determined by a court, how and where to meet may still be something over which the child and parent can exercise choice. Chapter 10 discusses more ways in which access between children in out-of-home care and their parents may be enhanced.

As explored in Chapters 5, 6 and 7, practitioners need to be culturally sensitive and competent if they are to work effectively with families from diverse cultural backgrounds. Child-rearing is heavily shaped by cultural norms and contexts – for example, the age at which it is appropriate for a child to be left alone or in the care of an older child or adolescent may vary greatly. At the same time, practitioners need to be aware of the risk of over-attributing child-rearing practices to cultural differences. This requires knowledge of and respect for cultural differences.

In some Aboriginal communities, there are painful historical legacies related to the removal of children that make it much more difficult for families to trust services. Cultural consultants can play a vital role in assisting workers to become 'culturally competent' when working with families with different backgrounds from their own, and acting as intermediaries in making services 'culturally safe' for families.

REFLECTIVE QUESTIONS

Think about the diversity of child-rearing attitudes and behaviours in your community and across different communities. What may be the 'grey' area between what is seen as 'family business' and what is seen as an obligation by the State to intervene on behalf of vulnerable children? Has this changed over time, and what may be the consequences of any changes?

What experiences and attitudes do you bring from your own family background that may assist you, or pose challenges for you, in working respectfully with vulnerable families with young children from different socioeconomic or cultural backgrounds?

■ Relationship-based practice

At the heart of family-centred practice is the quality of the working relationship with families (also see Chapter 8). Most of the research in this area has been on 'therapeutic relationships' in counselling and psychotherapy, but there is a growing body of research on working relationships across the human services. This includes how working relationships may be different for workers and families in rural settings and in organisational settings such as child protection, where clients are not voluntary.

Asay and Lambert (1999) have drawn on a broad range of studies on the factors responsible for positive outcomes in evidence-based psychotherapeutic interventions, including the meta-analysis by Lambert (1992a), which identified the degree to which positive outcomes can be attributed to different factors:

- 40 per cent: client factors and environmental factors such as social support
- 30 per cent: qualities of the therapeutic relationship
- 15 per cent: hope and expectancy of positive outcome
- 15 per cent: specific intervention techniques.

We do not have a similar body of research that specifically relates to family-centred practice with vulnerable families. However, these are the very same elements emphasised in intensive family-based services: environmental interventions, a therapeutic relationship based on rapport, nurturing hope and using evidence-based techniques (Whittaker et al., 1990). In any service responding to vulnerable families with young children, a supportive relationship with a parent can be valuable as an end in itself, as well as being a vehicle for specific intervention, enhancing social support or reducing situational stressors.

Scott and colleagues (2007) have pulled together some of the research on the importance of practitioner qualities in engaging families and have coined the acronym ERGO for the combination of empathy, respect, genuineness and optimism.

ERGO

- *Empathy:* Empathy is the worker's ability to understand what the client is saying and feeling, and is expressed through warmth, active listening and affirming and helping behaviours.
- *Respect:* Workers show respect in practical ways, such as arriving for a home visit on time as well as by being non-judgemental and treating people as unique rather than as 'cases' or numbers.
- *Genuineness:* Practitioners who can show humanity, humour and humility come across as individuals who are 'real' rather than in a 'role', even though they are 'in role'.
- *Optimism:* Practitioners who can feel and convey optimism will be more able to nurture hope in families.

Family partnership training is a model of care that enhances the provision of family-centred services (Davis, Day & Bidmead, 2002). It facilitates the development of respect, empathy and partnership among practitioners working with families. It turns the concept of expert-driven interventions on its head in emphasising the importance of parent-initiated and practitioner-supported changes that will be beneficial to family and child functioning.

In relation to child abuse risk situations, the research of Trotter (2002) suggests that it is also important to encourage pro-social behaviours directly and to have very clear roles and issues on which to focus.

Developing and sustaining relationships based on empathy, respect, genuineness and optimism under such challenging situations is not easy. Factors relating to the practitioner, the family, the service setting and the social environment are all important.

The practitioner

Each of us has a unique personality and our values, personal experiences and educational background shape the way we relate with others. There are times when workers struggle to feel and therefore to express empathy, respect, genuineness and optimism. None of us is immune from common mental health problems such as anxiety or depression. For example, high levels of depression in low-paid North American child care workers has been identified as a serious concern (Whitebook et al., 2004). Practitioners who are in close contact with children and who identify strongly with their suffering may understandably struggle to feel empathy for, or convey respect to, the parents.

The family

Each member of a family will influence the practitioner's capacity to offer and sustain a positive relationship. For example, parents whose own early history makes it hard for them to trust may take a lot longer to engage. Parents who have an insecure or conflictual relationship with their child may feel uneasy when they witness their child responding positively to a carer. The triangle of the worker–parent–child relationship can be a complex one and children may be very mindful of the tension in the working relationship.

The service setting

Service settings shape the working relationship. The physical nature and emotional climate of the service give strong cues about whether it is welcoming to children and adults, while the nature of the organisation powerfully shapes the relationship by defining the worker's role and mandate. Resources are also a vital factor and high workloads make it harder to establish rapport, as building good relationships takes time.

The social environment

The social environment shapes our working relationships too. Green, Gregory and Mason (2006) have used the metaphor of 'stretching the professional elastic' to describe rural working relationships on the continuum from 'professional, objective expert' to 'helpful friend'. This notion challenges traditional ideas of professional ethics, values and rules about professional boundaries as they relate to the development and maintenance of the working relationship. In rural and remote settings, the tyranny of distance also poses very practical challenges.

■ Conclusion

There is a large and growing body of knowledge that relates to working with vulnerable families with young children. This chapter has touched on some of the research, ideas and conceptual frameworks that can help us understand and respond to families struggling with their child-rearing roles. It is easy to be daunted by the level of knowledge that is available and by what we don't know. Just as we work best with families by building on their strengths, it is important to identify what we know and what we can offer. Being able to tap into the expertise of others to address gaps in one's own knowledge is an important skill. Perhaps the greatest gift we can offer families is ourselves – a working relationship based on empathy, respect, genuineness and optimism, and a willingness to ask them what might help.

■ Useful websites

Australian Centre for Child Protection: **www.unisa.edu.au/childprotection**

Australian Research Alliance for Children and Youth: **www.aracy.org.au**

Bernard van Leer Foundation: **www.bernardvanleer.org**

Circle of Security: **http://circleofsecurity.net**

Family by Family: **http://familybyfamily.org.au**

Raising Children Network: The Australian Parenting Website: **http://raisingchildren.net.au**

St Luke's: **www.stlukes.org.au**

St Luke's Innovative Resources: **www.innovativeresources.org**

The Australian Centre for Social Innovation: **www.tacsi.org.au**

The Family Action Centre: **www.newcastle.edu.au/research-centre/fac**

What Works for Children?: **www.whatworksforchildren.org.uk**

Wilfrid Laurier University: **www.wlu.ca/index.php**

2

Working within and between organisations

Dorothy Scott

■ Learning goals

This chapter will enable you to:

- **UNDERSTAND** current policy directions that are supporting more holistic approaches to working with vulnerable families who have multiple and complex needs
- **IDENTIFY** the practitioner, organisational and policy related factors that shape practitioner roles
- **CONSIDER** the potential for broadening practitioner roles so that they are more holistic and family centred
- **UNDERSTAND** the importance of working across professional and organisational boundaries and the factors that influence this
- **BE ABLE TO ACCEPT** and effectively manage the conflict that can occur in working across professional and organisational boundaries.

■ Introduction

WITH THE GROWING realisation that many varied and complex problems, from global warming to crime, infectious diseases, and child abuse and neglect, cannot be solved by one service sector or 'silo', there is an increasing momentum for 'joined up' approaches to tackle such issues. In relation to socially marginalised people, overarching 'social inclusion' policy frameworks in some countries are focusing attention on how sectors such as health, education, housing, employment and social services can work together more effectively.

This has two main implications for practitioners working with families that have multiple and complex needs:

1   Greater emphasis is being placed on redefining practitioners' roles and
    models of practice so that they are more comprehensive. The first part of this
    chapter therefore explores how practitioner and organisational roles may
    evolve to respond more holistically to families with multiple and complex
    needs.

2   Greater emphasis is also being placed on how service providers across
    different organisations, professions and service sectors work in partnership,
    so that more integrated and 'joined up' services are delivered. The second
    part of this chapter explores how practitioners need to understand and
    manage the potential for conflict when working across such boundaries if
    this goal is to be achieved.

■ Contemporary policy context

As the close relationship between problems such as poverty, mental illness, homelessness, substance misuse, unemployment, crime, antisocial behaviour, poor health, low literacy and child abuse and neglect is increasingly understood, new ways of thinking and responding to this challenge are emerging. Developing systems and funding models that get beyond the fragmentation and duplication created by 'single input services based on categorical funding' when trying to serve individuals and families with multiple and complex needs is a major challenge. At the service delivery level, a related challenge is how to tailor services to meet the individual needs of specific families and give the consumers of services a greater involvement in decisions about how these services are delivered; in short, how do we keep the family, and not the service, at the centre of what we do?

In countries such as the UK and, more recently Australia, 'social inclusion' policies have provided an overarching framework for understanding and responding to 'socially marginalised' individuals, families and communities. Hayes, Gray and Edwards (2008) describe the three commonly accepted forms of social exclusion as:

*   *wide exclusion*, referring to the number of people excluded on a single or small
    number of indicators (such as unemployment)
*   *deep exclusion*, referring to multiple forms of entrenched and deep-seated
    exclusion (such as a combination of unemployment, lack of accommodation
    and social isolation in addition to individual problems such as disability or
    chronic illness)
*   *concentrated exclusion*, referring to a geographical concentration of social
    problems. (For example, in urban areas where the manufacturing industry
    has declined, there may be a concentration of unemployment, poor housing,
    crime and child neglect.)

In relation to socially disadvantaged families with young children, there has been a great deal of interest in tapping the potential of locally accessible universal children's services to be unstigmatised 'platforms' from which early intervention and individually tailored intensive assistance can be offered. This has led to a greater emphasis on working with parents for those employed in traditionally child-focused services such as maternal and child health, and early childhood education and care (see Chapter 3). It has also led to a greater emphasis on such services working in close collaboration with one another, and on the co-location and integration of early childhood services as well as a range of family support and specialist early intervention services.

Until recently, less attention has been given to how traditionally adult-focused services in fields such as mental health, alcohol and other drugs, corrections, domestic violence and homelessness may become more responsive to the needs of their clients as parents and the needs of the children themselves. Given the emerging data on the high level of parental substance misuse, mental illness and domestic violence in the families of children involved with child protection services (Bromfield et al., 2010), this is becoming increasingly important.

In the field of mental health, the capacity of adult mental health services to be more responsive to the needs of the children of parents with a mental illness was identified as a significant issue in both policy and service delivery some years ago (Cowling, 2004; Australian Infant Child Adolescent and Family Mental Health Association, 2004).

This has resulted in the development of an Australian Government funded initiative – Children of Parents with a Mental Illness (COPMI) – aimed at strengthening the capacity of adult mental health services to address the parental roles of their adult clients and to respond to the needs of their children. A broad range of excellent resources for both service providers and families is available online (www.copmi.net. au). The Mental Health Professional Network also has online resources for mental health practitioners on family-sensitive and family-inclusive practice (www.mhpn. org.au). Similar developments are now beginning to occur in the alcohol and other drug sector. For example, the internationally acclaimed therapeutic program 'Parents Under Pressure', developed by Dawe and Harnett (2007a), is described in Chapter 9. Gruenert and Tsantefski (2012) have also recently explored the difference between family-sensitive practice and family-inclusive practice in the alcohol and other drug sector.

Family-sensitive practice occurs when service providers understand the family issues of their individual client and are sensitive to the needs of other family members. This may simply be a matter of scheduling appointments for parents so that they occur during children's school hours, but it can also mean understanding the stressors of parenting when struggling with substance misuse, or the potential motivational power of one's children.

Family-inclusive practice goes one step further, involving other family members directly and working in partnership with families. This may involve directly assisting the children of parents with a substance dependence in relation to both practical and psychosocial needs. Some useful resources to support service providers and managers in the alcohol and other drug sector in becoming more responsive to the needs of parents and children have recently been developed by NCETA, Australia's National Research Centre on Alcohol and Other Drugs Workforce Development at Flinders University (http://nceta.flinders.edu.au/workforce). These include a Family Sensitive Policy and Practice Toolkit and a checklist for organisations and practitioners. The latter was based on a survey undertaken with the Australian Centre for Child Protection and identified what family-sensitive practice meant to Australian alcohol and other drug workers (Trifonoff et al., 2010).

Some alcohol and other drug agencies have developed specific programs for parents and their children, such as therapeutic playgroups (Mohammed, 2003). Such approaches recognise the importance of seeing and responding to the needs of both parents and their children. 'Whenever the parents' interests and needs are regarded as antithetical to those of their children and relegated to second place, their incentive to cooperate with services in the care of their children is diminished' (Mohammed, 2003, p. 68).

In the field of homelessness, there is increasing interest in how best to respond to the needs of children accompanying their parents in emergency housing services, especially where children have been traumatised through exposure to family violence (Gibson & Morphett, 2011). A number of useful websites providing resources and tools, which workers in specialist homelessness services can use directly with parents and children, are listed at the end of this chapter. They include the program Safe from the Start, developed by the Salvation Army in Tasmania, and a resource created by the US National Center on Family Homelessness for caregivers working with children who have experienced traumatic stress.

The impact of family violence on children is also explored in Chapter 10, building on the earlier work of Humphreys (2006) concerning the need to strengthen the mother–child relationship following paternal violence. In the corrections field, the Victorian Association for the Care and Resettlement of Offenders (VACRO) has published a report that examines the unmet needs of children across the criminal justice system (Hannon, 2007).

While these are all promising initiatives, they are relatively isolated and recent examples in their respective fields. To achieve system-wide reform requires not only the right policies and funding models, but also a workforce in adult specialist services that has the values, knowledge and skills to work effectively with families with multiple and complex needs. This is a major challenge, requiring transformational reform. For traditionally adult-focused professions and services, such as mental health or drug treatment services, recognising the needs of children requires major changes. Similarly, for traditionally child-focused professions and services, recognising and responding to the needs of parents also requires major changes.

Through a major workforce development initiative funded by the Australian Government under the Council of Australian Governments' National Framework for Protecting Australia's Children, the Australian Centre for Child Protection has been working with partner community service organisations in 12 socially disadvantaged areas across Australia to strengthen child- and family-sensitive practice in both children's and adult services, and to strengthen collaboration between them. Further information on the initiative, *Protecting and Nurturing Children: Building Capacity, Building Bridges*, can be accessed through the website of the Australian Centre for Child Protection (www.unisa.edu.au/childprotection).

ACTIVITIES

Consider the policy changes now occurring in a field with which you are familiar. Are there any shifts towards more integrated and holistic approaches in the delivery of services? If so, what prompted this? Do you know how such changes are seen 'on the ground' by practitioners? What might such changes mean for service providers and for vulnerable children and their families?

Choose a traditionally 'child' or 'adult' focused field mentioned above with which you are not familiar. Using the internet, see if you can identify any recent policy directions in that field which may support an approach that is more 'child and family sensitive' or 'child and family inclusive'. Did you come across any terms and concepts that were new to you? How may you find out what these mean?

Map the traditionally child-focused and adult-focused services in a geographical area you know. Which ones may be serving the same families?

■ How we play our roles

Why is changing the way we provide services to vulnerable families so challenging? Perhaps most of us feel anxious when asked to perform a new role, especially one for which we may not be adequately trained or supported. When there is already a heavy demand on our time, it is even more difficult to embrace such change. On the other hand, extending our knowledge and skills can be stimulating and lead to greater job satisfaction, especially if we can see that it is of benefit to children and families.

Many factors influence practitioner roles: the history of different professions and services; organisational mandates, resources and procedures; professional registration and regulatory processes; industrial issues and occupational vested interests; legislation; the power of other professional groups; government policies and broader social attitudes. What clients using services on a voluntary basis are prepared to accept is also a major consideration. What at one point in time may be seen as a marginal role for a profession can become a core role, and what may once have been a 'core role' can become marginal or even disappear over time. For example, the recognition of 'new' social problems such as child abuse in the 1960s, the changing roles of women in the 1970s, advances in information and communications technology in the 1980s, the consumer rights movement in mental health in the 1990s, and the increased prevalence of depression and alcohol abuse in the past decade, are just a few factors that have led to significant changes in the roles of many professions and services.

It is possible to analyse service provider roles in terms of their 'core' and 'marginal' functions.

> ... core responsibilities are defined by society's central institutions, and these institutions possess powerful sanctions to ensure that they are fulfilled ... beyond the core are marginal areas in which much more variation is possible. The occupant of the role may ... limit his work to his core responsibilities or extend his involvement with clients to include other aspects of their situation.
>
> (McCaughey, Shaver & Ferber, 1977)

Factors relating to the individual service provider that may predispose them to perform 'marginal' role functions related to client wellbeing include their personality and their beliefs regarding the ideal of service (McCaughey, Shaver & Ferber, 1977). Individual practitioners differ in the degree to which they embrace tasks that transcend the 'bottom line' of their traditional professional role. For example, one child and family health nurse may prefer to stick to the traditional 'paediatric surveillance' role of weighing and measuring infants and checking for developmental disorders. In contrast, another nurse may use these important tasks as a means to other ends, developing a trusting relationship with parents and responding to psychosocial problems such as postnatal depression, domestic violence and social isolation (Scott, 1992).

Service providers within a particular occupational group or a service sector can probably be placed along a spectrum of role performance from narrow to broad, similar to that suggested by McCaughey, Shaver & Ferber (1977):

- narrow – core role only ('it's not my concern')
- somewhat narrow – core role and assessment of 'other needs', leading to referral for the latter ('it's a concern but someone else's job – refer on')

- somewhat broad – clients' 'other needs' are incidental but unavoidable ('not my core role but I need to do it if I am going to do my core role')
- broad – 'other needs' are an intrinsic part of the core role ('it's all part and parcel of my job').

The breadth with which a practitioner plays his or her role is not just an individual matter but is also shaped collectively by the profession or occupation. Role definition is at the centre of occupational identity: 'As an occupational group seeks to establish itself as a profession, it focuses its role around the specialised areas for which its members have training and expertise; in the process marginal tasks are excluded as inappropriate' (McCaughey, Shaver & Ferber, 1977, p. 166).

In response to scientific and technological advances and emerging community needs, professional roles need to evolve and it can be hypothesised that tasks perceived as 'higher status' marginal roles will be more likely to be adopted than tasks perceived as 'lower status' marginal roles.

The way practitioners work is not just a reflection of their individual and professional predisposition. Practice occurs within an organisational setting, a service system context and a particular social policy environment (Figure 2.1). Organisations often compete with one another for scarce resources, and they typically belong to sectors such as 'health', 'education' or 'social services', each with their separate funding sources and policy priorities. This can lead to narrow and rigid silos and 'single input services based on categorical funding'. The emergence of new 'whole of government' approaches to policy and service delivery that attempt to transcend sectoral silos is a source of hope.

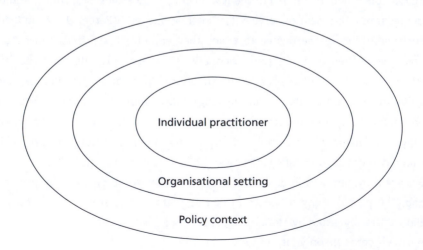

Figure 2.1   Levels of analysis for breadth of service provider role performance (based on Scott, 2009)

Professional boundaries can reflect and reinforce sectoral boundaries. The fields of health, education and social services can differ in their values, knowledge and skills, as well as in legal obligations, mandate and status. Such differences may be a great strength in terms of the depth of expertise they bring, but can also be a great weakness in terms of competition and a narrowing of roles and responsibilities. The emergence of an overarching bio-psychosocial perspective across professions working with children and families is another source of hope in addressing these challenges (see Chapter 1).

Other contextual factors that may influence an organisation's capacity to provide a more family-centred service for vulnerable families include:

- legal requirements, such as mandatory reporting of suspected child maltreatment, which may inhibit a service provider from getting 'too involved' in children's needs for fear of endangering a fragile therapeutic relationship with the parent
- privacy constraints on information-sharing between organisations, which may inhibit a comprehensive understanding of family needs
- 'single input services' based on categorical funding models, which will limit the capacity to provide comprehensive responses to families with multiple and complex needs
- resource scarcity, which may lead to increased 'gatekeeping' in relation to resource-intensive cases where there are multiple and complex needs
- strong centralised reform drivers in government and budget pooling across sectors and portfolios that may support broader, family-centred service delivery
- good cost-effectiveness data, which demonstrates the value of providing a broader service, can provide evidence to support such initiatives (Scott, 2009).

REFLECTIVE QUESTIONS

What are the key historical events that have shaped occupational roles in your field?

What are the main influences currently determining what are 'core' and 'marginal' roles in your field? Where would you put yourself on the narrow-to-broad spectrum in relation to how you 'play your role'? Has this changed? What factors determine whether you are able to perform a broader role?

◼ Working together

Organisations work together in many ways, ranging from the informal to the more formal. This spectrum has been described as beginning with cooperation, with increasing levels of formality, proceeding to coordination, collaboration and integration (Konrad, 1996).

- *Cooperation*, in which practitioners in different organisations may informally exchange information about their expertise and services to assist one another to meet the needs of their clients. Being located on the same site can increase the opportunity for people from different services to know one another and cooperate in such informal ways. For example, a preschool teacher may contact someone at a migrant resource centre to get information that may assist a non-English-speaking refugee family, who have just moved into the area, to access the services they require.

- *Coordination*, in which interactions between organisations are governed by formal organisational protocols, such as those relating to the release of information or the making of a referral. For example, in accord with an inter-agency agreement, a child and family health nurse may accompany a parent to a family support service and participate in the intake interview, so that both services and the parent are in clear agreement on the case plan and how information will be exchanged.

- *Collaboration* is sometimes used as a general term for working together, but it is also used in a more specific way to describe how services work side by side in an initiative auspiced by both agencies. An example of inter-sectoral collaboration between a child welfare service and a drug treatment service was the establishment of an innovative therapeutic playgroup for parents and their young children within a Sydney methadone clinic (Mohammed, 2003).

- *Integration* occurs when a new organisational form is created, sometimes merging what were previously separate services, or when a new structure is created. For example, in order to reduce duplication of intake services and to ensure that families would be referred to the most appropriate service, a single entry point into all the non-government family services funded by the government in a geographical area was developed (Leung, 2003).

White and Winkworth (2012) have developed a 'rubric' to help local networks of services assess their readiness to collaborate, and to identify the areas that may need to be strengthened to achieve successful and sustainable collaboration. They outline three drivers of partnership building: a shared commitment to collaboration; a common vision of what can be achieved through collaboration; and the capacity to sustain collaboration. White and Winkworth emphasise the importance of an 'authorising environment': one in which the collaborative efforts have legitimacy and support, and where the vision is embraced at all organisational levels – senior executive, operational managers and frontline staff.

Working across organisational boundaries in a family-centred way can be very challenging, because organisations may have different members of a family as their primary clients and there may not even be a consensus on the need to communicate or work together. For example, collaboration between a drug and alcohol treatment service and a statutory child protection service raises complex ethical and professional dilemmas (Scott & Campbell, 1994). For the drug and alcohol treatment agency, the parent is the primary client and there may be a realistic apprehension that sharing information with a child welfare service could frighten parents and lead to their withdrawal from a voluntary treatment service.

At the same time, professionals have a 'duty of care' to others, such as children, who may be harmed by their client. The priority of the child welfare service, on the other hand, is to assess if it is safe for a child to remain in the home, or whether restoring a child in care to their family is a viable goal. At the same time, they need the parent to remain effectively engaged with a treatment agency in order to maximise the child's safety. While there is a growing body of research on inter-agency collaboration between these two specific fields (for example, Smith & Mogro-Wilson, 2008), there are no simple solutions. Protocols may help govern the interaction, but on their own cannot guarantee the skilled professional discernment and mutual respect that such complex and sensitive situations require.

While it is generally assumed that working together is a good thing, some researchers in this field have argued:

> From an agency's viewpoint, collaborative activity raises two main difficulties. First, it loses some of its freedom to act independently, when it would prefer to maintain control over its domain and affairs. Secondly, it must invest scarce resources and energy in developing and maintaining relationships with other organisations, when the potential returns on this investment are often unclear or intangible.
>
> (Hudson, 1987, p. 175)

That is, to meet their survival needs, organisations have to maximise autonomy and conserve resources. A certain level of conflict between organisations is therefore to be expected and this needs to be addressed rather than avoided.

Having a way of understanding such tensions can help depersonalise the situation and identify possible solutions. Scott (2005) undertook a qualitative study of inter-agency interaction in child protection cases, and identified five levels of analysis: inter-organisational; intra-organisational; inter-professional; interpersonal; and intrapersonal. These levels of analysis are not mutually exclusive, as there are often tensions at multiple levels.

Inter-organisational level

Organisations have a history of past interactions with one another. If the legacy is a positive one, there may be a good store of trust and reciprocity for service providers to draw upon. If the legacy is negative and laden with past conflicts, one organisation may be held responsible by another for the perceived acts of its predecessors. If this is the case, then it may be important to acknowledge the legacy and try to reduce the risk of the past contaminating current attempts to work together.

Understanding the primary source(s) of inter-agency tensions is vital. If the source of the tension is primarily inter-organisational or structural, then this will require a different strategy from one that is appropriate if the problem is primarily interpersonal. Undergoing the process of such analysis in itself may facilitate a shift in the perception of the problem and help defuse conflict. For example, what was originally seen as an interpersonal difficulty may come to be understood as predominantly structural in its origin. This is not to say that interpersonal conflicts do not play a significant part in inter-organisational tensions. There is the potential for such conflict in all human encounters. Practitioners need to ask themselves, 'If I changed jobs with the person in the organisation with which I am now in conflict, would we swap sides on this issue?' If the answer is 'yes', then the tension is likely to be structural, not interpersonal.

Policy and funding arrangements are obviously central to tensions arising between organisations. For example, in a service system in which there are many non-government organisations vying for limited government funding on the basis of competitive tendering, it is going to be harder for such organisations to work together in the interests of families.

We see strategies to conserve scarce organisational resources in 'gatekeeping', or in attempts to resist referrals from other organisations, particularly if they are likely to be 'resource hungry' and place pressure on staff. For example, organisations may require prospective clients to ring and make their own appointments. This may be justified in terms of principles such as 'client self-determination' and the need to ensure that clients are voluntary and motivated, but if we require this of highly stressed families with multiple and complex needs, they are unlikely to receive a service. The intended or unintended consequence of such criteria is often to exclude the most marginalised.

Some organisations have greater capacity to 'gatekeep' and to be more selective about the referrals they accept than others. Those with less capacity must nevertheless develop mechanisms to prevent being overwhelmed with demand pressures. For example, statutory child protection services may 'triage' referrals or raise the threshold of eligibility by accepting only those cases that are deemed to require legal intervention. When organisations making the referrals operate on a lower threshold of risk, as occurs when reporting all cases of suspected child abuse is mandatory, the large gap between the threshold for making a referral and acting on a referral can lead to enormous strain between organisations. This is one of the major sources of conflict in the child protection field.

Demand pressures on statutory child protection services, and the inevitable 'gatekeeping problems' this causes, have led to policy and service system reform in some jurisdictions. Victoria, New South Wales and Tasmania, for example, have all developed new non-statutory 'diversionary' routes through which families that are struggling to protect and nurture their children can be assisted to prevent statutory intervention becoming necessary.

New approaches to the sharing of information between services in relation to vulnerable children have also been implemented in many jurisdictions and between the Australian Government and State and Territory governments. Especially under conditions of resource scarcity, such broad policy and systems reform is difficult to achieve, and so practitioners need to continue operating in imperfect systems. Campbell (1999) has proposed some valuable principles and practical processes for building a more collaborative service network under such conditions. Daniel (2004) has also proposed a model for a 'protective network' in the field of child welfare in which help for a child can be accessed via any entry point in the network of organisations having routine contact with the child.

ACTIVITIES

Draw a diagram of a service network, depicting each of those organisations that have an overlapping client population as a separate circle. Insert lines connecting those organisations that you know have direct contact with one another. Why might some organisations that share an overlapping client population not have contact with one another? Answer the following questions for each organisation in the diagram and consider whether the answers help to explain the potential for inter-organisational conflict. Who does each organisation define as the primary client? How does each organisation define its 'core role'? Which organisations are more dependent on other organisations in the network (such as for funding, information or referrals)? Which organisations have the most power and influence? Which organisations are competitors (for funding or clients, for example)? Which organisations have overlapping or blurred mandates or roles?

Consult any documents you can access (say from organisational websites and practice manuals) that establish protocols for the way organisations need to relate to one another when they share clients such as a family with multiple and complex needs, as well as vulnerable children living in the household. What do you see as the strengths and weaknesses of the protocols? Have there been any recent changes to these protocols and, if so, what is the intention behind such changes? Do you think they carry the risk of any unintended consequences that may make it more difficult for families to receive the assistance they need?

Intra-organisational level of analysis

Sometimes the source of inter-agency tensions is related to dysfunctional dynamics within an organisation. For example, some teams and organisations generate internal cohesion by making another organisation into 'the common enemy'. This is perpetuated through staff telling 'atrocity stories' in which the narrative is always the same – the failure and incompetence of the other organisation. Such dynamics can also operate between different sections or programs within an organisation.

We have probably all been guilty of telling 'atrocity stories' about another service at some stage. This may seem innocent enough and may allow us to vent frustration, but it can also contaminate the attitudes of new staff before they have even encountered anyone from the other service. A high level of scapegoating of another organisation reflects poorly on the leadership of the organisation doing the scapegoating. Often the leadership skills needed to address internal tensions or generate cohesion by other means are sorely lacking.

There is usually resistance to looking closely at the factors within a team or organisation that contribute to inter-agency tensions. A change of leadership may sometimes be necessary to bring about a new climate for collaboration. While most management and organisational consultants do not usually operate across organisational boundaries, Roberts (1994) has described the value of consultation in dealing with inter-group rivalry and conflict between health and social services in the UK. Mediation and conciliation processes may also be helpful in addressing recurrent conflicts.

REFLECTIVE QUESTIONS

Can you recall telling or hearing an 'atrocity story' about an organisation? What function did this serve for those telling the story? What may be the long-term effects of such narratives on service providers and on families?

Have you ever been in a team or an organisation that seems to develop its internal cohesion by engaging in conflict with others? How may this be addressed?

Inter-professional level of analysis

Sometimes we work across professional boundaries and organisational boundaries at the same time. Tensions similar to those that can occur in a multidisciplinary team within an organisation (such as 'demarcation disputes', power struggles and different values), can also occur when professional and organisational boundaries are crossed at the same time. The difference is that, when inter-professional tensions occur within an organisation, there is a leadership structure that can potentially address the problem, but this is typically lacking between organisations.

Status hierarchies often get in the way of professions working together. For example, higher status may be accorded to those whose roles are defined as 'therapy' than to those who provide concrete or material services for families, or to those who provide direct care for a child. Those closest to children and families in their day-to-day lives are usually those who know them best, yet paradoxically they are usually those least heard in case conferences and least influential in decision-making.

There may be differences between professions in their styles of communication and decision-making, about which the participants are largely unaware. For example, in a study on child protection case conferences, it was observed that health professionals were cautious about interpretation and speculation, and that police found the discursive consensus-seeking culture of welfare services frustrating (Scott, Lindsay & Jackson, 1995). In such circumstances, just recognising and openly acknowledging such differences may help to defuse the problem.

REFLECTIVE QUESTIONS
Professions and occupational groups sometimes resemble 'tribes', providing their members with a sense of personal identity and belonging. Do you belong to such a tribe? Whose interests are served by in-group and out-group boundaries? What impact may professional tribalism have on our capacity to work together in the interests of children and their families?

Interpersonal level of analysis

Interpersonal factors can help or hinder working across organisational boundaries. This is true everywhere, but is particularly obvious in regional and rural settings, where personal social networks overlap with professional and organisational networks to a marked degree. This can be a great asset, with positive pre-existing relationships and goodwill facilitating cooperation. When pre-existing relationships are strained, however, inter-agency collaboration may be much more difficult than if people do not know one another. The fear of conflict erupting and rippling through dense social networks may act as a useful curb on conflict; but if it just leads to conflict avoidance, it may make it more difficult to address the underlying problem.

Families can also fuel interpersonal conflict between services. For example, a school or a child welfare agency can become the common enemy against which a usually fragmented family may unite. When a practitioner in another organisation joins forces with the family against the service that is the 'common enemy', inter-agency relationships are further weakened. This is not to say that services do not sometimes behave in ways that warrant another agency acting as an advocate for the family, but the risk of families 'splitting' agencies needs to be considered. Sometimes it is tempting to engage a family by siding with them against another organisation, but the gains are likely to be short-term and to reduce the social capital that is essential to inter-agency collaboration in other cases.

We need to use a high level of interpersonal skills when working across organisational boundaries. The capacity to communicate clearly, to show respect and to build trust, are as vital in establishing good working relationships with other organisations as they are with families. Supervisors and team leaders have a key role to play in supporting staff to develop and sustain positive working relationships with other organisations.

REFLECTIVE QUESTIONS

Can you think of an example of inter-organisational conflict where interpersonal factors exacerbated or reduced the level of conflict? What are the values and skills that a practitioner needs to work effectively across organisational boundaries?

Intrapersonal level of analysis

Working with vulnerable children and families can be very distressing and can evoke painful feelings for service providers. In the face of strong emotions it is common for defence mechanisms, such as projection and displacement, to come into play. This can intensify inter-agency and inter-professional tensions, and lead to destructive levels of conflict. In a study of inter-agency conflict in a child protection context, it was most intense in those cases in which practitioners felt impotent to protect a vulnerable child (Scott, 1997).

For example, when child neglect was a long-standing problem in the family, or when there were suspicions but little evidence that a child had been sexually abused, deep emotions were aroused in all of the practitioners involved. Each sincerely believed that it was beyond their organisation's ability to protect the child, but some strongly believed that another service had the power to do so, even when there was little rational basis for this view. While this may relate to a lack of understanding of the capacities and constraints of other organisations, another explanation is that we sometimes cope with strong feelings such as anger and guilt by projecting responsibility or displacing hostility onto others.

In another study that explored the attitudes of different professions to child sexual abuse vignettes, responses were contrary to those expected by professional stereotypes, leading the researchers to comment:

It may be that for the child welfare workers vis-à-vis the court, just as for mental health workers vis-à-vis therapy, repeated exposure to demanding, less-than-successful procedures breeds doubt, and procedures on the other side of the professional fence look brighter.

(Wilk & McCarthy, 1986, p. 25)

Others, using a psychoanalytic perspective, have tried to explain why it can be so difficult to 'take the position of the other' when strong anxiety is aroused in interactions between organisations.

The potential for dissonance and conflict increases the more splitting and denial (i.e., mental partition) is the dominant defence employed by shared clients or patients, and the more their problems occasion high levels of realistic anxiety, stimulating powerful unconscious phantasies in practitioners and their managers. The more threatening the anxiety, the greater and more rigid the practitioners' reliance on socially structured institutional defences and the more fraught it becomes to enter imaginatively into each other's working world for fear of losing hold of their own. Practitioners may then fall back on the 'bedrock' of a narrowly defined primary task.

(Woodhouse & Pengelly, 1991, pp. 229–30)

High-quality clinical supervision is vital for dealing with such charged situations. We also sometimes bring our own individual issues to these conflicts. For example, there may be personal reasons why we are drawn to identify very strongly with one family member and to work in a particular service, and this can lead to a greater intensity of conflict with organisations that are advocates for another family member. Of course, sometimes it is necessary to be an advocate for a vulnerable member of a family, such as in cases of family violence or child maltreatment, and in those instances a certain level of conflict between the organisations representing the interests of different family members is probably unavoidable. The task, then, is to manage the conflict in ways that are least destructive.

While it is important to acknowledge and address conflict in inter-organisational relationships, it is also important not to overstate it. A major UK survey of different professions involved in child protection found that, contrary to the picture portrayed in official inquiries into child abuse controversies, most professionals reported that local inter-professional networks functioned reasonably well (Hallet & Birchall, 1992). Australian research by Darlington, Feeney and Rixon (2004), which explored the interface of child protection and adult mental health services, also found that in at least half the cases shared by both services, collaboration worked well. If we knew more about the conditions under which organisations work together effectively, we would be better able to recreate these conditions in other settings.

REFLECTIVE QUESTIONS
Think about high-risk situations that may arise in relation to mental health, domestic violence or child protection issues. What might help practitioners deal with the anxiety such situations arouse so that safety can be maintained and inter-agency relationships not weakened? Can you think of a situation like this where people in different organisations managed to work together more effectively than one might have expected? What might have made this possible? Are there any lessons that can be learned from this example?

ACTIVITY
Adam is two years old and has a history of serious 'faltering growth' or 'non-organic failure to thrive' with no medical cause having been found for his poor weight gain. He is significantly behind in his motor and cognitive developmental milestones, and his language skills are very poor. Statutory child protection services have confirmed that Adam is suffering from neglect and 'cumulative harm'. There is an application before the court for an order to require the family to receive ongoing supervision and monitoring of Adam's condition. The identity of his father is unknown. Adam's mother, Alice, is 23 and is six months pregnant. She spent most of her childhood in State care and experienced multiple foster placements. Alice lives with her boyfriend Robert, who is the father of the baby she is expecting. Robert is unemployed and is on probation for drug-related offences. Alice appears depressed and anxious, and seems very emotionally dependent on Robert. They live in private rental accommodation in a large rural town and have no extended family support. A range of services is involved with the family (child and family health nurse, childcare centre, non-government family support service, general practitioner, drug and alcohol treatment service, correctional services and statutory child protection services).

   In a small group, explore the current and future needs of Adam and his family and consider the part each of the services involved may play by having these various services represented by different individuals or subgroups in the group. How may the services work together to assist Adam and his family? What may be the personal, professional and organisational challenges you could face in working together with this family? What may each practitioner need to fulfil their role to the best of their ability?

■ Conclusion

The current policy environment offers some exciting opportunities to redevelop professional roles and services so that they are more holistic and individually tailored to families' needs. There is increasing recognition that organisations need to work together, especially for families with multiple and complex needs. This is not just a matter of exhorting people to do so – that is much the same as saying to a troubled family 'Why don't you smile and try being nice to one another?' To improve how we work across organisations and sectors, we need to understand the obstacles, identify the opportunities and cultivate within ourselves and our own organisations the values, knowledge and skills to support working together. Given that our work with vulnerable families is so mediated through organisations, there is no alternative. Considering all of the obstacles, especially those at a structural level, it is to the credit of practitioners and a reflection of their commitment to the families they serve that they work with one another as well as they do.

■ Useful websites

Australian Centre for Child Protection: **www.unisa.edu.au/childprotection**

Australian Government – Social Inclusion: **www.socialinclusion.gov.au**

Australian Institute of Family Studies: **www.aifs.gov.au**

Children of Parents with a Mental Illness: **www.copmi.net.au**

Kids Central Toolkit: **www.acu.edu.au/about_acu/faculties,_institutes_and_ centres/centres/institute_of_child_protection_studies/kids_central_toolkit**

National Center on Family Homelessness: **www.familyhomelessness.org/ media/91.pdf**

Salvation Army: **www.salvationarmy.org.au/en/Find-Us/Tasmania/Safe-from- the-Start-Project**

Social Care Institute for Excellence (SCIE) resources for inter-professional and inter-agency collaboration: **www.scie.org.uk/publications/elearning/ipiac/ index.asp?**

Victorian Association for the Care and Resettlement of Offenders (VACRO): **www.vacro.org.au**

3

Family-centred practice in early childhood settings

Dorothy Scott

■ Learning goals

This chapter will enable you to:

- **RECOGNISE** the potential of early childhood practitioners in health and education settings to engage parents of vulnerable children in ways that will enhance their ability to nurture and protect their children

- **UNDERSTAND** contemporary developments in policy and practice in relation to family-centred early childhood services

- **LEARN** about some innovative exemplars of Australian family-centred initiatives in early childhood settings and consider what may be applicable to other settings

- **BE SENSITIVE** to the needs of children and parents from culturally diverse backgrounds

- **THINK** about how different professions and services can work together for *and* with vulnerable families and their children

- **REFLECT** on the professional and personal challenges that may be faced when responding to the needs of vulnerable children and their families.

■ Introduction

WE ARE IN an exciting era of innovation in early childhood services. With the (re)discovery of the importance of the 'early years', new ideas about how early childhood services can be delivered, regardless of whether they are traditionally seen as 'health', 'education' or 'social welfare' services, are blossoming. Strengths-based ways of working with families are influencing the way in which practitioners are reaching out to parents and enhancing their ability to nurture and protect their children. Policies, programs and face-to-face practice are all in the process of transformation. This chapter provides a background to, and overview of, some of these developments; describes innovative early childhood Australian exemplars of family-centred approaches and their common principles; and identifies some of the challenges involved in working in such ways.

■ Looking back to see ahead

The early 20th century witnessed major advances in 'child welfare', a term that was then used in a similar sense to the term 'child wellbeing' today, and which crossed the sectors of education, health and social services. The pioneers of the key professions involved were sometimes more family- and community-centred than those who followed, with the cumulative influences of professionalisation, credentialism and specialisation sometimes combining to narrow the roles of services and practitioners. However, there have always been some individual practitioners in early childhood services who have been passionate about working with families and communities and who have seen this as central to their work with children. In this chapter, we shall hear a few of their voices as well as those of parents participating in such services.

In the field of early childhood education, the ideas of Froebel, the father of the kindergarten movement, spread across the world in the late 19th and early 20th centuries (Rogers, 2003). Froebel tended to see the kindergarten as a haven in which children might be freed from parental control, whereas Lillian de Lissa, a pioneer of the kindergarten movement in Australia who went on to become an international figure in the field, embraced parents as partners. Historian Helen Jones has brought to light the way Lillian de Lissa helped mothers to become ambassadors of progressive ideas and practices concerning health and education in their local Adelaide communities.

> Through mothers' clubs, the first begun in Franklin Street in 1906, these women co-operated in ancillary tasks for the free kindergartens and also gained useful knowledge of child rearing and health. Most lived in very poor circumstances; their experience was widened through contact with the kindergartens and in seeing the improvement in their own children's physical development and general abilities. Out of the Franklin Street Free Kindergarten mothers' club came not only personal advantages for members, but their own acts of altruism which extended the benefits of kindergartens to others.
>
> (Jones, 1986, p. 173)

In the field of infant health, there is evidence of similarly progressive thinking by the founding mothers. During the economic depression of the late 1920s and early 1930s in Victoria, Dr Vera Scantlebury Brown and Sister Muriel Peck established the State-wide system of infant welfare centres (later called maternal and child health centres). Dr Scantlebury Brown was also responsible for Victorian preschools. In her 1940–41 *Director of Infant Welfare Report*, Dr Scantlebury Brown noted that parents' clubs, mothers' clubs, get-together clubs and infant welfare leagues were flourishing in some infant welfare centres and that there were large numbers of volunteer helpers (Victorian Commission of Public Health, 1940–41). She also noted the close collaboration between infant welfare centres, the Lady Gowrie Pre-School Child Centre and other early childhood services. Family- and community-centred practice in maternal and child health nursing, now commonly seen as a very recent development, had strong roots in its origins. Interestingly, it was often the same women who campaigned for and established both infant health and kindergarten services.

In the field of social services, much of the innovation in the early 20th century was the result of philanthropic, rather than government, initiatives. In the economic depression of the 1890s, the plight of unmarried mothers and their infants was dire (Swain, 1995), with no government benefits to protect them from destitution. Extreme poverty, lack of contraception and the intense social stigma surrounding illegitimacy resulted in the abandonment of many newborn babies in lanes and along riverbanks of our cities and led to the practice of 'baby farming' – the placement of several infants in private homes in impoverished neighbourhoods, where babies frequently died as a result of malnourishment and neglect (Swain, 1995).

In response to deep social concern about 'baby farming' and the plight of these children and their mothers, women of private means in places such as Sydney and Melbourne established charitable 'day nurseries', where infants and children under school age could be cared for while their unmarried mothers went out to work. These day nurseries were the earliest form of organised child care in Australia. One of these, the Sydney Day Nurseries Association (now known as SDN Children's Services), will be highlighted later in this chapter in relation to its innovative work among very vulnerable families with infants and preschool children.

Throughout the history of early childhood health, education and social services, there have been many changes, some resulting from advances in technology and knowledge. For example, by the 1920s the development of 'babies' homes' became possible because of the advent of infant formula. In some places, church organisations established homes to 'rescue' infants from the 'social evils' of the slums. Paradoxically, later developments in knowledge were an important factor in helping to close such institutions. For example, by the 1970s, research by Bowlby and others on the effects of institutional care on infants was influential in bringing about the closure of babies' homes, as well as liberalising the very rigid parental visiting policies and practices in children's hospitals.

The 1970s was an era of marked changes in social policy and human services in Australia. It also witnessed significant innovation within non-government organisations that had previously provided institutional care for children. For example, the Uniting Church in Victoria closed the Methodist Babies Home and replaced it with very high-quality early childhood education and care *and* parenting education and support for families. Located close to the inner urban public housing estates of Richmond and Prahran, a multidisciplinary team of trained early childhood education and care workers, social workers and child health nurses was developed. Staff reached out to vulnerable families, often collecting children from their homes, which provided informal opportunities to build rapport with parents. Many of the parents, mostly single mothers, were struggling to nurture their children under difficult circumstances, such as their own childhoods of deprivation and neglect, financial stress, substandard housing, and poor physical and mental health. The parents were strongly encouraged to come to the centre, which had a special room for them, and to participate in its activities. Children were not segregated by age, but belonged to home groups of five children, with two caregivers to each group, who were warm and consistent figures in the parents' lives as well as their children's lives. Many 'teachable moments' occurred every day, which provided opportunities for enhancing responsive and sensitive parenting. Unfortunately this service, similar in nature to the famous Perry Pre-School in the US, came to an end in the 1980s due to a loss in government funding. Three decades later, this type of family-centred early childhood service for very vulnerable children and their parents is the model that is being re-created by the Children's Protection Society in Melbourne in its Early Years Education Research Project (www.eyerp.org/background).

The 1970s also saw the emergence of the playgroup movement to provide enriched opportunities for parents and young children to interact with one another in a local setting. While most playgroups are self-governing, in 'supported playgroups' a paid facilitator is involved until the group is well enough established to become self-sustaining. Supported playgroups usually meet on a weekly basis and their aim is to reach families with additional needs, including those from culturally and linguistically diverse backgrounds, Indigenous families, families where a parent or a child has a mental illness or a disability, teenage parents and families who are socially isolated and disadvantaged.

Supported playgroup coordinators also provide parenting information and help to link parents to other services they may need. Playgroups are especially valuable in providing a non-stigmatised and accessible service for families with very young children who are in the age group that falls between the predominantly infant-focused child and family health services and the preschool or kindergarten services. A recent study based on three supported playgroups in western Sydney explored parents' views of the different types of social support they received from these programs, emphasising the strong relational and peer support as well as informational support parents gave one another and their children in these settings (Jackson, 2011).

■ Contemporary policy context

Political support and a strong policy framework are vital if family-centred early childhood services are to be sustained and 'scaled up' to reach all vulnerable children and their families.

New Zealand has shown leadership in developing strong early childhood services with high standards in relation to staff–child ratios. Most Australian States and Territories now have 'early years' policies, and some have pioneered the development of 'integrated' children's centres that bring together a range of programs and organisations, with a community development focus as well as direct service delivery. Historical divisions between the early childhood education and child care sectors, and between federal and state responsibilities, have been major obstacles to developing integrated early childhood policies and services in Australia.

In relation to child and family health services, known in some States as maternal and child health services, there is enormous variation across jurisdictions in the degree to which there are universal services that reach families with infants. There is also significant variation in the degree to which they are narrowly focused on paediatric surveillance (monitoring infant and child growth and development) or encompass the social and emotional wellbeing of families and communities. Furthermore, there is also variation in the degree to which such universal services have been developed to act as non-stigmatised platforms through which vulnerable families with complex additional needs can receive a more intensive and individually tailored service.

In some States and Territories, targeted child and family health nursing services have been developed and are offered to families with complex needs in their own homes. For example, in South Australia, all families of newborns are offered at least one visit from a qualified community child and family health nurse. Based on the service's knowledge of the family and on the family's responses to a standardised survey, the family may be offered a more sustained Family Home Visiting program. The structure and delivery of this program draws upon the learnings from Olds and colleagues' Nurse–Family Partnership Program and, for Aboriginal families, upon the knowledge of previous home visiting programs for Aboriginal families in metropolitan Adelaide (Arney, Bowering, et al., 2010). Trained child and family health nurses provide a service focusing on child health and development and parent–child attachment for up to two years. For Aboriginal families, Indigenous cultural consultants work in partnership with nurses to engage families and provide the service. Research has shown that the non-stigmatising method of engagement used by this program has been instrumental in linking Aboriginal families to a high-quality maternal and infant care service (Sivak, Arney & Lewig, 2008).

There are also centre-based initiatives. Panaretto et al. (2005) have demonstrated how an antenatal clinic in Townsville, designed specifically for Aboriginal and Torres Strait Islander women and delivered within an Aboriginal community controlled health service, can improve outcomes for women and their babies.

Some non-government organisations have pioneered the use of universal early childhood education and care services as 'platforms' from which more specialist services can be offered to families with more complex needs. Through the Australian Government's 'Invest to Grow' initiative, Lady Gowrie Centres have pioneered the 'Through the Looking Glass Project' www.gowrie–adelaide.com.au/cms/node/19, an early intervention strategy in five child care settings across Australia for families where there is an impaired parent–child attachment relationship. The 18-week program provides intensive support, therapeutic intervention and high-quality child care for families where there are multiple risk factors including anxiety, depression, social isolation and early trauma in the parent's own life. A therapist and child care worker collaborate closely with each other and the family. The program also helps to build social bonds between families.

ACTIVITY

Talk to people who work in the early childhood field and ask them how they feel about and see their role in relation to working with vulnerable parents, especially when they are caring for a child whom they can see is not receiving optimal care at home.

■ Innovative exemplars

There are many innovative exemplars of early childhood health and education services being developed by committed and skilful practitioners. While some of these have been subject to substantial evaluation, others are yet to be fully evaluated, so our understanding of whether they are effective and, if so, why they may be effective, is undeveloped at this stage.

While most program evaluations focus on the nature of the program's interventions and outcomes, there is increasing awareness that the people behind a program, and working together in ways that enhance high morale and hope, may be equally critical ingredients of success (see Chapters 8 and 13).

The following four exemplars have been subject to varying degrees of evaluation, and have been selected for their disciplinary diversity as well as their common values and principles.

Holistic and culturally competent services for refugee and migrant families

Families from culturally and linguistically diverse backgrounds may not be familiar with Western models of early childhood services and it is sometimes challenging for early childhood services to become welcoming and 'culturally safe' places for such families. An organisation that has led innovation in this field is VICSEG New Futures (www.vicsegnewfutures.org.au), initially known as the Victorian Cooperative on Children's Services for Ethnic Groups. An early focus of the organisation's work was to enhance the cultural competence of mainstream early childhood services in multi-ethnic communities through the placement of bicultural and bilingual staff for a day or so a week in these settings. The bicultural workers engaged refugee and recent immigrant families in the service system, and helped to enhance the cultural sensitivity and competence of mainstream early childhood health and education practitioners by working alongside them.

Bicultural workers were also trained to be facilitators for supported playgroups for refugee and migrant families and their young children. Recognising that parental participation in employment was vital to the future prospects of these families in Australian society, the agency became a registered training organisation, offering accredited vocational education in health and community services, aged care, child care, hospitality and business through its New Futures initiative. This is an impressive example of a community-controlled early childhood service evolving to respond to the broader social and economic needs of the families and communities it serves.

First-time parent groups, Victorian Maternal and Child Health Service

Maternal and child health services in Victoria are delivered by local government and largely funded by the State Government. It is a very well respected universal service with approximately 98 per cent of all families with an infant using the service in the first year. In the past few decades, the service has evolved from one that was almost exclusively focused on infant health and development to one that is also focused on family emotional and social wellbeing and on strengthening social support.

The capacity of maternal and child health services to strengthen social networks at the neighbourhood level is now recognised and all first-time parents in the State are offered the opportunity to join a series of approximately eight group sessions facilitated by their nurse at their local maternal and child health centre. Group sessions cover a broad and flexible range of topics such as: adjustment to first-time parenthood, women's health post birth, child safety in the home, infant 'settling' techniques, baby massage and nutrition. Two-thirds of first-time mothers join such groups (Scott, Brady & Glynn, 2001).

Victorian maternal and child health nurses have been trained to facilitate groups in non-didactic ways to maximise group interaction and cohesion so that they are likely to continue of their own accord (Edgecomb et al., 2001). A follow-up study in two outer urban local government areas of Melbourne found that over three-quarters of the groups were still regularly meeting on their own, mostly in group members' homes, 18 months to two years after the nurse-facilitated groups had ended. Where groups ended due to women returning to paid employment, significant one-to-one friendships continued in most cases (Scott, Brady & Glynn, 2001).

In-depth interviews with the maternal and child health nurses in two outer suburban government areas identified how nurses actively encouraged mothers to participate in the groups through the one-to-one relationship they had established with them in routine visits.

> The reasons nurses gave mothers for attending the group ranged from being child-focused (for example, the benefits to the baby of information on feeding or CPR) to mother-focused (for example, social contact), and nurses varied the reasons according to what they thought would appeal to the women. For example, one described how she emphasised the practical aspects of the content of the sessions saying that 'some of them don't want the gossip thing'. Another conveyed the idea of group participation as a normative expectation but did so in a subtle and unpressured manner. 'You promote it as something for all new parents and give some information and then gradually turn it around to meeting others and transition to parenthood issues. I think it would put them off if I wasn't low key.'
>
> (Scott, Brady & Glynn, 2001, p. 24)

Some nurses saw the purpose of the group as being primarily community-building, with social contact and peer support being more important than information provision. This was how some mothers saw it as well. The nurses therefore facilitated the group in informal and unstructured ways to help the group 'gel'.

> 'My overall aim is to get them connected with one another … I don't give information directly, I draw out their experiences' said one nurse. This was echoed by another who commented that 'Sometimes they don't want information and I have to balance that – they want the social experience …' Nurses facilitated participation in the group in a number of ways. Some introduced themselves as mothers, thus minimising the social distance between them and the other women, and modelling limited and appropriate self-disclosure ('I give a little anecdote and if people don't talk I'll tell them mine and draw them in'). Many nurses emphasised the importance of doing the introductions well and ensuring that the members actually got to learn one another's names … Some nurses deliberately underscored what the mothers had in common in order to strengthen the cohesion of the group, and avoided drawing attention to differences.
>
> (Scott, Brady & Glynn, 2001, p. 26)

Some maternal and child health nurses in this study were highly successful in engaging hard-to-reach groups such as fathers, young mothers and immigrant families. For example, one nurse in a low-income urban–rural fringe community wrote to all the fathers of new babies and invited them, along with their partners and babies, to come to an evening session on 'how to save your baby's life'. Offering practical skills in infant resuscitation was what got the men through the door but once they were there, the nurse used her warmth, humour and down-to-earth manner to engage them in more sensitive issues such as the impact of a new baby on couple relationships, and the serious risks associated with shaking babies. For many of the families, such evenings nurtured new friendships and so strengthened neighbourhood social support.

In relation to young mothers, one nurse confessed 'With the real teenage mum I haven't had much success – the one looking for Mum thinks I am wonderful but the one rebelling against Mum thinks I am terrible' (Scott, Brady & Glynn, 2001, p. 27). In contrast, another nurse had been able to engage young mothers in a group by not trying to mix them in with other women but offering a group especially oriented to their needs.

> These groups were described as being very different from other groups ('I serve coke instead of tea!') and less reflective and more action oriented ('we just sat on the floor and made toys and they loved it'). One nurse said she avoided using videos (DVDs) as the adolescent mothers just 'switched off as if they were back in the classroom'.
>
> (Scott, Brady & Glynn, 2001, p. 27)

Some nurses described working effectively with immigrant mothers, either linking them into ethnic-specific women's groups, which were mostly conducted in their own language, or having English-speaking groups for women from a range of different countries.

> One nurse was excited about one of her groups in which ethnic diversity was actually what gave the group its cohesion. 'There are virtually no Anglo-Australians and it's a real multicultural group and they're mixing really well together' she said, adding that the husbands had also joined in regular social occasions which the group had organised. Another nurse described how 'in one group there was only one "Anglo" and they were a very diverse group' … the most popular session she had run for that group was on the theme of 'parenting in a new land' in which the members had shared similar experiences.
>
> (Scott, Brady & Glynn, 2001, p. 27)

SDN Children's Services Parent Resource Program

SDN Children's Services, which originated as a subsidised day nursery association in Sydney over a century ago, has created a family support program within a mainstream early childhood service (Udy, 2005). It provides good nutrition and a high-quality early childhood program for very vulnerable children who do not usually use any form of child care, and reaches out to parents struggling with problems such as poverty, social isolation, drug and alcohol abuse, mental health problems and domestic violence. The program has four key elements (Udy, 2005):

- scholarships that enable children to attend up to three days a week at a mainstream early childhood education and care centre
- additional on-the-job training, coaching and professional supervision for early childhood education and care staff in how to work with 'hard to engage' parents who often present as 'demanding' and 'difficult'
- a warm and welcoming climate to encourage these parents to participate in information sessions where there are opportunities to make friends with other parents
- inter-agency networking and referrals to link families with the range of services they need, and help to coordinate an integrated response to the family's needs.

A range of positive outcomes for the children, families, staff and community have been identified in an evaluation of the program that has captured rich qualitative data on the perceptions of different stakeholders (Goodfellow et al., 2004).

Some of the feedback from parents about staff includes the following:

They seem to let you into their lives – the personal things. I think that it's really nice that they're open with parents. I like it. I think this is important because we're prepared to do it ourselves so it's nice to get it in return. I think that it's important that they can be honest.

The staff tend to be interested in talking to you not only about the child but even in you personally. Sometimes they ask 'How are you going?' and say 'This was a wonderful thing that happened today.' I notice that they take enough interest to remember things. And that's quite important. People sometimes treat things as a job and have their cut-off points whereas I don't find that here … I like the stability of the staff as well.

The staff always tell me things and that makes me comfortable. They always tell me what Alan has done in the day and they get his book out and show me the photos of what he has been doing. And his teacher will say 'he has done this today'.

Udy (2005) argues that, for such a program to become successfully integrated in mainstream early childhood services, the following elements are necessary:

- consistent, committed staff
- support and mentoring for staff
- a mix of professional disciplines
- inter-agency engagement and involvement

- time to release staff to attend meetings, receive training, reflect on their practice and spend time with families
- management expertise as performance expectations are raised.

'PaL' – family-centred Indigenous early childhood education

Over a decade ago in Napranum, near Weipa on the Gulf of Carpentaria in Queensland, a home-based outreach program called 'PaL' was developed by staff in the preschool centre in close partnership with local Indigenous women. Napranum is a very deprived community and parents had asked for help to prepare children better for starting school. PaL stands for 'Parents and Learning', and local women with preschool-aged children are trained and employed as tutors to deliver kits to participating families over a two-year period. The focus of the program is on coaching parents to do enjoyable exercises based on carefully chosen books and materials each week, in order to build their confidence in themselves as their children's first educators (parentsandlearning.com). The program is an 'Indigenised' adaptation of the original Israeli HIPPY Program (Home Instruction Program for Pre-School Youngsters – see www.hippy–international.org).

The PaL Program has two levels – preschool and the first year of primary school. Weekly PaL kits, each one developed in close consultation with community members, comprise a high-quality storybook, a related enjoyable educational activity and a simple-to-understand instruction card. The parent works with the child each week during the school term, reading the book and working through the activities. The PaL tutors deliver and pick up the kits each week and show parents how to use the materials, based on the training and support they themselves have been given.

While it is ostensibly an early literacy program, PaL is also aimed at strengthening parent–child relationships by creating opportunities for enjoyable interaction. A process analysis of the program found that the program operates in ways that build on the knowledge and skills within the community (Hanrahan, 2004). PaL has also provided opportunities for some of the women in the community to engage in paid employment and occupy respected roles, thus strengthening their ability as community leaders. By 2012, the PaL Program had spread far and wide and was operating in 17 sites across four States, with a Train the Trainer model and follow-up support for communities wishing to establish their own program. The program has received numerous state and national awards and been the subject of some initial evaluations with promising results (Fluckiger et al, 2012).

REFLECTIVE QUESTIONS
Imagine what it might be like for a preschool-aged child and their parents who do not speak the language spoken by the staff and most other children in an early childhood education and care setting. What would staff need to know to assist the child's adjustment to this setting?

■ Common principles

While the practices highlighted in these exemplars may not be possible to implement holistically in all early childhood services, the underlying principles that they have in common are applicable to all early childhood settings and are explored throughout this book.

They include:

- developing positive partnerships between service providers and families
- building on families' strengths and aspirations
- responding holistically to the needs of children and families
- strengthening links between families to create social support
- collaborating across professions and services to provide comprehensive responses
- embodying and expressing an ethos of hope and optimism.

REFLECTIVE QUESTIONS
If you were a parent, what elements in the physical environment and the emotional climate of an early childhood service would make you feel comfortable or uncomfortable? How might the barriers to parents feeling comfortable be overcome?

Read the notes below of a conversation with a group of maternal and child health nurses working in a 'standard' community service for all families rather than a special program for vulnerable families. Can you identify any of the common principles listed above in their approach to their work?

Over lunch a group of maternal and child health nurses (Patricia Glynn, Fiona Hunter, Vivienne Thomas, Carol McIntyre and Nicole Carver), who work in the outer western suburbs of Melbourne, talked about several issues relating to how their roles had changed in response to new demands, and how they grappled with the complexities and challenges of their work. I started by asking them about the cultural diversity of the communities they served. One nurse spoke about a Karen refugee family from Burma, who had been featured in a recent television program. It had shown the mother and her six children in an overcrowded refugee camp in Thailand, living in a tiny space and washing from a bucket surrounded by a sea of other families. Then the program showed the family arriving at Melbourne Airport and going straight to a four bedroom house in a new outer suburb. Her nurse remarked 'It was going from poverty and community to affluence and isolation.'

Another maternal and child health nurse spoke, with warmth and great admiration, about the massive adaptation that was required of such families. 'These are earth mothers. They are brilliant – wonderful, natural responsiveness to their children. "What can I teach them about parenting?" I said to the NGO worker running a group for Karen families who asked me to come and speak with them! But there were challenges for them – like not letting a four year old take care of a two year old, and the importance of road safety, and eight year old children not going out walking on their own as they would have in a village when collecting wood. This is a different context and creates challenges for traditional childrearing which works in a setting where neighbours would all care for the children of the community.'

We discussed the enormous isolation such families face, especially in new suburbs, where there was no contact with neighbours. 'It's about adjusting our expectations and our views as well – we're learning as much from them … we have to be careful not to be paternalistic,' said one maternal and child health nurse. 'They are so grateful – one of our Karen mothers named her child "peaceful country" in her language' said her nurse, who obviously derived a great deal of satisfaction from working with families from culturally diverse backgrounds.

The maternal and child health nurses were sensitive to how bewildering our services might seem – 'to have a health system that looks after you when you are not even sick!' There was an interesting discussion about how the families saw the nurses. 'Sometimes it is hard initially as the parents may be suspicious, feeling that they are under surveillance as some are so scared … and making the transition from being visited at home to coming to see us in the centre … sometimes it is a challenge to find their way by public transport – it can seem very daunting.'

I asked them how they engaged immigrant mothers in the First Time Parent Groups that they offered. One nurse spoke about a group she facilitated which had mothers from China, Sri Lanka, India, Iran and local Australian mothers, including young mothers, in which they all got along well. Another spoke about the importance of encouraging immigrant women to join the groups but that if this was not appropriate, for example, because of language difficulties, how they might still be able to connect them with another family from a similar background. 'Some mothers are not confident enough in their English to join new mother groups but we have been able, with their permission, to link them with other families from the same background on a family to family basis and that can work very well.'

Another challenging aspect of the work for the maternal and child health nurses in the communities in which they worked related to problems such as domestic violence, mental health, drug and alcohol *abuse and child protection. 'We need more one-to-one time with some families. Sometimes referring them to the enhanced maternal and child health service [a more intensive outreach service] is not desirable or possible as they have the relationship with us, but it can still be good to consult with the enhanced maternal and child health service about the situation.' Another nurse commented that 'maternal and child health nurses now get clinical supervision in a group on a regular basis and that is very helpful.'*

Another said that she needed to know more about what other services did. 'I don't know enough about what other people do – what child protection workers actually do for instance.' They contrasted this with how they had come to know about practitioners in some of the new co-located service centres. 'In the new co-located centres, it is much easier to make referrals – you just walk across the corridor and introduce the parent. The other worker is a real person, not just a name and a telephone number – to you and to the parents.' Another nurse said 'co-location means that others on the site can give you support. For example, the kindergarten teacher and I will go for a walk together at lunch time and we can talk about our families.'

■ Conclusion

Early childhood services have enormous potential to enhance the wellbeing of vulnerable children and their families. To fulfil this potential, skilful engagement of parents by practitioners, an organisational ethos of developing partnerships with other service providers, and supportive policy frameworks and funding arrangements are required. There are many promising family-centred approaches in early childhood services currently being developed in Australia. They need to be rigorously evaluated for their effectiveness and for their transferability to other contexts (see Chapter 13). Working with vulnerable families in such settings can be professionally and personally challenging but also immensely fulfilling.

■ Useful websites

Australian Centre for Child Protection: **www.unisa.edu.au/childprotection**

Australian Research Alliance for Children and Youth: **www.aracy.org.au**

Bernard van Leer Foundation: **www.bernardvanleer.org**

Centre for Community Child Health, Royal Children's Hospital, Melbourne: **www.rch.org.au/ccch**

Early Childhood Australia: **www.earlychildhoodaustralia.org.au**

HIPPY (Home Interaction Program for Parents and Youngsters):
www.hippyaustralia.org.au/

PaL (Parents and Learning): **http://parentsandlearning.com**

Playgroups Australia: **www.playgroupaustralia.com.au**

St Luke's: **www.stlukes.org.au; www.innovativeresources.org**

The Family Action Centre: **www.newcastle.edu.au/research-centre/fac**

Through the Looking Glass, Lady Gowrie Centre: **www.gowrie-adelaide.com.au/cms/node/19**

VICSEG New Futures: **www.vicsegnewfutures.org.au**

What Works for Children?: **www.whatworksforchildren.org.uk**

Wilfrid Laurier University: **www.wlu.ca/index.php**

4

Including fathers in work with vulnerable families

Richard Fletcher

■ Learning goals

This chapter will enable you to:

- **RECOGNISE** the potential of child and family practitioners in health and education settings to engage fathers (and father figures) of vulnerable children in ways that will enhance their ability to nurture and protect their children

- **UNDERSTAND** how community and staff perceptions, social policy and institutional practices may act as barriers to fathers' participation in child and family settings

- **BECOME FAMILIAR** with recent research evidence pointing to fathers' positive influence on children's wellbeing and consider the implications of this

- **RECOGNISE** the complexity of changing service procedures and practice to include fathers fully in a way that enhances family wellbeing

- **REFLECT** on the professional and personal challenges that may be faced when attempting to include fathers in services targeting vulnerable children and their families.

■ Introduction

INVOLVING FATHERS IN the lives of children is consistent with the goals of nearly all family services. Child and family services routinely declare that they wish to form partnerships with *parents* to ensure the best outcomes for children, and most practitioners would consider that having both partners involved in parenting programs is likely to be associated with better outcomes than if services rely on the mother to relay information and ideas to her partner. The reality, however, is that while staff may wish to see fathers involved, when services say *parents* they usually mean *mothers* and when evaluators record *family* involvement in the service it is the mother's involvement that is assessed. The focus on mothers reflects the history of public support for families with young children through maternity services and mothers' clubs and, while the language and naming of services has changed to reflect a broader view of family practice, the reality is that participants are overwhelmingly mothers and staff in child and family services are mostly women.

In previous times, the focus on mothers might not have presented a problem, but community values have shifted to endorse the involvement of fathers with young children and the science of infant development has challenged the exclusive focus on mother–infant interaction by demonstrating an independent effect for father–infant and father–child relationships. At the same time, however, increasing awareness of sexual abuse and domestic violence perpetrated by men has added to the complexity of involving fathers in child and family services. (More is discussed about this in Chapter 10.) In this chapter, the context of family service provision to fathers is explored before recent research evidence pointing to a new role for fathers in child development is described. Examples of practice are used to illustrate some of the complexity involved when family-related services begin shifting their practice to include fathers while also remaining committed to mothers' and children's wellbeing.

■ Has fathering changed?

It is now common to notice fathers in shopping malls pushing strollers or walking with children in the park and to see advertisements for everything from computers to life insurance including images of young, well-toned fathers nursing happy infants or holding happy young children. Community surveys regularly report strong endorsement of the value of fathers taking an equal share in the care of children, and governments in many countries advocate for parents to share home duties and work opportunities equally through gender equality quasi-government commissions, boards and the like. We have new services such as antenatal groups for fathers, fathers' parenting classes and fathers' websites and forums that did not exist for earlier generations. Recent changes to family law in Australia have stressed the right of children to an ongoing relationship with both parents in the absence of violence or abuse, and paid paternity leave is being offered to new fathers. The enthusiasm of the media for stories featuring fathers means that any changes in fathers' behaviours or new developments in fathers' roles are widely promulgated.

However, while the amount of time that fathers spend with their children seems to be increasing in most Western countries, the role of fathers in all societies remains clearly different from that of mothers. This is particularly the case in the period surrounding childbirth; it is mothers who develop a special relationship with their infant through the pregnancy – a relationship that cannot be duplicated by fathers. Another female domain is breastfeeding which, whether sustained or not, also clearly defines the mother as nurturer and the father as 'support person'. The different roles for male and female parents are reflected in work patterns surrounding the birth. Even in countries that have strenuously promoted gender equity policies and encouraged fathers to take leave from their work to care for their children, the primary role of mothers in infant care remains. In no country do fathers take as much time away from their work and careers to care for children as mothers do.

One way to gain some perspective on the changes in the social definition of fatherhood is to examine the content and interpretation of family law as it applies to fathers and fatherhood. Legislation covering the whole gamut of family relations, from inheritance and probate to incest and child custody, incorporate definitions of who is a father and what his rights and obligations are. By defining the 'father' through his roles, rights and responsibilities, the law sets in train a discourse that permeates into the fine grain of society; legal debate surrounding fatherhood can provide an indication of changes in our social definitions.

■ Fatherhood in the law

New legislation has been introduced in many Western industrialised countries that alters the legal basis of paternity and helps to shape fathers' options in rearing their children. Nordic countries have pioneered paid paternity leave for fathers as part of their efforts for more equal gender relations in families (Gíslason, 2007). A second wide-ranging shift has been led by the United Nations in its Convention on the Rights of the Child which emphasises, among basic needs for care and protection, children's right to ongoing personal contact with both parents in the event of separation. Countries that are signatories to the Convention (140 have signed) have made changes to their laws regarding children, including those dealing with separation and divorce. In 2006, Australia passed the *Family Law Amendment (Shared Parental Responsibility) Act 2006*, which made both parents responsible for decisions about their child through the concept of 'equal shared parental responsibility' (Caruana, 2006, p. 56). A third important change has been the development of artificial conception procedures that have required separating legal fatherhood from biological fatherhood. Legislation in some States of Australia, for example, expressly deems that a sperm donor should not be considered the father of a child conceived through the use of his sperm (Fletcher & Willoughby, 2002).

However, as historians have noted, new conceptions of social roles that may be incorporated into legislation are not universally adopted; rather than one idea of fatherhood being swapped for another, different or even contradictory notions of fathers and fathering may coexist for considerable periods of time.

■ The task for child and family workers

Those working in child and family services have to navigate between the competing notions of what society, and what individuals, expect of fathers. Clearly some aspects of fathers' roles have changed, but many have not. The evidence that most men and women in the community (including most service providers) want fathers to be involved and yet few fathers are engaged with child and family services suggests that involving fathers must be a complex task, one that cannot be accomplished by simply inviting fathers to participate alongside mothers. When staff or organisations make the decision to include fathers, it is important to appreciate the scope of the task and the considerable changes that may be involved.

Practitioners who have attempted to recruit fathers on the basis that everyone agrees with father involvement and therefore all that is required is an invitation, have often been disappointed in fathers' responses. In many cases, these practitioners have put in extra time and effort to hold the event after hours and often to prepare the food, displays and activities. When only a few fathers turn up, the staff are then tempted to conclude that there is no interest from the men and to withdraw from the task of including fathers, saying 'Get fathers in? Yes, we tried that ... it didn't work.' Two important, initial steps to include fathers are (a) to identify the barriers that currently exist to prevent services addressing the needs of fathers; and (b) to develop an evidence-based rationale for why fathers should be involved in the first place.

The internal, systemic and organisational barriers to including fathers are described in the following sections, along with implications for service providers. Recent research on father–infant and father–child relationships is then outlined to provide an evidence base for including fathers.

■ Barriers for fathers: internal constraints

Qualitative studies using convenience samples in the United States and the United Kingdom have documented men's feelings of frustration, helplessness, anxiety, discomfort and nervousness in the context of antenatal classes and their resentment at feelings of being ignored at the birth (Chapman, 2000; Henderson & Brouse, 1991; Jordan, 1990; Nichols, 1993; Smith, 1999). Australian research has also shown that new fathers are often unprepared for the relationship changes occasioned by the birth, and that they are unaware of services available after the birth that are able to assist families (Fletcher, Silberberg & Galloway, 2004). Yet, when expectant fathers are surveyed about hospital services, they are generally very positive and when a large representative sample (n = 1000) of Australian fathers was asked to identify their needs, the most common responses were 'don't know' (16 per cent) and 'nothing needed' (14 per cent), with only 3 per cent identifying a need for more assistance from services (Russell et al., 1999).

Rather than conceptualising help-seeking as an individual, singular decision, researchers in the mental health area describe 'help-seeking pathways' involving multiple social interactions to identify and assess the psychosocial need and multiple decision points leading to engagement with services and treatment (Aoun, Palmer & Newby, 1998). Services may underestimate the lack of informal knowledge among fathers about how family support services operate. Fathers may not seek help because they (correctly) believe that their infant's crying or their child's unsettled behaviour will probably subside over time. They may also expect that their own distress will be temporary. The father's lack of experience in managing family relationships with new children may also make the recognition of child development or relationship problems by fathers less likely. Fathers' perception of the risk of embarrassment may be another factor, deterring them from seeking help from services or preventing the discussion of help for parenting problems within their social networks.

■ Barriers for fathers: opportunity constraints

In contrast to mothers, who of necessity attend antenatal and postnatal services, fathers' attendance is optional. Fathers do not need to have health professionals assess their weight, blood pressure and so on, and so do not need to attend clinics for procedures or consultations. Work patterns and social values also mean that it will probably be the mother who contacts the health or welfare services for support with any problems to do with the children. As a result, a major obstacle to engagement with fathers is the lack of regular contact with health and welfare services.

Although there are no published statistics of fathers' attendance at perinatal health visits, men are less likely than women to visit general practitioners during the primary parenting years and are less likely to contact telephone parenting services for information and support. In the welfare area, the reluctance of practitioners to contact biological fathers or stepfathers in cases where a child is considered 'at risk' is well documented (Scourfield, 2006).

Fathers also face considerable time pressure. Fathers in the survey by Russell et al. (1999) most frequently cited lack of time and the competing demands of work as a barrier to becoming involved with their children. However, the lack of time is, to some extent, a subjective judgement influenced by the father's perception of the importance of the activity concerned. For example, the prediction of a father's involvement with children from the father's workplace demands – such as the number of hours worked – is relatively weak. The amount of involvement is not simply a result of his lack of availability. The experience of father-involvement programs is that, once the fathers see the point of the activity, then ways to manage work demands are often found (Fletcher, 2004). This is also explored in Chapter 3.

■ Barriers for fathers: service constraints

From the time when a pregnancy is confirmed, the mother becomes the client of the health service and her pregnancy becomes the focus of visits to her general practitioner or to the antenatal clinic. Hospital data collections may not record the father's name, and the materials given to mothers during their hospital stay may not even mention fathers, referring instead to mothers and their 'support person'. Analysis of popular commercial child-rearing information in North America found that fathers were rarely mentioned, and when they were their role was depicted as predominantly ancillary to mothers and voluntary (Fleming & Tobin, 2005). A recently completed review of parents' information needs in Australia found that perinatal parenting information is usually directed explicitly to mothers and that there is widespread recognition among service providers that the father's role is considered an 'add-on' and insufficiently addressed (Centre for Community Child Health, 2004c).

Evidence from a wide range of studies also suggests that the attributes of staff and the design of services may unintentionally inhibit a father's participation. A review of fathers' access to family services identified 13 barriers to fathers' participation (Fletcher, Silberberg & Baxter, 2001). Professionals' attitudes to fathers, their lack of skills to engage with men, and the lack of appropriate models of male service delivery were identified as hindering the involvement of fathers. A paucity of appropriate information and resource materials targeting fathers and a lack of knowledge among service providers about men were also noted (Fletcher, Silberberg & Baxter, 2001).The lack of knowledge about men may derive, in part, from the gendered nature of the workforce in health and family services. Although there is no evidence that male clinicians provide better care to males, the need for family services to reflect the diversity of the clients being serviced is gaining recognition. In Western industrialised countries, fathers are unlikely to encounter males in any of the front-line areas of midwifery and paediatric nursing, or among nurses making home visits in the weeks after the birth. Social workers, family workers and welfare workers also tend to be female.

■ Interaction of barriers

The way in which these factors may interact to marginalise fathers was described as part of an invited contribution to a special issue of the *Medical Journal of Australia* on men's health:

> When Michelle and Anthony attend Michelle's GP after the positive pregnancy test, Anthony expresses his support but asks few questions. When asked about the couple's intentions for pregnancy care Anthony's quick glance towards Michelle flags his uncertainty. For the next visits Michelle attends the clinic alone. Anthony does participate in the ultrasound consultation and he joins in when asked during the antenatal classes but he accepts that the emphasis throughout is appropriately on the mother and a successful birth. During the birth he wonders if he is in the way and is grateful in the end to have a healthy mother and baby. Post-birth, when the home-visiting nurse arrives, Anthony goes to make coffee and misses most of the discussion. His return to work precludes him attending the check-ups for mother and baby at the doctors.
>
> Anthony's minimal role with health professionals is mirrored at home and in social settings. Michelle reads the books, brochures and magazines and tells Anthony about popular names, baby development, and the dangers of SIDS [Sudden Infant Death Syndrome]. Anthony is affectionately ribbed by workmates about sleep deprivation and nappy changing and although one of his mates has just become a father Anthony has little chance to learn about the business of fathering. Social time with the new baby is dominated by eager mothers or girlfriends and there are few opportunities for Anthony to try out 'holding a new baby' without drawing attention to himself.
>
> (Fletcher, Matthey & Marley, 2006)

Developing new father-inclusive models of service will require addressing all of the above barriers: fathers' lack of experience with infants and children's care and poor understanding of services; the lack of contact between family-based services and fathers; and the paucity of father-inclusive models of service delivery.

■ Implications for services

There is an important lesson here for any family service that is attempting to attract men to activities or programs at a centre – check the walls to see what message they are sending to the families. Health and welfare centres, for example, frequently have posters about domestic violence or sexual assault, important issues that need to be raised. But for many services these are the only messages directly talking to men. Young Indigenous fathers told us, when we interviewed them about their experience of community services surrounding the birth, that all the posters in the waiting rooms were about domestic violence, sexual abuse, women being stalked or drug and alcohol abuse. As one father put it: 'All they think about when they see a father is the bad things he done' (Hammond et al., 2004).

Changing the messages from the walls is relatively simple. Over recent years a variety of posters promoting involved, positive fatherhood for services have been developed, including posters for specific groups such as Indigenous fathers, and many are available at a low cost (see the useful websites at the end of this chapter). Of course, posters are not the only channel for the environment to give a message to fathers. Some child and family centres have taken the next step of examining the colour schemes and general décor in the centre with a view to how they may appear to a father. Most centres strive for a soft pastel look that reflects the 'normal' environment for mothers and children. The colours that may make the space more male-friendly can be seen in advertising for products that are aimed at male customers – they are often bolder and include greater contrasts.

In other places, centres have created a 'dads' corner', where photographs of fathers using the centre and notices directed explicitly to fathers can be displayed. Using photographs of 'real' fathers has the bonus of underlining the normality of fathers' involvement. Posters or images of sports stars or celebrity fathers have their uses, but locally produced images of 'ordinary' fathers can send the important message that 'fathers who are just like you' get involved at this service.

Some services have used notices to make their processes, which mothers already know, clearer to fathers. For example, when a father who doesn't usually pick up his child arrives at the early childhood centre, he may not know whether he is supposed to take home all the material alongside his daughter's bag or leave it. He may not know where the sign-out book is, or that he should fill out the form for photographs or for tomorrow's excursion to the park and leave it in the box near the director's office door. Having clearly set out instructions (information that mothers who attend often will already know) can reduce the father's sense that he is out of place.

An extension of this idea is to examine how fathers gain knowledge of a service before they walk in the door or attend an event such as a parenting course or clinical appointment. What pamphlets, advertisements or publicity may they have seen that explains who the service is for? How does the induction or referral process suggest who is expected to attend? What comments may their families or friends have made about the style of the service that will help form their attitude to the service?

An important point to grasp in answering these questions is that, although services intend to include everyone when using the words 'parent' or 'family', that is not how these words are understood in the community. It would be usual, for example, for any letter arriving at the home addressed as 'Dear Parent' to be handed to the mother, who is the one most likely to be dealing with family matters. Services wanting to communicate with the fathers in the families have sometimes added 'Dad this means you' after 'Dear Parent' or added a 'Message for Dads' with a separate section highlighting information for fathers.

For many services, the first contact with a father may be by phone. The following scenario is one that I have used in many training workshops for early intervention staff wishing to hone their skills to effectively reach fathers:

SCENARIO

Kerry works at XYZ Early Childhood Service. Jennifer Farmer has been in contact with her, seeking a place on Monday, Tuesday and Wednesday for her two-year-old daughter Jasmine. Kerry is calling to inform the family that these days are now available and to ask if a place is still required. As it happens, Bill Farmer answers the phone. The following conversation takes place:

Bill Farmer: Hello?

Kerry: Hello – is that the Farmer residence? I am calling about a place for Jasmine …

Bill Farmer: Who is this?

Kerry: Hi. This is Kerry from XYZ Early Childhood Service. I am calling about a place for Jasmine …

Bill Farmer: Ummm …

Kerry: Your wife Jennifer put Jasmine's name down for Monday to Wednesday …

Bill Farmer: Oh … OK …

Kerry: And we'd like to know if you still want the three days for Jasmine …

Bill Farmer: OK. Hold on and I'll get Jenny for you …

Many child and family practitioners find this scenario very familiar. It is often mothers who search out which services are available and then negotiate the best arrangements for the family. The telephone contact with the father in this example presents an opportunity to convey to the father that he is also seen as important by the service.

In the father-inclusive practice training workshops, the participants role-play various ways of engaging the father in this brief window of contact. The task for Kerry in this scenario is to convey that, for this service, the involvement of Bill is seen as important. Strategies suggested during the workshops include asking him about the things that Jasmine likes to do, asking if he knows where the XYZ Early Childhood Service is located, or discussing who will be dropping Jasmine off or picking her up. In the role-plays, participants often falter when the role-playing father asks why the service wants to involve him, because his partner Jenny has always handled these things in the past. In spite of the enthusiasm for fathers' involvement with children's care, few services have developed any detailed rationale for including fathers and staff are frequently at a loss if they are required to articulate the thinking behind efforts to reach them.

ACTIVITIES

Consider how you would explain the importance of including fathers to colleagues who are concerned about their ability to work with fathers; to a manager who requests evidence for allocating resources to work with fathers; to a father who is unsure about whether to undertake a 'fathering' activity; and to a single mother.

   Visit a child and family service. Try to see the physical layout as a new, relatively inexperienced father might. What messages about the service would stand out? What, if anything, would tell the father that the service is actively seeking his involvement?

■ Evidence of fathers' impact

The task of involving a father in a home visit, in a parenting group or even in a conversation about the best course of action for his child may be made difficult because it takes place against a backdrop of previous experiences like those of Michelle and Anthony described above. If things are to change, it will require considerable effort and thought by practitioners wishing to refashion services to include fathers alongside mothers in supporting their children.

The question that follows is: 'Why should this service invest precious resources in implementing changes to include fathers?' Developing new procedures has cost implications, as including fathers implies taking on additional clients or additional tasks to support families. The evidence of the impact of fathers on children's development is therefore crucial in two ways. First, if services are to allocate resources to refashioning procedures, skilling staff to engage fathers and reaching out to fathers, then the evidence that this will improve family wellbeing is essential.

Equally important will be the practitioners' understanding of the differences between mothers' and fathers' roles. Shifting the basis of the work from 'mother as central and father as helper' to an approach that includes father–infant and father–child relationships will mean grappling with how fathers' interactions influence both the child and the mother–child relationship. The recent developments in our understanding of how fathers' positive interactions can foster children's development will be important knowledge for managers, service planners and practitioners alike.

Studies assessing fathers' impact on development have followed families over several years, measuring fathers' interaction at an early age and then children's wellbeing some years later. In a study by the National Institute of Child Health and Human Development in the US, which examined parental factors that predicted school readiness, children who had fewer behaviour problems and higher social skills came from families where the fathers were sensitive and supportive of autonomy. An emotionally intimate marital relationship also added to the positive effect of these factors (NICHD Early Child Care Research Network, 2004).

A more recent study, also from the US, compared the influence of fathers and mothers from a low-income sample on their children's cognitive development. Children with two supportive parents scored highest on measures of maths and language, while those whose parents were both unsupportive scored lowest. What was also clear, however, was that the positive effect of having one parent supportive did not depend on whether that parent was a mother or a father. Elevated cognitive abilities were just as likely to be apparent among children with a supportive father as among those with a supportive mother (Martin, Ryan & Brooks-Gunn, 2007).

Fathers' effects on wellbeing do not stop at childhood. As part of the US National Longitudinal Study of Adolescent Health, a nationally representative sample of adolescents was tested from Grades 7 to 12 to measure their relationship with their fathers and mothers, and their level of depression. Over the five years of the study the quality of the father–adolescent relationship, as judged by the adolescent, was found to be just as predictive of the adolescent's mental health as the mother–adolescent relationship (Videon, 2005).

Studies such as these provide a powerful argument for recognising a role for fathers separate from that of mothers, and for challenging the notion of father as 'helper' to the mother. It has long been assumed, for example, that the mother–infant bond was the template for the father–infant bond and that, while the relationship with the mother was fundamental to the children's wellbeing, the relationship with the father was an optional extra. For their part, fathers assumed that they had no role to play with young children until they could be physically active or could 'kick a footy'.

Recent research has challenged the assumptions of practitioners and fathers alike. Infants' secure or insecure attachment, for example, is now thought to be largely independent for mothers and fathers. When the results of several studies assessing the attachment of infants were analysed, it was recognised that, while many infants did have a secure attachment to both their mother and their father, they could be securely attached to the mother but insecurely attached to the father or the reverse. Contrary to the 'helper' notion of fathers, an infant may form a secure attachment to the father alongside an insecure attachment to the mother (van Ijzendoorn & De Wolff, 1997). What is more, when a new father is depressed (and therefore less responsive and affectionate), the effect on the wellbeing of the infant is similar to when the mother is depressed.

Since the early 1980s we have known that depressed mothers' early parenting, specifically their insensitivity to infant cues and inability to provide effective emotional regulation, is associated with the development of insecure or disorganised infant–mother attachment and subsequent reduced social competence and increased behaviour disorders (Ashman & Dawson, 2002). What has recently been established is that fathers' depression is also an important factor in children's development. When over 8000 fathers were tested for depression eight weeks after the birth and their children's behaviour assessed at three-and-a-half years of age, those children whose fathers recorded depressive symptoms in the clinical range two months after the birth were found to have double the risk of behavioural and emotional problems (Ramchandani et al., 2005). The effects of the father's depression were independent of whether the mother was depressed and independent of the father's later mental health, which suggests that having a depressed father in the early months of life can have a long-lasting negative effect on children's emotional and social development.

In summary, recent research shows that:

- father involvement can have a significant and important effect on the wellbeing of children
- fathers influence their children's development directly rather than solely as a 'helper' to the mother
- infants respond to fathers as well as mothers and benefit from their relationships with fathers independently of their relationships with their mothers
- infants/children do best when they have a secure relationship with both mother and father and when the relationship between mother and father is warm and affectionate.

■ What about 'bad' dads?

The evidence for early intervention with mothers is now strong enough for governments of all persuasions to endorse programs and policies that aim to support vulnerable families with young children. However, although the evidence for the impact of fathers on children's development is also now well founded, and in many areas policies and programs are moving to include a focus on fathers within early interventions for vulnerable families, the provision of support for fathers remains problematic. One reason for the faltering progress of father inclusion is described above: societies and individuals continue to hold contradictory notions of fatherhood and practitioners frequently underestimate the changes required to incorporate fathers fully into mainstream services. As well, the research on a father's role in child development is relatively new, so that training and theoretical support for father inclusion is still emerging.

However, there is also the important issue of violence and abuse to incorporate into any changes seeking greater father involvement. Particularly in vulnerable families, practitioners may be well aware that part of the difficulty facing the family is violent behaviour from the father. In this situation, it will be important to avoid any simplistic approach that ignores difficult issues of violence or abusive behaviour, thereby ignoring the needs of the mother. Equally futile, however, is the approach that ignores the father and his relationship with the children because the father is (or once was or might be) violent. In a recent example from my own work, a parenting skills program refused to provide educational sessions for parents in a housing estate program because there might be men attending the course. 'They'll be wife-bashers' was the only explanation offered for the refusal.

As part of the reconceptualising of fathers' roles, researchers have questioned the exclusive emphasis on providing safety and comfort for young children and have turned their attention to how parents can foster children's confidence and exploration. Fathers' 'rough and tumble' play has been identified, not only as common among fathers and children in many cultures, but as beneficial for child development (Paquette, 2004). There has also been the suggestion that fathers' interactions with young infants are typically less modulated than mothers' with more unexpected peaks of excitement, again with positive developmental implications (Feldman, 2003).

However, for those working with vulnerable populations, the notion of encouraging fathers' energetic play with children may seem too risky. Indeed, there is evidence to support practitioners' caution with simply encouraging more involvement (of any type) from fathers. A study of over 1100 fathers and their five-year-old children found that, for children whose fathers had high levels of antisocial behaviour, the more time they lived with their father the more behaviour problems they exhibited (Jaffee et al., 2003). In this study, the problematic fathers were defined as having high levels of antisocial activity warranting a diagnosis of antisocial personality disorder, and so would form a rather small group within the population of fathers. A potentially larger group among those coming into contact with child and family services are fathers who may be involved in domestic or family violence. However, practitioners in child and family services may feel ill equipped to address the complexity of issues in a situation of family violence or even of family anger. (See Chapter 10 for more detail.)

As a UK volunteer expressed during a training session for home visitors:

… you go, to a house and you could hear dad shouting inside, what would you do? Well I'm sorry but I'm only a volunteer – I keep saying that to myself – I would get back in the car and I would ring the office. It's not our place to go into somewhere where (a) we don't know the situation and (b) we could be putting ourselves in danger …

(Evangelou et al., 2008, p. 74)

The risk of confronting antisocial or angry behaviour should be taken seriously when providing family-based services. The possibility of encountering an angry or even violent parent requires care in the overall design of the service, in training and support for staff, and in establishing safety protocols and procedures. However, the risk that there may be domestic violence should not preclude the family having contact with services, nor should it prevent the service including strategies for engaging with the father around his role in the family. Addressing violence and conflict as part of a comprehensive response to family difficulty can enhance the effectiveness of services with families facing serious disruption and stress. For example, this is how the manager of an all-female early intervention service for families with multiple problems (substance abuse, criminal history, parental history of abuse and neglect) described the effects of adopting a focus on fathers:

> There was a lot of domestic violence and the emphasis on fathers actually led to us developing a much better policy around domestic violence … We'd talk to the whole family about it not being safe in the family and that we weren't willing to send a worker into the family until things were safer, but we would still see them in a café or at our rooms. We didn't drop them and we made it clear that we really wanted the man to work on his own stuff. … We also asked two male therapists to talk to us about our own issues – about how we [the staff] didn't talk about our own fathers, and how the women staff members felt quite confronted by working with fathers.
>
> (Edwards, 2004)

■ Strengths-based practice with fathers

The notion of 'strengths-based practice' has been coined to describe ways of interacting with families that do not ignore any risk of harm to children, or the need at times for outside agency involvement, but which assume that family members have the capacity to develop supportive and healthy relationships that will enable their children to flourish. Applying this approach to fathers in vulnerable families implies a shift in emphasis from seeing the father as simply a problem – the irresponsible or drug-abusing father who is a major cause of the child's vulnerability – to picturing a father with his own vulnerabilities and needs as well as someone whose behaviours may be damaging to family wellbeing.

As described in the 'Barriers for fathers' sections above, a number of factors may make it unlikely that fathers would be involved in initial assessments or discussions. However, practitioners' training, experience and skills can also influence how inclusive services are of fathers. In the following account, an experienced family worker describes how she encourages the father's involvement once it has been established (through telephone contact with the mother) that there is no current violence between the couple.

> When I first visit a family I would see the person who made the referral, generally the woman, we'll call her Betty. The first visit would probably happen within business hours, during the day when the kids were at school and Betty's husband (or partner) was at work. The husband generally knew that I was coming. For example, I generally asked, 'Does your husband know that I am coming today?' If Betty responded 'Yes', I then might have said, 'What does he think about you asking for an agency's support around this?' Betty might have said something like, 'Oh he's okay, he doesn't really like talking about these sorts of things but he doesn't mind if I do.'
>
> From here, I would talk with the woman about how she thought I might be able to support them and generally the woman would have some ideas about that. For example, I might have asked Betty what her husband thought, and for her husband's name. Let's say, for example, Betty's husband is John. What I tended to do then was to include John's name in the conversation a lot. I would say something like, 'If John was here now, what would he be telling me about what's happening between you two?' Betty would then say something like, 'Well, he thinks it's probably my fault because I get depressed and I get down and I get fairly dependent and I can't cope.' And we would continue to talk.
>
> Those first visits were often short because I established that the work went a lot better if the man was present. For example, I would ask the woman when her husband would be willing to participate, and the woman would generally say that she had to ask him. My intention at this point would be to convey to the woman that I was interested in her husband's opinion as well, that I was interested to see both of them together, and, that I wanted both of them to be comfortable with me. I would make a time for the next visit, which may have been after hours.
>
> (Cantwell, 2004)

The ongoing work with vulnerable fathers as part of the support for families will, of course, require more than one conversation and may take a variety of forms, depending on the service type and target. There is now recognition, for example, that modifying services to include father or father figures of families where children have disabilities may enhance the wellbeing of all family members. Two examples of ongoing work with fathers, one through home visits and one through centre-based group work, are described below. In the first, a pilot attachment-based program for fathers, utilising videotaping of father–infant interaction, is described. In the second, a group program for men addressing anger and violence offers insights into how facilitated discussion can shift fathers' ways of handling family tensions and conflicts.

■ A pilot home visiting service for fathers whose partners have postnatal depression

The service was advertised as 'a free service for new fathers' who may have 'a wife or partner who is not doing so well'. No specific therapy or subsequent action was promised; however, a home visiting model (with a male visitor) was offered at the first interview if appropriate. The practice framework for the intervention, which was developed with mothers, uses videotape to record the parent doing 'whatever they enjoyed' with their infant and then viewing the tape together to discuss questions such as 'What is the baby thinking here?' Father-specific aspects of the intervention were guided by the emerging research on fathers' roles in infant development: fathers' attachment styles with their infants are likely to develop independently of those of mothers; fathers' use of play interactions will be particularly important; and negotiating a place in the father–mother–infant triangle is a key task for fathers.

A father contacted the service three months after the birth of his child requesting help to be a 'better father'. Although his partner had suffered severe postnatal depression, she was not requesting or receiving any professional support at the commencement of the home visits. During the 10 home visits, the father's interactions with his infant were videotaped and reviewed in an attachment-based framework. At the conclusion of the home visits, the mother and father were interviewed about their experience of the program. The father concluded:

> being a good parent is something that you can train yourself to do … anybody can change a nappy, anybody can pick him up if he is crying … but what I am looking for out of this is the interaction that you are missing … and that's what I am picking up. Through the DVDs and the video I am picking up those little signals that William wants to interact. Which I think in the long run will bring William and I a lot closer and improve our relationship and that's the whole point of the exercise.
>
> (Fletcher, 2009 p. 99)

In this case, the positive outcome for the father also had a 'knock on' effect for the mother's relationship with their infant. The mother reported:

> I think that you [indicating the father] taught me to be more aware. I think that I spent the first months going 'Oh there is this to do and that to do and everything to do' and because [the male home visitor] would ask you 'What do you think he's doing there?' then you would ask me 'What do you think that he is doing there?' and it actually made me more aware that he is actually thinking about things … not this lump that just … I think that made me love him even more because I stopped thinking about all the things that had to be done …
>
> (Fletcher, 2009, p. 100)

■ A group program for men to end violent and abusive behaviour

Stuart Anderson coordinates the Men's Resource Centre in Northern New South Wales. Using transcripts from men's groups (recorded and transcribed with their permission) he describes the potential for group processes that engage men on the challenges of parenting. Names have been changed to ensure anonymity.

The course offered for men focuses on ending violent and abusive behaviour. An alternative way to describe this focus is that the course assists men to increase safety, trust, respect, care and love within their family. Parenting issues and skills are addressed in the program, not because it has dedicated parenting segments, but because the desire to be a better dad comes up in nearly every group session. It's like a steady undercurrent that each man is struggling with in some way. One man telling a story about his children fires up all present to think about the dilemmas and frustrations involved in parenting. Even the men who don't have children are stimulated to participate as they recall traumas in their own childhood. It's very rare to hear any of the men talk about a violence-free childhood.

Here is an example of how the group process can assist fathers to rethink their approach to fathering.

Geoff begins with his concern about his wife yelling at their children:

Geoff: *Case in point, two girls in the back of the car coming home the other night, yabba yabba yabba. Told half a dozen times by their mother to keep quiet. They're starting to tick me off. I've been driving for four hours. I just put my foot on the brake two kilometres from home, stopped the car. 'Would you girls like to get out and walk now?' 'What for Dad?' 'Because you just won't shut up.' 'We'll be quiet Dad.' Off we went, peace and quiet. I don't want to yell at the girls, I don't want to have a confrontation. It is a conscious choice, I don't want to do this. I just came around the problem in a different way. Their mother was already tense and tired, she was up the anger scale.'*

Others in the group acknowledged that Geoff made a significant shift from how he used to yell and berate his kids. That he kept his voice calm was seen as great. The facilitators were keeping an eye on this, would others in the group speak up or would they intervene with some further questions? As it happened this group had several men who had attended for a few months and they found it easy to challenge each other. Gary thought that Geoff could do better.

Gary: *Do you think you were threatening your kids?*

Geoff agreed there was an element of threat in it, but said his voice was calm and he was not angry at the kids himself. He talked about his fear that his wife would abuse the kids because he could see her rising anger. In the following discussion several ways for Geoff to get the message across to his kids were explored.

Fred who has a back injury and, therefore, is the house husband said that he was in a similar situation the other day. He told the group that at that time he said, 'You are making your mother very angry, is that what you want to do?'

This response was thought by group members to have that same old language that seems to indicate that the kids are responsible for mum's anger. They asked Fred what he would say if he was taking responsibility for his own feelings. Fred struggled with this shift of focus. His habit was to blurt out his ideas on what and who was wrong. It took several attempts before he could name his feelings of anxiety and fear. In that session he only partially succeeded in putting together a sentence that satisfied the other group members. Another man, Nick decided that telling his own story might help Fred.

Nick is a creative steel and metal worker who speaks quietly and firmly. It would be easy to assume that he had never had a problem with anger or abusive behaviour. He related how much of a relief it was not to buy into other people's stress. He used to yell at his wife and daughter to try and stop them arguing.

Nick: It's just easier to stay out of the fights. I'm here if they've finished the fighting and come and talk sense, I'm here for that. I'm not here to get dragged into their fights. My wife said to me, 'It was so great that when we were having that fight you didn't get involved.' It really sunk into her that while she and my daughter were having that fight I was sitting over the other side of the room calmly having a coffee. My quietness allowed her to see what she was doing. She came over and said: 'Thank you. I appreciate that you stayed out of it and looked after yourself, that allowed me to have some insight.'

One person taking care of themselves had an effect on the whole family or household. The discussion continued exploring the benefits of a relaxed, calm, whole-picture view rather than the tunnel vision that develops as anger rises.

Nick: It's funny isn't it? When we start putting pressure on ourselves we start falling apart, then all the rest start falling apart and it multiplies – it makes it worse and worse. What I've found is a calmer approach has made everything else calmer. Even the kids are looking at me different, which is good.

(Anderson, 2004)

ACTIVITY

Helen is seven years old, and has been displaying very challenging behaviours such as frequent tantrums, fighting with other children, stealing and swearing at her teachers. She lives with her mother Julie and half-siblings, whom she is made to care for (four-year-old twins and a two-year-old). An unsubstantiated report notes that Helen was left alone in the house to care for her siblings during the day for some hours in the school holidays.

Julie received several periods of respite care when she was unable to cope with Helen. With the new baby (three months old) Julie requests respite with the same Department of Community Services carers as before, as Helen liked them. Julie did not want another child but is against abortion. After having the twins, she was diagnosed with postnatal depression; however, no record is available on any treatment or support offered to her or taken up.

Julie's mother lives two hours away and sometimes helps out, but finds Helen's behaviour distressing. She said she won't come to stay, as Helen gets on her nerves.

Eduardo is the father of Helen but not Julie's other children. He has been away working interstate for the last four years and returned home some months ago. He has taken Helen out occasionally. Eduardo shares a house with his mate and lives close by, but the house is too small to have Helen over to stay. There is conflict between Julie and Eduardo; however, Eduardo pays child support when he can and always remembers Helen's birthdays and Christmas.

Eduardo emigrated 10 years ago, but all his family still live in Ecuador. He works regular day shifts at the local petrol station three days a week and is hoping to get work in the Goodyear franchise next door.

Julie is advised by the duty child protection case worker that there are no respite carers available. After discussions with Julie, the case worker contacts Eduardo and asks if he would be willing to regularly read to Helen at bedtime to help her settle into a routine. Eduardo agrees and for the first week arrives at the arranged time to read Helen a bedtime story. After one week he misses a night, then reads again for three nights then misses a night, then reads for two and misses a night, reads for one night and then stops coming. Julie rings the caseworker and explains that 'He is too unreliable.'

What is your first guess at why Eduardo stopped the reading sessions? What factors or experiences might push Eduardo away from staying connected with his child? Who or what might encourage Eduardo to stay connected with Helen?

■ Conclusion

While the damaging effects of children experiencing or witnessing abusive behaviour deserve continued recognition, the potential of fathers to promote positive development in children justifies concerted action to expand the ability of services to include fathers. Maximising support for vulnerable children will require shifting the policies, procedures and practices in child and family services to be inclusive of fathers.

■ Useful websites

About the Fathers Program, Family Action Centre, University of Newcastle provides training, resources and research on father-inclusive practice: **www.newcastle.edu. au/centre/fac/efp**

European Fatherhood presents research and policy on improving gender equality for fathers: **www.european-fatherhood.com**

Fatherhood Institute (UK) provides policy and practice materials for father-inclusive practice: **www.fatherhoodinstitute.org**

Head Start is a national program in the US that promotes school readiness: **www.acf.hhs.gov/programs/ohs**

Mensline Australia provides 24-hour family relationships counselling: **www.mensline.org.au**

The Canadian Father Involvement Initiative develops policy and resources for father-inclusive practice: **http://dadcentral.ca/**

The Institute of Family Practice provides training courses relevant to men and family relationships: **www.ifp.nsw.edu.au**

5

Parenting in a new culture: working with refugee families

Kerry Lewig, Fiona Arney, Mary Salveron and Maria Barredo

■ Learning goals

This chapter will enable you to:

- **UNDERSTAND** the experiences of refugee and newly arrived migrants

- **REFLECT** on the personal and professional challenges that may be faced when responding to the needs of refugee and newly arrived migrants

- **DEVELOP** an understanding of the cultural and parenting differences that may contribute to parents and families from refugee backgrounds being involved with the child protection system

- **RECOGNISE** the potential of practitioners to engage parents from refugee backgrounds in ways that will enhance their ability to parent in Australia

- **LEARN** about an innovative exemplar of working with refugee families

- **THINK** about how different professions and services can work together for and with refugee families.

■ Introduction

The house was full of women and children and since we were one of the last ones in, we had to sleep under the roof. It was very unsafe where we tried to fall asleep. We lay next to an open area, which looked down on to the first floor. Since the house wasn't finished it didn't have a fence on the stairs or that area where we slept. The noise of grenades and guns made it impossible for us to fall asleep because they were basically falling somewhere near us. You could feel them and sometimes it felt that bullets were knocking on the roof, which was right above our heads. I was lying there on the floor covered by my mother's body, praying to God that one of those grenades or bullets wouldn't hit through the roof.

(Zana Mujenovic, aged 17, in Dark Dreams, 2004)

AS A RESULT of political upheaval and persecution in their own countries, many people (individuals and families with children) are forced to flee to neighbouring countries for asylum, where they are placed in refugee camps. Many of those recognised by the United Nations Refugee Agency (UNHCR) as refugees eventually go back to their own country and a number will be assisted to resettle in a third country such as Australia, Canada or the US.

As well as contending with previous traumatic experiences such as loss of family members, torture, displacement and starvation, resettled refugee families may also face many complex challenges, including parenting in a new culture. For some refugee children and adolescents, parents represent the only consistent feature in their lives. However, parents who are refugees face significant additional challenges to those of other parents in Australia. Many of the factors associated with parenting difficulties in mainstream Australian families are also experienced by refugee parents (parental mental health problems, poverty, physical health problems, social isolation, children's behavioural problems) (Centre for Community Child Health, 2004b). In addition, refugee parents confront stresses associated with the experience of torture and trauma, separation from or death of family members, resettlement, language difficulties and different cultural expectations about behaviour and parenting (Gonsalves, 1992; Lamberg, 1996).

Working with families from culturally and linguistically diverse (CALD) backgrounds can pose a number of challenges and opportunities. When families have had to flee their countries of origin because of persecution, war or natural disaster, this can add to the level of complexity. The unique circumstances of refugee families pose a special challenge to practitioners working in child and family services. Drawing on the published literature and interviews with child protection practitioners and members of refugee communities, this chapter provides a background to, and overview of, the refugee experience and presents practitioner and refugee community perspectives on working with refugee families.

■ Who are refugees?

The 1951 United Nations Convention Relating to the Status of Refugees defines a refugee as someone who:

> owing to well-founded fear of being persecuted for reasons of race, religion, nationality, membership of a particular social group or political opinion, is outside the country of his nationality and is unable to, or owing to such fear, is unwilling to avail himself of the protection of that country; or who, not having a nationality and being outside the country of his former habitual residence as a result of such events, is unable or, owing to such fear, is unwilling to return to it

> (UNHCR, 2007 p. 16)

Table 5.1 Major source countries of refugees at the end of 2011 (UNHCR, 2011)

Country	Number of refugees
Afghanistan	2 664 400
Iraq	1 428 300
Somalia	1 077 000
Sudan	500 000
D R Congo	491 500
Myanmar	414 600
Colombia	395 900
Vietnam	337 800
Eritrea	252 000
China	205 400

According to the United Nations High Commissioner for Refugees (UNHCR), at the end of 2011 there were 42.5 million forcibly displaced people worldwide. Of these people, 10.4 million were classified as refugees under the UNHCR's mandate and a further 895 000 were classified as asylum-seekers (persons seeking to be recognised by the UNHCR as a refugee). Also included among these displaced persons were 4.8 million Palestinian refugees registered with the United Nations Relief and Works Agency for Palestine Refugees in the Near East and an estimated 26.4 million internally displaced persons, some of whom were receiving assistance or protection from the UNHCR, and many more who fell into these categories but who were not helped by the UNHCR. According to currently available data, the UNHCR estimates that women and girls constitute 48 per cent of refugees and that 46 per cent of refugees and 34 per cent of asylum-seekers are children below 18 years of age (UNHCR, 2011). In this chapter we will use a wider sense of the term 'refugee', as it is accepted, more broadly to include all those who have fled their countries of origin to seek safety from harm (such as from war, violence, poverty and natural or man-made disasters).

Not surprisingly, most refugees come from countries experiencing conflict and/or human rights abuses (see Table 5.1). You can find more information about the UNHCR and the plight of refugees on their website (www.unhcr.org).

■ Australia's Refugee and Humanitarian Program

Australia has been accepting refugees since 1938, when it became a signatory to the Evian Conference that organised asylum for Jewish refugees fleeing from Nazi Germany (Richards, 2008). The signing of this document was controversial at the time and subsequent refugee policies have generated as much debate and controversy among Australians as this one did. Australia's immigration history is further outlined in *Destination Australia* (Richards, 2008). Australia provides humanitarian resettlement for refugees under the Humanitarian Program. Details of the visa categories, as was the case in 2012, are outlined in Box 5.1 (DIAC, 2012).

■ Resettlement in Australia

During the mid to late nineties the majority of refugees who resettled in Australia came largely from the former Yugoslavia, the Middle East, South-East Asia and Africa. From 2003 to 2005 there was a large increase in humanitarian entrants coming from African countries and in particular Sudan. Africa remains a key focus

---

BOX 5.1   Australian Humanitarian Program visa categories

Offshore resettlement

The offshore component of the Refugee and Humanitarian Program has two categories.

- Refugee Category – for people who are subject to persecution in their home country and who are in need of resettlement
- Special Humanitarian Program (SHP) – for people outside their home country who are subject to substantial discrimination amounting to gross violation of human rights in their home country. A proposer (known as sponsor under the Migration Program) who is an Australian citizen, permanent resident or eligible New Zealand citizen, or an organisation that is based in Australia, must support applications for entry under the SHP.

 There are five Refugee and Humanitarian visas: Refugee Visa, In-country Special Humanitarian Visa, Global Special Humanitarian Visa, Emergency Rescue Visa and Woman at Risk Visa.

Onshore protection

The onshore component of the Refugee and Humanitarian Program aims to provide options for people who are in Australia and wish to apply for protection (or asylum). The Protection Visa is available for people arriving by air or boat (Irregular Maritime Arrivals) who are found to have protection obligations by Australia either under the United Nations Convention on the Status of Refugees or the complementary protection criteria. 'Complementary protection' is the term used to describe a category of protection for people who are not refugees but cannot be returned to their home country, in line with Australia's international obligations, because there is a real risk that the person will suffer certain types of harm.

 The Department of Immigration and Citizenship's website (www.immi.gov.au) provides more detail about Australia's refugee and humanitarian program.

of Australia's current humanitarian program alongside the Middle East and South-West Asia, with refugees coming predominantly from Afghanistan and Iraq. Since 2005, Asia has also become a focus of Australia's humanitarian program, with resettlement of Burmese refugees from Thailand and Bhutanese refugees from Nepal (DIAC, 2011).

Many of these refugees would have spent some time in a refugee camp. For example, just over 48 per cent of refugees resettling in Australia in 2005 had spent time in refugee camps. Of these people, nearly 92 per cent had spent at least two years in refugee camps, 49 per cent had spent over five years in camps, and just over 36 per cent had spent more than 10 years residing in camps (DIMIA, 2005).

In Australia, refugees are generally settled as close as possible to family members or friends, if they have any who are living in Australia. Where refugees have no extended family or social networks in Australia, settlement location is influenced by factors such as settlement needs, availability of settlement services and support from communities with a similar background, accessible health services and accommodation, and sustainable employment opportunities (DIMIA, 2005).

■ The refugee experience

Despite all the humiliation my mother went through she maintains her dignity. She is a dignified woman. She is a strong woman but my brother and I made her even stronger. She knew she had to be able to fight to protect us and some day, with or without our father, provide a stable home. The strength she had I've never seen. Seven days without eating, giving me and my brother the last crumbs she found in her pockets, drinking poisoned water and being beaten and still she managed to stay straight on her feet. It was admirable.

(Zana Mujenovic, aged 17, in Dark Dreams, 2004)

For most refugees, the process of migration to a new country has been a painful one involving stressful and often traumatic pre-migration, transition and resettlement experiences (Fazel & Stein, 2002; Pine & Drachman, 2005). It is important to remember that, during these experiences, refugees have demonstrated incredible strength, determination, courage and resilience.

To be able to work effectively with clients from refugee backgrounds, it is important to have an understanding of their ethnic, religious and cultural backgrounds. It is also important to have some knowledge of the experiences that refugees may have lived through (such as war, famine, or time spent in refugee camps) and to be able to acknowledge and understand how these pre-migration and transition experiences, together with post-migration challenges (such as mental health, grief and loss, and adjusting to a new culture) may impact on parenting and child wellbeing in a new country. It is also important to recognise that some experiences that are normative for people born in Australia, such as receiving an education or gaining employment, may have been denied to refugees. By no means is this to imply that refugees are a homogeneous group, but rather to emphasise that developing knowledge and understanding of the range of experiences of this client group is essential to effective practice.

Pre-migration experiences

Exposure to torture, trauma and family separation

In their countries of origin, adults and children may have been exposed to or have experienced rape, killing of family members and friends, suicide attempts, concentration camp experiences, torture, brutality, starvation and displacement (Berk, 1998). In some cases, acts of violence may have been perpetrated by people known to them (Berk, 1998). Recent studies of the pre-migration experiences of refugees from a range of backgrounds settling in Australia report that, in almost all instances, refugees describe experiencing or witnessing human rights violations, extreme deprivation, separation from or loss of family and friends, trauma and periods of lack of food and water (Allotey, 1998; Brough et al., 2003; Momartin et al., 2002; Momartin et al., 2006; Schweitzer et al., 2006; Silove & Ekblad, 2002; Sinnerbrink et al., 1997). In some cases, women and children are abducted and forced into servitude (for instance, as sex slaves or child soldiers) with their persecutors (Wessells, 2006).

Deciding to leave

The safety and wellbeing of children is a very significant factor for many families, if not most, in seeking to flee their countries of origin and establish new lives in other countries. Making the decision to leave can itself be a source of great stress. Individuals and families may have to abruptly flee their country of origin, or may be forced into exile. Others may choose to leave of their own volition. For some families, harrowing decisions must be made about who will leave and who will stay. Once the decision to leave is made, a long period of waiting may follow (Pine & Drachman, 2005).

Transition experiences

The journey from the country of origin to a place of resettlement can be short for some and a long and perilous process for others, and may include multiple countries of resettlement (Pine & Drachman, 2005). Children and adolescents may be separated from their families either by accident or as a safety measure, and many are given to people-smugglers to ensure escape (Fazel & Stein, 2002).

Some refugees spend many years in refugee camps or detention centres (Fazel & Stein, 2002; Millbank, Phillips & Bohm, 2006). Experiences in refugee camps have been shown to have a negative impact on the psychological wellbeing of children. This is particularly so for children who have had traumatic experiences immediately prior to displacement, and children without parents or who have a parent or parents who are not coping well (Ajdukovic & Ajdukovic, 1998).

High levels of anxiety, depression and post-traumatic stress symptoms have been observed among adult asylum-seekers who have been held in Australian detention centres (Keller et al., 2003; Procter, 2005; Steel & Silove, 2001). There is also evidence that asylum-seekers held in detention may have suffered levels of trauma greater than those refugees who are not in detention (Procter, 2005).

Resettlement experiences

Refugees coming to Australia face unemployment, language, housing and cultural barriers, and may experience anxiety about friends and loved ones left behind, racism and discrimination, lack of mainstream social networks, boredom and loneliness (Allotey, 1998; Brough et al., 2003; Chiswick & Lee, 2006; Keel & Drew, 2004; McMichael & Manderson, 2004; Momartin et al., 2006; Rosenthal, Ranieri & Klimidis, 1996; Sinnerbrink et al., 1997). Refugees settling in regional areas may also be more susceptible to isolation, poverty and vilification (Millbank, Phillips & Bohm, 2006).

Health

Some refugees arrive with specific health needs (in some cases, for diseases that have never been present in Australia or that have not been present for a long time). Although people settling under the humanitarian programs have access to health services and trauma counselling, it has been argued that the level of understanding of those providing these services is inadequate or culturally inappropriate (Benson & Smith, 2007; Correa-Velez, Gifford & Bice, 2005; Harris & Zwar, 2005). Access to effective health care is also limited by cultural factors, including distrust of government services, doctors or authority figures, having little or no English language skills, poor finances, and the low priority that is often given to health in the early period of resettlement (Kisely et al., 2002; Murray & Skull, 2003; Neale et al., 2007; Sheikh-Mohammed et al., 2006).

Unemployment

Unemployment is of particular concern to refugees who have been in Australia for less than five years. People who have recently arrived in Australia are often at a disadvantage when looking for work, despite the settlement services available to them.

A range of factors influence the likelihood of finding work (or finding work consistent with employees' skills and desires) including lack of English language skills, non-recognition of qualifications, racial and cultural discrimination by employers, and a lack of mainstream social networks (Colic-Peisker & Tilbury, 2006). This is especially the case for those with Middle Eastern and African backgrounds (Millbank, Phillips & Bohm, 2006). Research indicates that refugees, regardless of their level of skills, are most often employed in low-status, low-paid jobs such as cleaning, aged care, meat processing, taxi driving and building and labouring (Colic-Peisker & Tilbury, 2006).

Changes in family roles

Changes in family roles resulting from the loss of family members or long periods of family separation significantly impact on refugee family wellbeing. Children and adolescents may be expected to take on the role of adults in the family because they have lost a parent or because a parent cannot fulfil their normal parenting role (Punamaki, Qouta & El Sarraj, 1997). Children may also become family advocates when they have greater English language skills than their parents. The expectations of these children may also reflect their roles and expectations of children as a part of traditional cultural practices (such as looking after younger children and contributing to family livelihoods). Family members may feel pressure to adopt 'non-traditional' roles, such as working outside the home or doing tasks previously done by servants. Families who have been reunited after a long period of separation may find that family members have had very different experiences while separated from one another, which may be accompanied by feelings of abandonment or betrayal. Cultural gaps may exist between family members, and some may need to rebuild their identities (especially those who have been traumatised). Children who have been separated from their families, and who have grown up in refugee camps, may experience cultural dislocation due to a lack of role models (Centre for Multicultural Youth Issues, 2006; Gray & Elliott, 2001; Guerin et al., 2003; Rousseau et al., 2004).

Trauma and mental health

Refugees (and migrants, more broadly) show a U-shaped curve of adjustment after resettlement. After the initial relief and elation at finding safety in their host country, the 'honeymoon period' may then wear off as the realities and challenges of resettlement are faced, and as previous traumatic memories gradually resurface. This downward turn is then usually followed by periods of adjustment and readjustment as people settle into the new culture (Sims et al., 2008).

In addition to affecting individual mental health, the consequences of trauma can also affect family roles and obligations, communication (for example, past experiences are not talked about); relationships between family members (survivor guilt and manifestations of trauma, for instance, can place strains on relationships), language acquisition, and connections with local communities (Weine et al., 2004). Parents may be in need of help to deal with their own problems and those of their children after the experience of torture and trauma. Concern has been expressed that Australia is not adequately prepared to cope with the special needs of refugees arriving from Africa who may have poor education, health and language skills, and a history of trauma and brutalisation (Millbank, Phillips & Bohm, 2006). It is also important to recognise that refugee children and adolescents may arrive unaccompanied (due to family separation or the death of both parents and other family members), which presents special challenges for practice, as these children will need to be placed with families (usually from different cultural backgrounds). Unaccompanied minors are more likely to have significant attachment and mental health problems due to the loss of their primary figures of attachment.

Acculturation

Acculturation refers to the process of adjusting to a foreign culture, and often involves changes in identity, values, behaviour, thoughts, attitudes and feelings (Chung, 2001). For many refugee families, this means the difference between living in collectivist societies (that is, societies that stress human interdependence and the importance of the group, rather than the importance of separate individuals) in their countries of origin, and moving to societies that are highly individualistic such as Australia, the US, the UK and Canada. Making these changes can be a source of stress for many refugees, and highly urbanised Australian environments can be especially challenging to refugees from non-Western and/or rural backgrounds (Chung, 2001; Colic-Peisker & Walker, 2003). Women may be more likely than their husbands to find jobs because of their willingness to work in low-paid sectors (Snyder et al., 2005). Conflict within the family can occur when women obtain work outside the family and are exposed to the influences of Australian culture. In addition, men may feel acutely their loss of social status and the ethnic and social boundaries that have thus far defined their role as fathers and husbands when women become the family breadwinners (Snyder et al., 2005).

Parent–child conflict is also likely to occur as children and young people rapidly adapt to their new culture and their behaviour is no longer aligned with their culture of origin (Kagitcibasi, 2003). Added to this pressure, newly arrived refugee parents may find that parenting styles that were normative in their country of origin are not endorsed in their new society (Azar & Cote, 2002). For example, many Western cultures do not view multiple or communal parenting as a common way to raise children. A lack of validation of such parenting beliefs and practices can lead to additional stress for parents in a new culture (Ambert, 1994; Azar & Cote, 2002; Kotchik & Forehand, 2002; Multicultural Perinatal Network, 2000).

■ Working with refugee families

Morland et al. (2005, p. 793) highlight:

> [the] potential for tragic consequences to newcomer refugee families when cultural differences, misunderstandings, language barriers, and a lack of cooperation exist between public child welfare, newcomer refugee families, and refugee-serving agencies.

There is little published literature about good practice when working with children and families from refugee backgrounds to strengthen family functioning. However, Pine and Drachman (2005, p. 538) argue that, by understanding the experiences of refugee families, child welfare professionals are better placed to understand and assess the needs of these families and to provide effective prevention, protection, permanency and family preservation services.

> Social workers who provide child welfare services must identify sources of support and stress in the relationships between families and their environment, and develop their intervention strategies accordingly. To provide effective services for immigrants that are family-centred and culturally competent, child welfare practitioners must understand the child and family's experiences in both emigration and immigration.

Pine and Drachman contend that understanding the experiences of refugee families:

* encourages awareness of the resilience and strengths of refugee families
* makes more salient the mental health issues that can develop out of traumatic pre-migration experiences
* allows examination of the social supports in the refugee service communities that can facilitate family preservation
* encourages communication with the refugee communities that can inform child welfare workers on cultural issues such as gender roles, parenting practices, views on health and mental health, and help-seeking behaviour.

This last point is particularly important, as some refugee families often do not seek help outside their communities and some do not seek help outside their families. Sometimes issues such as domestic violence can be hidden inside the family. Also, the Western concept of 'mental health' is unfamiliar to many refugees, as is the concept of counselling to address mental health and relationship concerns.

In 2006–07 the Australian Centre for Child Protection undertook a research project in collaboration with the then South Australian Department for Families and Communities to examine why refugee families were coming into contact with the South Australian child protection system and to identify the best ways to support parenting needs in refugee families settling in South Australia. This was the first study of this nature. Part of the project involved surveys and interviews with child protection practitioners about challenges and strategies for working with refugee families, and focus groups with refugee community members to explore refugee parents' and community members' views on raising children in Australia and to identify strategies and resources that have supported them, or may support them, in their parenting role. The refugee communities who took part in the focus groups came from Africa (Sudan, Somalia, Democratic Republic of Congo, Liberia, Burundi), the Middle East (Iran and Iraq) and Vietnam. The following sections will discuss the challenges of parenting in a new culture, the challenges practitioners face in their work with refugee families, and strategies identified by practitioners and community members for working successfully with refugee families in child and family services (the full report can be located at www.unisa.edu.au/childprotection).

■ The challenges of parenting in a new culture

Refugee community members identified a number of challenges that they face as parents in a new culture. The most significant of these included: the changing expectations of their children in regard to their roles and responsibilities; understanding Australian laws and norms about parenting; the perceived influence of schools and police on their children's behaviour and attitudes; and changes in the sources and structure of social support.

Changes in children's roles and responsibilities

When refugee community members were asked about parenting in Australia, their overwhelming response was that Australian culture had significantly challenged their traditional expectations about the role of children in family and society (see Williams, 2008 for a more detailed exploration of role expectations, parenting and filial piety in families from refugee backgrounds being resettled in South Australia). In part, this reflects the changes from moving from collectivistic societies to individualistic societies and the differing rates of acculturation of children and adults, as described earlier. All of the 130 community members who took part in the focus groups came from cultural backgrounds where family roles (including expectations of children to contribute to the family) are well-defined and reflect the traditional, economic, environmental and religious characteristics of their society. As one Madi Sudanese man explained:

We have a collective culture back home where we depend on each other. So much relies on the extended family. Below six years of age, the children are mostly attended to by older sisters and brothers and grandparents. The men and grown up boys go hunting and dig around and the ladies, if strong enough, do the weeding. The kids are surrounded by older sisters, brothers, cousins, uncles and aunties.

Refugee community members expressed that in their countries of origin children are normally expected to remain in the family home until marriage, unless they have to study or work away from home. According to community members, there are also well-defined rules and expectations between boys and girls regarding dating and sexual relationships. Children are also brought up to respect and obey their parents and to be respectful to other community members. This means not answering back or challenging and questioning parents' decisions. Most community members viewed children as having obligatory roles to their parents.

In Africa, we bring children up to be polite e.g., they need permission to go out. The child is brought up to respect that.

Burundian and Congolese focus group participant

In our country the children need to obey the adults, even women need to obey their husbands.

Vietnamese focus group participant

The age of marriage is about 20–25 years for boys and girls. This depends on schooling and refugee camp movements. Sex before marriage is not allowed for girls (girls are severely punished, labelled, and this diminishes her capability to find a partner). Boys are not labelled but severely punished. This act can lead to a breakout of diseases. We talk about Toumi which is a local shrine when a curse or misfortune befalls you. There might be an outbreak of diseases … Toumi is a superstitious belief that instils fear in young people not to have premarital sex. This prevents unwanted pregnancies.

Madi Sudanese Men's focus group participant

Parents and community members were very concerned about the independence that children have in Australia and about the impact that this was having on their children, themselves and their community. Families may see their children as leaving a cultural way of life.

… young men over there are just brought up in a kind of culture so they are not preoccupied about when they are going to obtain independence so they are not clashing with their parents there. In their mind they have been scheduled to be very good persons. Even if they have left their home or get married they will be in good contact with their parents. But here they are already preoccupied that they can be independent later on, and they will not need their parents. And the community tells them to do so, but in our culture, the community on the reverse told them to stay with their parents rather than to go out because they consider it a stigma. So it is quite different. Our understanding is that it is happening here and some of

the young men are totally independent from their family just because of the reality of the new situation here in Australia.

Iraqi focus group participant

I have experienced difficulty with young adults when they turn 18 years and become independent. In our culture, children are brought up to remain in the family. When married they still remain in the families and support them. In Australia, when you are 18 years old you are independent. Why is it that in Australia parents complain about their children not leaving home? Why are parents finding solutions for children to go away? That's not how we were brought up. With us, we want our children to stay home. The situation creates a problem for us because we do not want our kids to think that we want them to leave.

Madi Sudanese Women's focus group participant

Peer influence, the education system and Australian culture in general encourage children to be independent. Consequently children from refugee families are exposed to things they would not necessarily experience in their country of origin. This can make parenting difficult, as parents are confronted with parenting situations that are unfamiliar and for which they are very likely to be unprepared.

With regards to the culture here … We love Australia, we love this country, the weather is beautiful but the culture is problematic for us. We see this especially for our children when they go to school. People ask a lot of questions – 'did you go out on the weekend? Who with?' In our culture, this is not appropriate. Dating, for example, is very different in both cultures.

Dinka/Nuer-speaking Sudanese focus group participant

… Now in Australia, our social networks are already broken. We no longer have the extended family to help with disciplining the children. The new situation also exposes parents to confront children which wasn't done before. Children meld into society easier. It is much harder for older people.

Madi Sudanese Men's focus group participant

The perceived increased independence of adolescents from refugee backgrounds was closely linked with financial independence, as some young people were eligible to receive youth allowance payments from the Australian Government. Many community members were angry or distressed that their children were able to receive financial support to live independently from their families. Parents were concerned that children did not know how to handle their financial independence and were worried about their safety and wellbeing. They felt that children were drifting away from the guidance of parents and those children who lived away from their families were more likely to encounter drugs and other negative influences. Some parents also expressed concern about how their children and families were being perceived in the mainstream community.

Teenagers leave home easily. [There is] no social support. In Vietnam, it is harder for our children to move out of the house. Here in Australia, the financial support creates difficulty for parents and removes their power.

Vietnamese Established Community focus group participant

I worry about drugs, alcohol, coming home late. I used to sleep on the floor near the front door, worried about her safety and where she is.

Iranian focus group participant

We want our children to grow up and develop the country! So that we can bring other people! The government don't allow our people to come now … If they see our children the way they dress. [Demonstration of how the youth dress and talk]. We want people to say he is a doctor, a lawyer, he is at university, he is a refugee child. They will be happy to help the community if they see this …

Liberian focus group participant

However, Vietnamese focus group members, who had been in Australia for some time, acknowledged that their community had grown to accept their children's freedom to express themselves, although they did not always find it easy to do so.

The Australian way has influenced our own culture and we have adapted to this new way because of freedom that is available in this country. There is freedom for children to express themselves and school encourages them to do that. Sometimes, the kids don't respect their elders. We do agree with freedom to express themselves but still have to guide them using our culture and that can be difficult to do so. Freedom of speech is difficult to accept but we have to accept.

Vietnamese Established Community focus group participant

Parental perceptions about the rights given to children according to the Australian law and the broader Australian society were also raised. A large number of refugee parents articulated feelings of disempowerment, frustration and sadness caused by the rights, privileges and entitlements that had been granted to their children in Australia, and were unclear as to what their rights as parents were.

Parents feel disempowered. In Australia, being placed on the same level or table as kids (where there is equality between parents and children) and this puts parents in a very difficult position. In our society, there is a hierarchy. This causes the biggest trouble as it is difficult for parents who were initially the head of the household to be on the same level of negotiating with the children.

Madi Sudanese Men's focus group participant

But my heart is being broken more than in the war-zone – where we bring up children to respect us, grown ups. Parents have power. In Australia it is a different story.

Burundian and Congolese focus group participant

Understanding Australian laws and cultural norms regarding parenting

All refugee community members also believed that Australian law played a powerful role in how parents bring up their children in Australia, although there was confusion between what was perceived as being Australian law and what were Australian cultural practices. For all refugee groups, the role of government in Australia was quite different from that of government in their country of origin.

> *Coming from our country, we see the state or government as enemy. In our country, there is no role of state/government, no institution to take care of children. If something goes wrong, relatives take over. The Sudanese stakeholders are the relatives. If parents cannot look after children the relatives take over the role. In Australia the stakeholders are the government. This can sometimes be difficult for us as parents.*
>
> Dinka/Nuer-speaking Sudanese focus group participant

> *A problem in Australia is the law, this is the main problem. In Iran, the government and the law support the parent and trust the parent. In Australia, a parent with a problem they don't trust. They don't trust the parent to do something good for their children. I don't think the government love my children more than me. When my children do something wrong, when children make big mistakes, they make a problem for the family.*
>
> Iranian focus group participant

Refugee community members spoke about the tensions that arose primarily as a result of different cultural practices in the disciplining of children. The majority of the focus group participants came from countries of origin where the use of physical discipline was accepted as an appropriate parenting practice and a reflection of parental authority (as it was in Australia until relatively recently). It is worth noting, however, that while attitudes toward the physical discipline of children have changed, some forms of corporal punishment are still legal in Australia.[1] Parents felt not only powerless, but also that their authority was challenged when they could no longer use such techniques to discipline their children.

---

[1] Corporal punishment in the home is regulated at state level and is lawful throughout Australia under the right of 'reasonable chastisement' or similar (Australian Capital Territory under common law; Northern Territory Criminal Code Act s27; Queensland Criminal Code Act 1899, s280; South Australia Criminal Law Consolidation Act 1935, s20; Tasmania Criminal Code Act 1924, s50; Western Australia Criminal Code 1913, s257; Victoria under common law rule). For more information, visit www.endcorporalpunishment.org

In Australia, for us Africans, there is a lot of freedom; we cannot punish children when they do bad. This is hard for parents as they cannot control children without punishing them. The Australian Government doesn't allow punishing and so children do what they want. Parents do not have power as it is automatically not allowed.

Madi Sudanese Men's focus group participant

Here the government supports children not to listen to or respect their parents. We would like the government to let us bring up children the way we were doing it, for example, hitting a child – we don't hit to cause harm, it is a slighter hitting, we are not punishing them, it is a way for them to know what they did was wrong.

Burundian and Congolese focus group participant

The perceived influence of schools and the police on children's behaviour and attitudes

Many refugee parents believed that their rights as parents were undermined by schools and that the schools encouraged their children to be independent and to challenge them. For some parents, the schools were seen as interfering with or challenging parental authority.

More important – in Iran, when children go to school from the first year they are taught to have respect for their elders and parents, to be kind and helpful. But in Australia they don't teach them this – the opposite – if your parent does this, call the police, if they do that, call the police.

Iranian focus group participant

Communication breaks down because of people in the schools – well intentioned people always asking the children how is their situation at home – triggering doubts on them as they feel they are so different – young people start questioning their tradition because of this.

Dinka/Nuer-speaking Sudanese focus group participant

The role of police was also of concern to refugee community members. A number of parents were horrified that their children would call or threaten to call the police if they felt that their rights were being challenged by their parents. Parents believed that the schools encouraged children to call the police and were concerned that teachers and the police did not confirm with them the version of events that had been told to them by their children. The threat of having a child taken away was seen as a real one and was understandably distressing to parents. It should be noted that the results of a case file analysis revealed child removal to be a rare occurrence in families from the same countries of origin as those included in the focus groups (for more detail, see the full report at www.unisa.edu.au/childprotection).

We are also finding it hard to communicate with our children. We feel like we cannot sit down and talk about what they have and have not done. Now, we don't know how to talk to the child because if they become upset and start saying 'You shouldn't say or do that, then we will call the police.' The police do not listen to the parents.

Burundian and Congolese focus group participant

But when a parent, for example, is used to having the last word inside the family and when his son or his daughter comes to him and says if you don't do what I want I will call the police, 000. He will come and talk to you and the police will come and take you away! This is, in our community, the worst thing that can happen to a parent.

Iraqi focus group participant

We have nine year old children ringing the police. Where does he get that from? The school? It feels like the authority is against us.

Dinka/Nuer-speaking Sudanese focus group participant

Changes in sources and structures of social support

The refugee communities who participated in the focus groups came from cultures where parenting ranged from being the responsibility of the biological parents through to being the responsibility of the wider community. All of the refugee groups had experienced diminished support, albeit to varying degrees, in their parenting roles since arriving in Australia.

Here in Australia, we don't have blood relatives but people who speak some of our own language become family. The kids come together and there is a lot of noise. The kids might be playing together and the neighbour construes it as noisy and them causing trouble. Kids won't associate freely … The teen boys come together as a group and they feel great all walking together and a passerby sees this and automatically thinks they are a gang, vandalising things and getting up to no good. This is a dilemma when kids cannot even play with family members. There are a lot of misunderstandings. We are easily misunderstood …

Madi Sudanese Women's focus group participant

Back home there is family support – brother, sister, friend, neighbour – when they see a problem, they will talk to the child and the family straight away. People don't have support here. They are alone. It is bad to ask for support, bad for their reputation – it may be in a police report … and sometimes they will not know the law – their rights and children's rights. No information is given to people when they come to Australia about children's behaviour and the law.

Iranian focus group participant

The absence of, and separation from, immediate and extended family members puts additional strains on parents adjusting to the new culture. This was particularly noted in cultures where family problems are kept within the family and help from outside agencies would not normally be sought. One Iraqi woman, for example, spoke of the shame that children's misbehaviour can bring to the community.

> Parents will say okay, they will follow the law but they will never talk about the issue in front of any of the community. In front of the community, all things will continue normally as if nothing is happening.
>
> Iraqi focus group participant

Somali focus group participants spoke of the isolation of women, especially sole parents, due to the religious practices of their Somali community. The Somali participants described how their religious beliefs do not allow single women to seek help from unrelated men within their own community or from the broader community. Somali women spoke of the difficulty of obtaining a driver's licence because they could not find women to teach them. This meant that they found it difficult to take their children out on weekends and were often isolated at home with their children. Somali women also spoke of the difficulty in becoming involved in activities such as swimming, going to the gym and other sports because their religion does not allow them to mix with unrelated men.

■ Challenges in working with families from refugee backgrounds

Child protection practitioners related that they encountered a number of challenges in their work with refugee families, including the following issues.

Cultural challenges

Differences in cultural practices and values between other cultures and the Australian culture presented considerable challenges to practitioners in their work with refugee families. This was particularly evident in the differing expectations of practitioners and families around parenting and family roles more generally. As discussed earlier in this chapter, the roles and expectations of children in refugee and other immigrant families can be quite different from those in Western cultures.

Language and communication issues

Practitioners and community members noted the difficulties that communication and language issues presented in working together to support refugee families. Practitioners commented that a lot of information is provided in written form and in English, thus presenting a substantial barrier to non-English-speaking refugees. Working with refugee individuals who had some English skills was also seen as challenging because it allowed room for misunderstandings and misinterpretations. These communication issues make the dissemination of information about alternative parenting practices and appropriate services difficult.

> *And the way the information is provided may not be appropriate. A lot of the information is provided in written form and in English. And it is provided just once as well with no follow up.*
>
> Practitioner focus group participant

> *Well, it's really frustrating when you've got someone who has limited English and we also use interpreter services. Trying to explain things, when if it had been delivered properly in the first place, is frustrating and not necessary. It's frustrating, it's embarrassing for the client and it's frustrating for us. So, it's about ensuring that the information provided is accurate and that the customer understands it.*
>
> Practitioner focus group participant

Perceptions of government agencies

The perceived differing expectations of families compared with staff about the role of government agencies is an issue that practitioners found challenging. Some families from other cultures are not familiar with government agencies whose role is to support parents and families in their parenting roles. As described earlier, some families are suspicious and fearful of government agencies because of their previous experiences in their countries of origin.

> *The barrier is that we're the government and so firstly people tend to shut down. Secondly, families have linked us as Families SA to child protection and you're the agency that takes children away from their families and thirdly, it's recognised that we're statutory which has sometimes turned against us and affects our ability to engage.*
>
> Practitioner focus group participant

Organisational issues

A number of organisational issues were identified by practitioners as impeding their work with refugee families. These included lack of time in casework to become familiar with the cultural background of families; little time to engage and develop trust with refugee families; competing priorities; staff turnover and lack of cultural awareness, knowledge and training.

■ What helps practitioners in their work with refugee families?

Child protection practitioners were aware of the many issues facing the refugee families with whom they work. Practitioners reported on the previous experiences and histories of some of the refugee families such as mental health issues, alcohol misuse and financial difficulties, and highlighted the need for ongoing support. They recognised that the interplay of these challenges, in addition to cultural differences, all impact on the transition of refugee families to a new culture.

Practitioners and community members highlighted a range of strategies and approaches that would help individual practitioners in their work with refugee families. These included the personal and professional characteristics of practitioners, obtaining information about cultural and religious backgrounds, developing community links, using interpreters correctly and fostering internal and external collaboration. These will be discussed in more detail below. The strategies and principles of culturally sensitive practice with Aboriginal and Torres Strait Islander families are also relevant to working with families from refugee backgrounds (see Chapter 6). It's also important that these strategies should be considered in line with what O'Hagan (1999, p. 273) has highlighted as the six sources needing to be considered in practice to promote cultural aspects of the families with whom they are working:

- new legislation
- agency policies and guidelines derived from legislation
- professional and/or ethical codes of the numerous professions involved (for example, child and family health nurses, social workers and community mental health nurses)
- training at both the pre-qualifying and in-service phases
- employment and integration of family and child care staff from different cultural backgrounds
- pressure groups and community consensus within areas served by the agencies.

Personal and professional characteristics

In the Australian Centre for Child Protection's research, the personal and professional characteristics of practitioners identified as facilitating their work with families from refugee backgrounds were consistent with the principles of relationship-based practice outlined in Chapters 1 and 11. Respect, adaptability, a sense of humour and determination to build and nurture trusting relationships were considered essential personal attributes for practitioners working with refugee families. In addition, meeting the clients' needs, an ability to work with interpreters, increasing clients' participation and negotiation skills, and building clients' social support all contributed to developing effective working relationships with families from refugee backgrounds.

Developing trust with families was seen as key to being able to obtain information that could be used when working with, supporting and developing case plans for families.

> *I mean a lot of these sole parents are not really sole parents. There's a father there and a mother because of the polygamy. So, you've got two parents with two separate lots of children and a brother that comes and stays overnight every now and then and they try to hide it and that's another barrier to us working with them because they feel they need to hide that. That's difficult because if they actually come out and tell me the truth then I'd be more able to assist.*
>
> Practitioner focus group participant

Being well informed about clients' cultural and religious backgrounds

Practitioners reflected that it is important to be well informed about the cultural and religious backgrounds of clients in order to understand their behaviour and respond in a sensitive and appropriate manner. At the same time, practitioners emphasised the importance of not making assumptions about behaviour on the basis of this information. Practitioners discussed the importance of preparation and the recognition that each culture is different and that each family and individual comes with their unique experiences.

Practitioners noted the importance of receiving up-to-date and regular feedback and education about the different histories and cultures of refugees and their previous experiences, such as torture and trauma. Also, being able to consult with professionals with expertise in working with refugee families was considered a useful resource.

Developing community links

The development of community links, particularly with elders and community leaders, was recognised as a key factor in supporting practitioners who work with refugee families and communities. With such support, practitioners were able to suggest techniques and services (such as counselling) that they might otherwise not have done for families from refugee backgrounds.

> *When we access someone from community, we use leaders … and this worked well because it helped explain child protection concerns, appropriately and in not too shameful a manner where they can understand. For example, there were allegations of domestic*

violence and physical abuse in a community. There were concerns about dad's mental health, mum could not speak any English, the kids were school age and came to school with injuries. The kids told the teacher about the violence at home. Successful dealings with the department would include knowing about the culture and the genocide that went on. Given dad's mental health issues, we went around there with the cops (as we do with domestic violence issues) and dad became violent, threatening and we were not to talk to the kids. Dad eventually calmed down but we were disrespectful about parenting, [we] separated mum which was really wrong. We managed to get community leaders (man and wife) to explain why we were there, why you cannot commit assault, we're a statutory organisation concerned about supporting children and families and were not there to kill them. We were too threatening.

Practitioner focus group participant

Using interpreters correctly

Engaging appropriate interpreters and knowing how to work with interpreters were considered very important when working with refugee families.

I think … it's really important for workers to know how to work with an interpreter. You know, to actually speak to the clients themselves and let the interpreter do their job and develop the relationship with the client and the client–worker relationship.

Practitioner focus group participant

Practitioners highlighted some considerations when selecting interpreters:

- It is important to be aware that interpreters may be members of the communities with whom they are working.
- Interpreters or bicultural workers can be placed in a difficult position and may be hesitant to intervene in families, especially around sensitive topics such as child protection.
- Interpreters who have knowledge of the area of child protection and are keen to engage in these professional relationships were seen as particularly valuable.

The Women's Health Policy and Projects Unit (2007) suggests these considerations when using interpreters:

- Always use a trained interpreter. It is not appropriate to use partners or the client's children to interpret. A member of the client's community may also be inappropriate because of confidentiality.
- Use an interstate telephone interpreter if the client is concerned about confidentiality within his/her community group.
- Use short sentences and focus on one point at a time. Talk directly to the client, not the interpreter.

For an excellent reference on working with interpreters, see Lisa Aronson Fontes' book, *Interviewing Clients Across Cultures* (Fontes, 2008).

Internal and external collaboration

Practitioners identified the importance of both internal and external collaboration as strategies to improve their work with refugee families. The importance of strong inter-agency partnerships with key people and the need to develop networks with other agencies, both inside and outside their organisation, were highlighted. In addition, external collaboration with settlement services and other support services such as the Migrant Resource Centre, Lutheran Community Care and the Australian Refugee Association were emphasised. Sims and colleagues (2008) provide an excellent summary of what mainstream and culturally specific services can do to work more effectively with families from culturally and linguistically diverse backgrounds, and to work well with each other.

Suggested strategies

A range of strategies were suggested by refugee community members to help address some of the challenges they were facing as parents in a new culture. These strategies involved a number of agencies including schools, police and child protection and family support services, as well as having implications for community members themselves. The proposed strategies included:

- encouraging parents to communicate with their children (especially adolescents, to open channels of communication between parents and children)
- encouraging collaborative work between families, communities and schools to address problems between children and families in a consistent manner (these included establishing parenting committees to resolve parenting issues)
- providing information for newly arrived families about parenting in Australia at a time and in a manner that suits the needs and preferences of families (such information could include providing a consultative function in which parents can anonymously seek assistance as required to address parenting difficulties)
- developing flexible and culturally responsive ways of working that allow for two-way interactions between government agencies and families (these ways of working include talking with parents *and* children when dealing with child protection concerns, and engaging with community leaders and elders)
- enhancing access to culturally responsive child care.

The ABCD Program

There are many promising programs being implemented across Australia that attempt to address some of the parenting issues encountered by refugee families. The ABCD Program, delivered by the Parenting Research Centre in Victoria, has shown some encouraging results. The Program was designed for parents who have children between 10 and 14 years of age.

The Program has a number of aims, including:

- strengthening parent–child relationships
- improving family connectedness
- empowering parents to enhance their child's development and resilience by building their communication and problem-solving skills.

The program is designed as a weekly group program delivered in either a four-week or a six-week format. A range of topics are covered in the program, from understanding adolescents, to connecting and communicating with teenagers, to setting effective limits, to dealing with risky behaviour. In the group sessions, a trained facilitator works with the parents to develop their skills and parenting strategies. The sessions last from two-and-a-half to three hours and parents are encouraged to practise the strategies learnt in the groups at home between sessions. The program is available in five community languages: Arabic, Macedonian, Spanish, Turkish and Vietnamese. The ABCD Program has now been delivered to over 4000 families across Victoria from English and non-English-speaking backgrounds.

A group-based ABCD Program has also been delivered to parents of adolescents in Victoria's Somali community by trained Somali facilitators. Findings from the evaluation suggest the program is relevant, informative and enjoyable for Somali parents. Limited quantitative data obtained also indicated that parents found the program acceptable and gained some benefit, with a reduction in disagreements with their adolescents (Burke, Ward & Clayton, 2007).

REFLECTIVE QUESTIONS

If you were working with refugee families and newly arrived migrant families, what types of problems and issues may they be experiencing? Consider: previous traumatic experiences related to their country of origin; the process of migration; settlement into Australia; and cultural differences.

What kind of support is available for children, parents and families from refugee backgrounds? As a practitioner, what kinds of attitudes/beliefs may you bring that impact on the way you work with refugee families? How might you address these? How can practitioners engage and support refugee families? What kinds of services already exist that work well – and how can we make them better?

ACTIVITY

Kaela's husband was killed in Somalia, as were her sister and mother. She has no relatives in Australia and has little social contact. Kaela has been suffering from depression since emigrating to Australia with her three children (aged three, five and nine). Kaela has a number of appointments during the week and leaves her nine-year-old daughter in charge of the younger children, as she has no-one else to care for them. Kaela came into contact with the child protection system after reports were made concerning her three children being left alone for extended periods of time. A neighbour also reported that Kaela's two younger children had been found wandering the streets on a number of occasions and that they had asked for food a few times.

As a practitioner, discuss the issues you think you may encounter when working with this family. What approaches do you think may be most useful when working with this family/client?

What resources do you think may help you work with this family?

What other services and resources could be engaged to assist this family?

■ Conclusion

Refugee families experience a multitude of complex challenges as they start a new life in a new country. Drawing on the national and international literature, this chapter has attempted to provide a description of the experiences of refugee families during the pre-migration, transition and resettlement phases. In addition, this chapter has drawn upon the voices of refugee parents and communities as they speak about the challenges of raising their children in Australia, and documented the challenges that child welfare practitioners have encountered in their work. When refugee families come to a new country, they bring with them their own culture and way of life. As acculturation occurs for these families, tensions or problems emerge, especially when there is a mismatch or clash between cultures and norms. A mismatch between norms related to roles of family members, parenting styles, disciplining of children and roles of government and support services can all impact on parenting ability. This is compounded by language and communication barriers and organisational restraints. There are promising approaches and strategies that have been found to be effective. For parents, these include improving communication with their children and actively seeking information about parenting in Australia. For practitioners, these include forging trusting relationships and being well informed about the cultural and religious backgrounds of the families with whom they are working, developing community links, and engaging in collaborative work with other services.

LIVERPOOL JOHN MOORES UNIVERSITY
LEARNING SERVICES

■ Useful websites

Australian Centre for Child Protection: **www.unisa.edu.au/childprotection**

Bridging Refugee Youth & Children's Services: **www.brycs.org**

Foundation House – The Victorian Foundation for Survivors of Torture: **www.foundationhouse.org.au/home/index.htm**

Parenting Between Cultures: The Primary School Years – A program for parents from culturally and linguistically diverse communities: **www.marymead.org.au/publications**

Parenting in a New Culture Program – Spectrum Migrant Resource Centre (MRC) in Victoria: **www.spectrumvic.org.au/Settlement-Family/Parenting-Family**

Raising Children in a New Country: An Illustrated Handbook: **www.brycs.org/documents/RaisingChildren-Handbook.pdf**

6

Working with Aboriginal families

Gary Robinson and Sarah Mares

■ Learning goals

This chapter will enable you to:

- **CONSIDER** what constitutes vulnerability for families and children in different settings

- **DISCUSS** the interaction of cultural, historical, community and individual family and child factors that contribute to vulnerability

- **OUTLINE** an approach to engagement with communities and families as a prerequisite to any form of family or parenting intervention

- **RECOGNISE** the key elements of successful parenting and family interventions and how these may be adapted for delivery to families in remote communities

- **BE FAMILIAR WITH** Let's Start as an example of a family intervention that has shown positive outcomes with Aboriginal children and their families

- **IDENTIFY** qualities of practice and the training and supports required to successfully deliver family interventions with Aboriginal children and their families.

■ Introduction

THERE IS GREAT diversity in the composition, role definition and functioning of Australian families. This is true for Aboriginal and non-Aboriginal Australian families. Australian Aboriginal cultures were founded on practices of child-rearing dating back many thousands of years. These have been subject to pervasive change in response to the direct and indirect effects of European settlement; they are influenced by policies specifically targeting Aboriginal families, by processes of change affecting all Australian families and by changes and adaptations within Aboriginal communities themselves. There is considerable evidence that family functioning and parenting quality are core determinants of children's health, development and physical, cognitive, social and emotional outcomes. They shape the strengths and vulnerabilities that the children carry with them into life. Aboriginal parents and children differ greatly in their circumstances, their strengths, their resources and their vulnerabilities, and practitioners engage with them in a wide range of service settings and social contexts. It is important that models of effective practice are developed that are responsive to this diversity.

This chapter will outline some of the cultural, historical and social factors that shape the context of Aboriginal families and parenting today. It will briefly review some of the Australian and international evidence on effective early intervention and draw on the example of a parenting program for Aboriginal families that has been implemented in divergent social and community settings.

■ Demography

The Aboriginal and Torres Strait Islander population comprises around 2.5 per cent of the Australian population (ABS, 2012). The largest number of Aboriginal and Torres Strait Islander Australians live in New South Wales, followed by Queensland and Western Australia. Over half of the Aboriginal and Torres Strait Islander population live in cities, with about a quarter living in remote communities. In the Northern Territory, over 30 per cent of the population of approximately 230 000 people are of Aboriginal descent and of these, 40 per cent are aged younger than 18 years. Over 86 per cent of the Northern Territory's non-Aboriginal population and 46 per cent of the Aboriginal population live in the major centres of Darwin and Alice Springs, the remaining 54 per cent living in remote and very remote towns and communities spread over the Territory, where variants of traditional cultures and practices continue to be observed and access to basic services is often very limited.

The Indigenous population of Australia is young, relative to the general population, and the most recent national maternal and infant health data report that Indigenous women have a higher birthrate: 2.6 babies, compared with 1.9 for all women in Australia. This report also notes that motherhood during the teenage years is much more common among Indigenous girls: 21 per cent compared with 4 per cent of all births (AIHW, 2012). There is also a higher burden of illness and loss than in the general population. Aboriginal and Torres Strait Islander babies and children have higher rates of mortality and morbidity, particularly due to infection and injury. The most recent National Aboriginal and Torres Strait Islander Social Survey reported that almost one-third of Aboriginal and Torres Strait Islander young people and adults (those aged over 16 years) reported high or very high levels of psychological distress, more than twice the rate of non-Indigenous Australians. Three-quarters (77 per cent) of Indigenous adults reported that they or their close friends or family had experienced at least one life stressor in the previous 12 months and more than one-quarter of Indigenous adults reported they had recently experienced discrimination (AIHW, 2012).

The Northern Territory's Indigenous population is particularly disadvantaged in multiple senses. The Australian Early Development Index (AEDI) is a measure of children's development at the point of entry to school across domains of physical health and wellbeing, cognitive and social-emotional development. Based on this measure, five times as many Indigenous children in the NT are developmentally vulnerable compared to other Australian children, with those from remote communities and speaking languages other than English the most disadvantaged (Silburn et al., 2011; CCCH & TICHR, 2009). Nation-wide AEDI scores appear to be partly associated with the levels of investment in services and supports for families in each jurisdiction (Brinkman et al., 2012). However, other social and cultural differences are equally important for Aboriginal populations in the Northern Territory.

Child protection notifications and substantiations provide another measure of the disadvantage and vulnerability of Aboriginal children and families. Aboriginal and Torres Strait Islander children in Australia are over-represented in the care and protection system at a rate of 9–10 times that of non-Aboriginal children (AIHW, 2012). While some regard this over-representation as possibly reflecting a disproportionate response by the child protection system (Tilbury, 2009), others identify that the scale of need and the absence of alternatives to statutory investigatory responses mean that child removal is a significant reality in communities in which social adversity, family breakdown, chronic stress and ill health, and low levels of education and employment are reproduced in a 'vicious cycle' of disadvantage (Delfabbro et al., 2010).

■ Policy context

The impacts of the colonisation of Australia by Europeans over 200 years have been compounded by policies of intervention and welfare measures applied to Aboriginal families. Past practices of child removal resulted in the forcible separation of children of mixed descent from their families and communities. The impacts of these past policies were recognised and addressed in an Inquiry into the separation of Indigenous children from their families (NISATSIC, 1997; Silburn et al., 2006). The historical experience of the 'Stolen Generations' contributed to concern that contemporary levels of intervention and child removal were routinely repeating these experiences of separation for children, and that welfare agencies disregarded the needs of Aboriginal children and families. The Aboriginal child placement principle (AIHW, 2011; Lock, 1997) sought to moderate the impacts of intervention by ensuring that, wherever possible, Aboriginal children subject to removal would be placed with Aboriginal families in various out-of-home care arrangements. However, the capacity to provide quality of out-of-home care with Aboriginal families is not always able to meet demand. The recommendations and resources flowing from the Inquiry's 'Bringing them Home' report and the Aboriginal child placement principle were aimed largely at remediation of impacts of past practices, and moderation of contemporary practices of removal, rather than at dealing with the ongoing problems of vulnerability and developmental disadvantage among Aboriginal children.

The effects of social change on family functioning and wellbeing of children are acutely felt in communities of remote and rural Australia, along with the impacts of disproportionate or inappropriate intervention. A report commissioned by the Northern Territory Government, called *Ampe Akelyernemane Meke Mekarle*, or 'Little Children are Sacred' (Wild & Anderson, 2007) provided a picture of widespread sexual abuse of Aboriginal children in communities of the Northern Territory. It drew attention to widespread problems of alcohol abuse, gambling and violence that compounded the risks to child safety and wellbeing. A perceived lack of action by the Northern Territory Government saw the Commonwealth Government intervene on multiple fronts. It constructed a legislative framework for what it called the Northern Territory Emergency Response (NTER). The NTER included compulsory acquisition of land and suspension of Northern Territory laws and elements of the Commonwealth Racial Discrimination Act (1975). The 'Intervention', as it came to be known, created a mobile workforce of personnel from the Australian Defence Forces, Federal Police and members of other bureaucracies. Actions included prohibition of alcohol in prescribed communities, establishment of community safe houses, increased spending on primary health care and on specific child protection measures to provide therapeutic services for children affected by neglect and abuse. A centrepiece of the strategy was the introduction of 'income management', a system of welfare payments in which a proportion of income was sequestered into an account from which purchases of prohibited goods could not be made (Arney, McGuinness & Robinson, 2009). Similar programs have been implemented on a lesser scale in other jurisdictions: for example, a trial of income management and other child protection measures has been implemented in four 'welfare reform' communities in Cape York, Queensland.

The NTER has been replaced by a legislative framework called 'Stronger Futures', which sets out Commonwealth and Territory commitments to ongoing development of services by Commonwealth and Territory governments. The potential for these measures to contribute to longer-term improvement of outcomes for Indigenous children, much less to reduce the demand for statutory intervention and child removal, is unclear.

Of those policies (national, state and territory) concerned with the impact of adverse circumstances on child development and life chances, some apply pressure on parents, seeking to define desirable or rather minimal goals and standards for children's care and education and to coerce parents and caregivers to take responsibility for meeting them. These policies simultaneously legitimate and regulate the rationing of scarce welfare resources within a framework of moral ideas about accountability, responsibility and entitlement to welfare support. Aboriginal leader Noel Pearson (2000) first articulated these ideas for the Indigenous domain.

However, although such policies are justified by their intention to improve outcomes for Aboriginal families and children, they define a conditional entitlement to welfare in terms of punitive responses when parents fail in their responsibilities. Thus, child welfare measures for Aboriginal families and children after the NTER entail an extension of surveillance, regulation and control, combined with measures to ensure compliance, such as withdrawal of benefits if children do not attend school. In the case of many Aboriginal families, these measures potentially compound a sense of marginality, exclusion and inadequacy. The coercive or regulatory side of state welfare policy does not of itself support the capacity of parents and families to meet the required standards. It must be offset by strategies that aim to support families and to promote their strengths. These supportive measures include interventions to prevent later or more serious difficulties by identifying early signs of risk or vulnerability; they may take the form of universal measures for all members of a community or population, and targeted measures for higher-risk families and children. The Stronger Futures legislation that replaced the NTER, and the national partnership agreements for all jurisdictions under the Closing the Gap framework,[1] have moved towards more systematic implementation of such strategies.

---

[1] The Closing the Gap strategy is the long-term Indigenous reform agenda endorsed by the Council of Australian Governments (COAG) with the aim of improving the lives of Aboriginal and Torres Strait Islander Australians, and in particular Aboriginal and Torres Strait Islander children. The strategy focuses on reducing disparities in life expectancy, infant mortality, access to early childhood education, reading, writing and numeracy, Year 12 attainment and employment. A number of National Partnership Agreements have been agreed through COAG committing governments to a common framework of outcomes, progress measures and policy directions to guide Indigenous reform in specific policy areas. For more information, see www.fahcsia.gov.au/our-responsibilities/indigenous-australians/programs-services/closing-the-gap

■ Parenting and family functioning

Core dimensions of parenting and family functioning can be defined as (a) care (meeting the child's needs for physical, emotional and social wellbeing and safety); (b) control (setting and enforcing appropriate boundaries) and (c) development (realising the child's potential in various domains) (Hoghughi & Long, 2004). These tasks are influenced by:

- child factors, such as the child's age, health and temperament
- parental factors, including the parents' models and understanding of their parenting role, and ability to understand their child's emotional and psychological needs
- contextual sources of stress and support in the extended family, community or in the service sector, and the family's interaction with these (Reder et al., 2003).

The tasks are carried out according to the goals and expectations of parents and caregivers and their cultural values and expectations. Parental and contextual influences are highly variable, according to cultural differences and across social settings. There is little agreement about what constitutes optimal family functioning or how this should be objectively measured (Walker & Shepherd, 2008).

It is unlikely that any single risk factor or domain of risk adequately explains poor child outcomes, although parenting behaviour is a strong predictor of child maltreatment, and of problem behaviour and attachment security. Parenting mediates – and can protect against or exacerbate – the impact of genetic as well as environmental risk factors such as poverty. DeKlyen & Greenberg (2008, p. 640), propose a model that includes four domains of risk: child characteristics, including temperament and biological vulnerabilities; child–parent attachment quality; parental management and socialisation strategies; and family ecology including adversity. Tests of a similar model found that child problem behaviours at age five could be predicted by the interaction of gender, perceived support of caregiver, disorganised attachment of the child to parents at 15 months, child anger-proneness and negative parent–child interactions (Smeekens et al., 2007). Disorganised infant–parent attachment at 15 months was the strongest predictor of child behaviour problems (see Chapters 1 and 11). Parenting styles associated with past or current trauma predict disorganised attachment in the child.

■ Parenting interventions

Parenting programs have become increasingly central to strategies to improve child outcomes for disadvantaged families. Among the most well known is The Incredible Years (Webster-Stratton, 1998), which has been a mainstay of the Headstart programs for disadvantaged children in the US and has been widely adopted internationally.

There is also evidence for the effectiveness of a number of other parenting interventions (Reid, Webster-Stratton & Baydar, 2004; Eyberg, Nelson & Boggs, 2008). In Australia, the Triple-P Positive Parenting Program is the most widely adopted and rigorously evaluated parenting program and has been implemented at scale in many Australian and international locations (Sanders et al., 2000; Wise et al., 2005). Numerous other examples have been developed in recent years, albeit without the wide implementation of Triple-P.

Garland et al. (2008) have identified the common elements of effective psychosocial treatments for children to include therapeutic content (such as behavioural techniques, problem-solving), treatment techniques (such as role-playing, homework), aspects of the therapeutic alliance (including collaborative or consensus goal-setting) and treatment duration (at least 12 sessions at weekly intervals). Parenting interventions tend to be more effective when children are younger, when there are fewer other problems for the family or the child, when child behaviour problems are less severe and – where there is less psychosocial disadvantage – no history of parental antisocial behaviour and the family have supports. There is some evidence that maternal depression, parental substance abuse and sole parenthood reduce the effectiveness of parenting interventions (Fonagy & Target, 2004).

Scott and Dadds (2009) emphasise that standard parent training based on social learning theory and behavioural approaches may be ineffective for families or parents with multiple or significant problems. In these cases, therapeutic, attachment systems-based and motivational approaches may be more appropriate. Where there is a history of significant psychosocial risk, as is true for disadvantaged Aboriginal families, or where children have experienced maltreatment or attachment trauma, targeted support in several domains may be required. Treatment of parental mental illness, drug and alcohol misuse, or conduct problems needs to be included in the intervention, as well as attempts to address the impact of cumulative disadvantage and adversity experienced by these families (see also Chapters 9 and 10).

■ Culture and parenting

Social and psychological research has drawn attention to the extraordinarily wide variation in patterns of child-rearing and family functioning across cultural contexts. Cultural values of parents, families and communities determine how children are nurtured and protected, what risks and privations they are normatively exposed to in order to learn, and how they grow into emotionally competent adults who can in turn sustain intimate relationships and nurture their own children. Children learn about culture from birth through the daily caretaking rituals and behaviours of, and interactions with, their caregivers. This includes how they are held, touched, talked to and looked at, as well as feeding, weaning and sleeping rituals and arrangements. These experiences may include a dominant role for parents, or may involve many other caregivers.

For example, Kruske et al. (2012) describe how parenting in north-east Arnhem Land involves many caregivers from birth, with no separation of the parent and child dyad from the wider group and many people participating in the interactions between parent and infant. Nevertheless, infants do form stable attachments with their mothers as the primary caregivers. One of the most commonly observed cultural differences in parenting is in response to crying. Common advice to parents in the West has been to let babies cry and learn to self-soothe when they are fussing, wanting contact or having trouble getting to sleep. Kruske et al. note that this is intolerable to Aboriginal parents and family members. Robinson (2005) reframes this observation by noting that Aboriginal parents often do not respond to a baby's crying, but that this is in part to activate concern and support for both parent and infant among others in the family group, and that cultural values and norms in any society allow a wide range of behaviours and practices, including responses that expose small children to strain, risk or difficulty. This is often a culturally rationalised 'benign neglect' that is thought necessary in order to promote self-reliance and independence. For example, when parents refuse to respond to a child's crying or demands for food, this may be with the expectation that other family members should respond or that the child should learn to ask aunties or uncles for food or support.

While families in all cultural contexts may have clear values relating to safety and protection of children and seek to promote healthy growth according to culturally formed goals and expectations, chronic adversity and disadvantage can impact on these practices and place children at risk in ways that go well beyond what is acceptable within any normative or cultural frame of reference. The family may then become an unstable, unsafe or unresponsive environment that exposes children to serious risk.

REFLECTIVE QUESTIONS
Think about the values that underpin the way that your family of origin understands children and child-rearing. Can you think of families where different practices and values apply? What domains of care, protection and nurturance do these relate to? Consider whether this is influenced by cultural differences.

■ Adaptation of mainstream and evidence-based programs for Aboriginal families

Standards of evidence for the best credentialled parenting interventions have been developed in large-scale trials with rigorous randomised designs. These have been difficult, if not impossible, to implement for Aboriginal people, because of the scattered and diverse circumstances and interconnected ways in which Aboriginal people live. Nevertheless, intervention programs targeting Aboriginal families are increasingly being offered and delivered across Australia, many of them based on adaptations of international models. Evidence for the effectiveness of such interventions based on systematic adaptation for Aboriginal parents and families remains limited.

The Incredible Years has been widely implemented across diverse cultural groups in the US and in New Zealand, where a version has been culturally adapted for Maori families (Wille, 2006). The Nurse–Family Partnership Program (Olds et al., 1986) has been implemented in Australia as the Australian Nurse–Family Partnership Program (ANFPP) by Aboriginal Medical Services in a small number of trial sites. One of the most highly researched programs, the Triple-P Program, has been trialled with Aboriginal families and reported positive outcomes in the treatment group compared to controls (Turner et al., 2007). However, this was a small-scale study with high rates of attrition, which cases doubt on its effectiveness and wider applicability for Aboriginal families, at least without further attention to engagement of clients and improvement of their retention in the intervention.

Cultural adaptation of evidence-based programs

Reporting on the adaptation of a parent training program for Indigenous peoples of North America, BigFoot & Funderburk (2011) suggest that cultural enhancement should be:

> ... mindful of the family's cultural context and can be applied case by case, variable enough to melt into the needs of each family while maintaining the integrity of the evidence-based treatment. The concept of the child as the center of the circle stresses the importance of support provided by caregivers and family, the importance of attending to and listening to children, the importance of telling about experiences (e.g., through storytelling or ceremony), the relationships among emotions, beliefs and behaviors; and the importance of identifying and expressing emotions and developing self-control.
>
> (BigFoot & Funderburk, 2011, p. 316)

Identification of the key elements that contribute to program effectiveness should guide decisions about adaptation of an evidence-based intervention. Elements of cultural adaptation can be differentiated:

- development of specific strategies of community engagement, including engagement of client groups, contextualisation of the intervention with regard to local leadership and collaboration or integration with local frameworks of community organisation, services and programs

- cultural competence and safety training for staff, including specific capacities and skills required to deliver an intervention for members of a particular group (Lau, 2006; Self-Brown et al., 2011)
- modification of selected content to aid delivery and comprehension (for example, language translation or use of specific local examples and ideas, specific use of art, drawing or narrative) in a particular context, without modification of the intervention's key elements (Stock et al., 2012)
- review of the intervention's program logic and its theory of change: do core elements of the intervention need modification, because of significant cultural differences in respect of parenting and child development and their outcomes? Adaptation of core elements of the intervention may depart from the original, and ideally should be rigorously evaluated at a sufficient scale to be confident of effectiveness (Robinson et al., 2012).

Some or all of these levels or aspects of adaptation may be required in some combination to ensure effective implementation. At a minimum, interventions for many Aboriginal populations would require adaptation at the first three levels, while for Aboriginal families using services in many settings, the second element may be sufficient.

Parenting and family interventions, including those intended to reduce the risk of child abuse and neglect, need to be especially sensitive to cultural differences, given wide variations in parenting practices and family values. Responding to families and individuals with complex, multiple problems is challenging and requires a clear intervention model, adequate attention to family engagement and training, and ongoing support for staff.

There is an accumulating literature advocating culturally appropriate strategies and approaches to work with Aboriginal and Torres Strait Islander families (cf. Milroy, 2008 and Walker & Shepherd, 2008). Arney, Bowering and colleagues (2010, p. 112) refer to the need for service delivery that is:

- informal – encouraging informal talk and activities
- community-based – respectfully identifying and valuing the role of community
- culturally respectful, relevant, competent, safe and welcoming to Aboriginal clients
- supportive of families – recognising the diversity of families
- inclusive of Elders – recognising their respected status
- community-controlled, or with elements of community control – acknowledging the importance of community and the goal of self-determination

- delivered by learning organisations – prompting good practice that evolves to meet changing needs
- holistic – integrating spiritual, emotional, physical and cultural aspects of life.

It is important to have a model that informs work with families. Many family interventions in Australia and internationally, and particularly those that include home visiting, are informed by the Family Partnership Model. This emphasises the quality of the relationship established between the worker and the family (Davis Day, & Bidmead, 2002).

Family engagement and change are seen as dependent upon the relationship that is established between the helper and the parent. The necessary qualities of the helper identified by this program align with those qualities of Nurse Home Visitors identified as most helpful by Aboriginal families included in the South Australian Family Home Visiting Program (Arney, Bowering et al., 2010).

■ Identifying and responding to vulnerability in remote and urban contexts

In this section, some of the themes of work with families are illustrated with examples from Let's Start, an early intervention program for Indigenous parents and children in the Northern Territory and from a hospital setting in Sydney.

The Let's Start program is a manualised group parenting program that was specifically designed for Aboriginal families in the Northern Territory. Based on a model originally adopted by a community-controlled health service on the Tiwi Islands, it has been trialled in a range of quite divergent urban, rural and remote settings. It has a multi-group format that involves group sessions with a number of child–parent dyads, engaging in play and collaborative exercises to promote improved responsiveness and communication between parent and child, and sessions for parents to discuss children's behaviour and parenting. It takes referrals from multiple sources, with a number of parents self-referring. It runs for two hours a week over ten weeks, coinciding with a school term. To date, it has been implemented in eight remote Aboriginal communities, involving different language and cultural groups in two different regions of the Territory; it has been implemented in Darwin in two versions, one for both Aboriginal and non-Aboriginal participants, and another specifically for residents of Darwin's Aboriginal urban 'town camps' or special lease communities (Robinson et al., 2011).

In remote towns and communities and in major cities, there is not only diversity for Aboriginal and Torres Strait Islander people in terms of community history, ethnic composition, organisation, culture and language, but also in terms of patterns of kin relationships and the ways in which families function and relate to each other. Sources of vulnerability in families may be similar, but need to be understood in terms of the characteristics of each setting. For example, working in new remote locations, Let's Start typically works over many months to engage families, community leaders and service providers before beginning to implement the program. Sources of strength and vulnerability are identified at referral and throughout the program, and these are examined at four levels.

1   Sources of vulnerability within the family have the potential to adversely affect children's wellbeing, development and conduct. These influences may include the impact of parental mental illness or antisocial tendencies; suicidal behaviour or violence within the family; marital conflict; or tensions or conflicts involving other family members, such as older siblings or members of the extended family network. Parents who have experienced trauma and have been exposed to harsh or inadequate early parenting and care are very often unable to adequately care for their own children.

2   The family is a system of balancing demands and reciprocities in which tensions or conflicts between one or more members may be transmitted to others, causing them distress or anxiety; their behaviour may stand out – and be a reason for intervention – but is an effect of the behaviour of others. Important processes of adjustment within families may have important consequences for the wellbeing of children: break-up of the relationship between a child's parents; death of a parent or other family members; or other separations, such as the removal of a child. Such events may cause stresses and adjustments within relationships that affect children – over and above the direct effects of loss or conflict on the child. The impacts on children of the death of a caregiver, separation of parents or conflict between them are often unnoticed by adults preoccupied with their own responses to these events. Children's adjustment needs are often not recognised and are poorly met by parents or family members under stress.

3   Threats or stressors may arise from within the community: these may include violence, suicidal behaviour, substance misuse and a lack of concern for child safety or wellbeing. These may be reinforced by inadequate regulation of social behaviours linked to adolescent peer activity, availability of alcohol and other drugs, or response to social conflicts by Elders or police. Children may be directly exposed to these community stressors; stressors are also mediated by the relationships between family members and other community members, and communicated by parental anxiety and distress to children (cf. Linares et al., 2001).

4   Above or outside these spheres of concern – community relationships, family processes and individuals – exists the framework of institutions and

organisations, both within and connecting with the community and more widely in the society as a whole. These shape organised responses to the pattern of needs and difficulties of families and individuals through provision of needed services. These may themselves influence community stress through their effects on violence, alcohol and other drug use or their failure to promote positive social participation. Ill-judged child welfare interventions can cause children serious psychological distress with consequences for healthy development. Poorly coordinated services may be unable to provide continuity of care for vulnerable children and in this sense are an unintended source of risk and vulnerability.

These potential contributors to vulnerability may be summarised as shown in Figure 6.1.

For the Let's Start Program, quite different processes of engagement with some locally adapted content have been developed for each location: remote communities, town camps and the general mixed program. The aims are to build partnership with leaders, organisations and services as a basis for working within the community setting, and engaging families on their terms. Meetings and workshops are held with community leaders as well as with teachers, health workers and other service providers. These not only discuss processes for collaboration between services to deliver Let's Start, but also take the form of workshops that present information on child development relevant to the aims and objectives of the program. The team also conducts open workshops on early brain development and the importance of parenting and early social interaction for the children's growth. This includes interactive activities for parents and children such as those found within the intervention program. These workshops aim to

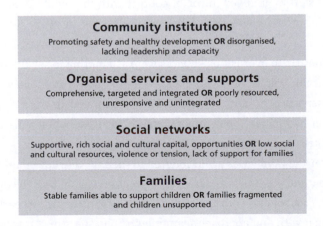

Figure 6.1   Potential contributors to vulnerability

generate community interest and significantly increase parental willingness to attend the program.

However, not all of the strategies adopted have been equally successful: for example, in Darwin many families facing marked adversity live in disadvantaged town camps where there are high levels of community tension. Many of these families were not successfully retained in the program, despite intensive preparation (Robinson et al., 2011). More substantial modifications of the program format are needed for these contexts.

In the following sections, some case material from Let's Start and a hospital-based intervention in urban Sydney is presented to illustrate some of the themes of family vulnerability outlined above, and the ways in which services can respond to this vulnerability.

Coordination and support over time: a child in a remote community

A mother, Stella, and her five-year-old son Roy, living in a remote community, were referred to Let's Start by school, child protection and health workers because of concerns about Roy's bizarre and disruptive behaviour. Roy rarely attended school and often appeared to be very anxious, hiding under furniture or disturbing the class. He was known to child protection services because of involvement in sexualised behaviour between children at school, and there was a current investigation. The father was often absent with work. There had been past family violence. In the community, there was both widespread concern about the boy and also resignation, as if nothing could be done. After being contacted by the Let's Start team, the parents agreed to come but, despite many follow-up contacts, did not do so.

Let's Start staff maintained informal contact with the family. A year later, Stella was functioning more confidently and had obtained part-time work. Service providers continued to express concerns about the quality of care received by Roy and his younger brother. Up to five visiting services were attempting to see the family (school counsellor, health clinic, family violence service, therapeutic services, learning assessment service). The now six-year-old Roy continued to miss school and the truancy officer had joined those professionals seeking to contact the family in the community. Stella again declined to attend Let's Start.

A year later, the family was again referred to the Let's Start program as a result of concerns about the younger son, Junior. The program was to be delivered in a room away from the school and both Stella and Junior began to turn up early each week and also to chat with and approach team members in the street at other times. Roy and his father also came to family lunches, so that there was benefit for the whole family as a consequence, allowing the need for an assessment of Roy to be discussed and agreed upon. Supportive contact with the team over time was necessary for this family to eventually accept opportunities for help. However, a simple matter such as relocation of the program away from the school was also important: the school had been a site of conflict and shame for this family because of criticism of the children's lack of attendance. Engagement with the family now occurred through the younger child, Junior. In one sense this was not ideal, since Roy's needs had not at first been directly addressed. However, the family was now in contact with services that could offer support to him.

This is an example where community members and several services held concerns about a family but there was no coordination and little change. Agencies tended to 'drop the ball' as soon as the family refused to respond. The Let's Start team's open-ended persistence, and sensitivity to the significance of program location, provided the critical link to treatment and care. This example demonstrates the importance of maintaining a consistent, interested and non-judgemental approach and – in non-statutory services – working at the pace that suits the family, even when anxiety about a child is high.

Adjustment issues within family relationship systems

A ten-year-old boy, Russ, was referred to the Let's Start program because of aggression and fighting in the classroom. His mother, Alberta, was impatient with him and angry at his behaviour. He would come to her workplace, take food from the store without paying, throw things to the floor and run off if she questioned him about it. She was attempting to have him leave for another community to stay with an aunt, and so at first did not want to attend Let's Start. She eventually agreed to participate, saying 'I want to understand what makes him like that.'

Some of the background issues became clear. Russ's father had died a year before. Alberta was frequently out drinking with others at the local club. Relocation of her son was part of her desire for more freedom of movement. During the group program with other children and parents, some incidents touching on his behaviour (for example, throwing stones at his mother when she wouldn't come home) were made the subject of role-plays. After this, he told a story about how he had helped prepare food in the home with his grandmother, and how he had carefully put a plateful aside for his mother. Early in the evening when she was thinking about going out drinking, she dismissed the food and said she wasn't hungry. Russ later became hungry and ate it himself. Later, Alberta came home a little drunk and then growled at the boy angrily because he hadn't saved any food. When telling his story to her in the group, he protested, 'You changed your mind! You changed your mind!' Alberta burst into tears.

At the end of the program, she was decisive. She decided to keep Russ living with her and to make other adjustments to living at home (sending other relatives to live elsewhere), so that her household was just for her, her own mother and her sons. His behaviour rapidly improved and by the end of the intervention, Russ was again at the front of his class and won a prize for leadership at the school. In this case, the mother and son were undoubtedly both in their own ways still dealing with bereavement; a critical loss, but also a change in status for the mother that had consequences for her relationship to her son. During the program, each made spontaneous disclosures and achieved an awareness of the emotions of the other, and the mother acted decisively in recognition of her son's needs.

Families make complex adjustments in response to the death of a member or the breakdown of a marriage relationship, re-partnering of a parent or other major changes. The consequences for children are often unrecognised, as people preoccupied with their own concerns simply react to their challenging behaviours.

Transgenerational parenting issues: a child in kinship care in urban Sydney

Katie was aged five-and-a-half years, the youngest in a large family where there had been repeated notifications to child protection services about parental alcohol abuse, neglect and exposure to family violence. She had never gone to preschool or school. The older children were in care with an uncle or had run away and returned home. Katie was placed with an auntie and uncle under a court-ordered kinship carer arrangement. Auntie had grown up with Katie's parents in a community about 500 kilometres from Sydney. Also in the family were Katie's younger sister, aged four (who had been informally 'given' to the aunt and uncle at birth) and their birth son Jeff, aged 14. The aunt's older daughter and grandchildren lived across the road and were often in the house. She and her husband were educated, worked and both had a lot of community responsibilities. They maintained cultural connection through regular family yarning and other activities, including big cook-ups and trips out bush. They shunned any involvement of 'the welfare' and were fiercely independent.

Katie was referred to a service for children in care in Western Sydney when the aunt and uncle approached the caseworker because of the effect her behaviour was having on the family. She often walked out of the house and away on her own or 'got lost' at the shops. Sometimes she stole things. She hoarded food, was over-familiar with strangers and displayed some sexualised behaviours. Auntie said Katie 'didn't know how to play' and 'seemed to have no spirit'. She often lost or broke toys and any new clothes she was given. She was reported to 'vague out' and 'not listen' when being told off and to be disobedient and rude. She also had some language and learning delays. These behaviours are not uncommon for children who have experienced inadequate care and protection, but they placed great stress on the family and there was a risk of Katie's placement breaking down.

Initially Auntie wanted Katie 'fixed', saying 'I didn't make the problem. Why should I come? I'm busy.' Auntie had health problems and community responsibilities, including absence for funerals that took a lot of family time. An Aboriginal case manager was then appointed who regularly brought Katie to play and speech therapy sessions. There were three-monthly case conferences with everyone involved with Katie's care. As Auntie wouldn't attend the clinic, meetings happened informally with her for a coffee and chat, and she started to talk about how caring for Katie had made her think about her own family history of separations and neglect and of hiding from the welfare, in case she and her siblings were 'taken'. Auntie was committed to Katie but also afraid that Katie would destroy the family she and Uncle worked hard to support, or that she would run away. Katie's behaviour was distressing because it reminded Auntie of her own family background. After this discussion it became easier to arrange occasional family meetings and the placement seemed more settled. Decisions were made to support regular supervised birth family contact in a way that allowed Katie to know her family, to settle in with Auntie and Uncle and attend school regularly.

This example of work with an Aboriginal family in a large city shows the importance of recognising what may make it hard for a family to attend or engage, even when supports and services are available; the way in which a caregiver's own history can be triggered by a child's behaviour and distress; and the possibility of solutions and healing occurring if respectful time is taken to understand the experience of all family members. It has also highlighted how specialised mainstream services can work with Aboriginal staff and services so that the child and family receive the interventions and support that they need.

Working with Aboriginal families

Drawing on the preceding examples from both remote and urban settings, it is clear that some criteria for appropriate practice are common to work with all vulnerable families. In addition, services must be sufficiently flexible to take into account specific needs and circumstances of Aboriginal families in particular social settings (see Box 6.1).

Working with individual families in therapeutic or supportive interventions requires attention to principles of practice that are essential to the engagement and retention of Indigenous families in the intervention, and to its effectiveness in achieving desirable outcomes (see Box 6.2).

BOX 6.1   Practice points: working with communities

- Engage communities and leaders and ensure that the program of work is thoroughly understood and is consistent with community needs and wishes.
- Develop local links with key partners in the community: traditional owners, councils, and health and community service organisations. Build consensus about the aims and processes of the program.
- If necessary, conduct preliminary meetings and workshops to pilot processes or adapt materials.
- Build community member involvement or employment within the program as cultural consultants or trained paraprofessionals or professionals.
- Ensure that there is feedback or that evaluation reports are provided to the community on a regular basis.

BOX 6.2   Practice points: working with individuals

- Clarify how the individual or family was referred – did they refer themselves and, if not, do they know about the referral?
- Be direct in addressing concerns about safety of family members, including children as a result, for example, of violence and/or substance use, and inform the family about mandatory reporting requirements at the outset.
- Take time to make sure they know who you are and why you are visiting them or offering an appointment. More than one contact may be required. When there are a lot of services visiting a community or family and English is not a first language, it may take time to understand what your service offers and to make room for it.
- When needed, refer Aboriginal people to appropriate services, where possible to those that are Aboriginal-controlled or where there are Aboriginal staff.
- Be reliable. Turn up when you say you will and do what you have said you will do.
- Keep in mind the history of Aboriginal people in Australia, including forced separations and family disruptions and negative experiences of 'welfare', and also local customs and cultural practices, but do not assume you know anything about any individual family, its particular history and its concerns.
- Be interested and patient; allow trust to develop before you expect intimate and personal issues to be discussed.
- Support parents in a non-judgemental way: help them to be interested in and to think about their children's needs and experiences.
- Notice when parents and children seem to get things right and mention it.
- Pay careful attention to ending, debriefing, feedback and any needs for follow-up contact. Build this into the intervention.

ACTIVITY

Think about a service for families and children that you work in, or with which you are familiar. How many Aboriginal families use this service as a proportion of the overall client group? Looking at the lists in the boxes above; for each item, describe how well this service meets these strategies and approaches. Discuss with others at the service what could be done that might increase the accessibility and/or relevance of the service to Aboriginal families.

■ Conclusion

There is great diversity among Aboriginal families across Australia. In some places families are adapted to modern, fast-paced, urban lifestyles, while in others family life is shaped by experiences of living in relatively closed or isolated small communities where traditional cultural practices, ceremonies and traditional forms of marriage and kinship, often combined with mission and church influences, are still strong.

Work with vulnerable families must be based on practices of engagement that acknowledge the local community, its values, its leadership and its resources. However, there is often far more variation between the needs and difficulties of individuals and their families than there is between community or cultural settings. In addition to showing respect to culture and community history, the key principles of practice must emphasise a high degree of responsiveness to the individual family, parent and child. In a sense, a language must be found that enables parent and practitioner to find a common understanding of important things in the family's life and experience. A crude emphasis of cultural ideas can sometimes impede the development of this understanding. What culture may mean to the individual may be more important than what it might mean at the general community level of understanding. Further, there is sometimes a need to ensure that a confidential and safe space needed for work with families, free of shame, can be shielded from the impacts of organisational politics, conflicts and tensions at the community level.

The current safety of the child and family must be ensured within culturally informed and accessible, targeted interventions that address quality of parenting and family relationships in order to address the child's individual needs. Parent training programs are identified as first-line interventions for uncomplicated presentations to address parents' needs to acquire skills to deal with behavioural challenges and to help their children prepare for school. However, there needs to be careful attention to the development of models for therapeutic practice and preventive early intervention to deal with the more complex needs and adversities in people's lives.

■ Useful websites

Lohoar, S. (2012) Safe and supportive Indigenous families and communities for children: A synopsis and critique of Australian research – Child Family Community Australia paper no. 7, 2012 **www.aifs.gov.au/cfca/pubs/papers/a142302/ index.html**

Mildon, R. & Polimeni, M. (2012) Parenting in the early years: effectiveness of parenting support programs for Indigenous families. Resource sheet. Closing the Gap Clearinghouse no. 16, 2012. **www.aihw.gov.au/uploadedFiles/ClosingTheGap/ Content/Publications/2012/ctgc-rs16.pdf**

Price-Robertson, R., McDonald, M., Lewis, P. & Bamblett, M. (2011) Working with Indigenous children, families, and communities: Lessons from practice Child Family Community Australia (CAFCA) practice sheet, 2011 **www.aifs.gov.au/ cafca/pubs/sheets/ps/ps6.html**

7

Family decision-making approaches for Aboriginal and Torres Strait Islander families

Fiona Arney, Alwin Chong and Kate McGuinness

■ Learning goals

This chapter will enable you to:

■ **UNDERSTAND** the impact of government policies and practices regarding Aboriginal and Torres Strait Islander people on families across generations

■ **RECOGNISE** the potential of family decision-making models in enhancing the roles of Aboriginal and Torres Strait Islander families in the protection of children

■ **IDENTIFY** the components of best practice family decision-making models

■ **LEARN** about the application of Aboriginal family decision-making in the Australian context.

■ Introduction

SEVERAL OF THE chapters in this book have described the over-representation of Aboriginal children in care and protection systems. In the Northern Territory, it has been estimated that 15 per cent of Aboriginal children per annum are the subject of a child protection notification (Guthridge et al., 2012; Northern Territory Government, 2010). South Australian data has projected that in that jurisdiction, by the time they are 16, as many as 80 per cent of Aboriginal young people will have been the subject of a notification to a child protection service (Delfabbro et al., 2010).

Aboriginal and Torres Strait Islander children are over-represented in out-of-home care systems at a rate 10 times that of other Australian children (Australian Institute of Health and Welfare, 2012). However, nationwide only 50 per cent of Aboriginal and Torres Strait Islander children removed from the care of their parents are placed with extended family members (Australian Institute of Health and Welfare, 2012).

Given this, there are grave concerns about the removal of Aboriginal children from their families and communities, and the absence of connection of Aboriginal children to culture, country, language and family (Libesman, 2011).

The experience for many Aboriginal and Torres Strait Islander families across generations has been one of loss and fragmentation of family through colonisation practices such as murder, genocide, protection and assimilation policies, and removal of children from families. It is essential to have an understanding of how the past has impacted, and continues to impact, on the lives of Aboriginal and Torres Strait Islander people.

■ What can we learn from the past?

One of the most ruthless practices has been Protectionism, which resulted in the loss of rights and freedoms as Australians, and severely impacted on the health and wellbeing of Aboriginal and Torres Strait Islander people. In recent times, 'The Stolen Generations' has become the term used when referring to the protective period, but Protectionism has been much broader than the removal of children from their families.

The Stolen Generations period began in the mid 19th century with the introduction of the South Australian Protector of Aborigines Act (1836), the Victorian Aborigines Protection Act (1869), the Queensland Aboriginal Protection and Restriction of the Sales of Opium Act (1897), the Western Australian Aborigines Act (1905), the New South Wales Aborigines Protection Act (1909) and the Northern Territory Aborigines Act (1910) (DECS Curriculum Services). By 1911 all States and Territories, with the exception of Tasmania, had introduced protection laws with the emphasis on restriction and segregation. This was based on the assumption that the Aboriginal people were a 'dying race'. Over time the Acts became more draconian, with the various Chief Protectors being given wide-ranging powers – from being the legal guardian of all Aboriginal children to having supervision control over all matters affecting the welfare of Aboriginal people. For example, Aboriginal women were not able to marry without the written permission of the Protector, and individuals were not able to get a job without a licence.

The Federal Constitution in 1901 reinforced the powers of the States and Territories. The Constitution excluded Aboriginal people as Australian citizens. It read:

> The Parliament shall, subject to this Constitution, have power to make laws for the peace, order, and good government of the Commonwealth with respect to:- [...]

> 'The people of any race, other than the aboriginal race in any State, for whom it is deemed necessary to make special laws'. Constitution, section 51, clause 26, pre-1967

> (Lee & Winterton, 2004)

This meant that the Federal Government could make laws for all Australians, except the Aboriginal population. The States therefore retained their power over Aboriginal Affairs (Australian Museum, 2012).

By the 1930s, assimilation and integration policies were being introduced that allowed some Aboriginal people free movement by means of exemptions and permits. 'Assimilation' meant that Aboriginal people were expected to attain the same manner of living as other Australians, enjoying the same rights and privileges, accepting the same responsibilities, observing the same customs and influenced by the same beliefs as other Australians (Australian Museum, 2012).

In the era of Protectionism, Aboriginal people were rounded up and sent to reserves and mission stations that were established throughout Australia. Reserves differed from missions, in that reserves were established by the government and the missions were managed by Christian organisations. Ultimately, though, they had the same purpose and were controlled by the various Aboriginal Protection Boards.

Aboriginal people from different cultural groups were herded together. Many people experienced forced confinement, the imposition of strict religious observance, separation from and removal of their children, the breakdown of traditional values and the banning of their languages and cultural practices (ABC, 2012). People were made to speak English and then eventually classified and separated on the basis of biology or skin colouring, and referred to as full-blood, half-caste, octaroon and so on.

Maternal and child health was markedly affected during this period. Young girls becoming mothers for the first time had very little support or education from their mothers, sisters, aunts or grandmothers because they were struggling to survive in a cruel, harsh environment. Often family members were physically separated and men excluded from child-rearing altogether.

Initially, there was an assumption that Aboriginal people would die out and that the purpose of the reserves and missions was 'smoothing the pillow of a dying race' (Osborne, 2001). By the 1920s, with the increase in the 'half-caste' population, it had changed to saving some souls, mainly by removing children at a very early age. This approach was reinforced by the assimilation and integration policies.

■ The Stolen Generations

'The Stolen Generations' refers to the practice of forcibly removing Aboriginal and Torres Strait Islander children from their families by the Australian federal and state government agencies and missions, under Acts of their respective parliaments. The removals occurred in the period between approximately 1869 and the late 1960s, although in some places children were still being taken in the 1970s (Human Rights and Equal Opportunity Commission, 1997).

There are often debates about the extent of the removal of children and the reasoning behind it. Some of the justifications for removing children included child protection; beliefs that, given their catastrophic population decline after white contact, black people would 'die out'; and a fear of miscegenation by full-blooded Aboriginal people. Documentary evidence from newspaper articles and reports to parliamentary committees was used to support these rationales.

However, in 1997 the *Bringing Them Home: Report of the National Inquiry into the Separation of Aboriginal and Torres Strait Islander Children from their Families* was tabled in Federal Parliament. It revealed the extent of the forced removal policies, which had gone on for 150 years into the early 1970s (Human Rights and Equal Opportunity Commission, 1997).

The Report revealed the devastating effects of these policies in terms of spiritual, emotional and physical trauma as a direct result of the broken connection to traditional land, culture and language, the separation from families and the effect of these on parenting skills (Human Rights and Equal Opportunity Commission, 1997).

The majority of Aboriginal and Torres Strait Islander people in every State and Territory had been 'protected', effectively by being wards of the State. The protection was done through each jurisdiction's Aboriginal Protection Board through the appointment of a Chief Protector. In Victoria and Western Australia these boards were also responsible for applying what were known as Half-Caste Acts (Luker, 2008).

■ Intergenerational/transgenerational issues

The Bringing Them Home Report revealed the transgenerational impact and damaging impact of the forced removal of children from their families and communities on Aboriginal and Torres Strait Islander families and communities into present times. It continues to be an overwhelming part of Aboriginal and Torres Strait Islander people's lives (Dudgeon et al., 2010). Haebich (2000) describes the removal of children as being not a single event, but a process stretching from colonisation to the present. The transgenerational effects of the policies of forcibly removing children have had a profound and enduring effect on the emotional and social wellbeing of Aboriginal and Torres Strait Islander people.

Aboriginal and Torres Strait Islander families were subjected to poor diet, poor living conditions, limited education and a lack of regular health checks. These conditions combined with poverty ensured that, when people moved from the reserves and mission stations into towns, they had limited job opportunities – the majority of work during this period was labouring or housekeeping. Children were being told that education was a waste of time because they would only get low-skilled jobs, like their parents and there were few opportunities to break this cycle. When many of these children became parents themselves, the cycle was repeated. This process is likened to the cycle of poverty that traps so many poor families. A number of disadvantages combine to work in a circular process, with risk and disadvantage accumulating over time, making it virtually impossible for an individual to break the cycle. Poor people do not have the resources to do this; they are disadvantaged and their poverty increases (Marger, 2010).

Research has demonstrated that poorer people have fewer financial and other forms of control over their lives (Aboriginal and Torres Strait Islander Social Justice Commissioner, 2009). The perception of control or lack of control can be influenced by:

- factors such as racism and other forms of discrimination
- addiction in the community most closely observed in relation to alcoholism
- trauma, particularly accidents, violence, natural disasters and the like.

There is also very solid research evidence that has demonstrated an association between an individual's social and economic status and their health. Poverty is clearly associated with poor health (Aboriginal and Torres Strait Islander Social Justice Commissioner, 2009). For example:

- Poor education and literacy are linked to poor health status and affect the capacity of people to use health information.
- Lower income reduces the accessibility of health care services and medicines.
- Overcrowded and run-down housing is associated with poverty and contributes to the spread of communicable diseases.
- Poor infant diet is associated with poverty and chronic diseases later in life.
- Smoking and high-risk behaviour are associated with lower socioeconomic status.

Over the years the intergenerational issues have grown worse and are now referred to as transgenerational issues, because they have gone beyond the initial two generations. The well documented and highlighted large gap between Indigenous and non-Indigenous life expectancy is seen to be a result of transgenerational influences. Two additional examples of transgenerational influence that greatly affect Aboriginal and Torres Strait Islander people are evident in their experience with the criminal justice system and trauma.

Robert Depew (1996) describes how Aboriginal and Torres Strait Islander people continue to experience disproportionate involvement in the criminal justice system as well as considerable frustration in trying to satisfy their goals in relation to justice and to their needs and aspirations as historical societies, despite decades of intervention by the States. It is no surprise, then, that Aboriginal people believe that the justice system discriminates against them, and marginalises and trivialises the importance of their cultures and community circumstances to their justice concerns.

Atkinson, Nelson and Atkinson (2010) write about how the effects of trauma are passed on within and across generations. The authors attempt to explain the impact of lived or transferred trauma in the lives of Aboriginal and Torres Strait Islander families and communities. One example they use is the intergenerational issue and the lack of appropriate government response to the overuse of alcohol and/or drugs by men in an attempt to cope with their loss of cultural identity and diminished sense of worth. The government's response was to remove offenders to reservations without any support to overcome their problems with substance use. The reservations were later replaced by prisons, by which time violence within Aboriginal and Torres Strait Islander communities had escalated and governments felt vindicated by incarcerating these men.

REFLECTIVE QUESTIONS

How familiar are you with what has been described in this chapter? How would you find out further information on the past policies and practices in your own State or Territory?

■ The involvement of Aboriginal families and communities in contemporary child protection systems

Societal, environmental and poverty-related risk factors for children exist across all of society. However, when looking at risk factors impacting on Aboriginal children in child welfare the impacts of intergenerational experiences of dispossession, cultural erosion and policies of child removal must be considered. These issues not only impact on families, but also on the ability of families to seek or accept help from a system perceived to have caused or contributed to problems in the first place.

(Northern Territory Government, 2010, p. 116)

In recognition of the impact of past government policy on the contemporary experience of Aboriginal and Torres Strait Islander peoples, there has been an increasing focus on establishing Aboriginal-controlled child and family services and the devolvement of child protection functions (particularly family support and out-of-home care) to these organisations. For example, in Victoria:

The impetus for establishing Aboriginal & Islander Child Care Agencies came from the Aboriginal Legal Service in Victoria during the 1970s, which identified a need for an Aboriginal child placement service. It observed that approximately 90% of its Aboriginal clients seeking assistance for criminal charges had been in some form of placement – foster, adoptive, or institutional placement. The formation of the Victorian Aboriginal Child Care Agency (VACCA) became a reality following the First National Conference on Adoption in 1976. This conference saw the issue of the adoption of Aboriginal children forced onto the mainstream agenda for the first time.

(VACCA website: www.vacca.org)

Similar agencies were established across Australian States and Territories. In 1981 the Secretariat of National Aboriginal and Islander Child Care (SNAICC) was formed as the national non-government peak body in Australia representing the interests of Aboriginal and Torres Strait Islander children and families. SNAICC has grown to have a network and subscriber base of more than 1400 organisations and individuals – mostly Aboriginal and Torres Strait Islander, but also significant numbers of other community-based services and individuals and state and federal agencies with an interest in Aboriginal and Torres Strait Islander families and children (www.snaicc. org.au).

Also, in recognition of the harm and suffering caused by the removal of Aboriginal children from their families and communities, the Aboriginal and Torres Strait Islander Child Placement Principle (ATSICPP) was developed (Lock, 1997). The Principle has been adopted in legislation or policy in all Australian States and Territories. It upholds the rights of the child's family and community to have some control and influence in decisions being made about their children. The ATSICPP prioritises the placement options that should be explored when an Aboriginal or Torres Strait Islander child is placed in care. These are, in order of priority, as follows:

- with a member of the child or young person's family
- with a member of the child or young person's community or language group
- with an Aboriginal person or Torres Strait Islander person who does not have a familial or kinship relationship to the child.

If a child cannot be placed with any of the above people, alternative placement choices can be made. Other options then include placing the child with a carer who is not Aboriginal, but is considered to be capable of promoting the child's ongoing affiliation with the culture of the child's community (and, if possible, ongoing contact with the child's family). Wherever possible, Aboriginal or Torres Strait Islander children should be placed with carers who live in close proximity to the child's family and/or community (Lock, 1997).

So, while healing for parents requires giving back a place that they have lost, for children, healing requires teaching us that there is a place.

(Williams in SNAICC, 2012, p. 7)

Many community-controlled organisations are establishing innovative approaches that are based on an understanding of the impacts of intergenerational trauma, Aboriginal cultural practices and the interconnectedness of Aboriginal families, and provide the best start for Aboriginal children to break cycles of disadvantage. Aboriginal and non-Aboriginal organisations are working together to establish the evidence base for these innovative approaches. To enable this knowledge to be freely shared across Australia, the Closing the Gap Clearinghouse (www.aifs.gov.au/closingthegap) was established in 2009 as an initiative of the Council of Australian Governments (COAG).

■ The role of family decision-making

Culture, land and spirit are tied together so closely that you can't have one without the other, but it's not a complete story without family – it's like building a house without mortar, it makes it the right shape but there's nothing to hold it together

(Williams in SNAICC, 2012, p. 8)

Since their inception, family decision-making models (such as Family Group Conferencing) have been developed and implemented in a number of Australian jurisdictions and internationally (Arney et al., 2010; Brown, 2003; Harris, 2008). These models have spread widely because of the appeal of the values underpinning them. This includes the promotion of families' rights to participate in decision-making about their children, and children's rights to have involvement with their families (Barnsdale & Walker, 2007; Brown, 2003; Sundell & Vinnerljung, 2004), the congruence of the model with the Aboriginal Child Placement Principle, participant satisfaction with the elements of the model, and the perceived adaptability of the model to different contexts (Arney et al., 2010).

One of the most well-known family decision-making models is Family Group Conferencing (see Connolly, 2010). A family group conference is a family decision-making model between the family, family group, their community and the statutory agency with an independent facilitator. The model aims to put decision-making around child protection concerns in the hands of the child's immediate and extended family, providing resources for the implementation of a Partnership Plan with the family.

Originating in New Zealand and growing from Maori cultural practice, Family Group Conferencing was developed as a family decision-making model to promote the wellbeing and safety of children involved in the child protection system (Connolly, 2007). Family Group Conferencing aims to empower families by increasing the capacity of the family, family groups and their community to make choices in partnership with the statutory organisation, and transform these choices into action to keep children safe and promote their wellbeing. The Family Group Conferencing model, in itself, aims to redress the power imbalance in child protection matters by providing an alternative forum where families are active participants in the decision-making process. Family Group Conferencing principles are based on collective responsibility, mutual responsibility and shared interest. The process emphasises the importance of kinship, extended family and community connections in finding solutions and implementing plans that support the safety and wellbeing of the child. In this model, a successful conference results in a Partnership Agreement or Plan that must ensure the care and protection of the child; that is an agreement between the parents and other 'interested parties'; and that must always include the child protection service. The Partnership Agreement is then incorporated into the child's case plan or care plan.

The American Humane Association (American Humane Association, 2008, p. 2) has developed criteria for exemplary family decision-making practice. These include the following:

- An independent (that is, non-case-carrying) coordinator is responsible for convening the family group meeting with agency personnel. When a critical decision about a child is required, dialogue occurs between the family group and the responsible child protection agency personnel. Providing an independent coordinator who is charged with creating an environment in which transparent, honest and respectful dialogue occurs between agency personnel and family groups signifies an agency's commitment to empowering and non-oppressive practice.
- The child protection agency personnel recognise the family group as their key decision-making partner, and time and resources are available to convene this group. Providing the time and resources to seek out family group members and prepare them for their role in the decision-making process signifies an agency's acceptance of the importance of family groups in formulating safety and care plans.
- Family groups have the opportunity to meet on their own, without the statutory authorities and other non-family members present, to work through the information they have been given and to formulate their responses and plans. Providing family groups with time to meet on their own enables them to apply their knowledge and expertise in a familiar setting and to do so in ways that are consistent with their ethnic and cultural decision-making practices. Acknowledging the importance of this time and taking active steps to encourage family groups to plan in this way signifies

an agency's acceptance of its own limitations, as well as its commitment to ensuring that the best possible decisions and plans are made.

- When agency concerns are adequately addressed, preference is given to a family group's plan over any other possible plan. In accepting the family group's lead, an agency signifies its confidence in, and its commitment to, partnering and supporting family groups in caring for and protecting their children, and to building the family group's capacity to do so.

- Referring agencies support family groups by providing the services and resources necessary to implement the agreed-upon plans. In assisting family groups in implementing their plans, agencies uphold the family group's responsibility for the care and protection of their children, and contribute by aligning the agency and community resources to support the family group's efforts.

The model recognises the deep relationships within kith and kin networks, and the reciprocity of relationships within Aboriginal and Torres Strait Islander cultures (Ban, 2005). Kin relationships, mutual obligation, roles and responsibilities of multiple caregivers, family leadership and consensus decision-making are also cultural practices honoured as part of the process. The Family Group Conferencing process also recognises the multiple caregiving roles that family members may have:

> Our families are essential to our children's experience of, and connection with, their culture and thus their healing. Aboriginal and Torres Strait Islander people learn and experience our culture and spirituality through our families: whether through our knowledge, stories, and songs from parents, grandparents, Elders, and uncles and aunts, and through everyday lived experience of shared values, meaning, language, custom, behaviour and ceremonies.
>
> (Williams in SNAICC, 2012, p. 8)

Family Group Conferencing and other family decision-making models actively encourage men who are significant in children's lives (such as fathers, grandfathers and uncles) to participate in decision-making about the safety and wellbeing of their children, even if they are not present in the home. This is not always possible in other child protection processes, as there may not be adequate resources to locate men who are no longer living in the family home; there may be safety concerns; men may not wish to engage in the process; or it may not be valued as a priority by workers (Goff, 2012). This is particularly a concern when working with Aboriginal families, both for the potentially valuable role that men's involvement can have (see Chapter 4), and also because Aboriginal men's protecting and nurturing roles have been significantly curtailed through processes of colonisation and marginalisation.

Family decision-making models for Aboriginal families are gaining momentum across Australia. From initial work in Victoria (Ban, 2005; Linqage International,

2003), Aboriginal Family Decision Making now operates as part of the child protection system in every region of that State. This model uses traditional cultural approaches to decision-making, with Aboriginal Family Decision Making meetings co-convened by a Child Protection Best Interests case planner and a Community convenor from an Aboriginal organisation. The meetings involve extended family and respected Elders in decision-making and case-planning for Aboriginal children and may be used in family preservation and reunification processes (Department of Human Services, 2007).

The remainder of this chapter describes an approach to incorporating family decision-making for Aboriginal and Torres Strait Islander families in child protection processes that was trialled in the Northern Territory.

■ Family Group Conferencing in Alice Springs: a case study

In response to escalating rates of notifications and substantiations of concerns regarding the health and safety of Aboriginal children in the Northern Territory, and the high proportion of Aboriginal children placed with non-Aboriginal carers (66 per cent – Australian Institute of Health and Welfare, 2012), legislation[1] was passed that emphasised the role of families involved with the care and protection system in collaboratively developing plans for vulnerable children. In the Northern Territory, 80 per cent of children in substantiated child protection reports and out-of-home care are of Aboriginal and Torres Strait Islander descent. After an extensive consultative process, the Family Group Conferencing model was identified as the most appropriate model to support family involvement in decision-making regarding child protection matters in the Northern Territory context. Funding for a pilot project to trial and adapt the model over a 30-month period was obtained from the Australian Government through the Alice Springs Transformation Plan (Northern Territory Government, 2010).

---

[1] *Care and Protection of Children Act 2007*, Division 6 s48–49. This section relates to Chief Executive Officer (CEO, NT DHF) arranged mediation conferences as a model of decision-making in child protection proceedings. A Mediation Conference is a service that the Department of Children and Families may offer families for a protected child. The object of a Mediation Conference is 'to ensure that, as far as possible, the wellbeing of a child is safeguarded through agreements between the parents of the child and other interested parties'. A Mediation Conference can be convened if (*Care and Protection of Children Act 2007* s 49):

(a) concerns have been raised about the child; and

(b) the CEO reasonably believes the conference may have addressed those concerns; and

(c) the parents of the child are willing to participate in the conference.

The Alice Springs Regional Office for Children and Families (the statutory child protection service) receives approximately one-quarter of the total number of notifications of child protection concerns in the Northern Territory (Northern Territory Government, 2010).

The initial implementation of Family Group Conferencing in Alice Springs was supported by an Advisory Group, which included representatives from Aboriginal community controlled organisations and other non-government organisations from Alice Springs, as well as the funding partner, the project partners, the evaluation team and the Northern Territory Children's Commissioner. The role of the Advisory Group was to provide advice to support implementation and evaluation to the Family Group Conferencing team and to support community engagement. The Advisory Group was very active in this role and brought a high level of expertise and commitment to the service.

The program logic developed for the Family Group Conferencing pilot in Alice Springs by the Advisory Group emphasised key principles of the Family Group Conferencing process, as well as considerations about the Family Group Conferencing process in this context. These included:

- That Family Group Conferencing processes will shift the balance of power to families and communities, and that families will feel listened to and respected; however, this relies on the process being voluntary and professionals being supported by their organisations in respectful, flexible and trusting ways (Barnsdale & Walker, 2007; Huntsman, 2006).
- Family involvement may increase the child protection worker's capacity to implement plans in practice when there is a partnership approach adopted by professionals and families (Barnsdale & Walker, 2007).
- The engagement and facilitated participation of children in the Family Group Conferencing process signals that they are valued, important and are being listened to, but care must be taken to ensure that children's voices aren't lost in a process that involves many adults and that children's participation doesn't involve risks to their wellbeing.
- The strengths of having Aboriginal convenors are manyfold and include greater likelihood of locating and engaging extended family members, building trust, providing guidance on cultural and family customs, assisting in communicating concerns and outcomes needed for addressing the concerns (also in Aboriginal languages and Aboriginal English), providing an understanding of family dynamics, and an awareness of Aboriginal service providers.
- Partnership Agreements developed from Family Group Conferencing processes will be more comprehensive and more realistic than traditional

case plans because more people contribute their perspectives and resources, and family members know whether relatives will deliver and family members can say whether something will work or not; however, the quality of information sharing is crucial to the family's ability to develop appropriate plans that are acceptable to professionals (Kiro, 2006).

- The outcomes of a conference will depend on organisational system factors such as having the time for effective case planning and relationship building; and the autonomy of workers to make or endorse decisions made (Darlington, Healy & Feeney, 2010). Organisational factors such as caseloads, time constraints and unsupportive work environments are barriers to participatory practices.

- Family Group Conferencing may develop collective efficacy, provide social support/social capital (Presser & Van Voorhis, 2002) and encourage collective accountability (Huntsman, 2006). Family Group Conferencing processes may also provide leverage and motivation for parents to seek help for long-term problems such as substance use (Huntsman, 2006). However, it is important to note that the process may not work for parents who feel alienated from their families or who grew up in care and for whom connections with extended family members are not strong (Huntsman, 2006); and that intra-family dialogue is almost never free from power dynamics.

- Family Group Conferencing can lead to improvements in communication between families and child protection agencies (Huntsman, 2006), because families develop a greater understanding of their involvement in the process and reasons for child protection involvement. They may also provide additional insights into the risks that face a child and times when additional supervision or support may be necessary. Honest and transparent information-sharing means that common understandings are developed and misunderstandings addressed.

- The potential effectiveness of Family Group Conferencing will be affected by the degree to which Partnership Agreements are implemented – if this implementation is not supported and monitored, then this is likely to lead to adverse outcomes including re-notification and child removal. Results from Family Group Conferencing will only be observed if there are high-quality services and supports to refer families to (Sundell & Vinnerljung, 2004).

The Family Group Conferencing team

The Family Group Conferencing Unit included a Senior Convenor, a Convenor, an Aboriginal Co-Convenor and an Administrative Officer. The high-calibre team included staff with extensive experience in mediation, child protection, family support and Family Group Conferencing child advocacy, and includes Aboriginal and non-Aboriginal staff with extensive family and professional connections in Central Australia. All convenors in the Unit attained mediation accreditation; for some staff this accreditation was achieved during the course of their employment with the Family Group Conferencing Unit.

In addition to accreditation and experience, the Family Group Conferencing Unit convenors and co-convenors had demonstrated skills and abilities required to engage with families in sensitive, difficult and often lengthy conversations. The skilled Family Group Conferencing team were also able to:

- support all participants fairly and be in a space that could present as unbiased, but recognise that their position might place them in positions of internal personal or professional conflict and that this might require removing themselves from the process
- search for points of agreement between people who might have had conflictual relationships
- read nonverbal communication during the process (understanding what an individual or family might be saying without saying it)
- be alert about what signals were being picked up, and checking that what needed to be said was said and that people in the room were hearing each other (that there was clarity in what was being said).
- demonstrate fairness and neutrality and help families determine what needed to happen to get the best for their children
- get behind someone's position in a situation and apply communication skills to help someone move to a shared position.

The stages of the process

Family Group Conferencing includes a number of well-defined phases:

- the referral and consent of families: to gain a clear picture of what is happening for the child, the concerns to be addressed, the decisions to be made, details of the family and who will be participating from the Department. Information in the referral regarding the purpose, concerns and possible outcomes of the conference is provided to the parents and the parents have the ability to appoint the conference convenor
- the preparation phase: this time is specifically to connect with as many family members as possible, including children; to ensure that family understand the purpose and process of the conference; to ensure that there is clarity about the concerns to be addressed at the conference; and for the

convenor to work out with the family who are the appropriate people to attend and when and where the conference is be held. Further, it is the time for the convenor to build professional relationships with child protection staff, other service providers, child advocates and interpreters and to ensure all professionals are clear about their roles and responsibilities at the conference.

- the conference itself: the conference is held in a neutral location as decided by the family, and food is provided to family members attending the conference; many conferences involve families travelling from remote locations or interstate

  - information-sharing – the philosophy of the family group conference is that family should have access to all information that will help them, to understand not only the issues/concerns but also what services may be accessed. The case worker will present information about information to the family about the concerns/worries for the child; what the needs of the child are; what they would like the family to consider, emphasising that decisions need to be made ensuring that the care, supports and safety of the child are at the forefront of the family's decisions. Family members are able to ask questions and discuss the concerns, and the convenor will check understanding. A child advocate will also present the child's view and their wishes for the meeting.

  - private family time – this time is for families only; however, some families may be hesitant or nervous when 'private family time' comes around about spending time together without any professional guidance. The family may nominate a support person (maybe a professional person) to provide support to the family and not be part of the decision-making. He/she may spend some time in private family time as a scribe for the family; other than that he/she will play no other role. During private family time the family discuss, among themselves, what they have heard and how they might turn things around. There is no restriction on how long 'private family time' takes, as it is during this time that the family have the opportunity to work together to develop a plan.

  - coming to an agreement – when the family indicates to the convenor that they have finished their discussions and have a plan ready to present and negotiate, the convenor invites all participants back to the conference. The convenor facilitates the discussions around the family's plan, between the family and the child protection service. Other professionals may need to be included. This facilitation process includes reviewing the plan point by point, highlighting any decisions in the plan that lack clarity or where the child protection issues have not been sufficiently explored, and then to facilitate negotiations around these points until agreement is reached between all participants and people are clear about their role in the plan. The child advocate plays a very important role in this phase, as he/she will ensure that the child's wishes and views have been taken into account, as long as they are realistic and do not compromise the wellbeing of the child. The child advocate will also be able to talk to the child after the meeting to explain what happened. The plan is then recorded in the form of a Partnership Agreement which, where possible, is signed by all parties at the meeting itself. At this stage it is also determined whether the matter is to go to court for child protection orders or whether the family is willing for the document to be presented in court so the court can see that the family has attended a conference and has come to an agreement with the department and other interested parties.

- plan implementation and review – the Partnership Agreement is then provided to management in the child protection service for their approval. There may still be some negotiation at this time, although this is less likely if team leaders (in addition to case workers) participate in the conference. Once signed off, the plan is implemented and monitored over time through a review process. The review process includes going through the Agreement point by point, and discussing to what degree the plan has been implemented; the child's outcomes as a result of the plan; and any new concerns that may have arisen. A review conference will also be held so that all parties can contribute to the discussion.

The conferences

In a six-month period, the Family Group Conferencing Unit received 28 referrals from a range of sources within the child protection office (for example the youth team, the out-of-home care team, the child protection team). The bulk of the referrals related to finding a safe and secure placement for the child that was in accordance with the needs of the child and the wishes of the family, or for regular and safe contact visits with family members and the establishment of cultural care plans. In a smaller number of cases, the referrals related to the desire for safety plans for children who were not the subject of court orders. This highlights the potential use of Family Group Conferencing in making decisions about care arrangements for children, but there is the potential, used earlier in the child protection process, to avoid the necessity to place children in out-of-home care.

Of the 28 referrals, 22 were designated to proceed to a family group conference, with six referrals having a conference pending at the time of writing this report. Of the 16 convened conferences, all resulted in a valid Partnership Agreement established by all parties.

Six referrals did not proceed to a conference for a range of reasons:

- In one case the reasons for referral were resolved between the family and the Department before a conference could proceed.
- In four cases the conference did not proceed due to an inability to locate key family members to gain consent, including mothers not making contact.
- In one case the referral was declined because the parents did not provide consent, as they did not agree with the child protection concerns as outlined by the Department.

Most conferences were convened within a month of the referral, with some being convened within as short a time as two weeks. Twenty-seven children were represented at the 16 convened conferences, with child advocates (representing the children's views and wishes) attending all but one of the conferences. Seventy-six family members participated in Family Group Conferencing, with on average five family members attending, but as many as 15 family members present. Female relatives who participated included mothers, maternal and paternal aunts, great-aunts, grandmothers and great-grandmothers, a sister and a cousin, and male relatives included fathers, maternal and paternal uncles, great-uncles and grandfathers. Men's participation from jail was also facilitated.

Half of the conferences also included professionals who described services and supports available to families at the conference. These professionals included family support workers, alcohol and other drug workers, residential care workers, sexual assault workers, mental health professionals and nutrition and speech specialists.

Feedback from participants in the process was very positive.

We know all the kids and what they are like. Sometimes welfare don't understand why kids are like that – doing things European way. They need to talk to grandmothers because instead of it just being welfare treating that child European way, grandmothers can help that child Aboriginal way and then we help that child together. This family group conference should be for other kids too to stand up together to help the child.

Grandmother

The difference of this meeting to other meetings with [the child protection service] in the past is there is accountability and it's realistic about a partnership between families and the Department.

Support person to family

You can feel the trust and the belief from families that it can work. I like to see it when the families make the shift – get that they are in a position to say what they really want to happen and to be heard, rather than saying what they think they should say. I like that I get to know the outcome as the child advocate and I really enjoy working with the convener.

Child advocate

It is really good to have conveners who can help families get all the information and then think for a plan themselves for our child.

Grandmother

It is good for the case workers to come to these meetings to learn more about Aboriginal way so we are putting our two cultures together.

Auntie

Before this meeting I never knew I could take my child home. I thought they were with welfare for good.

Mother

This meeting is good. Before I did not know these kids was in so much trouble. Now we are talking.

Father conferencing in from prison

This is a good meeting.

Grandfather

This meeting makes me feel good because I know where my baby is and that she is going to be with family.

Father conferencing in from prison

Using words like respectful, thoughtful, considered and inclusive, family group conferencing enables people to have authority over their own kids. The process and associated language cuts through legalistic and intimidating approaches used with families here.

Service provider

■ Conclusion

This chapter has described the transgenerational impacts of the removal of Aboriginal families from their families, communities, land, language and culture. It also spoke of the healing that needs to occur across these generations to allow children and their families to thrive. In contemporary child protection systems, returning decision-making to the hands of the family through a process of family decision-making is a step to harnessing the power of families in the nurturance and protection of their children. It takes many hearts and many hands to raise a child. Harnessing the warmth, love and commitment of family members through family-inclusive practices such as family decision-making and Family Group Conferencing should be a cornerstone of practice with vulnerable families.

ACTIVITY

Think of a child from a vulnerable family that you may know. Who might be the family members and significant people in that child's life who could be invited to participate in a family group conference? Write down the stages of the conferencing process as described in the Alice Springs case study. What would be the considerations for each of the family members you identified at each stage of the process?

■ Useful websites

Aboriginal and Torres Strait Islander Social Justice Commission: **www.humanrights.gov.au/aboriginal-and-torres-strait-islander-social-justice**

Australian Centre for Child Protection: **www.unisa.edu.au/childprotection**

Australian Institute of Aboriginal and Torres Strait Islander Studies. Mission and Reserve records **www.aiatsis.gov.au/fhu/missions.html**

Bringing them Home Report: **www.humanrights.gov.au/publications/bringing-them-home-report-1997**

Closing the Gap Clearinghouse: **www.aihw.gov.au/closingthegap/**

Kempe Center: **www.ucdenver.edu/academics/colleges/medicalschool/departments/pediatrics/subs/can/Pages/ChildAbuseNeglect.aspx**

Secretariat for National Aboriginal and Islander Child Care (SNAICC): **www.snaicc.org.au**

The National Center on Family Group Decision Making: **www.americanhumane.org/children/programs/family-group-decision-making/national-center**

8

The relationship between family support workers and families where child neglect is a concern

Elizabeth Reimer

■ Learning goals

This chapter will enable you to:

- ■ **DISCUSS** the key worker qualities and behaviours that underpin effective working relationships with families where child neglect is a concern

- ■ **UNDERSTAND** how effective working relationships can help families with such concerns to engage with supportive services

- ■ **IDENTIFY** the kinds of underlying issues that families where neglect is a concern may experience when you attempt to build and maintain working relationships with them

- ■ **IDENTIFY** some of the key challenges you may experience when building working relationships with families struggling with their parenting, and what may support you in overcoming these

- ■ **REFLECT** critically on your approach to working with families where neglect is a concern and identify areas for professional development.

CASE STUDY

'Bernadette' has had many years of experience working with social welfare practitioners, having been removed from her family of origin as a young child and placed into a number of out-of-home care placements. Recent difficulties with her child, including an accusation that her parenting was neglectful and subsequent fear that he would be removed from her care, had prompted her to visit the family service in the regional town in which she lived. In the following excerpt, Bernadette describes her experience of building a working relationship with a family worker against the backdrop of this personal history.

I had previously lost a child. I hadn't dealt with that. And having my son, who has ADHD, he was very challenging. So it was time. I admitted defeat. And that's how I would describe it … I had previously done that and counsellors were not understanding. Were very cold … Turned me off a lot of counsellors. So coming in I was very, you know, 'Is this one gonna work?' I was really reserved that they weren't gonna be able to help me. Weren't going to understand where I was coming from. So, I wasn't really up for it. But in order to keep my children … I had to do something. So I did that for the kids. I didn't necessarily do it for me … In all honesty I didn't think I needed counselling.

I remember meeting Martha and feeling extremely reserved. I was nervous. I always feel judged in counselling. So therefore I usually watch what I say. Because, I don't want to be judged more. I don't want to be told what I am doing right or wrong. I just wanna be able to talk. And when I came in that day and met Martha, I was quite reserved. But she allowed me to talk. For quite a while all I did was talk about everybody else. Not about my problems. Martha was very understanding. She used to prompt me to, you know, 'What else is going on?' or, 'Would you like to discuss it?' … When finally, she confided in me that something had happened in her life that was very similar to mine.

Parent

REFLECTIVE QUESTIONS

Take a moment to think about the insights of this mother. What does she identify as important considerations for practitioners charged with building a relationship with parents for whom child neglect concerns are noted?

■ Introduction

NEGLECT IS OFTEN a persistent and recurrent problem (Berry, Charlson & Dawson, 2003; Daro, 1988; Stone, 1998; Tanner & Turney, 2003; Wilson & Horner, 2005), and parents for whom child neglect is a concern experience multiple barriers to providing adequately for their children. Common parent characteristics include mental health and other related issues, such as parent stress (Minty & Pattinson, 1994), anxiety (Cash & Wilke, 2003), poor self-esteem (Cowen, 1999; Crittenden & Dubowitz, 1999) and depression (Cowen, 1999; Dore & Lee, 1999; Polansky et al., 1981). Other common parent characteristics include reduced intellectual capabilities, which may lead to rigidity in parenting approach (Connell-Carrick, 2003; Erickson & Egeland, 1996) and parent substance abuse (Dunn et al., 2002; Trocme et al., 2003). Key risk factors relating to child neglect with respect to the family environment are poor family functioning, physical environment and physical health, along with family relationships involving much conflict, chaos, conflict, stress and crisis (Cowen, 1999; Polansky et al., 1981; Stone, 1998). On a wider social level, poverty has been found to be a major risk factor for child neglect in so far as it exacerbates other factors relating to neglect (DiLeonardi, 1993), but not necessarily as a direct cause.

Working with families where child neglect is an issue is very challenging, due in part to the difficulty experienced in engaging parents (Berry et al., 2003) and cumulative patterns of behaviour that make building and maintaining relationships difficult (Stone, 1998; Tanner & Turney, 2003; Wilson & Horner, 2005). This may explain why 40 per cent of families where child neglect is a concern have been found to withdraw prematurely from service involvement, which is a much higher rate of premature disengagement than with families where concerns relate to other types of child maltreatment (Daro, 1988). Given this, it is important to focus on the 'helping alliance', or client–worker relationship, as crucial to effective engagement and intervention with families where neglect is an issue (Dore & Alexander, 1996).

The role of the working relationship has intrigued social workers and clinicians, researchers and theorists since the early social casework literature of Mary Richmond (1899) in the late 19th century. The nature of the relationship was later reconceptualised by psychoanalytically influenced therapists and social workers in the early 20th century (Robinson, 1930) and then by proponents of non-directive and humanistic strains of psychology such as Elizabeth Zetzel, Carl Rogers and Ralph Greenson (Horvath & Luborsky, 1993). However, despite the long-established connection to practice in the social and human services sectors, promoting the central role of the relationship seems to have fallen out of favour for the better part of the past 50 years. This may be partly due to the rise of business principles underpinning modern ways of working with social welfare clients, which has resulted in a preference for practice that provides more easily measurable client outputs (Doel, 2010; Ruch, 2005). Nevertheless, a critique is emerging and the refocusing on the relationship in social work and welfare practice is leading to an emergent professional dialogue and a growing body of research evidence on the working relationship as a central feature to practice. With this in mind, the current consensus is that the nature of the working relationship is central to the professions of psychotherapy (Lambert, 1992b) and social work (Howe, 1998; Ruch, Turney & Ward, 2010) and in the field of child welfare (de Boer & Coady, 2007; Kroll, 2010). This repositioning has been assisted by the findings of Lambert (1992b), who examined the outcomes of evidence-based practices and, as outlined in Chapter 1, identified that characteristics of the working relationship account for 30 per cent of positive outcomes in therapeutic interventions.

Much of the research examining the working relationship has been in the area of psychotherapy and therapy services. While there is a small collection of empirical studies that have explored perspectives on the relationship in statutory child protection (de Boer & Coady, 2003; Drake, 1994; Ribner & Knei-Paz, 2002), there are very few publications that explore relationships with families where neglect is a concern using rigorous research evidence. Although there is a body of evidence on the importance of the quality of the working relationship in facilitating family engagement in child neglect-related interventions (Berry et al., 2007; DePanfilis, 1999), much remains to be learned of the processes (Girvin, DePanfilis & Daining, 2007), especially with regard to how workers and families actually experience their relationships.

This chapter will explore how family workers can successfully build and maintain working relationships with parents for whom child neglect is a concern. Lessons from the research will come to life through the voices of parents, family workers and supervisors who described their experiences of eight relationship dyads during in-depth interviews for a qualitative study that took place in a regional area of New South Wales (Reimer, 2010) and was undertaken at the Australian Centre for Child Protection at the University of South Australia. Interviews took place after the family work intervention had ceased and were conducted with parents, workers and supervisors independently of one another, with the exception of one parent couple who were interviewed together. While the working relationships varied in duration, all were medium- to long-term and lasted from over one year in all cases, to over five years in two cases.

All of the parents attended the family service for neglect-related concerns and experienced a variety of factors commonly experienced by such families. These included mental health issues (6), drug and alcohol misuse (5), unstable housing (5), family and domestic violence (4), homelessness (2), limited and at times hostile and unsupportive extended family and social networks (2) and intellectual disability (1). In addition, all parents reported receiving government financial support as their primary income. The parents experienced various combinations of these factors both prior to and during the relationship period.

The workers and supervisors involved in the study were continuing a tradition of family support work in NSW spanning more than 30 years. The original underlying principle of these services was to meet the needs of families who could not access informal supports, or who found that previously established statutory social welfare services could not adequately meet their needs (Wolcott, 1989). Contemporary family services connected to this tradition continue to operate in much the same way, providing an ongoing important social network function, as introduced in Chapter 1. They provide a professional environment that is characterised by practice which is strengths-based, community-embedded, empowering and which includes building connections to the broader community through universal support mechanisms such as playgroups (NSW Family Services Inc., 2009). Furthermore, although an important principle is that of voluntary access to services by clients, work with families occurs in a statutory child protection context. While workers are clear that parents are not mandated to attend, and that the service is not explicitly an agent of the statutory child protection system, parents usually feel, at least initially, that the threat of child removal is real.

Family services deliver multiple programs such as home visiting, information and referral, playgroups, parenting groups, centre-based support, and counselling services (NSW Family Services Inc., 2009). The eight workers in the study had from two to over 30 years' work experience in this type of setting, while the supervisors had from three to 12 years' experience supervising family workers, and three had also spent considerable time as family workers prior to becoming supervisors. All of the supervisors and five of the family workers had completed higher education courses in social welfare-related fields such as social science, social work and community work, while the three other workers had completed diplomas in community welfare.

This chapter will draw on the eight parent–worker relationship stories to explore parent attributes workers may expect to encounter when working with parents for whom child neglect is a concern, and crucial dimensions of successful working relationships, specifically trust and collaboration. In addition, the chapter will cover practitioner attributes and environmental factors, such as the work environment and supervision, which support parent–worker relationships with families where child neglect is a concern.

■ Parent characteristics

As described by 'Bernadette' at the beginning of the chapter, it is clear that many factors precede the process of building working relationships with families where neglect is a concern. This shows how the effects of prior experience, or the way in which 'past worlds affect present worlds', as described in Chapter 1, is an important consideration for workers, as it may help explain why some parents are slow to trust and unwilling to engage.

Relationships in families can be marked by a history of negative communications, conflict, and lack of warmth and empathy (Coohey, 1995; Gaudin et al., 1996), as well as difficulties being responsive within relationships (Wilson, Kuebli & Hughes, 2005). While the direction of causal relationships is complex, in terms of the degree to which child neglect is caused by lack of social support or results in social isolation or both, evidence for social isolation and lack of support as contributing factors for child neglect is now recognised (DePanfilis, 1996). Many researchers have noted that families where neglect is a concern lack social support, feel lonely, and have fewer people to approach for assistance and support with personal and family issues and with parenting (Garbarino & Collins, 1999; Polansky, Ammons & Gaudin, 1985). Others report that neighbours indicate that they distance themselves from neglecting families (Gaudin & Polansky, 1986), and families where neglect is a concern are known to offend potential sources of support (Crittenden, 1985), including viewing professionals offering help with suspicion (DiLeonardi, 1993). Furthermore, a sense of demoralisation and hopelessness associated with depression can manifest as, among other things, child neglect and poor relational skills (Wilson et al., 2005; Winefield & Barlow, 1995; see also Chapter 12).

Given such research findings, workers attempting to build working relationships with parents for whom neglect is a concern should expect parents to approach them with heightened feelings of vulnerability. This includes having fears related to child removal into State care, being judged and feeling stigmatised by, but pressured to engage with, the child protection system. They may also experience feelings of desperation, anger, hurt and lack of motivation related to the prospect of having to build yet another working relationship (Reimer, 2010).

Combined and confusing feelings such as these may result in relationships that evolve, following varying timeframes, from distrust to trust via ambivalence and testing. Feelings of ambivalence, and testing the worker's trustworthiness, can cause parents to withhold information related to deeper and more significant issues. This includes parents discussing obvious or publicly known issues, issues related to immediate and concrete needs they want met, or issues they think may shock the worker until they decide the worker is 'right'; for example:

> It is up to me. It's about, if I'm going to confide in somebody, I have to judge who I'm confiding in … you've got to reassess whether this person is right for you.
>
> Parent

While some parents may quickly put aside their fear and allow workers to prove why they are trustworthy, building working relationships with other parents may include extended periods of testing. This may involve parents engaging in activities that help them avoid, interrupt and even attempt to sabotage the developing working relationship and claim back some power they perceive they have lost (Reimer, 2010; Tanner & Turney, 2003; Zeira, 2007). It may help if workers reconceptualise such resistance as a healthy protective response that any reasonable person would have under similar circumstances, rather than considering parents untreatable or deficient. Instead, the hope is that parents may become aware of their limited ability to improve their life circumstances, yet desire to do so; and as soon as they acknowledge outside help as a way to achieve their desire, they may become willing to engage with the worker.

■ The key is trust

Building trust is central to developing a working relationship and increases parent willingness to engage with workers, as this supports parents in being open and cooperative with workers (de Boer & Coady, 2003; Fernandez & Healy, 2007; Reimer, 2010; Zeira, 2007). When parents for whom neglect is a concern identify with or find some similarities with the worker, it seems to mark a turning point in building trust. It also influences the degree to which the parents open up and are attentive and responsive to workers regarding their needs and making life changes. Knowing a worker is 'right' through identifying with them in some way builds a point of connection and a sense of feeling comfortable. It helps parents move from unwillingness to willingness.

Once trust is established, the focus can shift to setting and meeting goals and then, later, to challenging parents about the extent to which they are working towards the goals; and continually renegotiating the set goals as parents meet some of them and as new issues and needs arise. Indeed, until trust is established it is unlikely that parents will confide deeply and respond positively to worker probing and challenge, as noted by one parent:

> You've gotta connect with somebody. And then you go to counselling. And you sit down and talk. And you build a relationship with the counsellor. And all of a sudden you feel more comfortable and you start talking about your subjects. And the more you offload the better you feel. And the more confident you feel with this person and more willing to open up to them. And before you know it you start working on the problems that you have got ... Until that relationship's there, until you are willing to trust the people, there's not much use in trying to work towards your goals because you're not going to.

■ Being 'real in role'

Building the kind of relationship where trust can occur requires workers to convey their professionalism informally (de Boer & Coady, 2003; Reimer, 2010). It involves workers being '*real*' while in the professional *role*. In being 'real', workers try to avoid being distant professionals, and instead maintain an authenticity that displays their personal or human qualities and brings these qualities into the foreground of the interaction.

> I think that's often where the connection is. That people want another human being to treat them like a human being. Regardless of what the problem is, or regardless of the background or anything else. It's just another human being.
>
> Family worker

While such personalised role issues within the parent–worker relationship have been discussed sporadically since at least the 1970s, awareness of and discussion about this way of working seems to have been gaining attention only in the past few years, especially in the area of 'relationship-based practice' (Ruch et al., 2010) and 'use of self' (Ward, 2010). When parents and workers emotionally connect, this enhances parents' feeling of being human, instead of making them feel like 'clients' with no human identity in and of themselves (de Boer & Coady, 2003; Drake, 1994; Maluccio, 1979; McMahon, 2010; Ribner & Knei-Paz, 2002).

This equates with the notion of 'genuineness' (the 'G' in 'ERGO' outlined in Chapter 1). Being 'real', or genuine, assists workers to understand what parents need, and how to tailor their response accordingly. It also helps parents to focus on their children's needs, aspects of themselves and of their parenting to change, and on positive aspects of working with the worker, rather than on fear brought about through imposed or threatened child removal. Furthermore, it assists parents to become aware of life understanding, experiences and interests that they share with their worker. Thus parents can identify with workers as human beings; that is, as fundamentally similar to them, and with similar experiences of life.

Others have reported on the notion of parents and workers mutually liking one another, and that similarities in areas such as life experiences, socioeconomic background and values help (de Boer & Coady, 2003; Fernandez & Healy, 2007; Maluccio, 1979). Some have also found that parents respond more favourably to workers whom they know have been parents (Maluccio, 1979; Paris & Dubus, 2005; Riley et al., 2008; Taggart, Short & Barclay, 2000). Importantly, self-disclosure does not have to be of a deeply personal nature, which might raise concerns about testing professional boundaries. For example, even though Bernadette's worker disclosed losing a child, she did not provide personal details about this. However, disclosing something known publicly is usually sufficient, such as a common experience of parenting, being a smoker, or having similar interests or hobbies. Parents perceive such an approach to mean that workers have drawn on their real-life experiences, not just theoretical knowledge, to meet parents' needs. This is explained by one parent, who perceived the following in the worker despite the worker's disclosing nothing of her life to him,

> You just listen to Jane, listen to the way she talks. You listen to such a wide range of ideas. You can almost see she has dug herself up from a very big hole from a very young age. She has been quite with it from a very young age and got herself trained and put herself through uni. And all the rest of it when she was a lot younger. Just something there just tells me that she's, when she was younger, she lived quite a life.
>
> Parent

The essential elements for parents and workers to engage in this type of relationship involve workers being perceived by the parents to be supportive, genuinely caring and interested, informal and keeping their confidence. In the study, parents reported that effective workers were essentially like them in their humanness and not distant 'expert' professionals; that is, that there was a friend-like element to the working relationship. Likewise, others have reported on the notion of the relationship being 'friend-like' (de Boer & Coady, 2003; Doel, 2010; Drake, 1994; Lynn et al., 1998; Ribner & Knei-Paz, 2002), compared to relating to workers who just took a friendly approach, and how professional distance may actually be harmful to people using services (Doel, 2010; Green, Gregory & Mason, 2006).

This relates to the importance of being empathic and caring in order to build successful relationships (Fernandez & Healy, 2007; Maluccio, 1979; Paris & Dubus, 2005) (noted as the 'E' in 'ERGO' as outlined in Chapter 1). In the study, parents reported that when workers displayed genuine care and empathy, they felt cared for and this helped build their trust and helped them to open up. It enabled the parents to focus on what they shared with the worker and on the issues impacting their life and parenting. In many ways, this reinforced the nurturing type of approach that has been found to work with families where neglect is a concern (DePanfilis, 1999; Gaudin, 1993).

However, the parents in the study distinguished between professional relationships and friendships by arguing that, unlike in a friendship, the worker was completely attentive to them and did not expect any support or attention back. This highlights a very important aspect of highly personalised working relationships, which is that all of those involved are aware of the *professional* dimensions to a relationship. All participants must be very clear that these relationships are professional relationships explicitly for the purpose of professional work. One parent in the study explained the difference in the following way:

> Don't get too friendly. There's a level of professionalism. One of the people who used to come out to the farm years ago, she just got too personal. And she ended up talking to me about her and I knew everything about her … I mean Leo said a certain amount about himself. But obviously he knew when to stop. It was much more about me than it was about him … he was still able to give enough personal information without being too personal. The thing is that we, having a connection, made the connection stronger to know that … And he was able to relate to that directly by giving me his personal experience without getting in-depth with it.

When working with parents for whom child neglect is a concern, this means that each participant must carry out their role with the goals of parental growth and protecting children. Workers can achieve this through clear communication concerning the participants' roles, limitations and expectations at a level parents can understand (de Boer & Coady, 2003; Drake, 1994; Ribner & Knei-Paz, 2002), including ethical, professional and legal boundaries (Kenemore, 1993). During this time it is important to be empathic, although not excessively so, which requires balancing empathy with objective distance (Kenemore, 1993; McMahon, 2010; Trotter, 2006). This is to avoid a situation where workers over-empathise with parents, which could result in a tendency to let inappropriate behaviour go unchallenged (McMahon, 2010; Trotter, 2006).

Professional boundaries, reinforced through good supervision, can provide support for workers and benefit parents (McMahon, 2010; Reimer, 2010). In the study, the roles defined by boundaries were a continual reminder about the primary reasons for the relationship's existence. Most workers reported how this helped them negotiate the ambiguity that characterised the professional involvement in private lives. The boundaries created the structure that provided for a safe working relationship. In addition, the parents noted that the professional dimension to the relationship kept the relationships 'not as complex' as friendships because, unlike in a friendship, they felt they did not need to reciprocate a supportive role.

ACTIVITY

Returning to the case study at the beginning of the chapter, how did the worker demonstrate being 'real' in her professional role? If applicable, identify instances when you have been 'real' in the professional role. What challenges did you experience and did they relate to your expectations of 'proper professional behaviour', as well as those of the parent, your supervisor or the profession?

■ Achieving a collaborative approach

Another important factor when working with parents for whom neglect is a concern involves workers facilitating a *collaborative* approach (DePanfilis, 1999; Zeira, 2007). Following on from being 'real' in 'role', being collaborative involves workers presenting as equal to the parent in certain ways and supporting the parent to achieve their goals. It involves acknowledging that this is the parent's process, and negotiating the process together, as a 'team'. Collaborating with parents to set and work towards certain goals is important for building parent empowerment and developing parenting skills (de Boer & Coady, 2003; Drake, 1994).

In being collaborative, workers can draw parents into a professional relationship that becomes grounded in trust and focused on parental change and empowerment. Others describe how participants can engage in equal partnerships rather than developing a 'client' and 'expert' positioning (de Boer & Coady, 2003; Drake, 1994; Kirkpatrick et al., 2007; Ribner & Knei-Paz, 2002). This involves ongoing negotiation between parents and workers about the process and their expectations. It also involves workers being clear about the degree to which intrusion into parents' private lives is necessary (Fernandez & Healy, 2007).

However, it also involves workers understanding that there is a power differential, yet actively and consciously negotiating its use in a considered way (de Boer & Coady, 2003), as explained by a parent in the study:

> She just came across real. She just came across as the person you wished was living next door to you. There was no airs or graces. It's like this is me and that's you and I can meet you on the same level. I'm not above you. I don't have all the answers but I might have some things that can help … She didn't take control off me. She tried to help me get more control. It wasn't that I felt powerless. It was more that I felt empowered. Then the more we went along, the more I felt like that.

Collaboration requires giving parents some degree of authority over the process, as long as the ultimate focus is that of the parent working towards meeting the goals that have been identified as negatively impacting on their parenting. This relates to workers holding parents accountable, and challenging them to solve the identified problems, for example:

> I used to have to challenge her sometimes. But how I do it is in a way … that they don't end up feeling judged … I have the relationship built first, and the trust there, and hold them in a safe and secure place … I think if I don't set myself as the expert … I'm open about the challenges but without judgement. I pick up on the strengths they do have as much as possible. And always acknowledging that she wanted the best for her kids even though sometimes some of her patterns got in the way.
>
> Family worker

Workers can achieve collaboration through listening to parents' perspectives and meaning, and working hard to understand them, focusing on their strengths and successes and providing choices. In the study, feeling empowered was described as a time when the parents began to believe in themselves and experience themselves as capable of meeting their own needs, and of continuing the personal development work they had begun with the family worker. Underlying this is a belief that parents are agents in their own life decisions. This involves creating a safe environment where the parents' solutions to their issues can emerge, supported by the worker providing reflection and support.

However, empowering parents is not always clear-cut. In rare situations workers may need to act on behalf of the parent in relation to another service, after challenging and supporting the parent to try to deal with the issue themselves. This supports the notion of Tanner & Turney (2003) that, rather than conceptualising dependency as poor practice, it can be managed as a useful therapeutic tool. This was described in the study as workers acting on behalf of the parent, or 'doing for'. It only occurred when situations arose where not acting this way would have led to substantial loss of confidence in the parent. Practice in these instances involved finding a balance between empowering the parent to try, and consequently grow in confidence to push themselves further next time, and disempowering them, should they fail and lose confidence to try in the future. This was noted as particularly difficult where completing the task or solving the problem was outside the parent's capacity at the time. Workers needed to remind the parent of their prior learning and successes, of professional expectations about parental change and growth in competence and confidence, and to reinforce and renegotiate the parent's goals.

It is important for workers to hold the ideal of parent empowerment but adapt the extent to which they let the parent try to deal with the issue, before stepping in and helping; and for supervisors to support workers in this. It requires parents and workers to share responsibility for the goals being set and met and then later, towards the end of the period of intervention, have an increasing expectation that the parents will meet their needs more autonomously. Improving the channels of communication to enhance accessibility has been found to help this process, along with the practice of being informal when relating to parents when working towards parenting goals. This may involve following the parent's lead, as this may help the parent feel comfortable and thus enable them to be more responsive.

■ Important worker characteristics

A number of worker attributes and actions facilitate good parent–worker relationships with families where neglect is a concern. They include attentiveness, responsiveness and support, respect, a non-judgemental approach, patience and flexibility, positiveness and hope, and professional confidence and competence. Although discussed separately here, in practice these coexist in complex ways to create the conditions that shape the relationship between families and their workers.

It is very important that workers are attentive and responsive to, and supportive of, parents very early in the development of the relationship, as this helps parents to form favourable initial impressions and to decide to engage, for example:

> I knew if she was going to listen to what I had to say, and she was willing to help, I knew Lorraine was the right person to come to and try to get her to help me even more with things … When she started to tell me how she got people to help me get out of that house, I thought, 'That's a good sign. Maybe I should stick with Lorraine and see how we go.'
>
> Parent

Being attentive, supportive and responsive helps parents and workers 'connect' and keep lines of communication between the parents and workers clear and open. As such, it is important for these qualities to remain present throughout the relationship. It involves active listening, interpretation and reflection (Ackerman & Hilsenroth, 2003), along with approaching the building relationship tentatively (Fernandez & Healy, 2007). It also involves workers responding to the immediate issues and needs parents identify, including providing practical and emotional support (Taggart et al., 2000; Zeira, 2007) and social support (Ribner & Knei-Paz, 2002). However, an important aspect of this also involves workers being prepared to focus on issues much broader than the referral or presenting neglect and other child protection concerns (Reimer, 2010).

Mutually *respectful* behaviour in workers and parents alike towards the other party is another fundamental attribute of the relationship, and is present within open and trusting personalised relationships with parents (Altman, 2008; Drake, 1994; Ribner & Knei-Paz, 2002). Respect helps workers and parents negotiate the process of working together, with parents thus feeling they have agency over decisions. For parents who are not voluntary clients, this is particularly important. Respectful behaviour involves workers communicating openly and transparently about not only what they are doing, but why they are doing it. This also requires workers being patient and not 'pushy' or 'bossy'; allowing time and space for parents to open up at their own pace; not being judgemental; accepting differences of opinion and not forcing their views on parents. Above all, being respectful involves workers treating the parent like, as in the words of one parent, 'a person' and not 'a number'.

> If they're gonna pull-out number 4567, you know, take me into the room. They are gonna charge me $200 for an hour's visit. And they're gonna put 4567 back in the box and they're going to go on to 4653. It just doesn't mean anything to them. It doesn't mean anything to me. And it's completely empty. Where Jane doesn't put across the idea that you are a number. She, you know what I mean, you're a person. You've got a name. You've got an identity. You've got a life. And she never loses sight of that.

Importantly, this involves workers following advice and information about the parent from the parent rather than giving precedence to others' opinions, as noted here.

> Often when clients are referred to me ... I've been asked, ... 'Do you wanna look at the record?' And I say, 'No.' Because I don't find that helpful for me. I want to find out what the people are like first-hand. I've got my own way of joining with people and then if I think I need to, then I'll ask ... because that's often their side of the story ... Often what I find, what [the statutory agency] want and what the client actually wants and what's actually going on (pause), it doesn't really help with that relationship ... I think it puts a real judgemental attitude going into that first meeting.
>
> Family worker

As noted by this worker, another significant contributor to building a working relationship with families where neglect is a concern involves workers being perceived as *non-judgemental*, and to approach parents empathically and with an *open mind* (Altman, 2008; de Boer & Coady, 2003; Drake, 1994; Fernandez & Healy, 2007; Reimer, 2010; Zeira, 2007). Non-judgemental workers validate parents and show understanding rather than condemnation. Being non-judgemental may involve holding a view that most parents wish to provide the best circumstances for their children, and providing opportunities for parents to express themselves creatively without judging them or forcing opinions on them. It facilitates dialogue about parents' experiences of the process and of their journey towards development in self-awareness and behaviour change, and about challenges they are facing. A non-judgemental approach also helps parents explore a wider range of options than if workers close dialogue through being judgemental.

Furthermore, given parents' possible unwillingness to engage, it is important for workers to show *flexibility* and *patience*. Worker flexibility involves being prepared to talk about a diverse range of issues and life experiences and interests, and being able to pitch communication at a level that parents can relate to and understand (de Boer & Coady, 2003; Friedlander, Escudero & Heatherington, 2006; Priebe & McCabe, 2006).

Flexibility and patience has been found to help create a safe environment for parents for whom neglect is a concern, and help them feel more in control of the process and consequently more empowered (Ackerman & Hilsenroth, 2003; Friedlander et al., 2006; Priebe & McCabe, 2006; Reimer, 2010). These are particularly important when building trust. However, it may also be necessary to anticipate that parents will feel unfamiliar with new issues and changes in their life circumstances as they work with the worker, and that they may withdraw from the worker during these times. Patience is required when parents lose confidence, feel overwhelmed by new challenges, and/or resist goal-setting and change that relates to themselves and their children's needs and timelines.

> *She just needed time … There would be sessions where I felt like I didn't achieve anything, but planting the seed which probably wouldn't be cultivated for a long time. But I felt like that's what needed to happen. There in the beginning I think it went for about a couple of months where I basically just took the line that, every time I tried to work on strategies or 'Let's look at other ways of doing things.' I was just completely blocked. So I just got to the point where I thought, 'Okay. I'm just going to let her talk.' … I think that to build that trust I think you needed that time. You need flexibility. You need to be able to adapt to the client's needs.*
>
> Family worker

This is consistent with the findings of research, which encourage workers to be calm (Drake, 1994), to persevere and be patient and not to take such setbacks personally, as this may put further pressure on the parent (de Boer & Coady, 2003).

Other worker factors that support parent–worker relationships with parents for whom neglect is a concern include *positiveness* and *hope* (or 'optimism', the fourth element noted in the 'ERGO' acronym regarding relationship-based practice in Chapter 1). Celebrating achievements, using positive reinforcement, expressing feelings of hope for the parents' future and focusing on parents' strengths throughout the relationship, support the relationship by facilitating motivation in workers and parents alike (Reimer, 2010). As noted by one parent in the study, 'when I achieved something he said he was happy *for* me. And that was, it *really was*, supportive. Encouraging. Motivating. It was good. Somebody cared.' The benefits of worker humour, hope and positive reinforcement have been observed previously (de Boer & Coady, 2003; Drake, 1994; Paris & Dubus, 2005; Trotter, 2006).

Building on this, there is emerging evidence that while parent positivity and humour can help motivate the worker, so too can parents' feelings of despair and hopelessness, which can motivate workers differently, depending on the source of the negativity (Reimer, 2010). For example, where parents may feel despair due to staff from other organisations erecting barriers to support, workers may rally to support them. Alternatively, where parents express hopelessness due to the weight of their situation, workers may also feel burdened and helpless. Sometimes workers even experience both in relation to the same family's situation. This may be an example of workers taking on board the feelings of parents; however, it may also reflect the complex nature of the relationship when people empathise strongly with those with whom they have connected when engaging in personalised practice. In this event, worker hope and positive reinforcement of parents can help both parents and workers sustain the relationship. On the other hand, negative feelings or feeling overwhelmed may reduce the optimism of both parties.

Finally, worker confidence and competence also influence the working relationship in that it supports parent responsiveness and willingness to engage.

> I felt that she was competent. And that sort of gave me confidence because I knew I knew nothing but I knew that she knew her stuff … It wasn't like you met the business first. It was like I met Imogen first … She came across relaxed and humorous. That played a big part, because like you're already nervous … She came across as a powerful woman but she wasn't going to put any of that on me. She wasn't power trippin'. She get didn't come across like she knew everything and was going to fix everything, and I knew nothing. It was that, more of a question, 'Can I help you?', not, 'you need to do this'.
>
> Parent

It is well known that parent perceptions of worker competence and depth of knowledge positively influence working relationships (Ackerman & Hilsenroth, 2003; Altman, 2008; Kirkpatrick et al., 2007; Maluccio, 1979). For parents for whom neglect is a concern, confident workers can help parents feel safe and comfortable. This involves workers acting assertively regarding their professional role in the relationship, remaining open to what parents need to raise, and responding flexibly. Furthermore, confident workers are prepared to cover a wide range of issues and interests beyond parenting and child protection, as well as reflect on their practice and learn from colleagues and parents alike. This confidence is a significant contributor to both building and maintaining relationships and includes workers having good intuition, sound skills and self-esteem (de Boer & Coady, 2003; Reimer, 2010).

Additionally, confident workers are likely to challenge parents to meet their needs themselves and stay focused on their goals, or to negotiate new ones as others are met. They are also ready to persevere in those instances when they perceive parents are unwilling, and exercise the professional discretion required when there is escalation of risk. However, it is likely that these are not possible without a close connection and some level of understanding of how the parents might respond.

ACTIVITIES

Drawing on this chapter, and the case study at the beginning, discuss what may have been going on for Bernadette and how Martha, her worker, developed an open and trusting relationship with her. You might like to think about:

- what Bernadette was going through as the working relationship developed; in particular what inhibited her working with Martha
- qualities Martha demonstrated and what she did to build the working relationship with Bernadette
- how this compares with what you identified at the beginning of the chapter as important to consider when building working relationships
- challenges Martha experienced and how she overcame these.

Think about working with a parent with whom you need to focus on child neglect concerns. Identify the attributes and actions you bring to that relationship and the extent to which these will help you develop a collaborative working relationship with the parent. What are the challenges you could experience? Critically reflect on your approach in light of the chapter content and explain what you might do differently in future work with parents with child neglect concerns.

Stressors that emerge for workers

Being a confident professional, and being able to develop the approach, qualities and skills discussed throughout this chapter, requires having a thorough grasp of issues that arise for parents while not losing a focus on the needs of children subject to neglect. This is challenging. Working with this group of families may diminish workers' morale and sense of professional accomplishment (Watson et al., 2005). It is also important to note that the personal way of relating discussed can be emotionally demanding of workers (McMahon, 2010). This is because, by engaging in personalised ways in professional relationships, workers open themselves up to parents, investing in parents' lives and genuinely caring for them. In addition, being invested in and thus obligated to parents may mean workers experience many of the emotional highs and lows parents experience, and requires a level of trust that parents will acknowledge the professional context.

Furthermore, at the same time workers may experience pressure from professional norms to maintain distance (Green et al., 2006; Maidment, 2006). The type of relationship-based practice discussed can create stress for workers, as they may feel they are behaving unprofessionally or unethically at times; and yet believe that without such a friend-like connection, they are less able to access the more fundamental issues for the parent. They may feel it is not possible to perform the professional role to its fullest potential without connection through a personal and human interaction.

It is useful to learn from research into practice in rural and remote locations, where workers in such settings grapple with 'the challenges of providing accessible, ethical and competent practice in ... multi-layered networks' (Green, 2003, p. 210). Although some have argued that strict professional boundaries reduce the risk of negative outcomes (Heaman et al., 2007) or unethical practice (Daley & Doughty, 2006; Zur, 2006), others have found professional distance to work against the relationship (Green et al., 2006; Kirkpatrick et al., 2007; Lynn et al., 1998). Some authors discussing working in rural settings describe the way in which rural contexts can have a 'humanising effect' on relationships (Pugh, 2007), and that workers provide a less professionally distant (Green et al., 2006) or more personalised and informal approach (Ginsberg, 1998; Martinez-Brawley, 1986). Lynn et al. (1998), have further detailed a rural Aboriginal and Torres Strait Islander construction of the relationship. They describe the relationship in terms of 'deprofessionalism'.

> In a deprofessional approach, friendship, yarning, recognition of your common humanity with the client, sharing of stories, sharing of self, including spirituality and humour, are recognised and valued techniques. A relationship characterised in this form works with power and equality in a more complex way than the present approaches within social and welfare work
>
> (Lynn et al., 1998, p. 79)

Further to these kinds of ideas, Green et al. (2006, p. 450) argue that it might be more useful to conceptualise relationships in rural contexts as 'a stretchy piece of elastic'. By this they mean a continuum between the 'professional objective expert' and the 'helpful friend' rather than the dichotomy of professional and non-professional that is often presented, and that practitioners be allowed to choose where they are on the continuum as they respond to the unique situations they face with clients and professionals alike. This includes challenging, rethinking and 'stretching' traditional notions of professional ethics, values and rules about professional boundaries as they relate to the development and maintenance of the relationship. Given the breadth of stressors that may emerge for workers, it is important to utilise outside sources of support, such as those available within the work environment.

■ Conclusion

There is much evidence to show a range of parent and worker qualities and behaviours that facilitate effective working relationships with families where child neglect is a concern. By drawing on the literature, across Australia and internationally, and by exploring the perceptions of parents, workers and supervisors, the values, knowledge, skills and environmental factors required for creating and sustaining effective working relationships with vulnerable families have been identified. Families struggling to provide for their children's needs prefer to build relationships with workers who provide a safe space to work together in a trustworthy, transparent, respectful, non-judgemental, optimistic and empathic fashion – much like the kinds of relationships that most of us hope for.

■ Useful websites

Child Family Community Australia (CFCA) information exchange – hosted by the Australian Institute of Family Studies (AIFS): **www.aifs.gov.au/cfca/index.php**

Child Welfare Information Gateway: Family Centred Practice – **www.childwelfare. gov/famcentered**

NSW Family Services Inc.: **www.nswfamilyservices.asn.au**

Positive Partnerships with Parents of Young Children; Australian Research Alliance for Children and Youth (ARACY): **www.aracy.org.au/publications-resources/ area?command=record&id=83**

9

Working with parents with substance misuse problems

Sharon Dawe and Paul Harnett

■ Learning goals

This chapter will enable you to:

- **UNDERSTAND** the outcomes for children raised in families with substance-misusing parents

- **APPRECIATE** the effectiveness and key elements of interventions that have been developed to work with parents with substance misuse problems

- **IDENTIFY** the elements of the Parents Under Pressure program and how the Parents Under Pressure Integrated Framework can be used to plan an assessment and intervention

- **UNDERSTAND** the importance of setting goals.

■ Introduction

PARENTAL SUBSTANCE MISUSE is a serious problem that does not occur in isolation but is typically accompanied by a range of parental and lifestyle problems. This often leads to a family environment that lacks structure, routine and emotional regulation and features lifestyle stressors associated with financial problems and drug or alcohol use. The outcome for children raised in such chaotic and uncontained environments is often poor, with problems compounding as children move from early infancy through to adolescence. There has been some attempt to develop interventions that aim to improve child outcomes in such families. The Parents Under Pressure Program is one of several programs that have an evidence base demonstrating success, at least in the short term. In this chapter, we provide an overview of the key outcomes for children living in families with parental substance misuse, discuss the evidence for successful interventions and provide an overview of an integrated framework to guide assessment and intervention when working with complex family presentations. We present a case study to illustrate the use of the Integrated Framework in practice.

■ Outcomes for children in families with parental substance misuse

Babies exposed to substances *in utero* experience a range of difficulties (see Harnett & Dawe, in press). While the direct effects of some substances on development appear to be limited, others such as alcohol are profound and lifelong, with problems associated with foetal alcohol spectrum disorders (FASD) well documented (see Mattson, Crocker & Nguyen, 2011). Prenatally exposed infants may experience neonatal withdrawal symptoms, and may show compromised autonomic nervous system functioning in the early months of life (Porges & Furman, 2011). These babies are then hard to soothe when distressed, unsettled during feeding, and irregular in their sleep patterns. These 'difficult' behaviours are stressful for the parent, creating from the outset an environment that is fraught for both infant and caregiver and can set the scene for early attachment difficulties. When these behaviours combine with other problems in the family, many infants raised in such environments begin to show developmental difficulties in the early toddler years, with high rates of insecure attachments to primary carers. During middle childhood, behaviour problems such as non-compliance, poor attention and concentration, and early school failure emerge. By adolescence, these problems can lead to school truancy or dropping out and early initiation into substance use (Dawe et al., 2007).

It is important to stress that these problems are not solely attributable to parental substance use. Typically parents will have other psychological problems, such as depression or anxiety-related disorders. Many have had traumatic childhood experiences that included neglect or abuse and current life stressors can include severe financial difficulties and social isolation. There are often high rates of conflict between adults in the family and a parenting style that can be either neglectful or authoritarian (Suchman & Luthar, 2000; Mayes & Truman, 2000). As a consequence, family life can feel uncontained and unpredictable for children. It is not surprising that many children living with substance-misusing parents come to the attention of statutory child protection services. Parental drug and alcohol misuse is a key issue for 50 to 80 per cent of children who are placed in care (Walsh et al., 2003; Scannapieco & Connell-Carrick, 2007; Delfabbro et al., 2009). However, in a review of 498 children aged 0–2 that examined their first placement in the care system, approximately 60 per cent were judged to be in need of more formal entry into out-of-home care (as opposed to respite placement) and of these children, almost three-quarters came from families in which four or more risk factors were present (Delfabbro et al., 2009). Substance misuse is a serious problem, but cannot be treated in isolation from the associated problems facing these socially isolated families, who are living in poverty with psychological challenges to their health and wellbeing. (See also Chapter 10 regarding children in the midst of family violence.)

■ The intervention context: a brief overview of interventions that help families with parental substance misuse

There is a growing recognition that providing interventions to families where a parent is involved with a substance misuse treatment service may provide a critical opportunity to reduce multiple risk factors present in a child's life. Indeed, there is now growing evidence that early enrichment of a child's environment is a key factor in ameliorating some of the negative effects associated with prenatal exposure (Harnett & Dawe, in press). There is no doubt that the treatment for substance misuse is associated with considerable reductions in illicit drug use and associated crime (Prendergast et al., 2002). This underscores the importance of early intervention for substance-misusing families.

However, while substance abuse treatment helps parents gain control of their substance use, improvements in other domains of family functioning do not automatically occur (Dawe et al., 2000). Additional family-focused interventions need to be incorporated into existing substance use treatment services, or parents need to be able to access support through referral to programs developed specifically for high-risk families. The former strategy has been more widely evaluated. Early work by Catalano and colleagues combined parenting skills and relapse prevention with home-based case management services in a program called Focus on Families for parents enrolled in methadone maintenance. At 12 months an improvement in parenting skills, conflict management and parental drug use was observed in those who received the service, compared to those who had only received standard care. Notably, there was no change in children's behaviour (Catalano et al., 1999). However, when the children were followed up almost 15 years later, boys whose families had received the intervention had a lower risk of developing a substance use disorder, compared to boys who had been in the no-treatment condition. There was no difference in the risk of substance use disorder among the girls from both groups (Haggerty et al., 2008).

Luthar and Suchman (2000) described an intervention designed to increase maternal reflective functioning – the capacity to recognise and understand one's own and others' thoughts, feelings and behaviours – with the aim of helping parents provide more responsive and sensitive caregiving. In their early work, Luthar and Suchman (2000) reported a significant reduction in the risk of child maltreatment for women on methadone maintenance. In later work by this group, however, initial gains observed in the immediate post-treatment period were not sustained at six months (Luthar et al., 2007). While it is difficult to account for this discrepancy in results, it is notable that the age range of children in both studies spanned 1–16 years. It seemed that for families with older children, who had displayed poor parenting and compromised care over many years, improvement was more difficult. A series of studies now suggest that working with families with younger children may hold the most promise.

Suchman and colleagues (2011) developed an intervention called the Mothers and Toddlers Program. As with Luthar's early work, this program is theoretically underpinned by the concept of reflective functioning. Working with substance-using mothers and their toddlers, gains were sustained at least in the short term at six weeks post treatment. Belt et al. (2012) provided pregnant women with a choice of one of two treatments and compared outcomes at 4 and 12 months on maternal drug use, depression and the quality of caregiving. The active treatment consisted of psychodynamically oriented group treatment, again focusing on reflective capacity, compared to a more general supportive intervention. Gains were found with both interventions, although it is notable that there was a reduction in mothers' hostile and intrusive interactions only in the psychotherapeutically oriented treatment group..

In parallel with much of this work, the authors of this chapter have been developing an intervention, the Parents Under Pressure (PuP) program, aimed at improving family functioning in families with parental substance abuse with children from birth to eight years. The PuP program was developed as an intensive, home-based intervention integrating (1) attachment theory to provide a focus on the central importance of a safe and nurturing relationship with a primary carer(s); (2) parenting skills to ensure that parents have a repertoire of skills that they can use; and, critically, (3) a focus on parental emotional regulation. The quality of the parent–child relationship and the parent's capacity to provide consistent and appropriate parenting skills is seen to be dependent upon the parent's ability to understand and manage their own emotional state. Mindfulness strategies are incorporated into treatment as a strategy parents can use to help manage their emotional state.

The effectiveness of the PuP program was evaluated in two series of case studies, one with parents on methadone maintenance (Dawe et al., 2003) and the other with families referred by child protection services (Harnett & Dawe, 2008). A randomised controlled trial (Dawe & Harnett, 2007b) compared the effectiveness of the home-delivered PuP program with a clinic-based, brief parenting intervention and standard care in families on methadone maintenance. Substantial changes were found for families receiving PuP in all three reports. Of particular interest in the randomised controlled trial was the finding that child abuse potential significantly decreased in families receiving PuP at six months follow-up. The average age of the children in the study was four years, once again suggesting that targeting families with younger children may be associated with positive outcomes.

This brief overview highlights the point that interventions that have been trialled with parents with substance misuse problems can make a difference and that it may be particularly important to focus treatment as early as possible in a child's life. In the remainder of this chapter, we describe the way in which the Integrated Framework from the PuP program can be used to assess and aid in planning an intervention for families with parental substance misuse. Box 9.1 introduces the reader to a case situation to which the Integrated Framework will be applied.

BOX 9.1   The case of Julie and Beckie

Imagine that you work in an Intensive Family Support service. Julie, a 26-year-old mother of three children (James, age 10; Melissa, age 6; and Beckie, age 18 months) has been referred to your service following concerns regarding her parenting of her youngest child. The two older children have been living with their maternal grandparents under a court-ordered kinship carer arrangement for the last four years. Child protection services originally became involved after concerns were raised about neglect, excessive parental alcohol use and a failure for James to attend school regularly. Julie sees the children most weeks and there is no plan to return them to the full-time care of their mother, as there is a view that they are doing fine with their grandparents.

Julie was in contact with treatment services throughout her pregnancy and reportedly abstained from alcohol use. However, following the birth of Beckie, she began to drink regularly and concerns were raised that resulted in the removal of Beckie at four months and placement with her maternal grandparents. As a consequence, Julie re-engaged with treatment services and Beckie was returned to the full-time care of her mother at 12 months since Julie appeared stable, was managing not to drink and was continuing to attend the Drug and Alcohol Service and Alcoholics Anonymous.

Since Beckie was returned to her care, Julie has continued to have some contact with the drug and alcohol service, although this is sporadic. Her case worker left the service six months ago and she has seen several different people whom she has not 'clicked with'. Annoyed with the service, she has increasingly failed to attend appointments.

Recently concerns were raised about Julie's potential drinking by a neighbour, who believed that she had seen Julie drunk on several occasions with Beckie in the pram. A notification to child protection resulted in a visit from a social worker. Julie denied drinking alcohol and there was no evidence of this in the home. Nonetheless, the home was starkly furnished; Beckie's bed appeared to be with her mother on a mattress on the floor. Julie told the social worker she didn't want any help from anyone, but appeared flat in mood and reluctant to discuss how she was managing. She said everyone had 'written her off as a bad parent' and she didn't need anyone else telling her what a bad mother she was: she knew that by now. She admitted that she often felt judged by her mother and wouldn't ask her for help looking after Beckie; having to have her look after the older two was shameful enough.

During the visit the social worker noticed that Beckie was sitting on the floor holding a doll and watching a children's program on the television. She seemed absorbed in the program, but when it had finished she went up to her mother and said 'Up Mummy, up'. Julie helped her climb onto her knee, stroked her hair and gave her a cuddle and kiss. After five minutes Beckie started to squirm. Julie put her down, saying, 'She's a bit whiny because it's near her nap time; I'd better feed her before I put her down.' The social worker followed Julie to the kitchen, which was untidy with rubbish on the bench and around the unemptied bin. The floor was unclean, although the kitchen stovetop appeared to have been wiped recently. The social worker noted that there was little food in the cupboard or fridge. Beckie was given a drink of milk in a baby's bottle.

Beckie appeared small for 18 months. However, she was walking quite well for her age, and had a vocabulary consistent with her age. It was noted that the environment was lacking stimulation, with no evidence of age-appropriate toys, picture books or soft toys. There were three DVDs Julie said Beckie really enjoyed. Julie described Beckie as a fairly easy baby. Julie said Beckie had not received any immunisation since she returned to her care and that she had not been taken to her 12-month check-up with the child and family health nurse.

Following a case conference with Julie, the drug and alcohol service, the local child and family health nurse, the social worker and team leader, a decision was made to seek from the court a statutory order that enabled Beckie to remain in her mother's care under supervision and on the condition that she accepted a service from your organisation.

■ The PuP Integrated Framework: a model of assessment to guide clinical practice

It is not uncommon for practitioners to feel overwhelmed by the number of problems in the lives of the families they are asked to help. To make sense of what feels like a chaotic and complex interplay of forces intrinsic and extrinsic to the family's current situation, we developed the Integrated Framework (Harnett & Dawe, 2012). This practice framework, informed by existing models of child development and family functioning (Cicchetti & Cohen, 2006; Sameroff, 2010), moves beyond simply identifying the presence of risk and protective factors to articulating *how* and *why* specific risk and protective factors are important for a particular family. For example, it is easy to assess that a family is experiencing considerable financial and other life stressors, that the parents employ poor coping strategies to solve difficulties, maybe experiencing problems with low mood or other severe mental health issues, and are abusing substances. What is more difficult, but essential, is understanding how these factors interact and operate to reduce a parent's capacity to meet the needs of the children in the family.

The Integrated Framework integrates information obtained from talking to families, the results of assessments using self-report measures, and observations of the quality of the parent–child relationship and the child's home environment. The aim of the assessment is to identify the key issues that are likely to impact on child outcomes. These issues are used to define clear and measurable goals that represent the changes a family will need to make in order that their children have the best chance of achieving their full potential.

Overview of the Integrated Framework

The underlying principle of the Integrated Framework is that a healthy parent–child relationship is essential in promoting a child's development. An extensive research literature has demonstrated that responsive, sensitive, nurturing caregiving from a primary carer is essential for good child outcomes (see Chapter 11). The early years – indeed months – matter greatly and lay the foundation for the development of self-regulatory skills in early childhood and an understanding of relationships across the life span (Slade, 2005). Parents who are able to provide an optimal caregiving environment are able to tolerate and contain an infant or young child's extreme fluctuations in emotions. This, in turn, allows a child to feel safe in expressing these emotions. Sensitive and responsive parents structure the environment with predictable routines and consequences to help the child organise their behaviour and emotions. They are able to show genuine warmth and nurturance that allows the child to feel loved, and present opportunities and scaffolding to promote cognitive and physical development. However, the extent to which a parent is able to provide an optimal caregiving environment is dependent on a range of factors that are both intrapersonal and situation-specific. The Integrated Framework provides a model in which these various influences can be clearly articulated and both the strengths and areas of difficulties in different domains can then be viewed as potential focal points for intervention.

Assessing developmental outcome

The starting point of the Integrated Framework is to understand the forces at play that will impact on the capacity of a child to reach their full potential across multiple domains of functioning (see Figure 9.1). Thus it is important to first assess how a child or infant is currently faring in relation to their social, emotional, behavioural, spiritual and cultural development. This can be done through consultation with a general practitioner, health visitor or child health nurse, or teachers, and by the use of developmental charts. There are a number of these charts now available on the internet and they are designed as resources for parents and practitioners alike (see 'Useful websites' at the end of this chapter). They give a reasonable indication of whether a child is developing as expected and allow for both the celebration of milestone achievements and the identification of areas of potential delay. In addition, there are more general measures of child or infant emotional social and behavioural wellbeing, many in the public domain. The Strengths and Difficulties Questionnaire (Hawes & Dadds, 2004; Goodman, 2001), for example, is a good measure of child behaviour problems and is appropriate for children from the age of 2 years. More specialised assessment by appropriately trained professionals is sometimes indicated. This may include an assessment of childhood disorders such as autism or attention deficit disorder and a comprehensive assessment of cognitive and adaptive abilities (language, self-care) if developmental delays are suspected. Importantly, beginning with a focus on a child's current developmental status allows the parent and practitioner to develop a clear understanding of the child's strengths

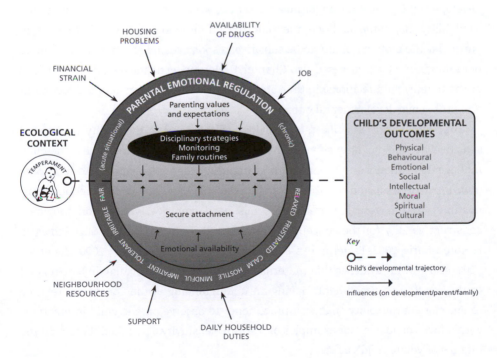

Figure 9.1 The Integrated Framework

LIVERPOOL JOHN MOORES UNIVERSITY
LEARNING SERVICES

as well as difficulties, and emphasises that the intervention is ultimately for the benefit of the child. Some examples that we have found in our own work have been the identification of potential problems with language or motor development, and difficulties in cognitive development. Equally, we often find areas of great strength that can be shared with the parent, such as a baby who is clearly an early walker, or a toddler whose language seems well advanced for their age.

Emotional availability and attachment

A fundamental premise underlying the Integrated Framework is that the quality of the relationship between a child and their primary carer(s) is critical to the development of the child. This relationship may be with a biological parent or parents or with extended family members. What we do know is that there needs to be someone who is able to provide an environment that helps a child feel safe and loved. The construct that is proposed to underpin this is 'parental sensitivity', which can be directly observed by watching the quality of the relationship between child and primary carer. There are also a number of formal observational coding systems that have been rigorously tested to ensure that they do indeed capture this critical quality of caregiving. One of the most comprehensive ways to measure parental sensitivity is the use of a systematic coding system such as the Emotional Availability Scales developed by Zeynep Biringen (Biringen, 2000, 2004). Biringen proposes that emotional availability shapes the quality of the maternal–infant interactions and influences; in particular the mother's ability to be sensitive, responsive and emotionally in tune to her infant's or child's cues (see also Chapter 1). Her model delineates the dimensions of the parent–child relationship that predict the quality of parent–child attachment and other child developmental outcomes.

Four dimensions describe the behaviour of the parents: the ability to respond sensitively to the child (sensitivity); the ability to provide structure to help the child manage their emotions and behaviours (structuring); the ability to promote autonomy (non-intrusiveness); and the ability to minimise angry and hostile interactions (non-hostility). In this research area, there has been empirical verification providing construct validity for the concept of emotional availability (Aviezer, Sagi-Schwartz & Koren-Karie, 2003; Easterbrooks & Biringen, 2005; Swanson et al., 2000; Ziv et al., 2000) and growing evidence that maternal and child emotional availability are related to the security of attachment. Having an understanding of the constructs relating to emotional availability enables a practitioner to observe parent–child interactions with a focus on looking for examples of warmth, sensitivity and an ability to read the infant's or young child's cues.

Assessing parenting values and expectations

A parent's own upbringing embedded within cultural and spiritual beliefs will shape a parental value system. One of the ways of beginning a conversation around values can be asking a parent what they would like their child to be like in two or five years' time. This will elicit different responses and it is then possible to draw from this response some of the underlying parenting values. For some parents, this may be more socially focused – having friends, having fun, being loved. For others, it may relate to connection to culture, or to educational attainment. Helping a parent articulate their own hopes and dreams for their child provides an opportunity for both parent and practitioner to develop a shared understanding of the values that matter to this parent. Setting goals that explicitly build on an underlying value system will both enhance the therapeutic relationship between parent and practitioner and increase the likelihood that the parent will actively engage with steps needed to reach a goal.

Practitioner values can also set a stage for parents' feeling judged. Having strong views about, for example, domestic hygiene, nutritional practices, substance use patterns and immunisation status (to name a few) can at times drive practitioner-identified rather than parent-identified goals. Perhaps there are times when it is actually in the best interest of the child that the goals identified by the practitioner are set, such as school attendance. In such situations, linking the goal explicitly back to parental values and helping the parent see how a goal can achieve multiple outcomes that are going to benefit a child may be the therapeutic component of the intervention. For instance, a parent who values family ties may be helped to see that school attendance gives their child the opportunity to take part in cultural activities, or perhaps become closer to cousins and other family members attending school.

In addition to the construct of values is the importance of understanding parents' expectations around their child's developmental capacity. A parent who does not understand normal child development may have unrealistic expectations of their child – both behaviourally and emotionally. For example, a mother may smack her 12-month-old child for pushing buttons on a television, demonstrating both a failure to appreciate that the child does not have the cognitive capacity to understand why they have been smacked and the use of inappropriate disciplining. Unrealistic expectations are associated with an increased risk of child maltreatment (Milner, 2003). Helping a parent develop realistic expectations of their child requires an understanding of normal child development, which may need to be a focus of the intervention.

Parenting skills, family routines and monitoring

The Integrated Framework acknowledges that a parent's repertoire of parenting skills is an important influence on child development. Do the parents know what to do in a challenging parenting situation? It is important to ascertain whether there is:

1   a skill deficit – the parent does not know what they could do in particular circumstances

    OR

2   there is skill inhibition – the parent knows what they should do but for a range of other reasons is not able to put these skills into practice.

Thus, the first step in this component of the Integrated Framework is to ascertain whether there is indeed a skill deficit, or rather a skill inhibition. Clearly the former would lead to helping the parent acquire parenting skills. However, the latter implies that there are other factors in a parent's life that are preventing the parent putting the skills that they possess into practice. It is surprising the number of parents we have worked with who actually know 'what to do' but are not able to do so. Sending parents in this category off to another parenting program is undermining; their existing repertoire of skills has not been acknowledged. It also fails to identify the impediments to using the skills and thus is unlikely to change parenting practices.

For parents who fall into the first category, provision of parenting skills is central to improving the outcome for the child. There is a substantial literature on the effectiveness of behavioural parenting skills in improving child behaviour (Wyatt Kaminski, 2008), underscored by the sobering statistic that 60 per cent of 3-year-olds with conduct disorders still exhibit problems at the age of 8 years if left untreated. Further, at least half of these children will have significant problems in adulthood, including antisocial personality disorder (NICE, 2007). Thus, helping children learn how to behave by providing clear and consistent parenting is a key aspect of helping children develop to their full potential.

Included under the heading of parenting skills is the importance of family routines for younger children and infants. These are also important because they provide a sense of harmony and predictability in young children's lives. While behavioural models of parent training have their theoretical roots in learning theory, the need for structure in a child's life is integral to the concept of emotional availability. Within the Integrated Framework we conceptualise the capacity of a parent to provide structure through family routines and effective, non-punitive discipline, which are important in promoting a child's sense of security. This enables a child to develop a perception that their parents are capable of containing and regulating both the child's behaviour and their emotional state (see Katz, Maliken & Stettler, 2012).

It should be noted that, while behavioural parenting skills are helpful for families with parental substance misuse, there is now clear evidence that group-based parenting programs are not effective for complex families with children (NICE, 2007). This suggests that programs are more effectively delivered on an individual basis, although a caveat must be made regarding the appropriateness of providing parenting interventions within a context of family violence (see Chapter 10). Individually focused parenting programs need to be responsive to a range of family issues that impact on a parent's ability to put parenting skills into practice. Most proximal is the capacity for a parent to remain calm and to manage a range of intense emotions in challenging parenting situations.

Parents' state of mind

The Integrated Framework places considerable emphasis on the parent's state of mind. By this we mean the parent's capacity to be calm and emotionally in control, as this directly impacts on the way in which parenting skills are practised. A parent who is unable to control extreme mood states, such as anger, or who typically acts impulsively, will be less consistent and more punitive in their disciplining style (Dawe et al., 2007). Equally, a parent's state of mind will impact on the extent to which the parent accurately perceives their infant's or child's cues. For example, a depressed parent typically fails to notice their child's cues and is less sensitive to signals of distress.

Determining how and what to assess about a parent's state of mind depends in part on the nature of the intervention and on the areas of concern that are believed to be impacting on parenting capacity. It is generally considered good practice to administer a tool to measure parental mood as recommended, for example, in the UK Department of Health Framework for the Assessment of Children in Need and Their Families (see 'Useful websites' below). Anxiety and depressed mood are clearly linked to parenting capacity and so a measure such as the Depression Anxiety and Stress Scale (Lovibond & Lovibond, 1995) would be a useful tool to gauge parental mood (see 'Useful websites'). Importantly, this measure is also sensitive to change, so it is possible to determine whether there has been any change in scores across the course of the intervention. In addition to measuring the symptoms associated with depression or anxiety, it is also possible to measure a wide range of beliefs, attitudes and other psychological constructs.

The wider social context

Finally, the Integrated Framework incorporates the extensive literature that demonstrates how living in chronically stressful conditions (such as overcrowded homes, domestic violence and poverty) leads to a variety of adverse outcomes. These outcomes for children include heightened emotional and physiological reactivity, social problems with peers, and poor problem-solving ability – factors that can lead to failure at school, the increased likelihood of antisocial behaviour, and health problems (Repetti, Taylor & Seeman, 2002). Importantly, the evidence shows that these negative outcomes are not inevitable. Studies of resilient children (children who display positive developmental outcomes in the face of adversity) have identified that the ongoing presence of a nurturing primary caregiver during infancy, positive parent–child relationships, high parenting efficacy, and consistency in the use of fair disciplinary practices by the parents are important factors in promoting resilience (Cowen et al., 1990; Masten et al., 1990). Thus, while the wider social context is important to assess, there may be other ways of improving family functioning that can militate against contextual issues that are not amenable to change.

ACTIVITY

Reread the case study of Julie and Beckie in the text box above. While there is clearly a need for much greater assessment of this family, use the Integrated Framework above to reflect on the areas of potential strength and difficulty when considering how best to support Julie. Afterwards, check whether you have identified all of the areas of strength and difficulty by looking at the Integrated Framework in Table 9.1.

■ The importance of setting goals

In the process of using the Integrated Framework to guide an assessment, you will have identified many areas of strength and significant challenges for the family. This will allow you to set specific goals for change with the parent. Goals can be identified by asking the question, 'What needs to change in the family for this child to meet his or her developmental potential?' The goals for change should be mutually agreed. Both the parent and practitioner should have a shared understanding that they are working towards an agreed-upon outcome and a commitment towards achieving the goal. Goals that are assigned tersely and without a clear rationale ('Do this') and goals that are perceived as imposed and unjustified lead to frustration, anger and resistance. Including the parent in the identification of goals typically leads to greater goal commitment (Locke & Latham, 2002).

Goal commitment would be particularly important when working with Julie. She does not necessarily want to be involved with your service and one of the key aspects of relationship building in this case would be to hand control over to Julie to make

Table 9.1 The Integrated Framework: considerations for assessment and intervention

Domain of functioning	Areas of potential strength	Areas of potential difficulty
Child Developmental Outcomes	Appears to be meeting milestones including walking, talking. Is able to settle for appropriate amount of time watching age-relevant program on television. Goes to mother with clear expectation that she will be warmly received.	Small for age. Has not organised immunisation or 12-month check-up. Check diet – some evidence that this may need to be improved, given that lunch was a bottle of milk and not much food in the kitchen. Cognitive development may need to be considered: Little evidence of age-appropriate toys, picture books, so perhaps limited stimulation in environment.
Emotional Availability	Sensitivity – notices Beckie's bids to be picked up; interprets whining as cue Beckie is tired. Responsivity – picks Beckie up for an appropriate length of time, recognises hunger cues – provides bottle before her nap. Warmth – gives her kiss and cuddle. Structuring – some evidence that she is able to respond to hunger cues and has regular sleep times.	Low mood exacerbated by limited social support may interfere with her capacity to be consistently emotionally available at times.
Parenting Values and Expectations	Wants to be a 'good mother' for Beckie – committed to her.	Unclean house inconsistent with her values, but lacks energy to clean regularly.
Parent's State of Mind (emotional regulation)	Does not display hostility towards Beckie.	Annoyed at drug and alcohol service for changing staff. Low mood likely to be related to moderate depression. ? Drinking as a means of coping.
Ecological Context	Adequate housing.	Financial difficulties. Due to the shame she feels in not being able to cope with two older children, she does not turn to or accept support from her mother.

some decision on how to address the concerns raised by the statutory services around her capacity to parent Beckie. This process should also be empowering for the parent, as she is making decisions rather than simply following instructions such as 'You need to go to counselling' or 'You need to do a parenting course' (Davis, Day & Bidmead, 2002; see also Chapter 8). Success in attaining the goal is critical, so ensuring that all is in place to maximise success is essential. Attaining the goal will also help build trust and a working alliance between the parent and practitioner.

Framing the meaning of the goal is also important. One could question, for example, the meaningfulness of a 'clean floor'. Is this simply a practitioner's set of values around household cleanliness? If you and Julie have both decided that cleaning the floor is the first goal, then the context for this goal needs to be clearly articulated for both Julie and for professionals involved in the case. The following could be one such scenario (see Box 9.2).

BOX 9.2   Julie's first goal

You have spent several hours with Julie and Beckie and identified a range of areas of strengths and difficulties. Julie commented on several occasions that she feels overwhelmed by the state of the house – she can't believe that it has got so bad and it just goes to show what a bad mother she is... Julie has many negative beliefs about herself as a mother, including guilt about her inability to provide a good home for her two older children, her drinking following the birth of Beckie and the current involvement of statutory services. She knows she can't change what has happened in the past but feels overwhelmed and immobilised, with no sense that she can create any good out of disorder and mess.

You have discussed the strengths you have observed. Further, rather than trying to solve any of the very significant issues raised above, you have acknowledged that they are influences that are making it tough to be a good enough parent.

You then talk about taking some small, practical first steps towards making things a little better. You get Julie to talk about how Beckie learnt to walk, in gradual stages achieving small goals along the way: rolling, crawling, holding herself up with the furniture, tiny first steps. You talk about how Julie helped along the way, but ultimately it was Beckie's job to do the walking.

The use of this metaphor is obvious to Julie and so, when you suggest that just for today you both identify what would be the equivalent of 'rolling' for Julie right now, Julie agrees. Julie considers what could make a difference – what the very first small step may be. Let's say in this case Julie says the dirty kitchen floor bothers her a lot. She hates having Beckie sit on a dirty floor and she hates the idea that there are ants and other insects that crawl across the floor. Together you make a very practical plan around cleaning the floor; maybe you even help in executing the plan.

Framing this goal within the Integrated Framework: Julie showed a commitment to change by developing a meaningful and manageable goal with the practitioner. The goal was driven by Julie's concern for her baby's health and wellbeing (Child's Developmental Outcome). Achieving the goal made Julie feel that a small change was possible (Parent's State of Mind) and she felt supported by someone (Social Support) who was going to be there for her to help achieve bigger gaols (Development of Therapeutic Alliance). What may initially seem trivial (Julie washed the kitchen floor) is in fact an important first step in helping frame goals that are achievable, manageable and meaningful to Julie.

◼ Conclusion

This chapter provides an overview of the Integrated Framework to help guide practice and intervention planning for complex families. The framework guides intervention planning for the PuP program, but it is not linked to only one program. It is possible that many different programs could be conceptualised as fitting within the Integrated Framework. In the case of Julie, there may be both adult mental health services involved to assess and treat depression, perhaps using a Cognitive Behavioural approach. If alcohol does indeed appear to be a problem, this could be addressed using Relapse Prevention, with a re-referral to a drug and alcohol agency. There may be further issues around housing, or support with finances, that help improve living conditions. Ultimately, from a parenting perspective, the support Julie receives to deal with all these issues will influence her capacity to parent. What we can glean from this brief scenario is that Julie has a capacity to respond sensitively and warmly to her baby and that she appears to have been able to provide sufficient structure to help Beckie reach her developmental milestones. Along the way, Julie has done much that is right. She, like many other families with whom we have worked, is struggling with her own complex history around child protection and substance use problems. She and daughter Beckie deserve the best chance of being supported to overcome adversity, and to help Beckie reach her potential.

◼ Useful websites

Australian Centre for Child Protection: **www.unisa.edu.au/childprotection**

Babycenter website, information about developmental milestones and other useful information: **www.babycenter.com**

DASS, Information about the depression, anxiety and stress scale: **www2.psy. unsw.edu.au/DASS**

PuP program website, for further information about the PuP program: **www.pupprogram.net.au**

UK Framework for the assessment of children in need and their families – the assessment framework, practice guidance, questionnaires and scales, assessment recording forms: **www.dh.gov.uk/en/Publicationsandstatistics/Publications/ PublicationsPolicyAndGuidance/DH_4008144**

Youth in Mind, information for researchers and professionals about the Strengths & Difficulties Questionnaires: **www.sdqinfo.com**

10

Children in the midst of family and domestic violence

Cathy Humphreys and Menka Tsantefski

■ Learning goals

This chapter will enable you to:

- **UNDERSTAND** that children living with family violence are of cross-sectoral concern, as these children appear in the case loads of child protection, alcohol and other drug, mental health, disability and family services, as well as services in the housing and specialist domestic violence sectors

- **SITUATE** your practice within a gendered understanding of family violence

- **RECOGNISE** the impact of family violence on children and how children live in different contexts of protection and vulnerability, often including other adult issues of alcohol and other drugs and mental health problems

- **UNDERSTAND** the ways in which family violence constitutes an attack on the mother–child relationship

- **ASSESS** risk and safety factors consistent with your role in responding to women and children living with heightened vulnerabilities

- **CONTRIBUTE** to the development of safety plans for women and children escaping violence, recognising that their needs are both separate and interdependent

- **RECOGNISE** that working with children living in the midst of family violence requires multi-agency working within complex legal contexts.

■ Introduction

CHILDREN LIVING IN the midst of family violence experience high levels of fear and confusion as they watch, or become aware of – and sometimes embroiled in – the abuse and violence (physical, emotional, sexual) of the key caring adults in their lives. This 'wicked problem', which defies any easy solution, is essentially a gendered social problem in which the primary victims of violence and abuse are women and their children, though we note that this is the dominant, but not the only, pattern of abuse. This chapter is divided into two parts. In 'Understanding the knowledge base' we address key issues in relation to gender, prevalence and the impact of violence on the lives of women, children and men. In 'Practice responses' we attend to the demands of the practitioner response from the first point of engagement through to supporting safety and accountability within a multi-agency context.

While family violence is a challenging field of practice, it can also be one of the most rewarding. There is a long tradition in domestic violence intervention that has been led by survivors and the women who stood beside them to name and expose this form of violence against women and their children (Hague, Mullender & Aris, 2003). Men have also played an important role in speaking up for relationships without violence and affirming that respectful relationships are at the heart of masculinity (Fisher, 2011). The issues for children were slower to surface (Mullender & Morley, 1994). It is important that their safety and wellbeing be understood to be linked to, as well as separate from, the safety of their mothers (Howarth et al., 2009). We would argue that there are few areas of practice where the individual and the social, the psychological and the political are so closely entwined. As intervention in domestic violence increasingly draws on mainstream organisations (child protection, courts, police, family services), it is essential that practitioners continue to understand their work as being connected to the politics of the social movement, which names domestic and family violence as a deeply rooted social problem that needs to be actively identified and resisted (Nixon & Humphreys, 2010).

■ Understanding the knowledge base

Definitions and terminology are contentious, since they serve to both include as well as exclude significant concepts. Terms such as 'intimate partner violence', 'domestic abuse', 'family violence', 'abuse by known men' and 'batterer violence' are used to explain violence and abuse in intimate relationships. A standard definition is provided in the *Family Violence Protection Act (Vic) 2008*:

> Family violence is any behaviour that in any way controls or dominates a family member that causes them to fear for their, or another family member's, safety or wellbeing. It can include physical, sexual, psychological, emotional or economic abuse and any behaviour that causes a child to hear, witness, or otherwise be exposed to the effects of that behaviour.

This definition emphasises the core element of coercive control and a range of tactics to achieve it and, importantly, includes the impact on children. Other definitions may include mention of the gendered aspects of family violence:

It is most often violent, abusive or intimidating behaviour by a man against a woman.
(NSW Department of Health, 2003, p. 4)

However, for women and men with disabilities the definition needs to include those abused within an institutional setting (which is their home) and by carers who may be intimate in terms of their access to personal space but are not their partners or ex-partners (Healey, Humphreys & Howe, 2013, in press). In the Australian context, the complexity of Indigenous kinship relationships alongside the impact of colonisation and assimilationist policies provides another lens that also needs to be acknowledged:

> *For many Indigenous people the term family violence is preferred as it encompasses all forms of violence in intimate, family and other relationships of mutual obligation and support.*
>
> *(Laing, 2000, p. 1)*

The definition across Australia is contested. We have chosen to use 'family violence' to ensure inclusion of Aboriginal perspectives. However, in making this decision we reiterate that this does not diminish our understanding of the gendered nature of the problem, which will be reflected in the language used. When referring to victims/survivors, female pronouns will be used and perpetrators will generally be referred to as male.

■ Prevalence and gendered issues

The prevalence of family violence and the dominant pattern of men's violence against women and children are generally accepted, but this analysis is not without critics. A number of features of family violence are uncontested. The data from services and organisations that respond to family violence shows an entirely consistent gendered pattern. Women are in the majority of victims seeking help, while men are much more frequently named as the perpetrators of violence and abuse. For example, Victorian data shows that in 2009–10 adult victims included 25 296 women reporting family violence incidents to the police, compared with 6992 males (Diemer, 2012). This pattern is repeated in police data across international jurisdictions; the data consistently shows a pattern of a female victim and a male perpetrator in around 80 per cent of intimate partner violence incidents (Holder, 2007; Scottish Government Statistician Group, 2010).

The data on domestic homicide is also unequivocal. Women are much more likely than men to be murdered by their partners or ex-partners. Australian data is consistent over time and shows women to be the victims in 78 per cent of domestic homicides (Virueda & Payne, 2010), while the 2009/10 British Crime Survey found that 54 per cent of female homicide victims aged 16 or over had been killed by their partner or ex-partner, while this was the case for only 5 per cent of male victims (Smith et al., 2011).

The gender symmetry debates (Dobash et al., 1992) revolve not around the service use data, but whether there is a large group of hidden male victims who are not accessing services. Large population-based surveys and crime surveys are consistent in demonstrating that family violence is a widespread social problem (Mouzos & Makkai, 2004; Smith et al., 2010); however, prevalence rates and the gendered analysis are very dependent upon what and how questions are asked and the approach to data analysis. British Crime Surveys, which use a self-completion model, show that approximately one in four adult women in England and Wales experience some form of non-sexual domestic abuse, including financial and emotional abuse, from the age of 16 (Walby & Allen 2004). However, the surveys also show (using the same definition) that 17 per cent of men report being victims of domestic abuse since the age of 16. The strong gendered differences emerge when the severity of abuse is examined: 81 per cent of all incidents involved male violence towards women; of those who had experienced four or more incidents, 89 per cent were women. Furthermore, women were three times more likely to be living in fear and three times more likely to be injured (Walby & Allen, 2004).

Of equal importance and concern is the data that relates to children living with family violence. Consistent prevalence data is shown in both Australia (Indermaur, 2001) and the UK (Meltzer et al., 2009), with approximately 25 per cent of children and young people reporting having ever lived with family violence, which for 5 per cent was chronic and ongoing.

An understanding of the gendered nature of family violence is significant for practitioners intervening in the area. Many family service practitioners are trained to be gender neutral and fail to recognise that safety may be compromised for women and children if patterns of dominance and control are not recognised and understood in combination with a knowledge of family history and the different perspectives of men, women and children confidentially gleaned from individual interviews.

■ Issues of diversity

This chapter is informed by an approach to diversity that highlights not only the issues of gender but also those of race, class, age and disability. We are drawn to the ideas of 'intersectionality theory', which originally drew strongly from feminism and particularly those women from outside the white mainstream (Almeida &

Lockard, 2005). Intersectionality refers to the interaction between various social divisions such as gender, 'race' or ethnicity, class, ability, age and sexual orientation and describes how each form of oppression 'intersects' with and compounds the effects of others. More recently, these ideas have been used to also take account of the social and structural location of men and the tendency towards 'identity politics' that can underplay the strength of structured relationships of power (Sokoloff & Dupont, 2005; Nixon & Humphreys, 2010). Intersectionality considers how each form of oppression, in combination with others, influences outcomes among women, men and children. Issues of power and privilege are addressed within this framing and can provide a more specific understanding of social location. For example, issues such as the higher prevalence of family violence among some ethnic minority groups largely disappear once socioeconomic factors are controlled for, which results in a more nuanced understanding of the patterns of inequality (Sokoloff & Dupont, 2005). While domestic violence is widespread and cuts across ethnicity and sociodemographics, individual women's vulnerability to, and experience of, violence is mediated through social divisions such as 'race', class, gender and (dis)ability. As an example, women with disabilities can be subjected to different forms of abuse, such as withholding of medication (Nixon & Humphreys, 2010). Men's unemployment increases the likelihood of perpetration of violence, while employment among women buffers exposure to abuse (Walby & Allen, 2004). The finding that employed women are less likely to experience domestic violence has significant implications for groups of women who traditionally lack access to paid employment: women with disabilities, Indigenous women, women from ethnic minority groups, older women and women with young children. Those at the intersection of multiple forms of oppression may be more likely to be subjected to prolonged or more severe violence due to their inability to escape (Nixon & Humphreys, 2010).

The experiences of Indigenous Australian women, among whom violence is likely to be more severe and to have greater impact, can be taken as a case in point (Nixon & Humphreys, 2010). Indigenous women have been found to have a significantly greater risk of hospitalisation for injuries sustained through interpersonal violence, mostly perpetrated by intimate partners rather than their peers (Berry, Harrison & Ryan, 2008). As this is most pronounced in remote areas, it is likely that socioeconomic factors associated with remote living are implicated in morbidity; for example, lack of access to health care, inappropriate housing and unemployment. In addition to poverty, the long-term effects of colonisation and continuing racism contribute to high rates of alcohol and other drug use and violence (Berry, Harrison & Ryan, 2008; see also Chapter 6).

Australian research illustrates how cultural, psychological, social and economic factors compound vulnerability to the effects and outcomes of violence among immigrant and refugee women. Rees and Pease (2007) used extensive qualitative methodology to examine the experiences of communities from Ethiopia, South and North Sudan, Serbia, Bosnia and Croatia, and Iraq. The experience of being a refugee increased women's isolation and reduced awareness of services and laws about domestic violence. Men perceived 'family conflict' to be related to women's new-found independence and to government intervention, which they saw as supportive of women while undermining male authority (see also Chapter 5). Female participants were almost equally divided on whether women are more or less at risk of family violence in Australia, with some arguing that laws are protective and others maintaining that those who seek assistance receive negative reactions from service providers and their own communities. There was evidence that most women do not seek help, due to shame and fear of isolation and poverty for themselves and their children, and due to lack of trust in mainstream domestic violence services. Women and men reported an association between men's unemployment and domestic violence.

■ Adult and child victims

Children may be directly impacted by family violence. However, their wellbeing and safety is also closely tied to the damage that domestic violence does to the relationships with their mother and their father, and sometimes other family members. Understanding the impact of family violence therefore requires attention to the effects on the adult victim(s), the children, and the relationship between the child and each parent.

Family violence is the leading contributor to preventable death, illness and disability for Victorian women under 45 years (VicHealth, 2004). Its severe impact on women's health may be as a direct result of physical trauma, but also can result from the vulnerability to poor health created by lack of sleep (Lowe, Humphreys & Williams, 2007), sexual assault (Heise & Garcia-Moreno, 2002) and serious and disabling acts such as strangulation and burns. To some extent, these detrimental health impacts have been overshadowed by the extensive damage to women's mental health and wellbeing. Study after study shows significantly heightened rates of depression, post-traumatic stress, self-harm and suicide attempts among women subjected to family violence (Golding, 1999). The important World Health Organisation study across 10 countries and 24 000 women showed highly consistent and troubling data about the undermining of women's mental health through exposure to domestic violence (Ellsberg et al., 2008).

The effects on children are clearly related to the disabling impact of violence and abuse on their mothers. In this sense, family violence represents an attack on the mother–child relationship, disabling the mother both directly and indirectly so that her capacity to parent is undermined (Humphreys, Thiara & Skamballis, 2011). Women struggling with depression, trauma and problems with their physical health may be compromised in their ability to respond to their children. Threats that involve children, such as abduction and threats to kill, also compromise 'normal' mothering behaviours. At its most serious, unborn infants are attacked *in utero*: double intentioned violence that abuses both the woman and the child (Kelly, 1994). However, abuse in the post-partum period is equally serious. An infant needs to be able to establish an attuned attachment relationship with their mother, and if she is undermined by physical and emotional abuse, the infant's survival emotionally and physically can be threatened (Jordan & Schetkey, 2009). At each age, children will be affected by the insidious ways in which the tactics of power, control and violence undermine their mother and therefore her ability to respond to their needs (Mullender et al., 2002).

Children and young people may be directly physically or sexually abused by the same person who is abusing their mother. There is also conflicting data about whether they are at increased risk of harsh parenting, with some studies showing an increased risk (Damant et al., 2010) and other studies showing no difference (Radford & Hester, 2006). The data on the co-occurrence of child physical abuse and intimate partner violence varies depending on the study, the site location and the severity of the intimate partner violence (Ross, 1996). Studies suggest that between 30 per cent and 66 per cent of children who suffer physical abuse are also living with domestic abuse (Edleson, 1999; Zanoti-Jeronymo, 2009). Such evidence suggests that, where there is child physical or sexual abuse, questions should be raised about the presence of intimate partner violence. Similarly, the presence of intimate partner violence should prompt exploration of child abuse.

However, the distinction between direct child abuse and its impact on the child may lead to an inaccurate assessment of significant harm. Research is now showing that children are involved in many different ways in the domestic abuse: they may be used as hostages (Goddard & Bedi, 2010); they may be in their mother's arms when an assault occurs (Mullender et al., 2002); they may be involved in defending their mother (Edleson et al., 2003) or they may become aware of the consequences or symptoms of abuse such as bruising or bleeding. Understanding these complexities has led to referring to children as 'living with family violence', rather than using the earlier framing of 'witnessing' violence.

Family violence occurs more frequently in households with children aged under five years (Tomison, 2000 in Richards, 2011). Not surprisingly, children in this age group are disproportionately present during incidents. They have been found to be more susceptible to exposure to severe forms of violence, including the use of weapons and the infliction of major injuries (Fantuzzo & Fusco, 2007). Violence is more likely in households headed by a single female and among minority groups; however, poverty is the overarching risk factor, rather than parenting status or ethnicity (Fantuzzo & Fusco, 2007). Risk of exposure to violence is also heightened when mothers use alcohol or other drugs or suffer depression and/or anxiety (Meltzer et al., 2009).

■ Poly-victimisation for children

Family violence and other forms of abuse frequently co-occur (Goddard & Bedi, 2010). The likelihood of direct violence towards children increases with the severity and frequency of family violence (Jouriles et al., 2008). The terms 'poly-victim' and 'poly-victimisation' are sometimes used in reference to a group of children subjected to multiple forms and repeat episodes of abuse, which occur across different contexts and within different relationships. For example, a child exposed to family violence may also be physically abused, and subject to bullying by peers and property crime. Psychological distress and symptoms are, understandably, extremely high among these children, among whom are a subset of sexually abused children. Poly-victimisation is implicated in the association between victimisation and trauma and poor mental health outcomes for children. This trauma is likely to be cumulative. Younger children are more likely to live with sole parents, while older children are more likely to be in stepfamilies (Finkelhor, Ormrod & Turner, 2009).

■ Issues for men as fathers

Comparatively little attention has been given to research on the attitudes and behaviour of domestic violence perpetrators towards their children (Bromfield et al., 2010). What research there is suggests cause for concern. Qualitative research studies and evaluations point to a significant group of domestic violence perpetrators who have poor parenting skills resulting from their sense of entitlement, self-centred attitudes and over-controlling behaviour (Bancroft & Silverman, 2002; Harne, 2011; Scott & Crooks, 2007) and overuse of physical forms of discipline (smacking) when compared with other fathers (Fox & Benson, 2004). They are more likely to be angry with their children (Holden et al., 1998), hold unrealistic expectations and have poor understanding of child development (Fox & Benson, 2004; Harne, 2011). The evaluation of a Canadian/UK *Caring Dads* program highlighted a subgroup of domestic violence perpetrators who developed a relatively responsive relationship with their children, and were in touch with their children's lives (for example, their health and education needs), but who actively manipulated and undermined the mother–child relationship, sometimes inciting children against their mothers (Scott & Crooks, 2004).

Notwithstanding the negative impact on children, men who use violence in the home continue to have a significant fathering role with their children or stepchildren. A US study of 3824 men who attended court-ordered evaluation after a conviction for assaulting an intimate partner showed that 65.5 per cent of these men had a continuing and direct fathering role (Salisbury, Henning & Holdford, 2009). Similar findings emerge when post-separation parenting orders are examined (Jaffe, Lemon & Poisson, 2003; Humphreys & Harrison, 2003); through consultations with practitioners (Featherstone & Fraser, 2012); and from some early evidence from Australian Men's Behaviour Change programs (Day et al., 2009).

The continuing fathering role that men who use violence play in the lives of children highlights the need for more effective intervention strategies in this area. While a plethora of programs has sprung up within a number of different sectors (men's behaviour change, healing programs for Aboriginal men and fathering programs that address the issues of abuse), the evidence base that can point to significant and positive shifts in attitudes and behaviour is still at an early stage (Stanley, Graham-Kevan & Borthwick, 2012). Moreover, family violence primary prevention campaigns that target the impact of violence on children have shown positive responses from men in the community who have been alerted to the destructive effects of their violence (Donovan, Paterson & Francas, 1999) and again highlight a positive momentum for change.

■ Further adult problems: drugs and alcohol and mental health

There is a well-documented association between substance use and all forms of violence, particularly when other drugs are used in combination with alcohol (Feingold, Kerr & Kapaldi, 2008). Substance-dependent women are more likely to be living with substance-dependent men (Horrigan, Schroeder & Schaffer, 2000). Use of alcohol and other drugs is higher among perpetrators and victims of intimate partner violence (Klostermann & Fals-Stewart, 2006) and increases the likelihood of violent death in the home, either by suicide or homicide, even among those who do not use substances (Rivara et al., 1997). Women are more likely to use as a consequence of violence, while men are more likely to use prior to perpetrating violence (Humphreys et al., 2005). Violence during pregnancy is more likely when men combine the use of alcohol and other drugs (Frank et al., 2002).

While there is general consensus that alcohol and other drugs are not causal, they are a contributing factor in violence. However, the role played is subject to continuing debate, as a range of personal and social factors appear to be implicated. Earlier theories argued that alcohol might contribute to intimate partner violence through reducing inhibitions or by providing social sanction for abusive and violent behaviour (Jewkes, 2002). Nevertheless, intimate partner violence occurs within a social context that includes beliefs and attitudes about gender and violence. Emerging evidence suggests that antisocial behaviour, which tends to be higher among men who use illicit or 'hard' drugs, is more predictive of intimate partner violence than the use of either alcohol or other drugs (Feingold, Kerr & Capaldi, 2008). Intimate partner violence has been found to be more severe among men who use drugs only, compared to men who use alcohol only. This may suggest an association between criminality and lethality (Willson et al., 2000). It lends further support to the relationship between antisocial behaviour and violence. Some substance-using men may be more lethal when sober, perhaps due to the process of withdrawal (Bennett & Williams, 2003).

Alcohol and other drug use, family violence and mental health are intersecting problems. Domestic violence exacerbates women's drug use by increasing the duration and extent of use (Martin, Beaumont & Kupper, 2003). Many women receiving treatment for substance dependence have a dual diagnosis of mental health problems. Women with co-occurring mental health and substance abuse disorders are more likely to report intimate partner violence than those who report only one issue (McPherson, Delva & Cranford, 2007). Exposure to family violence increases for children when mothers have more significant substance use and/or mental health issues. A study of children of mothers in residential rehabilitation for substance misuse revealed that 67 per cent had witnessed adults hitting each other in the home. Rates of violence were higher among children whose mothers reported more recent problems with alcohol and other drug use (Connors-Burrow, Johnson & Whiteside-Mansell, 2009). Similarly, mothers who report higher rates of psychiatric symptoms and related hospitalisations have been found to be more likely to experience intimate partner violence (McPherson, Delva & Cranford, 2007).

■ Practice responses

While family violence intervention has much in common with other forms of intervention in vulnerable families, there are a number of approaches to working with family violence that signify whether women, children and men accessing a service receive an appropriate response to the issue of violence and abuse, whichever agency they contact. This includes workers: engaging in the issues of safety planning and risk assessment; understanding the policy and legal context; and providing advocacy at both an individual and policy level to galvanise a multi-agency response.

Risk assessment, risk management and safety planning

An analysis of risk and the ability to manage risk configures much of the work with vulnerable children and their families (Houston, 2012). Work in the family violence area is no exception. A significant research effort has been undertaken to analyse domestic homicides and serious cases of violence and sexual assault to determine if there are commonalities and patterns in risk factors (Campbell et al., 2007). On the basis of this work, a number of family violence risk assessment frameworks have been developed. A common one in use in the UK concentrates on the risks posed by the perpetrator of violence to designate cases of high risk and potential lethality drawing from both professional judgement and an actuarial assessment.[1] This includes:

- 10 risk factors (from a checklist of 20)
- or 4 significant concerns (drawn from the top 5 risk factors, which include: partner/ex-partner criminal record for violence or drugs; current incident resulted in injuries; use of weapons; threats to kill; partner/ex-partner expressed/behaved in a jealous way or displayed controlling behaviour or obsessive tendencies)
- or 3 police call outs in 12 months
- or an assessment by advocates, police or the victim's perception that their risk is very high, even if they do not meet criteria outlined above (www.caada.org.uk/).

Such an approach is valuable in providing guidelines that help practitioners understand the seriousness of risk. However, there are a number of other issues that need to be considered.

First, the number of risk factors that come to light is almost entirely dependent upon the level of trust and context for the assessment. For instance, a snapshot of Victorian police data on family violence showed only 2 per cent of 886 cases had six or more risk factors. In the same period, a study of women accessing specialist family violence services (mostly referred from police) showed 34 per cent of women with nine or more risk factors. It is clear that, beyond the crisis of the family violence incident and in a different, more trusting context, the emerging story of abuse shows much greater cause for concern than might be revealed initially (www.cfecfw.asn.au/know/research/sector-research-partnership/partnership-projects/family-violence/safer/governance).

---

[1] Actuarial risk assessment refers to the use of a probabilistic tool to determine the likelihood of an adverse outcome.

A similar story could be told in understanding the data from any sector. Unless women are asked about their experience of family violence, they will not disclose the abuse they or their children are suffering. An early study by Hester and Pearson (1998) showed that the rate of family violence that was known about increased dramatically from one-third to two-thirds of women whose children were being seen for sexual assault counselling once assessment questions about domestic violence were routinely asked. Such evidence has led to the establishment of 'screening' for domestic violence, particularly in areas such as maternal and child health. The effectiveness of this strategy is still being explored and the evidence to date about the extent to which policies for routine screening are implemented in practice remains equivocal (Taft et al., 2012). It is clear from a randomised control trial in Victoria that cultural change to support routine questioning about family violence among maternal and child health nurses is difficult to achieve and that enhancements such as training, support and clear guidance are needed (Taft et al., 2012). Nevertheless, given the vulnerability of infants and their mothers in the post-partum period, the provision of access to help via a universal service such as maternal and child health is an opportunity that both government and the profession are recognising as essential.

Such findings raise the second issue that impacts on the effectiveness of risk assessment. This is, namely, that risk assessment needs to be undertaken with the woman and her children as an exploration of risk and protective factors, not as a checklist by a professional from a distance. Such an approach led one of the key exponents in the family violence field, Ellen Pense (2004), to eschew the 'checklist' approach and recommend instead that the establishment of a dialogue with the woman survivor was the most important aspect in the development of a safe and more accurate assessment of risk and an appropriate safety plan. She suggests that the following questions provide the basis for such a conversation:

- Do you think he will seriously injure you or the children? What makes you think that? If not, why not?
- What was the time you were most frightened or injured by him?
- Are things getting worse? Describe the pattern of the abuse (frequency, type severity, escalation).

The establishment of the protective strategies that have been used to date can flow from this dialogue. In this process, risk assessment can be used to establish a supportive relationship between child protection workers and other professionals and survivors of family violence, while still maintaining a focus on issues that are of crucial importance in protecting children.

A third critical issue is that there is a wide range of factors that need to be assessed in understanding risk assessment and safety planning for children living with family violence. For instance, Healy and Bell (2005) name nine areas for assessment:

- the nature of abuse
- the risk to the children posed by the perpetrator
- risks of lethality
- the perpetrator's pattern of assault and coercive behaviours
- the impact of the abuse on the woman
- the impact of abuse on the children
- the impact of the abuse on parenting roles
- protective factors
- outcomes of women's past help-seeking.

This framework draws attention to the fact that children live in different contexts of vulnerability and protection, and blunt assessments that fail to take into account risks (such as the escalation of violence on separation) may increase rather than reduce danger. Safety planning is therefore a critical aspect of practice in the family violence area and is the 'flip side' of risk assessment: a process that requires trust, time and the ability to establish an empowering conversation with a woman that will help her name, identify and assess the basis for her decision-making and the support she will need.

While engaging with risk assessment focused on women and children, the risk and safety of workers should also not be ignored. Workers have a right to feel safe and protected at work. Moreover, there is evidence that workers who do not feel safe are unable to function effectively (Littlechild & Burke, 2006). Their thinking and behaviour may mirror that of the victims of abuse whom they should be attempting to support. Minimisation, avoidance, rationalisation and denial may all feature as responses from workers who lack adequate supervision and are expected to engage in contexts in which their safety is inadequately addressed (Stanley & Goddard, 2002).

The undermining of the worker's effectiveness when their safety is threatened highlights the important role of management within organisations to establish a culture of safety. Strategies can include: having mobile phones; seeing men in the office rather than in the man's home; working in pairs; notifying and working with police where necessary; paying judicious attention to where workers are going and when they will be returning from appointments; checking in with managers on leaving a home visit; actively using risk assessment; recognising signs of immediate mental health problems and evidence of current alcohol and drug intake; and making prior checks of the man's criminal or agency history. The critical issue is that there is a culture of active implementation of safe work practices and consciousness of worker wellbeing established within the organisation.

■ Understanding the policy and legal contexts

Much of the violence and abuse that is perpetrated in intimate partner relationships is at the level of criminal activity or significant harm to children. Sexual assault, stalking, serious injury and the direct abuse of children requires police intervention. An understanding of the policy and legal context is therefore an essential aspect of good practice. Safety planning may well involve gaining access to an intervention order, ensuring that evidence has been collected and is available to the court, or that children have been appropriately referred in line with the legal obligations of the jurisdiction.

The legal context for children and their mothers living with family violence is particularly complicated. Women attempting to separate from violence will often find themselves in a legal quagmire, in which they will need worker support to negotiate their right to protection and to secure safe accommodation. A foundational aspect of family violence intervention in Australia is the Intervention Order (variously called an AVO, Injunction, Protective Order), a civil order granted to prevent future abuse rather than to prosecute for past violence. In most States, it can be taken out by police on behalf of the victim; children can also be named on orders as 'affected family members'. Research on protection orders shows a mixed picture. Women's views of protection orders suggest that a majority of women feel safer and more protected with an order in place (Logan & Walker, 2009). However, there is also a group of women who perceive that the violence became worse, possibly in retaliation for taking their case for protection to court (Spitzberg, 2002), highlighting how important it is to take into account the woman, her context and her fears. Furthermore, it appears there is a group of offenders for whom intervention orders provide little deterrence (Frantzen, San Miguel & Kwak, 2011). This includes offenders involved in stalking (Logan & Walker, 2010), with a previous criminal record (Spitzberg, 2002), who are unemployed (Ko, 2002), younger (Klein, 1996) and have previously seriously injured their victims (Frantzen, San Miguel & Kwak, 2011). Essentially, family violence perpetrators who believe they have something to lose should they be convicted of an offence are most responsive to a protection order (Ko, 2002). Enforcement of the protection order and sanctions for breaching also determine effectiveness. It is argued that consequences need to be timely, graduated and consistent if interventions are to be effective (Gondolf, 2002).

However, it is not only in relation to intervention orders that women and their children require legal advocacy and support. To secure protection and safety, *evidence of abuse* will be required at every turn: to increase the likelihood that children are not abused through post-separation child care arrangements; to protect women and their children from problematic immigration restrictions; to secure finances and limit aptly named 'STDs' (sexually transmitted debts); to action criminal prosecution; to protect children from significant harm; to be eligible for victim compensation; and to have access to safe housing. Because family violence is a largely hidden activity occurring behind closed doors, any worker who witnesses or is given specific evidence of violence has a responsibility to document and record their findings. The adversarial nature of 'his story' versus 'her story' is only able to be fully countered with evidence, and it may only be through this process of evidence-gathering that ongoing safety can be secured.

In some States of Australia, there is a mandate to report to statutory child protection authorities children who are living with domestic and family violence, while in the Northern Territory it is mandatory for every adult to report any family violence whether children are present or not. While there is no evidence to suggest that this is an effective strategy for most children (Stanley et al., 2011; Humphreys, 2008), it nevertheless remains important that workers understand their legal obligations, while recognising that they will need to do much more than refer to child protection to support the safety and wellbeing of children. Children have a right to live free from violence and abuse (Article 19, United Nations Convention on the Rights of the Child [UNCRC]). The shift to 'family sensitive practice', which advocates for the responsibility of all services to respond to children, even where the adult is the primary client accessing the service, has particular relevance when the problem is ubiquitous; and the tertiary child protection service can only respond to a very limited number of referrals. Children living in the midst of family violence will need greater access to community-based services if the aspirations of the UNCRC are to be realised.

■ Multi-agency advocacy at a strategic and operational level

Collaboration between the various services that come into contact with families is needed to prevent and respond to abuse of children (Gondolf, 2002). Furthermore, interventions for vulnerable families such as home visiting for new mothers can be undermined by the presence of family violence (Council on Community Paediatrics, 2009) However, the evidence from the specifically targeted UK *Safety in Numbers* domestic violence research that followed 2500 women with 3600 children over a two-year period demonstrated that an increase in the number of services that surrounded the woman and her children was reflected in a similar rise in the reported level of safety for both women and children (Howarth et al., 2009).

However, the success of the Independent Domestic Violence Advisers, whose role was to advocate to bring the service and domestic violence system around the woman and whose work was evaluated in the *Safety in Numbers* research, cannot be separated from the well-developed inter-agency forums that have been established in every local area of the UK. It is not possible to 'draw the system' around the woman and her children without the establishment of strong collaborative processes that allow responsiveness to referrals and effective intervention through the justice and health systems. These local, strategic, multi-agency partnerships provide the basis for planning as well as the regional network of structures that support flexible collaboration at the front line to provide effective intervention for women and children and accountability for perpetrators of violence (Javdani et al., 2011). However, the presence of a local family violence partnership does not guarantee effective collaboration. Research by Geddes (2006) in this area suggests that an interrelated set of characteristics (history of positive partnering, cohesive local community, strong local champions) create 'virtuous circles' of collaboration or, alternatively, 'vicious circles' (ineffective leadership, limited resources, unresolved accountability issues and the costs of partnership outweighing the benefits). The evidence suggests that translating strategic partnerships into collaborative processes at the front line that increase both safety and accountability is not straightforward.

A number of strategies have been developed that show potential to increase effective multi-agency collaboration. Holding a shared vision and agreed definition of domestic and family violence between organisations is an important starting point. A common risk assessment and agreed strategies for risk management can provide a shared basis for intervention as well as multi-agency training. These strategies may be supported by co-location of workers, shared budgets and strengthened protocols or memoranda of understanding between collaborating agencies (Banks, Dutch & Wang, 2008). Attention to the ways in which confidentiality is preserved and data shared in an area of high risk usually requires extensive discussion and the development of relationships of trust between different agencies.

Of particular importance is the way in which multi-agency working is inclusive of diversity. As previously mentioned, women with disabilities are at a heightened risk of the most severe forms of violence and abuse (Healey, Humphreys & Howe, 2013, in press), as are Aboriginal women and their children (Arney & Westby, 2012). The compounding effects of poverty, trauma, alcohol and other drug abuse and mental health problems contribute to entrapment and isolation and therefore increase the severity and chronic nature of domestic violence. Engaging these service sectors in multi-agency collaborations is essential to creating a more effective and strengthened response to family violence.

ACTIVITY

When she was 10 years old, Linda came to Australia with her mother, who suffers from anxiety. Linda developed few friendships. She dropped out of school at an early age and never held a steady job. As an adult, Linda presented at an obstetric clinic with bruising and cuts to her face after an assault by her substance-using partner, Max. Her unborn infant was notified to child protection for exposure to substance use and domestic violence. Child protection encouraged Linda to separate from Max and directed her to attend a residential early parenting program upon discharge from hospital. Hopeful that parenthood and the desire for an intact family would bring about lasting change in Max, and confident she had the resolve to leave should violence resume, Linda returned to the relationship. By the time her infant, Sophie, was six months old, substance use by both parents increased and violence intensified. Linda called upon child protection to help her escape. A safety plan was put in place. Linda was assisted to attend a detoxification service. The alcohol and other drug (AOD) worker helped her to access transitional housing at an undisclosed address. Child protection continued to monitor Sophie's safety and wellbeing while the AOD service provided counselling for substance use and parenting support.

With a colleague, discuss what barriers might have prevented Linda from leaving her partner. What factors facilitated her eventual separation? What might have been the issues for Sophie? What does this case study tell you about work with Linda and Max? What might be the long-term outcomes for Linda, Max and their daughter?

REFLECTIVE QUESTIONS

Think about a family with whom you may have worked where there was family violence. What factors increased the likelihood and severity of family violence? What form of risk assessment would you use? How confident would you feel about your risk assessment as the basis for risk management and the basis for safety planning to maximise the safety and wellbeing of those family members in jeopardy? Which child or children was/were at increased risk of exposure to violence? Which child or children might experience poorer outcomes? What was the impact on the relationship between the child or children and each parent? What other agencies, if any, were able to assist and how did the different agencies work together?

■ Conclusion

Intervention in family violence has commonalities with other areas of practice; however, particular characteristics highlight good practice in this area. These include: the establishment of a trusting context for assessment that enables exploration of individual risk and protective factors for women and their children; attention on the perpetrator of violence and not allowing other problems such as alcohol and other drug use and mental health issues to detract from a focus on abuse; and the development of safety plans that empower women to identify the basis of their decision-making and the support they require. We need to be reminded that children living in the midst of family violence are children living in the midst of fear. Supporting the safety of both women and children is critical to their human right to live free from violence and abuse.

■ Useful websites

1800 RESPECT: **www.1800respect.org.au**

Australian Domestic and Family Violence Clearinghouse: **www.austdvclearinghouse.unsw.edu.au**

Breaking the Silence: **http://nceta.flinders.edu.au/files/6513/5285/7437/EN469_Nicholas_2012.pdf**

Domestic Violence Resource Centre Victoria: **www.dvrcv.org.au**

New Zealand Family Violence Clearinghouse: **www.nzfvc.org.nz**

Queensland Centre for Domestic and Family Violence Research: **www.noviolence.com.au**

11

Attachment theory: from concept to supporting children in out-of-home care

Sara McLean

■ Learning goals

This chapter will enable you to:

- **DEVELOP** an understanding of attachment theory

- **LEARN** about the scope and limitations of what attachment theory can tell us about supporting vulnerable children

- **CRITICALLY** reflect on the use of attachment ideas and other theoretical perspectives to inform our work with vulnerable families

- **RECOGNISE** examples of practice that do not appear to be based on attachment theory

- **REFLECT** on what trauma and attachment may mean for decisions that are made about children's care.

■ Introduction

AMONG THE DOMINANT conceptual frameworks that workers use in working with vulnerable families and children are trauma, resilience and attachment theory (Bath et al., 2005, Daniel et al., 2009). It has been argued that attachment ideas, in particular, dominate our thinking when it comes to the needs of children in out-of-home care (Bath et al., 2005).

The early attachment experience is thought to be pivotal and influential in a child's development (see Chapter 1). Several types of attachment have been documented, most of which are not considered pathological and commonly occur within 'intact' families. Much of what we know about attachment 'disorder' comes from studies of young children hospitalised in the 1950s and infants and children raised in large institutions, rather than maltreated children placed in foster care or with members of their extended family as a result of child protection intervention. Nonetheless, these early orphanage studies have shaped our beliefs and assumptions about the attachment of children in foster care.

Notions of the concept of attachment can vary widely among the important players in a vulnerable child's life and this highlights the need for conceptual clarity and rigour in applying the concept of attachment to the care of vulnerable children (McLean et al., 2012). Therefore, this chapter will provide an overview of attachment theory and point out its strengths and limitations in supporting vulnerable children, especially those in out-of-home care. Examples of limitations in the translation of concepts into care will be discussed. The opportunity will be provided to critically reflect on concepts in child protection practice and on their application to practice.

■ What is attachment theory?

John Bowlby stated that, as part of evolution, human beings have developed a predisposition to initiate and form attachments (Bowlby, 1969; 1979). While this universal, lifelong drive to form attachments is initially focused by children on their primary caregivers, it can later be directed towards a range of individuals throughout a person's lifespan.

Attachment is defined as a strong disposition to seek proximity to and contact with a preferred caregiver (in Western societies, typically the mother) (Bowlby, 1969). The attachment figure is one who is responsive to the child's attachment needs. Bowlby later broadened the concept of attachment to include not just the child's need, but also the responsiveness and emotional availability of the caregiver. By doing so, he began to use the idea of attachment to account for individual differences in the quality of parent–child interactions.

■ Early experimental studies of attachment

Mary Ainsworth further developed the concept of attachment. She highlighted the cognitive aspect of the infant's world by further broadening attachment theory to take into account the infant's appraisals and expectations of whether or not the caretaker would be available in times of need.

Bowlby originally identified a child's attachment bond as either secure or insecure (Bowlby, 1969). That is, the child either was or wasn't securely attached to their primary caregiver. Since then, further classes of attachment were identified. By studying a child's behaviour during a classic experiment called the Strange Situation (Ainsworth et al., 1978), Mary Ainsworth identified three classifications of attachment organisation. In the Strange Situation experiment, the child's reaction to a stranger and the very brief separation from, and reunification with, the caregiver were carefully coded. See Ainsworth et al. (1978) for more information about the Strange Situation.

In this structured experimental situation, Mary Ainsworth identified three distinct, predictable (or organised) attachment patterns: one described as secure, and two insecure – insecure avoidant and insecure ambivalent (Ainsworth et al., 1969; Ainsworth et al., 1978). Each of Ainsworth's attachment styles was characterised by different attachment behaviour in this highly structured experimental situation. These three different ways of interacting with the caregiver upon separation and reunification were hypothesised to reflect different cognitive expectancies, or 'internal working models' regarding the availability of the caregiver under conditions of stress.

Children who are securely attached are thought to have experienced their caregivers as physically and emotionally available to them. Secure attachment is thought to foster a belief in the availability of the caregiver as a 'secure base' that allows for safe exploration and learning on the part of the infant or toddler. According to attachment theory, securely attached children are thought to have better developmental outcomes and less psychopathology than children with other attachment patterns (Zilberstein, 2006).

The insecure patterns of attachment (insecure avoidant and insecure ambivalent) are thought to represent organised strategies that attempt to maintain proximity to a caregiver who is inconsistently responsive or emotionally unavailable, in different but relatively predictable ways. In an assessment situation such as the Strange Situation,, the child whose attachment is deemed 'avoidant' in its organisation is thought to have developed an expectation of conflict or rejection in response to the expression of their attachment needs at times of stress, and therefore avoids expressing these needs to the caregiver. In this way the child can resolve their needs for proximity to the carer without angering or challenging the carer. The 'ambivalently' attached child, uncertain of their mother's response to their needs, demonstrates angry resistant or passive behaviour towards her. Both of these patterns of attachment behaviour are thought to represent organised (coherent) ways to maintain proximity to the caregiver.

Subsequently, Main identified and added a fourth attachment pattern, insecure *disorganised*, which was thought to reflect a lack of predictable, coherent organisation of attachment behaviour and representations, resulting in inconsistent attachment behaviour in the same stressful assessment situation (Main & Solomon, 1990). In the case of children who present as disorganised in their attachment behaviour, the caregiver is thought to have been simultaneously a source of comfort and fear, leaving the child in an impossible bind. Children with a disorganised attachment are thought to both seek proximity to the caregiver and also fear the caregiver. Accordingly, disorganised children exhibit apparently contradictory behaviour such as freezing, spinning or fearful apprehension towards their attachment figures in this structured assessment situation (Main & Solomon, 1990; Zilberstein, 2006). Children with disorganised attachment are thought to be at the highest risk for behavioural and emotional disorders (Zilberstein, 2006), possibly due to their lack of integration and organisation of behavioural, cognitive and affective attachment representations.

Another category of problem attachment is Reactive Attachment Disorder (RAD) (Diagnostic and Statistical Manual of Mental Disorders, 4th edition, American Psychological Association, 1994). In contrast to the situations described above, this type of attachment is thought to arise in situations of extremely aberrant child-rearing. Most of our information about this disorder comes from studies of children raised in poorly resourced orphanages, in which children were subject to prolonged and extreme emotional and physical neglect. In this type of early caregiving environment, children were observed to develop two different and problematic types of reactive attachment disorders: disinhibited attachment disorder and inhibited attachment disorder. Disinhibited attachment is characterised by poor social boundaries and attempts to gain attention and affection from adults, whether family or strangers. Inhibited attachment disorder is characterised by excessive inhibition and reluctance to express distress and accept comfort when distressed. As you might imagine, these difficulties may be extremely difficult for a subsequent adoptive or foster parent to manage. It is important to note that the situation of children raised under circumstances in which there is no specific caregiver and there is prolonged neglect is fundamentally different from the situation of most children who are placed in foster care, who have generally formed an attachment to a specific carer prior to removal. Nonetheless, the concept of attachment disorder has been influential in child protection.

■ Overview of attachment theory and child development

The attachment relationship that is formed with a child's caregiver is thought to be a powerful foundation for optimal development in a range of areas. Principally, it is thought to influence the development of the child's 'internal working model': a template that reflects the child's expectancies about safety, reliability and worthiness of self and others and acts as a 'filter' through which all other information about the world is processed (Bowlby, 1979). As the child develops, this internal working model becomes increasingly differentiated and elaborated (Sroufe et al., 1999) and is thought to influence many aspects of the child's social relationships.

DeKlyen & Greenberg (2008) have described four main areas of child development that are influenced by early interpersonal experience of attachment. First, attachment experiences form the basis of a child's cognitive development, through the development of the internal working model. Attachment experiences form the basis of the way the child thinks about self and others, the way the child feels about self and others in the world, and whether or not the child has positive expectations of others. Secure attachment is thought to translate to optimal opportunity for cognitive development and learning.

Second, attachment experiences form the basis of a child's capacity for emotional regulation by influencing their ability to experience, tolerate and regulate strong emotions. From early interpersonal interactions with the caregiver, the child learns how to correctly identify and label and express internal states such as emotions. Through this process of co-regulation and soothing on the part of the caregiver, the child learns how to manage and soothe their own emotions. The child who has a secure attachment to their caregiver is thought to experience emotions freely, have good emotional regulation (ability to soothe and calm self at times of stress) and good tolerance for emotions, including stress. Children who do not have optimal development may become emotionally under-regulated, be emotionally labile (sometimes described as overly dramatic) and experience difficulty in self-soothing. Others may become emotionally over-regulated and under-responsive (for example, not crying when hurt) and have difficulty experiencing emotions or even identifying the emotions they experience.

Third, children's behaviour towards caregivers and others is thought to be influenced by early attachment relationships. In very young children, the nature of their attachment is thought to influence their explorative and help-seeking behaviour; whether or not children feel free to explore and investigate the world or feel inhibited due to anxiety about the availability of the caregiver. A secure attachment relationship is thought to allow children to feel safe enough to explore and investigate the world, secure in their expectation about the availability and responsiveness of the caregiver in times of need. In contrast, some children's behaviour can be shaped in less adaptive ways because they have learned that the caregiver is not likely to be responsive to their needs, or is inconsistently responsive. Cooperative behaviour is thought to arise in the context of the capacity to delay gratification and take another's perspective, which in turn develops as a result of caregiver responsiveness and emotional attunement.

Fourth, the attachment experience is thought to influence whether or not a child develops a pro-social orientation in life (DeKlyen & Greenberg, 2008). Children raised with warm and responsive relationships may develop a generalised positive social orientation, be more likely to comply with parental instructions throughout their development (DeKlyen & Greenberg, 2008) and provide motivation and connection with others that deters them from antisocial behaviours (DeKlyen & Greenberg, 2008).

It is argued that this, in turn, determines whether or not social rewards are reinforcing for children.

REFLECTIVE QUESTIONS

Children may experience strengths and difficulties in these four areas as a result of their early caregiving experiences. What might difficulties as a result of early attachment experiences look like in these four main areas of development? What might strengths look like? Would these look different at different developmental stages? If so, how?

■ The importance of theory and evidence in child protection practice

Children who are living in circumstances of poverty, parental mental illness, family conflict, violence and substance abuse are extremely vulnerable to a range of developmental problems.

For some families, the complexities of these issues mean that children may be removed into care due to concerns for their safety. Children placed in out-of-home care may be placed in one of several alternative placements. These may be home-based care, such as foster care or kinship care (that is, with members of the child's extended family), or in small residential group homes.

These children are among the most vulnerable groups of children in the community. Despite the best intentions, placement in out-of-home care may threaten children's relationships, and relationships with family members, school friends, community and culture may be diminished or lost entirely. When children are removed into care, there is usually a focus on reunification of the child with their family and most children admitted to State care return to their parents' care. Ideally, parents are supported to address the issues that are preventing them from providing adequate care to their children so that children can return to them. However, in many cases children live in several different foster families while their parents are supported to address the safety and care concerns. Some may never return to live with their biological families. Sadly, a significant proportion of these children will experience 'placement drift'; that is, they will experience multiple placements for varying lengths of time.

In many cases, the distress these children experience can be expressed as challenging, defiant and self-defeating behaviours that are difficult for carers to manage, as well as being very challenging for parents following reunification. These behavioural issues, among other factors, can mean that children are moved from foster home to foster home, repeatedly experiencing loss of relationships, hope and self-worth. This continuing 'placement drift' and the lack of a stable home environment resulting from placement changes can further entrench children's difficult behaviour and make them more difficult to care for (Rubin et al., 2007). In this way, a vicious cycle can be set up in which past experience teaches them that relationships are not likely to last, and this in turn diminishes their self-worth and teaches them to expect the loss of important people in their lives.

At the present time, there are very few evidence-informed programs that are specifically designed to support children in out-of-home care (Craven & Lee, 2006). In the absence of these programs, children and families may be offered supports that are effective with other groups of children. The issues of children in out-of-home care are complex. They may have been exposed to abuse and neglect, have experienced loss of family and friends, have had repeated changes of school and placement and need to negotiate multiple relationships including relationships with foster carers, kinship carers and biological parents. These issues make it considerably more complex to translate what we know from theory and training, or what works for other children, into effective practice for these vulnerable children.

■ Limitations to our knowledge about the role of attachment for children in out-of-home care

While the theory of attachment is relatively well developed for certain populations, there are important limitations to our knowledge about the attachment needs of school-aged children and for children in out-of-home care and those who have been abused or neglected.

While the needs of infants and toddlers have been well explored, it is still unclear how to conceptualise and assess the attachment needs of older pre-adolescent children (Kerns, 2008). While we can be reasonably confident about assessing a very young child's likely attachment bond by observing their behaviour with their caregiver over a range of situations, this may not be as true for older children who have more developed cognitive, affective and behavioural strategies to cope with attachment needs.

Children entering care are often doing so at an age after which their selective attachments to parents/caregivers have already formed. For these children, the issue becomes the formation of a new attachment to the foster carer or kinship carer in a way that is different from a child's original attachment bonds. There is little systematic data about the age at which it may be difficult for children to develop attachment to new caregivers (Dozier & Rutter, 2008) and whether a child's new attachment relationships confer the same protection as attachment relationships with the child's biological parents (Dozier & Rutter, 2008).

Attachment theory is developmental theory. Much of what we know about the link between attachment and child outcomes is based on longitudinal studies of normal populations or studies of children raised in institutions and subject to long-term neglect in the complete absence of an attachment figure (Zilberstein, 2006). Attachment theory also offers little guidance for clinical interventions for children, especially those who have suffered disrupted attachments. 'Despite more than 20 years since the establishment of "disorders of attachment" there is still no consensual definition or assessment strategy nor are there established guidelines for treatment or management" (O'Connor & Zeanah, 2003, p. 241).

Some concepts from child development theory have such intuitive appeal that they are adopted without reservation. Examples of this are the concept of the traumatised child and the child with attachment difficulties arising from early caregiving experiences. The relevance of the insights from these theories and concepts are so widely accepted that the need to critically and empirically examine these concepts is only cursorily acknowledged (Tucker & MacKenzie, 2012).

Over time, the meaning of theoretical concepts can become broadened or blurred so that they become more of a 'general theory' (Tucker & MacKenzie, 2012, p. 2209) or general term (Werner-Wilson & Davenport, 2003) describing children's needs, rather than a specific concept applied to a well-defined group of children. This may be particularly likely when contemporary research becomes distant from the original source, and often derived from another discipline.

Over time, theoretical constructs can come to be applied to differing populations of children without qualification (Rutter & O'Connor, 2008). For example, a concept from normative child development can be adapted for interventions in clinical populations, more vulnerable groups of children, or children from different developmental stages from those about whom it was originally devised. This is the case with attachment theory. It is a theory of typical child development, whose principles have been applied to a wide variety of populations and age groups.

The way that we are socialised as a professional group during our training can also mean that concepts become understood and applied differently by different professions. Psychological theory can be viewed through a systems lens, or through the lens of psychopathology, child protection, health or child development, depending on the discipline involved. Each professional discipline draws on different practice frameworks, involving implicit assumptions about child development. New theoretical ideas may undergo modification so that they may be accommodated within existing disciplinary frameworks.

Workplace culture can also influence how theoretical concepts are introduced to staff, through prevailing norms, induction, training and supervision. In multidisciplinary and inter-agency settings, concepts may come to be understood differently by different players and this may have negative effects for children. For example, Salmon & Rapport (2005), in discussing the process of inter-agency meetings about children's behaviour, found that '[different] professionals use the same words as each other, but apportion them with different meanings, in the belief that agreement has been reached in conversation, when in fact those conversing are at odds with one another...' (p. 430). It may be critical to identify underlying beliefs about children's development and needs before effective multidisciplinary casework can begin (see Chapter 2).

For all these reasons, it is important to be clear about what it is that we are talking about when we are using these ideas in working with vulnerable children and families. This is important because we are often working with multiple players, and the potential for misunderstanding and miscommunication is great, with the potential to impact negatively on children's lives. It is important to be on guard against such slippage in the translation of theory into practice; or of concepts into care.

■ What examples of conceptual blurring are there in child protection practice?

Children being cared for by child protection services have typically experienced 'trauma' or have been 'traumatised' in one way or another. However, identifying and treating trauma in children in out-of-home care may be hindered by the wide variety of ways in which the term 'trauma' is used (Cameron, Elkins & Guterman, 2006; Klapper, Plummer & Harmon, 2004). In our everyday language the words 'trauma' and 'traumatised' can be used, variously, to mean an overwhelming experience to which it is difficult to adapt (Cameron et al., 2006); a particularly strong reaction to a stressful event (Cameron et al., 2006; Smith, Perrine & Yule, 1998); or a pathological outcome of an identifiable traumatising event (Cameron et al., 2006; Sparta, 2003). These multiple ways of using the term in everyday language make it difficult for us to be clear about what we are saying when caring for children.

To further complicate things, there are two main classifications of trauma that are described in the literature. These are Type I and Type II trauma. Type I trauma occurs when a child is exposed to a discrete traumatising event. For an event to be traumatising, the child must experience an environmental or interpersonal event that threatens their safety or the safety of others, and it must be associated with intense fear, helplessness or horror (DSM-IV; APA 1994). Symptoms of a Type I trauma include intrusive thoughts or images related to the traumatic event (such as flashbacks, dreams), attempts to avoid reminders of the event (such as numbing, avoiding people or places that share characteristics of the event) and increased physiological arousal (such as trouble sleeping, hypervigilance and concentration problems). In Type II trauma, the child is exposed to ongoing or repeated episodes of trauma to which the child may become normalised in some way (Terr, 1991).

The majority of treatment approaches that target the traumatised child conceptualise trauma as a discrete historical event in the child's life. Interventions for Type I trauma involve developing strategies to address the symptoms described above while encouraging the child to reprocess traumatic events in a supportive and safe relationship. Typically, we may think of a traumatised child in terms of having experienced a Type I trauma.

Unfortunately, most children who are removed from their biological families due to care and protection concerns have been subject to multiple and ongoing traumatic events. These may include exposure to domestic violence that they perceive as a threat to self and others. It may also include multiple episodes of sexual or physical abuse, living with chronic parental conflict, or repeatedly witnessing other frightening events involving parents, other adults or community. Therefore, it is important to think of children who are placed in out-of-home care as coming from a background of repeated exposure to trauma, which those children may have come to accept as relatively normal.

The distinction is raised here because it is an important one for working with vulnerable children and families. There are a range of behavioural difficulties associated with Type II trauma (also called complex trauma or developmental trauma disorder). Most importantly, children become physiologically and psychologically adapted to this environment, so that when we are trying to support these children we need to address more than a reaction to a discrete event, as in Type 1 trauma. We also need to address the 'dual problem of exposure and adaptation' to this environment (Arvidson et al., 2011; Spinazzola et al., 2005, p. 433). In situations of ongoing complex trauma, the simultaneous exposure to chronic frightening events and the child's adaptation to the fear response results in a more complex profile of difficulties. These children are likely to experience ongoing problems in regulation of feelings and impulses, memory and attention, self-perception and somatisation (physical symptoms resulting from a psychological disorder), and develop distorted views of self and others (Cook et al., 2005; Ford, 2005; Nader, 2011; van der Kolk et al., 2005).

There is good reason to believe that different approaches targeting these areas of vulnerability (Arvidson et al., 2011; Cook et al., 2005; Nader, 2011) are needed to support children who have experienced Type II or complex trauma (Ford & Courtois, 2009; Kira, 2010; Nader, 2011).

When working in a pressured child protection system, there may be a tendency to minimise the needs of traumatised children. One may think that removing a child from an unsafe environment where they are exposed to traumatic events and into a safe environment would provide sufficient conditions for the child to heal from trauma. Children who have experienced prolonged and cumulative trauma need specifically targeted approaches for each of the domains of development that have been affected. It is important to realise that the provision of safety alone may not be sufficient. In addition, for most children placed in out-of-home care, the removal into care in itself is traumatic. Following placement, many children may be exposed to subsequent trauma in response to repeated placement changes, or exposure to the violence and aggression of other children in placement. Therefore, it is important to be mindful that, when we talk about traumatised children in out-of-home care, the nature of the trauma is qualitatively different in this population, compared to those who have experienced a discrete traumatic event.

■ Attachment can be misunderstood in practice

This chapter has so far provided an overview of the basic concepts of attachment theory and an outline of some of the limitations to our knowledge about how to apply attachment theory and related theories in practice. This next section includes examples of some of the ways in which key stakeholders who support children in out-of-home care talk about the attachment needs of children when discussing their challenging and disruptive behaviour.

The role of attachment theory and attachment ideas have been extremely influential in our thinking about what constitutes the best interests of the child in a range of situations, including separation and divorce, blended families and adoption. It has also been extremely influential in relation to policy and decision-making about placements and reunification. It has been suggested that attachment constructs dominate our thinking and our practice with children in out-of-home care (Bath et al., 2005). This is understandable because we know that the children have often experienced early disruptions in their relationships.

In particular, challenging behaviour that can be exhibited by children in care is frequently accounted for in terms of a child's attachment disorder (Barth et al., 2005; McLean et al., 2012). Managing challenging and disruptive behaviour is a significant issue for carers (Chamberlain et al., 2008) and failure to manage behaviour has significant implications for the child's long-term outcomes in terms of education, employment, social relationships, mental health and likelihood of contact with criminal justice (Courtney et al., 2001). Because all children in out-of-home care have experienced a disruption in at least one early caregiving relationship, the appeal of attachment explanations is obvious. Yet the relationship between attachment experience and behaviour disturbance is complex.

A recent study conducted in South Australia examined how the theory of attachment was used to understand the behaviour and needs of children in care (McLean et al., 2012). The study specifically focused on decisions made about children over the age of four who were exhibiting challenging behaviour. In this study, attachment theory was the most common theory invoked by workers and foster carers when justifying decisions about the placement of children. Attachment theory featured strongly in discussions about whether or not a placement was stable and in deciding what the most suitable supportive relationships for the child were. These are no doubt complex decisions that courts and child protection case workers are regularly required to make in the context of a paucity of evidence and theory to guide decisions about children's lives. Some of the examples that were given in this study will be given below.

■ Practice example 1: some children don't need attachment

In practice, there can sometimes be a minimising or disavowal of the child's attachment needs. Children's challenging behaviour can come to be seen as reflecting limited desire or ability to form an attachment with carers. When children are viewed as having no desire for close and loving relationships with carers, their behaviour is seen as unlikely to change as a result of placement in care due to their 'inability' to form an attachment with a significant adult. Children who have had multiple placements may be especially likely to be discussed in these terms. These children may be assumed as not suitable for being placed in home-based care because there is a belief that they actually don't want to feel close to anyone.

Discussion about the placement and support needs of these children can also minimise their attachment needs. As a result, within the range of options available in out-of-home care, residential care can seem to be the best option for these children because of their attachment difficulties. In residential homes there may be several children living in the same environment and children may be looked after by several rostered staff. There may be less opportunity or requirement to develop long-term relationships with the number of carers in this setting. Placement in an institutional setting with multiple carers is seen to allow them to 'spread out' their attachment among more carers, thereby requiring only a superficial or shallow attachment to any one person.

Here is an example of the way in which the needs of one such child were described in a discussion about where the child should be moved to after the breakdown of the child's foster placement:

But he can't be placed in another foster home, because that will break down and he will go to another one, and another one. So the only option, I think we'll have, in order to prevent further attachment disorder from taking place, is to share the care [among many caregivers], so that in some sense he doesn't [need to] become attached to any one person.

Child welfare caseworker

Another describes her approach to managing children's behaviour:

I tried to always be about the attachment and it is flawed and at times you will never get it to work because the kids are so damaged [that] you will never have the relationship you can use... you can be with them for three years and still not have a relationship that is going to change their behaviour.

Residential care worker

These kinds of descriptions in which children are viewed as damaged and incapable of forming attachments may be frequently encountered in discussions about children in care, especially those with challenging behaviours. These kinds of accounts convey little hope that the child will form an attachment to any significant person. With the best of intentions, children may be denied the opportunity to form lasting relationships if they are seen to prefer not to have significant relationships in their lives. An assumption that a child feels more comfortable in the absence of a reliable attachment figure may serve to rationalise many potentially damaging practices.

REFLECTIVE QUESTIONS
What do you think? Discuss this with another person. Are there some children who do not have the capacity to form an attachment to a carer?

While these views may be commonly encountered in discussions about vulnerable children in out-of-home care, the accuracy of this belief about a child's attachment is challenged by what we know from research. Early studies of adoptive infants that suggested a critical age (6–8 months) after which adopted children had considerable difficulty in forming attachments to adoptive parents may have influenced this belief (Tizard & Rees, 1975). The notion that early neglect may mean that a child is unable to form attachments appears to persist. However, even institutionalised orphans who are subsequently adopted can form a secure attachment to a carer when provided with the right caregiving environment (Zilberstein, 2006)

While it is true that some children who have been institutionalised as infants for longer than six months in the first two years of life can fail to develop specific attachments (Zeanah & Smyke, 2005), a substantial proportion of institutionally deprived children do not show this pattern (Dozier & Rutter, 2008) and children raised in stable home-based care, rather than institutional care, do not show this difficulty with forming a specific attachment to a carer (Dozier & Rutter, 2008). It is also important to remember that the experience the neglected or maltreated child has in the biological family environment is likely to be qualitatively different from the experience of a child raised in institutional care. Even where children have been maltreated by their parents, they nonetheless appear to develop specific attachment relationships with them (Crittenden, 1985; Egeland & Stroufe, 1981; Dozier & Rutter, 2008). Despite this, the notion that some children are not able to form, or do not need, an attachment relationship, persists.

Perhaps most importantly, if we believe that the formation of attachment relationships is not possible or desired by children, it could make us less willing to persist in forming our own relationship with young people in care. Barth et al. (2005), for example, have suggested that an emphasis on attachment explanations among foster carers and professionals may encourage a pessimistic outlook with respect to the possible social and developmental outcomes for the child.

REFLECTIVE QUESTIONS
What might it mean for the child and for those supporting them if the child is seen not to need to form an attachment relationship? What might this mean for how much support the child and carer receive? What other explanations can there be for children who appear not to need or want contact with people?

■ Practice example 2: attachment is a close and trusting relationship

Sometimes attachment can become idealised solely in terms of a close, trusting and dependent relationship, together with the behaviour that demonstrates this intimacy. This is understandable: when we imagine the caregiving relationship between a mother and child, this image often includes the child who freely demonstrates affection and is trusting of the caregiver. In the context of the out-of-home care environment, however, children's less than ideal behaviour towards a foster carer can sometimes be interpreted as being a sign of lack of attachment to the carer.

This caseworker was asked her view about the cause of behaviours shown by children in care:

> It is all attachment-related behaviour, aggressive, the inability to form close relationships, they are hard to get to know, they don't trust, that inability to trust.
>
> Child welfare caseworker

This residential care worker also describes how she recognises attachment in terms of the formation of a close and trusting relationship:

The best thing that works good is relationship building and attachment stuff. So if the young people think that you care about them and you form a close relationship with them... that is when you get that mutual sort of [changed] behaviour.

Residential care worker

What might it mean if a child's attachment to a carer is viewed in terms of the child's capacity to trust and to tolerate affection and intimacy with the carer? This understanding about attachment might reflect an idealised notion of a secure attachment between a carer and a child, in which the child is comfortable to rely and depend on adults and able to form close, intimate relationships. Such an understanding about attachment is potentially problematic when one considers its possible impact in terms of support for the child. While a close and trusting relationship between children and their carers does reflect an attachment bond, the absence of a close and trusting relationship does not necessarily mean that the child has not formed an attachment relationship with their carer. The foster carer and the caseworker may interpret a lack of affectionate behaviour as a lack of attachment or to reflect a poor-quality foster placement.

It is important to emphasise that the absence of warm, affectionate behaviour towards the carer does not indicate an absence of attachment to the carer. You will recall that the behaviour exhibited by children whose attachment bond is classified as avoidant appear aloof, self-reliant and under-expressive of distress and do not seek out caregivers for comfort. Nonetheless, this pattern of attachment bond is relatively common, even among children in the general population, who have not been removed from their principal caregiver. Avoidant attachment is considered within the normal range, even if it does not conform to our idealised or desired notions of close and loving relationships between a carer and child.

REFLECTIVE QUESTIONS
What do you know about why a child may not freely express their emotions, and act as though the carer is not important to them? What might it be like for a carer or a biological parent on reunification, when love and affection is not reciprocated? How could you support carers and parents, as well as children, in this situation?

This kind of aloof behaviour, influenced by early attachment experiences, can be difficult for carers to understand. Seeming indifference to the carer's affection is understandably disheartening for the carer. Workers observing this kind of interaction may be tempted to mistake this extreme self-reliance as a lack of attachment. The child who has formed an ambivalent attachment style also poses a problem for the carer. They may appear overly dramatic in reactions to events, make unreasonable or excessive demands of the carer and be difficult to soothe. In this context, it may be easy for both the carer and the professionals supporting the child to think that the child dislikes the carer, when this may not be the case.

■ Practice example 3: a child should have one primary attachment

Another way in which a child's attachment needs can be interpreted within the out-of-home care sector arises in the context of the multiple relationships that these children are required to manage. A child's capacity for attachment can be treated as though it is somehow limited – that is, as though children can only have a limited number of attachment relationships. Many of those involved in children's lives, with good intentions, become concerned about managing a child's attachment relationships. With the best possible intentions, those supporting children attempt to shape a child's developing attachment so that the child becomes attached to the most suitable adult, rather than managing and negotiating the child's multiple relationships. This view then shapes decisions about children's relationships and placements.

> What happened [was] that around Christmas time, he became so attached to us, he wanted to come and live with us. So at that point, after Christmas, I had to say to everybody we have to review this… we need to have a transition where we have him come every four weeks, and then every six weeks cause his primary attachment should be with his long-term family and so that's what we did.
>
> Respite foster carer

In this example, a case plan was put in place to 'fade out' the respite foster carer from the child's life in the hope that he would become more attached to the long-term carer. There are plans put in place to prevent the child becoming 'too strongly attached' to the respite carer, whereas the more 'appropriate' attachment was deemed to be with the primary carer. For caregivers and professionals alike, this may also result in a belief in the need to remove themselves from the young person's life so as not to interfere with the formation of new (more appropriate) attachments.

> Another thing we had to do because I had him since he was 5 and he is now 14, so I spent about 8 years with him, so there was too much attachment – where it was good attachment but he was starting to become too reliant of me… I spoke to the social workers and I left… I still keep in contact with him once a month.
>
> Residential care worker

This kind of practice seems to come from an idea that a child should ideally be attached to only one person, and that the child's capacity to form attachment is somehow limited. There may sometimes be an assumption that their attachment to one carer automatically diminishes the 'strength' of their attachment to another significant person. Those supporting the child can then inadvertently encourage a child's attachment to one person over another. In the out-of-home care context, this may take the form of manoeuvring frequency of contact between a child and potential carers or relationships. This kind of approach can divert attention from the need to simultaneously maintain and strengthen the child's multiple attachment relationships (such as with parents, relatives, foster carers).

REFLECTIVE QUESTIONS

Take a moment to think about your own childhood. Did you have deep attachments with more than one person? How were these relationships formed? What would it have felt like to lose contact with significant people in your life?

Initially, it may be difficult to understand this practice. However, from the perspective of the workers involved, adopting an 'emotionally detached' style may be rationalised as minimising the distress of separation (Rutter, 2008, p. 960).

The idea that a child should be encouraged towards a primary attachment figure warrants examination. Bowlby described the infant's preferred caregiver as their primary attachment figure (in Western societies this has typically been the mother), and other caregivers as subsidiary, or tertiary, thereby introducing the notion of a hierarchical organisation to a child's attachment figures, or 'monotropy'. Bowlby was the first to introduce the idea of monotropy – in which infants form an initial or primary attachment to their mothers before forming later attachments to other people – and that this represented the optimal developmental conditions. This was a theory put forward, but subsequent research reviews have concluded that even infants can form attachments to multiple caregivers simultaneously, rather than sequentially (Lamb, 2012). The literature on cultural issues in attachment (for example, Ryan, 2011), multiple caregivers (Howes, 1999; Howes & Spieker, 2008) and attachment in middle childhood and beyond (Kobak et al., 2005; Kobak et al., 2007; Laible, 2005) call into question the necessarily hierarchical nature of attachment relationships and therefore the notion of a primary attachment figure and primary attachment needs for older children.

In reality, there is often great uncertainty about whether, and if, a child placed in out-of-home care will be reunited with their family. The role of the foster carer in the meantime is to provide safety, nurturance and emotional containment to the child at a time of great uncertainty. This is often a difficult task for carers. The worker's role may be to acknowledge, support and strengthen children's multiple attachments and support their loyalties to both foster/kinship carer and biological parents.

■ Enhancing practice in out-of-home care

This chapter has provided an overview of the basic concepts of attachment theory and an outline of some of the limitations to our knowledge about how to apply attachment theory in practice. It is not the intention of this chapter to argue that attachment difficulties and attachment history do not contribute to the difficulties of children in out-of-home care. However, it is important to highlight the limitations in our current knowledge about the attachment needs of children in out-of-home care.

Early disruptions in attachment relationships, arising from removal into care and subsequent placement drift, are undoubtedly a risk factor for later mental health and behavioural issues. But the relative impact of attachment issues is likely to differ according to the developmental stage of the child.

Rutter (2008) has also argued that the popularity of attachment theory has led uncritical enthusiasts to neglect the role of social relationships more broadly (see also Dunn, 1993; Stroufe, 1988) and has had a disproportionate influence on child welfare policy and decision-making (Rutter, 2008).

This raises the question of how to best draw on attachment ideas to inform work with vulnerable families, including foster carers and kinship carers.

First and foremost, in making casework decisions, we need to be mindful that children in care have had at least one disrupted attachment relationship. While their attachment to their parents may not have been secure, due to abuse, neglect or chaotic and frightening environments, they are likely nonetheless to have an attachment to biological parents, siblings and extended family members depending on their age. While the child may have been removed for their own safety, the child's attachment to a parent is likely to continue.

In supporting carers in their often difficult relationship with children, it may be to highlight the rewards of foster care by focusing on factors external to the child; for example, gaining satisfaction from watching the child play well with peers, rather than through the child being openly affectionate with the carer (McDonald, 2011). Fostering a child with insecure or disrupted attachment can be difficult (Golding, 2006, 2008; Howe & Fearnley, 2003) and can take a high emotional toll on carers (Golding, 2006, 2008; Howe & Fearnley, 2003; Nutt, 2006). Children may unintentionally invite new carers into parenting behaviour that echoes that of their earlier caregivers (Golding, 2006; Stovall-McClough & Dozier, 2004). As a result, carers may unconsciously make decisions about managing their attachment to and emotional investment in the child (McDonald, 2011; Nutt, 2006). Paradoxically, the experience of consistent, ongoing, responsive caregiving may be what is needed to support children with disrupted attachments (Golding, 2006); therefore it is important to support carers to appropriately balance the need for personal space and respite with the need to engage with the child.

■ Conclusion

In this chapter, the importance of drawing on theory and evidence in order to support vulnerable children has been explored. It outlined some of the ways in which child development theory needs to be interpreted carefully for children in out-of-home care, using examples from two key theories relevant to child protection: trauma theory and attachment theory. In translating dominant theoretical concepts such as trauma and attachment into practice, it is important to work in evidence-informed ways. Unfortunately, when dealing with complex issues and vulnerable families, there are significant gaps and limitations in our knowledge about the application of theory and research to specific children and situations.

In the pressured environment of child protection practice, it is critical to guard against slippage in the application of theory into practice. Working in a multidisciplinary setting presents particular challenges and the potential for miscommunication and misunderstanding of theory may be magnified. Collaborative partnership with other professionals and carers is needed to maximise support for vulnerable children in out-of-home care. This partnership should be based on sound understanding of normal child development needs, including the need to support the growth and maintenance of children's attachment relationships.

■ Useful websites

Australian Centre for Child Protection: **www.unisa.edu.au/childprotection**

Child Welfare Information Gateway Attachment Resources: **www.childwelfare. gov/can/impact/development/attachment.cfm**

Use of attachment theory when working with children in foster care: **www.community.nsw.gov.au/docswr/_assets/main/documents/research_ attachment.pdf**

12

Understanding the journey of parents whose children are in out-of-home care

Mary Salveron and Fiona Arney

■ Learning goals

This chapter will enable you to:

- **UNDERSTAND** the experiences of parents when their children have been removed and placed in out-of-home care

- **RECOGNISE** the various ways in which parental identity can be disconfirmed and interrupted after the removal of children from parents

- **UNDERSTAND** how parents negotiate and reconstruct their parent identities after the removal of their children and placement in out-of-home care

- **LEARN** how practitioners may engage parents whose children have been removed and placed in care and facilitate self-recovery

- **UNDERSTAND** the importance of parent–worker relationships and social support in helping parents reconstruct their parent identities and become better able to safely care for their children.

■ Introduction

THERE IS SERIOUS concern in Australia and other developing countries about the increasing rates of children living in out-of-home care (Bromfield & Osborn, 2007; Cashmore et al., 2006). The 2012 Australian Institute of Health and Welfare (AIHW) report on child protection has reported a twofold increase in the last decade from 18 241 children recorded in out-of-home care on 30 June 2001 to 37 648 children in care on 30 June 2011. Currently, the rate of children in out-of-home care in Australia is 7.3 per thousand children (37 648 children), although there is a very marked range between jurisdictions, with New South Wales having twice the rate of children in care as Victoria (AIHW, 2011). These statistics reflect similar increases in English-speaking countries such as England, the Republic of Ireland and the United Sates (Department for Education and Skills, 2006; Health Social Services and Public Safety, 2006). This is due to a combination of increasing numbers of child abuse and neglect notifications and problems associated with children not getting an earlier intervention, escalating numbers of children requiring care, the need to secure permanent placements in an arena with reduced placement options, and a crisis in recruiting and retaining suitable foster carers (Barber & Gilbertson, 2001; Bromfield et al., 2007; Bromfield & Osborn, 2007). Research has also revealed that children are staying in care longer and entering care at a younger age (Bromfield & Osborn, 2007). Disturbingly, compared to previous cohorts of children, the children currently entering out-of-home care present with more complex needs and problems, possibly because of prolonged exposure to maltreatment and disruption, and this is associated with placement instability (Bromfield & Osborn, 2007). Furthermore, this may also be related to an increase in the prevalence of parents with drug and alcohol problems, mental health problems and intellectual disability, and also to the recent inclusion of exposure to family violence as a form of child maltreatment (Richards, 2011). It is also a function of a trend in the increasing use of kinship care, which has a lower reunification rate than foster care (Winokur et al., 2008).

Given the lack of placement options for children, practitioners working in child protection, out-of-home care and child and family services are under enormous pressure. While the policy and practice preference is for children at risk of child abuse to remain safely at home or, if removed, to be safely reunified with their birth families, increasing numbers of families are presenting to child protection systems with a constellation of chronic and underlying issues including domestic violence, mental health issues and substance abuse that need to be appropriately addressed to ensure the safety and wellbeing of children (AIHW, 2009). These families can be challenging, hard to reach and difficult to engage.

When children enter care, a significant component of case-planning generally involves contact between parents and their children in care. However, the complexity of parent–child contact means that courts and child protection services must balance the degree and reasons for maintaining contact with the permanency needs of the child. If parent–child reunification is the goal, then frequent family contact between children and their family is usually prioritised to prepare both children, parents and significant others for the return home. On the other hand, if the case plan is long-term out-of-home care, less frequent contact may occur, with the main aim of contact being the preservation of the child's links, connections and ties with their biological and/or cultural heritage (Panozzo, Osborn & Bromfield, 2007, Scott, O'Neill & Minge, 2005).

Research has revealed that parent–child contact may: maintain the child's identity and connectedness to his or her family (Neil & Howe, 2004; Thoburn, 2004); impact positively on the child's psychological wellbeing (Barber & Delfabbro, 2004; Quinton et al., 1997); and maintain parent–child attachment (Barber & Delfabbro, 2004; Littner, 1975). The importance of contact is also evident in the context of adoption and fostering, where it has been found that some children seek out their birth parents (Logan, 2010; Macaskill, 2002; Quinton et al., 1997). It is, however, also widely acknowledged that parent–child contact may not always be a positive experience for children, with research showing that this is particularly the case for children whose parents have substance misuse problems and serious mental illness (Fanshel, 1975; Lawder, Poulin & Andrews, 1986; Taplin, 2005).

■ Characteristics of parents of children in out-of-home care

Currently, there are no national data available about why children are placed in out-of-home care (AIHW, 2011). A significant body of research has profiled families facing social disadvantage and chronic, multiple and interlinked problems associated with poverty, mental health issues, family violence, addictions, sole parenting, disabilities, homelessness, unemployment and isolation. The interplay of these social and environmental factors impact on parents' abilities to effectively meet the basic needs of their children, including food, shelter, clothing, health care and the provision of adequate parenting. In addition, these parents may have limited parenting knowledge, lack positive parenting role models and experience difficulties coping with stress (Bromfield & Higgins, 2005; Cashmore & Paxman, 1996; Fernandez, 1996; Fisher et al., 1986; Jenkins & Norman, 1972; Kroll & Taylor, 2000; Maluccio & Ainsworth, 2003; Marsh et al., 2006; McConnell & Llewellyn, 2005; Millham et al., 1986; Odyssey Institute of Studies, 2004; Rutman et al., 2002; Thomson & Thorpe, 2003). It is the accumulation of these risk factors that lead to child protection involvement (Schorr & Marchand, 2007).

Recently, Delfabbro et al. (2012) compiled a national profile (excluding Northern Territory, Australian Capital Territory and Western Australia) of parental characteristics of children in out-of-home care, revealing 69.4 per cent experiencing parental substance abuse, 65.2 per cent experiencing domestic violence and 62.2 per cent with mental health problems. Other characteristics include poor parenting skills (73.3 per cent), no protective adult (69 per cent) and an emotionally abusive environment (66 per cent).

The interlinked and intergenerational nature of these social and environmental stressors facing parents whose children have been placed in care also negatively influence their engagement with services and propensity to seek help (Kovalesky, 2001; D. Scott, O'Neill & Minge, 2005) Often, these parents have not yet recovered from their own childhood traumas of abuse, neglect, loss or social isolation, as many have themselves been in State care (MacKinnon, 1998; Thomson & Thorpe, 2003).The study by Delfabbro et al. (2012) found that approximately 6 to 18 per cent of children in care come from parents who themselves were also previously in out-of-home care.

The marked overrepresentation of Aboriginal and Torres Strait Islander children in comparison to non-Aboriginal children has been evident in child protection and out-of-home care services since data was first collected by the AIHW in 1990 (AIHW, 2011; Lamont, 2011). This overrepresentation has been attributed to an interplay of historical factors stemming from the legacy of past policies of forced removal from their families of some Aboriginal children (known as the 'Stolen Generations'), perceptions around differences in child-rearing practices, overcrowded and inadequate housing, family violence and alcohol and drug abuse (AIHW, 2011; Berlyn, Bromfield & Lamont, 2011). Compared to non-Aboriginal children, Aboriginal and Torres Strait Islander children are almost 10 times more likely to be removed from their families and placed in care (Berlyn et al., 2011).

■ Involving parents and families in care and protection practice

As outlined in the National Out-Of-Home Care Standards (Department of Families, Housing & Community Services and Indigenous Affairs together with the National Framework Implementation Working Group, 2011), out-of-home care services are designed to provide a safe environment for children, contribute to improving their developmental outcomes and assist in addressing issues that led to the out-of-home care placement. Across Australia, when children are placed in care, the relevant department in each State or Territory becomes the corporate parent and each child is assigned a case worker to represent, advocate and support them to meet their needs.

While much of the research in out-of-home care has rightly focused on meeting the needs and stability of children and supporting carers in their roles, there exists a major gap in existing support structures for parents, especially after children have been placed in out-of-home care (Hansen & Ainsworth, 2008; Schofield, 2009; Thorpe, 2007). However, while the structure of the child and family services sector across Australia is fragmented, there exist many promising, innovative and creative programs that support parents and families. Programs and services vary enormously between jurisdictions, and most are provided by community service organisations that receive short-term funding from governments through competitive tendering processes.

■ Maintaining connections between children in out-of-home care and their parents

The experience of child abuse and neglect and the process of removal from their parents and families has lifelong consequences for children (Bruskas, 2008). Children often experience confusion and emotional strain as they grapple to understand separation from their birth families and adjust to the out-of-home care environment. Facilitating contact between children and their birth parents requires an understanding of the emotional and psychological experiences of both children and their parents. This may shape the nature of the contact experience and its effects.

For some children, parent–child contact may serve as a traumatic reminder of the experiences prior to coming into care, as well as the event of removal and the experiences of separation itself (Taplin, 2005, as cited in Pithouse & Parry, 1997).

A consequence of parent–child contact can be the emotional distress experienced by children at various stages of the visit – before (distress linked to initial separation, or children not wanting to see their parents) (Haight et al., 2002) and/or after the visit (distress linked upon separation from parents or from re-traumatisation) (McMahon, 1998; Wilson & Sinclair, 2004). In these cases, some carers have deemed contact as problematic and disruptive, as children exhibited nightmares and aggression and displayed internalising and externalising behaviours (Moyers, Farmer & Lipscombe, 2006; Wilson & Sinclair, 2004). However, emotional distress in children may also be the child exhibiting attachment to the parent, and in such cases these behaviours need to be normalised and managed by the carer. The literature has, however, been consistent with regard to children and young people preferring to have more contact with their family while in care. A study in Queensland showed that nearly 17 per cent of Aboriginal and Torres Strait Islander children reported wanting more contact with their parents (Commission for Children and Young People and Child Guardian, 2013), and research from New South Wales has indicated that a significant number of children return to birth families when they leave care (Cashmore & Paxman, 2007).

The literature regarding parent–child contact has revealed quality contact to be associated with the child's emotional and behavioural wellbeing and intellectual development, in that children who have more frequent contact with parents also display better adjustment and good self-esteem, and exhibit fewer internalising and externalising behaviours (Barber & Delfabbro, 2004; Cantos, Gries & Slis, 1997; Fanshel & Shinn, 1978; Quinton et al., 1997).

Parent–child contact also affords opportunities to preserve links and the cultural identity of children in out-of-home care (Burry & Wright, 2006; Ellenbogen & Wekerle, 2008; Mapp, 2002; Thoburn, 2004). The preservation of these links is particularly important for Aboriginal and Torres Strait Islander children, given the

LIVERPOOL JOHN MOORES UNIVERSITY
LEARNING SERVICES

cultural significance of family and maintaining positive identities of children. Quality contact can promote the maintenance or building of attachment and meets the child's emotional needs for love and a sense of belonging, stability and continuity (Mason & Gibson, 2004). The same is likely to be true for children from culturally and linguistically diverse backgrounds, although this is an under-researched area.

■ Negotiation and reconstruction of parent identities after child removal

Very little research has explored the psychological impacts of child removal and related child protection intervention on parents, or on the ability or desire of parents to maintain relationships and make the lifestyle and parenting changes necessary for them to maintain a role in their children's lives. In the remainder of this chapter, we explore the findings from a qualitative study conducted by the first author into the identity trauma and recovery process experienced by parents who had had their children removed from their care (Salveron, 2012). This research involved a grounded theory analysis of 58 interviews with parents, carers and workers about the psychological factors that inhibit or promote the maintenance of relationships between birth parents and children through contact.

■ The impact of child removal on parental emotions and sense of self

Parents in this study spoke about leading lives that were better than they themselves were afforded by their own families. Parents, carers and workers also spoke of histories of parental trauma, previous poor attachments and relationships with their own parents. Parents described doing the best they could against benchmarks for parenting that might have been quite low. This mother of two spoke about her negative childhood experiences and poor connections with her mother.

> You know I always wanted a family, my mother was horrible and I always wanted to have kids so I could have a proper family because my mother, she wasn't very nice and when she was being nice she was being nice to other people. We didn't have a very easy upbringing. Most of the time we were just being ignored and I always just wanted to make up for all the lost play time and I've missed out on both of my kids learning to walk and things like that I can never get that back…

It is important for practitioners, parents and carers to differentiate the behaviours, family context and lifestyles of parents from the 'person who is parent'. Parents in this study spoke of experiencing a range of problems, including a combination of mental health issues (feelings of depression, anxiety, excessive stress, personality disorders), substance abuse (excessive drinking, regular use of illegal substances), domestic violence, relationship breakdown (multiple partners and relationships) and poverty (financial issues, not having money for food and basic essentials). Parents also spoke about not having stable housing and accommodation for themselves and their children (moving from shelter to shelter to different friends' houses) and poor physical health. Some of the parents also had intellectual disabilities, were isolated and had poor family and social support. For a majority of the parents, experiences of grief and loss, drug and alcohol abuse, family violence and mental illness may be responses or signs to previous histories of trauma/identity trauma. As a result, these behavioural coping responses may then interfere and overtake the caregiving role of parents, subsuming or numbing their identity as parent.

> I had a mental illness. Umm … I'd been beaten up and was living isolated in a house that wasn't of a living standard for a family to be quite honest. I had more on my plate than I could deal with because we had so many animals but I didn't know a way out. I was so sick. I couldn't see that there was anything wrong.
>
> Parent

For all parents the removal of their children marked a crisis that was accompanied by painful and intense emotions, as detailed in Figure 12.1. When asked how parents felt after their children were removed and placed in care, most reported strong feelings of distress, anxiety, grief, heartbreak, emptiness, worthlessness, insignificance and failure. Having children physically removed in front of them and/or children taken away without their knowledge (for example, children not being there when parents went to pick them up from school) was perceived by parents as unjust, unfair and wrong.

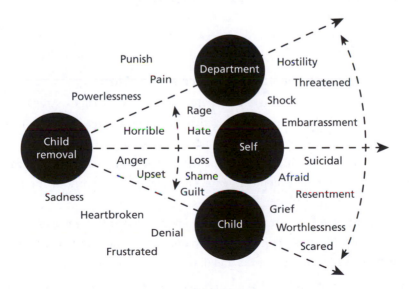

Figure 12.1   Parental emotions surrounding removal of their child or children and after removal

The removal of children from parents was experienced as highly traumatic, often signalling an enormous discrepancy between parents' perceptions of themselves, in particular whether they were still parents or not and how others would view them, as demonstrated by this parent and worker.

We weren't parents any more. They were taken from us.

Parent

Oh they've just lost everything … you know for some parents there's just nothing worth living for once the kids have gone … you've taken their life away from them because that's what they live for even though they don't know they haven't been good parents, they're still their kids and they still love them, no matter how bad they are, they still love their kids.

Worker

The emotions parents reported (such as sadness, devastation, grief, shock, failure and a deep sense of loss) when their children were removed were not only directed towards the statutory child protection service but also directed towards themselves and their responsibility or role in losing their children. Some parents had difficulty describing the actual time and events that occurred before and during removal, with two parents saying that they did not ever want to recall that time again. Some parents even spoke about ending their own lives.

I felt like I'd failed, to be quite honest. I felt like I had failed being a mum that I wanted to be and wasn't. I think that was the worst part of it when she actually got taken. Because I just broke down and cried. I couldn't stop crying that whole time. For the next few days I was just right downhill.

Parent

■ Fighting internal and external battles

The impact of child removal led to what parents described as a fight, struggle or battle for identity that had both positive–negative and internal and external dimensions (see Figure 12.2). This 'fighting' subsequently affected parents' interactions with others in the environment or context, including their relationships and engagement with workers, other family members, carers and, most importantly, their relationship and reconnection with their children.

Parents expressed hate, resentment and anguish towards the workers physically responsible for taking their children. Some parents chose not to engage with workers; some shouted, yelled, threw objects and did not cooperate with hem.

Some … plenty of parents hate us as you can imagine. Some get over that, some don't. I mean I like to think I get on with parents pretty well but they've all got baggage from the past.

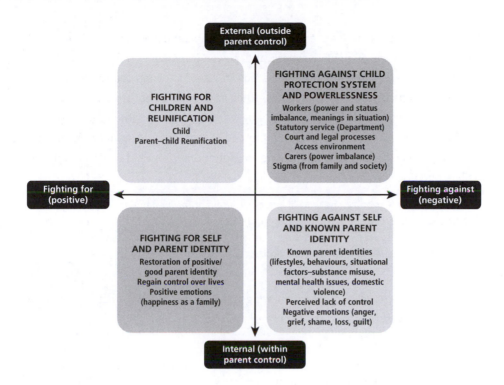

Figure 12.2 Aspects of parents fighting for and fighting against (with internal and external dimensions)

They've dealt with other social workers from [the child protection agency] who have had to do the awful process of removing their kids from them so you can imagine we're all tarred with the same reputation.

Worker

These strong negative emotions were associated with disengagement behaviours such as withdrawal, avoidance of workers, missed appointments, tardiness and what was interpreted as lack of motivation. Despite this worker's motivation and efforts to reunify the father with his children, engagement and connection with the worker and the process was difficult to achieve.

He wouldn't really engage in any part of the process. We were actually wanting to return the children into his care but he wouldn't participate in anything so we couldn't really assess whether he was able to and what we were seeing … he wasn't even able to come to the meeting to come and talk about the reunification plan so as much as he did love his kids and he was constantly on the phone to me, he just would not participate in any way of getting them back or have contact with them.

Worker

For parents, there existed an enormous power imbalance between workers and parents. The themes of powerlessness and power imbalances resonate with the findings of Dumbrill's (2006) qualitative study in Canada, which found two ways in which parents perceived worker power: either as a form of control or as support. Parents who viewed power being exercised by workers to control them fought openly with workers or 'played the game' and pretended to cooperate with workers. This mother highlights the power of the worker to deduct time from her access visit if she was late and also even end it altogether.

> I didn't like her – because she wasn't interested in me or in my daughter. She was just interested in the bookwork – whatever happened was written on paper. She would be on our case. She would deduct five minutes if we were late … stop access because I said the wrong thing – everything had to be perfect and clockwork.
>
> Parent

Another parent spoke of resentment, fighting and powerlessness against an authority that had the power to remove children from their families.

> You resent them enough as it is when they first take your kids away. [Child protection workers] say why do we fight with the Department so much, why do they think we fight them so hard because if I had known that strangers can just walk into your home and say 'we're taking your children and there's nothing you can do … there's nobody that you can go to' and say 'is this allowed?', you just take their word on it [crying]…
>
> Parent

On the other hand, parents who perceived workers to be using their power to support and help them developed positive working relationships and partnerships with their workers. Mandell (2008) maintains that the power imbalance will always exist and cannot be eliminated, even when workers exercise self-awareness and kindness and are careful in their interactions with parents involved with statutory child protection intervention. (See also Chapter 8 for a discussion of this in the context of family support work with families where neglect has been identified.)

As well as fighting against factors outside themselves, parents were simultaneously fighting against factors within themselves, including their lifestyles, behaviours and emotions. After the removal of their children, parents reported feeling a sense of shame, embarrassment, worthlessness and resentment. These emotions changed over time and because of the sense of grief and loss, some parents spoke of drinking and taking drugs that 'numbed their pain'.

The assault on their parent identities as a result of the removal of their children signalled a major disruption to their sense of self, and the lives they had learnt to live and know, which were now regarded by others as dysfunctional and bad (as reflected by external others such as statutory workers). This contradiction, according to Schofield and Ward (2011), leads to the cognitive dissonance that parents experience contributing to their psychological stress and negative emotions. The following worker speculates about the factors that inhibit parents from contacting their children in care and highlights the influence of internal elements.

> I think it has a lot to do with what's inside themselves, how they are functioning, how they are feeling. I think parents probably lose hope a lot of the time because it's too hard. I think people get overwhelmed, I'm thinking about one mother in particular who I'm working with at the moment, she's got a lot stacked against her and it's too much she has to change. I don't fully understand why you wouldn't come to your fortnightly visits, because she only sees him fortnightly anyway but why you wouldn't come for that hour in a fortnight but maybe … Could it be that there is [a] feeling that when everything is going downhill for that person the contact goes as well, maybe it's a shame factor, maybe because of the drugs she simply can't get herself organised to come up…
>
> Worker

Parents were fighting within themselves in order to regain control of their lives and restore their parent identities. Mansell and Carey (2009, p. 338) articulate that 'life is a constant process of comparing how things are with how we want them to be and if they do not match, doing something to make them closer to how we want them to be'.

> … what helps me in myself feel best about myself is being in control of myself and when they're running your whole life and including the kid's life, you feel like you're out of control of your own life because you don't have any say. Even what psychiatrist you see or you can't even talk to your family doctor about how you're feeling because you have to sign an agreement that everything you say to your doctor is for [the child protection service] and your psychiatrist. You don't have any private life any more. That's what makes it hard.
>
> Parent

For this young parent, her family and social support were critical in her positive struggle to be with her child again, and in reminding herself of her need and desire to be a good parent.

> My Mum and my Dad definitely. Both of my foster parents. They were telling me but as well as the last thing that Mum said to me was do you want [child] to grow up hating you? That I took to heart and I thought 'no I don't want [child] to hate me when he's older'. I need to be a good parent, I need to, I want to, I have to…
>
> Parent

The most obvious reason or motivation for fighting was for parents' children, specifically to have them returned to their care. This mother feels whole again when she is with her children, and emphasises missing parts of herself without them. She talks about being a proud mother when she is with her children.

> What made me really want to get the kids back is that I know I'm lost without them. There's a part of me that's not here. I need those little pieces to come back to make me whole again. I don't feel myself unless they're with me like when we see them, when we get to take them out, I feel whole, I feel proud, I can hold my head up, so to speak, while I'm walking around with the children because I've got them for three hours, I'm whole again. Can you understand? When they go, I feel a little bit sad and everything but each time that they go they take a little bit of me with them and they know that.
>
> Parent

REFLECTIVE QUESTIONS

Imagine you have just finished meeting with a parent whose three children have just been removed. What impact may removal have on their identity as a parent?

What emotions may the parent be feeling and what behaviour may they be displaying?

What may such emotions and behaviour evoke within you, and what may you need to help you work effectively with this parent?

■ Reconstructing parental identity and recovery after child removal

Face-to-face access and contact between parents and their children enabled parents to enact their parenting roles and achieve a progression from fighting against themselves and the child protection system and processes, to fighting for their children and for themselves and their parent identities. In negotiating the struggle, parents began the journey of self-recovery, which included getting in the right state of mind, reviving hope and strengthening determination and the management of their emotions (see Figure 12.3). Fighting constructively for their children and their parent identity assisted parents with the trauma of removal to engage with workers and begin the reconstruction of their identities. Fighting constructively meant harnessing their cognitive, emotional, physical and spiritual resources in their fight to get their children back.

> I put access number one. If I have got appointments or anything else they come after that. My daily life is built around the access days ... it's the only time I really get to see her. Like I don't get to see her on the weekends or anything like that. I don't have overnights, it's pretty much that's the only time that I have with her. I miss her ... I want to keep our bond strong and not weaken or deteriorate it.
>
> Parent

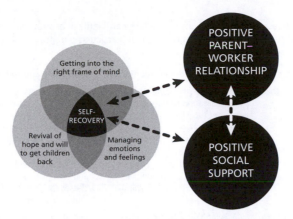

Figure 12.3 Negotiating and reconstructing parental identity after removal

Parents saw face-to-face contact visits as a chance to reconnect with their children, build on the bond they had before the children went into care or, for some parents, develop the bond with their children that may not have been initially established. While some parents recognised the importance of access for the children, all parents commented on how hard and distressing it was for them personally.

■ The role of parents

For parents, self-recovery was about dealing with what was going on internally, including their thoughts and emotions, and ultimately finding their sense of self again and reconstructing who they were as parents. Table 12.1 represents the underlying elements of self-recovery, cognitive and emotional tasks and individual strategies and behaviours employed by parents from their experiences. Focusing on the internal dimensions of the self and identity assisted in influencing the external dimensions, including contact with children and, in some cases, reunification with them, and relationships with child protection workers and carers.

In adopting the right mind set and focusing on what was most important, which was their children and the love they had for their children, parents began the recovery process. Part of the process of recovery was acknowledging their responsibility for the removal of their children.

> I know there were things in my life that had to change. I know that I wasn't doing the best job I could be doing because of the drug usage and everything ... but when I was on the drugs, I did try to be ... I was a good Mum ... the best Mum I could be at the time but things needed to change.

> Parent

Table 12.1 Processes, cognitive and emotional tasks and individual strategies and behaviours associated with self-recovery and negotiating and reconstructing parental identity after child removal

Self-recovery elements	Cognitive and emotional tasks	Strategies and behaviours
Getting in the right state of mind	Acceptance of child removal and realisation of the need for change; focusing on children and staying on track; making a decision to fight constructively; finding confidence, strength and faith within self; activating and strengthening own cognitive, emotional, physical and spiritual resources	Going to access visits and seeing their children's faces; hearing their voices on the phone; being involved in their lives; having photos of children around the house as a reminder; stopping drinking alcohol; taking medication; not taking medication, complying with court orders and care plan (attending parenting classes, anger management workshops, domestic violence counselling)
Revival of hope and will to get children back	Believing that positive change is possible; developing self-determination and motivation to make changes for children	Imagining being reunified with the children and being a family again; seeing self as a human being capable of positive changes
Managing emotions and feelings	Recovery from negative feelings and symptoms to acquiring positive feelings and actions through trial and error	Talking to a professional, family member or friend; self-talk; controlling emotions; reading books; learning about various topics such as alternative therapies (like drinking herbal teas) and effects of drugs and alcohol; writing thoughts and feelings down; prayer; forgiving self; exercise; vitamins

The right state of mind was focusing on what needed to be done and changed in parents' lives to get their children home. It was about gaining confidence and strength within themselves and knowing that change was possible. Getting in the right state of mind gave parents purpose, confidence and strength to head in the direction of their children. This parent talks about factors within herself that she needed to find and harness:

> … just finding the confidence and the strength within myself to do it, like because at the beginning I didn't have very much faith in myself but the more I fought and the more I talked to people … whether it be social workers, counsellors, friends, the more I spoke to people I just found it … that it is all possible…
>
> Parent

Another parent talks about getting in the right state of mind by concentrating on the pragmatic things that needed to be done for her child to come home:

> So you know as soon as he got taken off me and I got in the right state of mind, I was just like, I need to get a house, I need to get his room set up and I need to do all this in order to get him back, so yeah I've got my own house, my own car, got his own room.
>
> Parent

While parents' initial motivation for change in their lives may have been externally motivated (that is driven by factors outside themselves, such as court orders), workers were able to see the internal change in parents. As parents started to see the impact of the changes in their lives and their families, they began to internalise and acknowledge the benefit of the changes.

> ... often parents do jump the hoops because they've got no choice, they want the kids back, they'll do absolutely anything but it's almost irrelevant because once they do it and start to see the effects, the initial motivation for doing it is irrelevant as long as they do it and start to internalise it so it's not necessarily a bad thing and I tell that to a lot of parents, I say do what you've got to do.
>
> Worker

Parents in the study grasped on to the hope that they were going to get their children back. They focused on their will and belief that positive change was possible – that they were able to be determined and motivated to make the changes in their lives for their children.

> You know ... just the will to be back with my family, honestly that's enough for me. Even though it seems so far away until we're all back together, I know that if I buckled now, if I was to buckle now and think, fuck it it's all too hard, then it's never going to happen because when the kids are back in my care, there are going to be days when it is going to be too hard and I'm still going to have to keep going. There are going to be days when I'm not going to feel like getting out of bed but I'm going to have to ... so there's no point in buckling now because it might seem hard when I am away from my kids but it is going to be twice as hard when I'm back with them so that's one way I look at it ... If I can ... If I tell myself I'm never going to be back with my kids, I know that I'd end up somewhere that I don't want to be so if I keep reminding myself that I'm going to be back with my kids, each day is easier to live away from them.
>
> Parent

The revival of hope for parents involved noticing the changes and progress they were making in their lives. This worker talks about celebrating with parents, no matter how small the changes in their life may seem:

> ... You don't actually know that this woman never had a house and was sleeping on floors and being very transient, and then she come in yahooing [expressing happiness] because she's now got a one bedroom flat and you think big deal but to her it's a huge achievement.
>
> Worker

How parents managed their strong negative emotions and feelings was important, especially around access visits and how they related to case workers, carers and especially their children. When dealing with workers, parents learned through trial and error. Parents learned what worked and what didn't when it came to showing and expressing their feelings.

In the beginning I hated my workers, not personally but because they represented the loss of my kids. My anger was getting me shut out. My social worker would walk out of our meetings again and again because I was behaving badly. I would abuse her and not even listen. I learnt the hard way. Every time I did this, she stopped my access visit for that day because they said I was too angry and could not control myself. I soon had to learn to sit down and shut up if I wanted to see my kids. As soon as I started being more respectful things moved along like they hadn't before. We started to make some progress.

Parent

Over their journey, parents discovered new ways and strategies for managing their feelings and taking care of themselves emotionally. Some of the strategies included talking to counsellors and professionals, close family members and friends; learning about alternative therapies like drinking herbal teas and relaxation; writing their thoughts and feelings down; taking vitamins and drinking water; and praying. This parent articulates how she personally cares for herself cognitively and emotionally.

I'm learning to deal with loneliness and I'm learning alternative therapies like drinking herbal tea and I've started drinking herbal tea for relaxation. I've started reading books and I must admit moving house – into a house where I can turn the heater on and I'm more comfortable has made my life so much easier, not easier but – I still cry but at least I'm not going to be cold, shaking, emotionally a cripple. I'm just going to bed very sad.

Parent

■ The role of workers

While self-recovery must come from within the individual, many parents indicated needing support from others to kick-start or maintain the process. For example, the recognition of small changes and achievements parents made (such as celebrating with parents) helped maintain their motivation. This is especially essential 'when outcomes are distant and uncertain' (Kanfer & Schefft, 1988, p. 149) such as in child protection cases.

In most cases, the parent–worker relationship was crucial, as it was instrumental in beginning the process of self-recovery and facilitating contact between parents and their children. A significant number of participants in the study reported the relationship between the parent and the worker as a critical factor that either facilitated or inhibited engagement between parents and their children who had been placed in care, which was paramount when it came to orchestrating access visits and contact. As depicted in Figure 12.4 and described by all study informants (parents, workers and carers), workers who were seen as non-judgemental, respectful

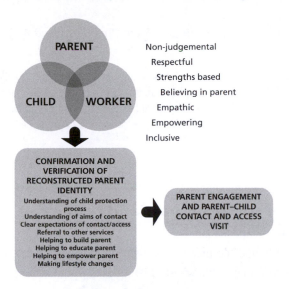

Figure 12.4   Characteristics of a positive parent–worker relationship

and empathic, and worked from a strengths base, believed in the parent's capacity to change and were inclusive, were able to engage with parents and develop positive working relationships. In turn, the development of positive parent–worker relationships led to various positive outcomes, including parents' understanding of, and inclusion in, the child protection process and educating and empowering parents to make major lifestyle changes.

> … to be able to tell them [parents] … what's actually going on, what your thoughts are, what's actually happening for this child at this point in time, where are we going, you have to be very clear with your goals … to involve parents in the making of those goals, for them [parents] to be active participants in the case plan, in the child's life as much as possible and doing certain things like if you have meetings to write down for a parent what you have agreed upon, what they have agreed to do, so that it is visual for them because when I meet with parents, they go away and they might remember a quarter of what you have talked about. So it's about going 'ok, this is what we agreed on today, you'll do this and we'll do that' … keeping those communication lines I suppose.
>
> Worker

The personal characteristics and qualities of workers described by participants in this study are consistent with the worker characteristics and competencies found throughout the child protection literature (de Boer & Coady, 2007; Drake, 1994; Gockel, Russell & Harris, 2008; Howe, 2010; Ruch, 2005; Scott, 2003; Trotter, 2006). Specifically, worker attributes such as empathy, respect, genuineness and optimism, as highlighted by Scott et.al. (2007), mirrored the findings in the study as key ingredients in forging relationships with parents of young children. Chapters 1 and 8 also explore this in greater detail.

> I think for me it's about having a belief. I think the worker has to have a belief in the parent that they can do this and with the right support they can do this. If the worker believes that the parent can't do it they've got no chance unless they've got other supports outside. They may have other counsellors or people that support them but I think it becomes very difficult if they can't.
>
> Worker

■ The role of social support and respectful relationships

While some parents had the internal motivation that something needed to change in their lives, it was widely acknowledged by all participants that parents needed the support to make such changes. Parents needed support from family members, friends, positive role models and workers to help and teach them new ways and strategies to recover in order for them to get in the right frame of mind and be emotionally strong for themselves and their children.

> I didn't talk to anyone … at all. I couldn't talk to anyone about it, it just made me feel upset to actually talk about it all. I didn't even think about it. We couldn't even bring up [child's name] in the house but in the end I had to talk about it and then got … through to [the child protection service] they gave me a counsellor because my Mum rang them because I tried killing myself after I lost my [child] because it just hurt so much. I couldn't talk and I just bottled it all up too much. My Mum rang [the child protection service] and said you need to do something, it would have been nice of you to offer her a counsellor or something instead of just leaving her. Like they didn't offer me a counsellor, they only offered me one February this year after Mum rang up [three months after child removed].
>
> Parent

The literature has been consistent regarding the power of therapeutic alliances and relationships as motivators for change (Herman, 1992; Kanfer & Schefft, 1988). This is because 'recovery can take place only within the context of relationships; it cannot occur in isolation' (Herman, 1992, p. 33). For parents in the study by Salveron (2012), the therapeutic relationships forged with workers, family support workers and positive family members and friends who empathised with them, believed in them, included them and respected them, led to a sense of empowerment that was vital for their self-recovery and identity negotiation and reconstruction. The process of self-recovery for parents in the study involved dealing with what was going on internally, including confronting thoughts about their children and what happened about removal, about their own upbringing and parenting, about their own families, their emotions, their capacities, their strengths, their weaknesses, their limits and so on.

According to Herman (1992), after the experience of trauma and for recovery to ensue, people need to connect with others with whom they can build healing relationships. These relationships must, however, be founded on safety and trust. In her research and clinical work with trauma survivors (including victims of sexual and domestic violence, combat veterans and victims of political terror), Herman (1992) details various stages of the recovery process, including the development of healing relationships, the establishment of basic safety and self-care, remembrance and mourning, and reconnection.

Much can be drawn from Herman's work to inform the child protection context, especially as regards engaging with parents involved with statutory child protection intervention, whose children have been removed. The importance of healing relationships that Herman espouses strongly resonates with the experiences of parents in this study who were able to find, connect and develop positive relationships with their workers or others to support them as they navigated the child protection process and maintained contact with their children in care. Herman (1992) describes that traumatised individuals seek emotional support from a range of people in their lives, and the relationships they establish take many forms that change throughout the recovery process. Herman (1992, p. 62) asserts, however, that 'assurances of safety and protection' are of greatest importance. This then paves the way for rebuilding their positive self-view and sense of self.

According to Herman (1992, p. 133), the establishment or renewal of such connections and relationships allow for the 're-creation of psychological faculties that may have been damaged by the traumatic experience. These faculties include the basic capacities for trust, autonomy, initiative, competence, identity and intimacy'. These connections and relationships provide a safe way through which parents can learn, re-learn or re-form these inherent cognitive and perceptual skills and abilities for themselves, and enhance the physical and psychological safety of their own children who have endured abuse and neglect.

■ The Parents Plus Playgroups: an innovative program for parents who have had their children removed from their care

In 2006, staff from the Australian Centre for Child Protection conducted an evaluation of the Parents Plus Playgroups, a joint initiative of Families SA (which includes the statutory child protection service in South Australia) and Good Beginnings Australia, a non-profit organisation that delivers universal and targeted early intervention programs to families with young children (Salveron, Arney & Lewig, 2010). The Playgroups are no longer funded by Families SA, but they provide a clear example of a service that gave support to a highly vulnerable target group: children in out-of-home care and their parents.

The Parents Plus Playgroups aim to provide a safe, engaging environment for parents to learn and use skills in parenting, and to maintain positive relationships and build happy memories with their children, even though the children may not return to their care. Facilitated by staff trained in early childhood development and supported by volunteers, the playgroups are run as structured weekly sessions in a community setting. In the sessions, parents participate in parenting education (for example, positive parenting, anger management, nutrition, grief and loss, learning through play and budgeting), a supervised children's playgroup and a debriefing session that provides an opportunity for parents to reflect on their learning and discuss their emotions.

Facilitators use a non-judgemental and positive approach to build trust and share their extensive knowledge of parenting and child development. Role modelling, demonstration and opportunities for parents to practise are frequently provided in the playgroup sessions, and parents set the rules and identify the topics to be discussed in education sessions. The facilitators also describe clearly their mandatory notification responsibilities to parents and display transparency in any interactions with statutory child protection services about the children and their parents.

Salveron and colleagues (2010, p. 235) described aspects of the program environment that were important to the groups' success:

- *having a safe and fun place for children to play;*
- *holding the playgroup in a community-based centre where the focus is on children (and separate to child protection offices);*
- *having a playground attached to the playgroup room;*
- *providing good equipment and lots of toys;*
- *being close to public transport; and*
- *having an open space for play.*

Parents participating in the Parents Plus Playgroups spoke of how the groups were non-stigmatising and allowed them to share experiences with families in similar circumstances. As Salveron and colleagues (2010, p. 239) note:

> Parents reported an improvement in their parenting knowledge, skills and confidence as a result of participating in the program. Parents related that learning a range of strategies when managing the behaviour of their children helped increase their strength and confidence in parenting and decreased their anxiety about the parenting role [a sense of becoming a 'better parent']. Confidence was further enhanced by the opportunity to interact with the children of other parents in the group. These changes in parenting approaches and confidence

were also noted by all of the interviewed workers, including Families SA social workers whose clients were attending the playgroups.

Perceived benefits for children included having fun, meeting new friends, improved attachment to parents, sense of routines, a sense of safety and the benefits of effective parenting and positive interactions with their parents [e.g., play].

Parents demonstrated an enhanced understanding of children's needs in the context of their development, including recognition of the importance of play in the early years. Parents also reported greater social support and improved interactions with other family members and service providers, including the statutory child protection service, as a result of their attendance at the playgroups.

■ Conclusion

The research described in this chapter has a number of implications for practice with families in the context of child removal. It sheds light on the dynamic interplay of psychological factors (including parental identity disconfirmation, emotions and cognitions) that influence parents' behaviours, motivation and capacity to engage and contact their children in care. First and foremost, the research has implications for the way workers (statutory child protection workers, family support workers and other practitioners) involve, relate to and engage parents in the child protection process. Given the trauma experienced as a result of child removal, both children and parents urgently require ongoing psychological intervention and support to deal with identity interruption, negotiation and repair of the parent–child relationship. The research affirms the significance of relationships in triggering the self-recovery process of parents. Therefore, workers who are able to develop helping alliances with parents and reaffirm and support the reconstruction of their identities can also create meaningful parent–child contact and access visit experiences. There needs to be greater understanding of parent behaviours in interaction as a result of identity disruption and negotiation.

Second, the research has implications for the conduct, structure and execution of contact (access visits) between parents and their children in care. Findings of the study have revealed the importance of reaffirming the identities of parents, which entails setting up visits that are meaningful, positive and identity-confirming for both parents and children. The research highlights the importance of preparation, understanding, communication, helping parents to comprehend the importance of their role as parents and teaching them more positive and constructive ways of parenting and relating to their children. Furthermore, helping parents to understand the aims of contact, provision of constructive feedback and clear expectations of contact and access visits; activities that help build the parent, empower the parent, and educate the parent all contribute to help them understand the child protection system. This in turn assists them to process, engage with support services and make lifestyle changes for themselves and their children.

Given the role of parent identity in parent–worker engagement and contact with children in care, specialised support for parents to initiate the self-recovery process is vital. Specifically, support needs to help parents express and manage their emotions, understand the child protection system and process, find confidence and inner strength, and develop a positive state of mind. These are the keys to parents' recovery and identity reconstruction and change.

ACTIVITY

Imagine you are going to be in a meeting with a parent who has recently had her children removed and placed in care. In preparation for the next face-to-face contact visit, what practical and psychological factors do you need to consider to maximise the opportunity to be therapeutic for both the parent(s) and the children?

■ Useful websites

Australian Centre for Child Protection: **www.unisa.edu.au/childprotection**

Child Welfare Organizing Project: **http://cwop.org**

Family Inclusion Network Websites across Australia:

Australian Capital Territory: **http://finact.com.au**

New South Wales: **www.fin-nsw.org.au**

Queensland: **www.fin-qldtsv.org.au**

Western Australia: **http://finwa.org.au**

Rise: Stories By and For Parents Affected by the Child Welfare System: **www.risemagazine.org**

Volunteers in Child Protection: **www.csv.org.uk/volunteering/mentoring-befriending/child-protection**

13

Spreading and implementing promising approaches in child and family services

Fiona Arney, Kerry Lewig, Robyn Mildon, Aron Shlonsky, Christine Gibson and Leah Bromfield

■ Learning goals

This chapter will enable you to:

- **RECOGNISE** the role that research can play in improving the lives of vulnerable families and their children

- **THINK** about how you might use research to inform your practice with vulnerable families and their children

- **UNDERSTAND** how evidence-informed programs and practices are spread and implemented in the child and family service sector

- **RECOGNISE** the factors that influence whether programs and practices will become embedded in service delivery with vulnerable families

- **UNDERSTAND** how a focus on high-quality implementation practices can support better outcomes for families.

■ Introduction

THERE IS AN urgent need to enhance outcomes for vulnerable children and their families, and the evidence base for strategies that can meet this aim is growing daily. But there are limits to the extent to which this evidence base is or can be embedded in policy and service delivery. As many of the chapters in this book have described, vulnerable families have highly complex needs and often live in chaotic circumstances, characterised, for example, by parental alcohol and drug misuse, parental mental health problems, and high levels of family conflict and violence (Bromfield et al., 2010; Dawe & Harnett, 2013; Mildon & Shlonsky, 2011). Evidence-based approaches to working with families in these circumstances are limited, with only a number of programs being tested through rigorous research methodologies.

Several of the chapters in this volume have highlighted promising approaches to working with vulnerable families in a range of settings. Some of these promising programs have been implemented beyond their site of origin, but many have not yet spread throughout the service system.

In the health field, it has been estimated that it takes an average of 17 years for only 14 per cent of new scientific discoveries to enter day-to-day clinical practice (Westfall, Mold & Fagnan, 2007, p.403). As a relatively new field of research endeavour with a burgeoning evidence base, the process for child protection interventions to reach a similar evidence standard could be expected to take even longer (Curran et al., 2012; Olson & Stroud, 2012). As described in Chapter 1, while there is an abundance of descriptive knowledge (knowledge about a phenomenon), there is far less prescriptive knowledge (knowledge about how to intervene with regard to the phenomenon).

Even more pragmatically, research evidence is but one of many sources of information and influence that inform practice, policies and service development. In recent research conducted by the Australian Centre for Child Protection regarding decision-making in child and family services, for example, the influence of competing sources of information, and political and organisational imperatives, were cited as the most frequently endorsed barrier to evidence-based practice and policy (Arney, Lewig, Bromfield & Holzer,2010; Humphreys et al., 2010; Lewig, Arney, Salveron et al., 2010; Lewig, Scott et al., 2010).

■ The role of implementation in improving outcomes for families

While the evidence base for programs and practice with vulnerable families is growing, the implementation and active delivery of these programs to children, parents and families vary in actual practice (Olson & Stroud, 2012). For example, in the US, it is estimated that between 80 per cent and 90 per cent of practitioners in the children's services system do not use evidence-based interventions, and if they are implemented they are often quickly adapted or changed, resulting in interventions potentially losing the key ingredients that were critical for their effectiveness (Forman et al., 2009; Palinkas et al., 2009). Indeed, this is reflected in the Australian Centre for Child Protection's recent work investigating the uptake of a range of promising programs. Programs that were seen as flexible and adaptable were more likely to 'diffuse' or spread across a range of contexts, compared to those whose program parameters were fixed through licensing requirements. However, it was this very perceived adaptability in the model that caused a potential dilution in the critical components of the intervention (Harris, 2008; Lewig, Arney et al., 2010). For example, due to time constraints practitioners might leave out elements that were seen to be vital to family-based decision-making (for instance, removing private family time from the intervention, or not inviting extended family members to participate).

Since the 1980s, evidence has grown about the impact of the quality of the implementation on outcomes for clients and families (for example, see Aarons et al., 2009; Abbott et al., 1998; DuBois et al., 2002; Durlak & Du Pre, 2008; Gottfredson, Gottfredson & Hybl, 1993; Grimshaw & Russell, 1993; Tobler, 1986). Implementation is the 'efforts specifically designed to get the best practice findings and related products into routine and sustained use' (Curran et al., 2012). One study, which collated evidence from more than 500 studies, estimated that high-quality implementation can enhance program outcomes for children and families by as much as 200 per cent (Durlak & Du Pre, 2008). In the field of child neglect, implementation practices supporting practitioners in the delivery of evidence-informed programs have been shown to significantly reduce staff turnover (Aarons et al., 2009).

A focus on implementation in child and family services has been identified as a pressing need in a field in which practice may be strongly affected by political imperatives, goodwill and intuitive appeal (Arney, 2012). This has at times resulted in the spread of harmful programs to children and young people. For example, the Scared Straight program, focusing on reducing offending behaviour in young people by exposing them to the more violent aspects of life in prison, has spread widely across the US because of its political attractiveness and intuitive appeal (see Box 13.1). This is despite repeated trials which demonstrate that participants are more likely to engage in offending behaviour than young people who do not take part in the program (Petrosino, Turpin-Petrosino & Buehler, 2003).

BOX 13.1   Scared Straight

The 'Scared Straight Program' was developed in the US in the 1970s to deter juvenile offenders and at-risk children from future offending. The program was started by life-serving inmates in a New Jersey prison and involved organised visits to the prison where participants were exposed to the more violent aspects of prison life in an effort to scare them away from a life of crime.

Following a television documentary about the program in 1979, in which a 94 per cent success rate for the program was claimed, Scared Straight was rapidly replicated across the US. Since then, Scared Straight type programs (that is, programs that use deterrence as their underlying theory) have become a popular method of crime prevention in the US and to a lesser degree internationally. It has been argued that these programs are popular because they fit with common beliefs about 'getting tough on crime', they are inexpensive, and they provide a means for prisoners to contribute to society.

However, research conducted over the past two decades, including randomised control trials and a well-publicised review of over 500 crime prevention evaluations undertaken by the University of Maryland in the 1990s, has shown these programs to be ineffective and in some cases harmful. Indeed, a recent systematic review of this research, undertaken by the Cochrane Collaboration in 2009, concluded that

> programmes like Scared Straight are likely to have a harmful effect and increase delinquency relative to doing nothing at all to the same youths. Given these results, agencies that permit such programmes must rigorously evaluate them, not only to ensure that they are doing what they purport to do (prevent crime) – but at the very least they do not cause more harm than good.(Petrosino, Turpin-Petrosino & Buehler, 2009, p. 2).

(From Lewig, Arney et al., 2010, p.250)

■ Developing a theory of change

One strategy that assists practitioners and policy-makers in the development and implementation of promising practice is the use of a theory of change or program logic. In the context of responding to the acute needs of vulnerable children, young people and their families, there can be limited opportunities for this type of reflection about why a particular practice strategy may be effective. For implementation efforts to be successful, the program, policy or practice must be clearly articulated and clearly linked to or determined by outcomes for a specified target group and community context.

> The logic model is a roadmap for program goals and objectives, but also serves as a framework for ongoing monitoring and continuous quality improvement ... Once a logic model is established and put into action, continuous quality improvement efforts are necessary to test whether the logic model is working and if not, to identify what adaptations are needed ... Utilising evaluation data to measure progress towards meeting goals as outlined in the program's logic model is an important and necessary step to ensure program improvement and sustainability.
>
> (Hodges & Hernandez, 2008, p. 101)

Segal and colleagues' (2012) review of 53 home visiting interventions for vulnerable families with infants identified that the level of success of these programs in preventing child abuse and neglect was dependent on the degree of alignment between four key elements:

• an explicit program objective with the prevention of child abuse and neglect as a primary aim
• the intended target population

- a theory of change
- program components.

Where there was alignment between these elements – that is, the program components were based on a clear theory of change for the target population with the aim of reducing child abuse and neglect – these programs were all successful in preventing abuse and neglect. Where there was a match between some of these elements but not all, only 60 per cent of programs were successful, and where there was no match between the aim, target population, theory of change and program components – no program was successful. While this may seem an obvious point, evaluation efforts in the sector have highlighted that the links between service activities, their intended target group, the issue they are intended to address and their anticipated outcomes are not always clear (Arney, McGuinness & Robinson, 2009; Segal et al., 2012).

> **REFLECTIVE QUESTIONS**
> Think of a program or practice you know well. What is the theory of change for that program – how will its different elements achieve its intended outcomes? Will it work well for all client groups? Will it suit different client populations (for example, families from refugee backgrounds, parents with learning difficulties, fathers)? Why?

■ Factors that influence program adoption and implementation

Several common factors influence an agency's decision-making about the adoption of a new program or practice and their efforts to implement it as part of standard practice. These factors also influence the extent to which individual practitioners are able to incorporate evidence from research into their daily practice with children and families. These factors relate to features of the practice or the program itself, characteristics of the practitioner, their organisation, and the wider environment that the organisation sits in. Due to the difficulties of conducting experimental research in such a diverse sector, our knowledge about these factors and how they influence implementation has been collated from individual or multiple case studies.

Research conducted at the Australian Centre for Child Protection described the role of these factors in the spread and implementation of seven promising programs across Australia through a survey with 223 child and family services across Australia and 92 in-depth interviews with individuals from those organisations (McLaren et al., 2008). The programs examined included a mix of 'imported' and home-grown initiatives selected because of their focus on significant issues in the child and family sector, the degree of interest external agencies had demonstrated in them and the fact that there was sufficient evidence to consider their utility (Lewig, Arney et al., 2010). This, together with findings from other research in the area, will be briefly discussed below.

■ The new program or practice

The perceived relevance and 'fit' of the new program or practice to the organisation and client population are understandably among the greatest predictors of whether they will be adopted and implemented (Lewig, Arney et al., 2010). Adopting or adapting a program that relates to the characteristics, needs and preferences of potential program recipients is of key importance when looking to reach vulnerable families who may not find it easy to engage with services (Salveron, Arney & Scott, 2006). Related to this is the notion of relative advantage – the new program or practice must be seen to provide better outcomes for clients, efficiency, cost effectiveness and so on if it is to be adopted over and above other new programs or an existing program being used by an agency. The extent to which a new program or practice resonates with the values of the organisation and practitioners, and to which it requires relatively small adjustments in practice or organisational systems, is also important (Greenhalgh et al., 2005; Rogers, 2003).

Interestingly, the country of origin of the programs and program developers influences to some extent how well they are known in the sector, and therefore the extent to which they may be adopted. In the study by the Australian Centre for Child Protection, imported programs were better known and in some cases preferred to their domestic counterparts. This is in part related to the extent of the evidence for a program and for the dissemination related to programs (such as tours by international program developers describing their programs, or championing of programs by Australian experts or leaders within the organisation).

> Our organisation is continually looking to support new program models from overseas which have been going for a few years and which have already built an evidence base and a reputation, self-fund them for the first five years and build our own evidence in our own region, then seek external funding to sustain the programs. From our experience, government funders are more likely to fund imported programs and are more likely to take their 'goodness' on face value because they are from the UK or the US. We know we are less likely to win funding for home-grown programs.
>
> (Lewig, Arney et al., 2010, p. 285)

■ The practitioner

The practitioner-related factors that influence the degree to which a program may be implemented include values, beliefs and assumptions, particularly in relation to evidence-based practice (Aarons et al., 2009; Brown, 2005). Some practitioners may actively seek out new knowledge to incorporate into their practice and more readily adopt new ideas.

> *Individuals come with their own skills, beliefs, values and experiences and are not passive recipients of new ideas or innovations. Rather, people actively seek out new ideas, experiment with them, evaluate them, make sense of them, develop positive and/or negative feelings about them, challenge and modify them, and aim to improve them.*
>
> (Lewig, Arney et al., 2010, p. 280)

New concepts and practices are more likely to be disseminated through practitioners who are part of networks and teams who share a common purpose, vision and values, and who identify with each others' contexts and needs (Salveron et al., 2006). Support for practitioners to implement new initiatives is particularly crucial. This will be discussed in more detail below.

■ The organisation

> *One of the main reasons cited for the lack of sustainability and replication of successful programs in child and family services is the failure to understand the institutions and systems within which programs are required to operate*
>
> (Lewig, Arney et al., 2010, p. 281)

In order to implement a new program in the way that it was intended by program developers, the organisation must engage in a change process, which focuses on its people, its policies and systems, and its ability to sustain the new practices. Leadership in the organisation, systems to support implementation, and the degree to which the new program or practice is seen as a priority by executive and management, and has resources dedicated to its implementation, are particularly influential in this regard (Greenhalgh et al., 2004; Lewig, Arney et al., 2010).

The culture or climate of an organisation (the norms, values and rituals that establish 'the way things are done') influence whether and how a program will be implemented (Hemmelgarn, Glisson & James, 2006). Organisational factors such as staff cohesiveness, shared vision and practitioner autonomy are more likely to be conducive to the uptake of a new program that has been endorsed by their organisation, whereas organisations characterised by high rates of staff burnout and turnover and highly bureaucratic processes are less likely to be able to implement a new program successfully (Barwick et al., 2005; Fixsen et al., 2005).

■ The wider service environment

Factors in the wider service environment can be highly influential in determining the outcomes of adoption and implementation efforts in child and family services.

For example, funding availability and politically imposed service criteria can strongly influence how government-run or -funded services operate and their ability to implement evidence-based practices (Arney, Lewig, Bromfield & Holzer, 2010; Chadwick Center, 2004). The level of collaboration or competition between services in a community is also a consideration in the implementation of new programs, particularly if the program depends on referrals from, or joint work with, other agencies, or if working with clients with multiple and complex needs (Bowen & Zwi, 2005; Dobbins et al., 2002; Greenhalgh et al., 2004; Plsek, 2003; Westphal, Gulati & Shortell, 1997).

■ Types of implementation frameworks

Implementation interventions (the techniques designed to enhance adoption of interventions) and implementation strategies (bundles of implementation interventions) have traditionally been applied with a focus on the practitioner developing knowledge, skills and competencies in a particular intervention. These practitioner-led implementation interventions often include training and clinical support in an intervention. These training programs are relatively easy to implement with a large number of practitioners; however, when practitioners leave or the organisation no longer supports the program, then these programs are no longer able to reach vulnerable families.

In New South Wales, the implementation of the Triple P , Positive Parenting Program included the training of 1027 practitioners. When the implementation of the program was evaluated, 'only 60% of trained practitioners had started delivering courses and only one third were delivering the expected number of courses … per year' (Nexus Management Consulting, 2011, p.7). Similarly, in the initial roll-out of the Healthy Start program, a parenting program for parents with intellectual and learning difficulties, only 30 per cent of the almost 400 practitioners who completed training commenced the program with families (Polimeni, Wade & Mildon, 2008). While a number of families are still receiving services as a result of these training and support initiatives, there is potential for far more families to benefit from these programs.

There are now a number of implementation frameworks that incorporate knowledge of the influential factors described in the previous sections and highlight strategies to support practitioners and organisations in the introduction and maintenance of a new program. For example, Meyers, Durlak and Wandersman (2012) have conducted a synthesis of 25 implementation frameworks developed across a range of research and practice areas. One of the best known of these models was developed from Fixsen and colleagues' (2005) seminal review of more than 700 research papers in the implementation literature and is known as the 'stages and drivers model' of implementation. The model identifies several key stages in the implementation process, each of which must be considered for successful and timely implementation (Fixsen et al., 2009). In each of these stages, the common factors that influence implementation across an organisation should be considered, understood and refined to drive the implementation process forward.

In brief, the stages of implementation outlined in this model include:

- the exploration phase – in which the best match between community need, strengths and preferences, desired outcomes, staff capabilities and evidence-informed program, policy and practice options is considered; as is the readiness of an organisation (and its staff) for change to a new way of working
- the installation phase – in which the 'drivers' of implementation are considered and put in place, and leadership prepares the organisation for the new way of working
- the initial implementation phase – in which the new program, practice or policy is trialled with early adopters and potential issues are identified; implementation drivers are also adjusted in this phase
- the full implementation phase – in which the program, policy or practice becomes part of regular practice and is seen as 'the way we do things around here'; continuous quality improvement systems are operating across the organisation to maintain high quality practice and inform about the outcomes of the new way of working.

Fixsen and colleagues (2009) also identify that sustainability should be a consideration across the life of the implementation process, to guide long-term improvements in outcomes for children and families. Innovation and adaptation are also important considerations, but must be done planfully in order to provide service improvements. As identified earlier, many adaptations or innovations occur without sufficient theoretical justification, or to suit organisational and economic requirements, rather than with a sound basis in evidence.

In addition to the stages of implementation, the implementation framework from the National Implementation Research Network outlines factors that drive implementation efforts forward, including those factors that support practitioner skills and capabilities in delivering evidence-informed services, and those organisational and systemic factors that provide supportive environments for these new ways of working (Fixsen et al., 2009). These drivers work together, and for effective implementation should be based on a clear understanding of the features of the new practice, program or policy.

The drivers include:

- staff selection – which includes recruitment and selection processes that are most likely to recruit staff from within and outside the organisation with skills and abilities to deliver the program or practice over the long term
- training – which includes evidence-based methods to promote knowledge acquisition, skill development and enthusiasm and confidence in the new way of working
- coaching and supervision – to ensure transfer of the skills developed in training in practice with families, and to promote clinical practice and judgement
- performance evaluation and assessment – which includes providing strengths-based feedback to practitioners about their performance with respect to the new practice or program, assists with measuring fidelity and informs the organisation about their selection, training and coaching processes
- data systems that support decision making – this includes the development of data systems that can provide feedback to practitioners and management in real time about the progress of clients on key outcomes
- facilitative administration including adaptive leadership – this includes management that supports the installation of the drivers across all aspects of the organisation, and the alignment of policies and procedures to the new way of working
- systems intervention – which includes leadership to support the new way of working across the various systems involved in the lives of children and families including service coordination, funding and so on.

Fixsen and colleagues (2009) have also noted the potential benefits of using team-based structures ('implementation teams') to drive the implementation process forward within and across organisations. These teams include key decision-makers in implementation (such as executive staff, managers, funders and implementation support personnel) and focus on enhancing the organisational and practice environment to maximise the sustainability of implementation. The teaming process is a social process and the relationship between service providers, program developers and implementation support providers is also an important consideration. Palinkas and colleagues (2009, p.9) have identified features of the relationship between researchers and service providers that could contribute of implementation success:

- possession of similar goals (for example, the wellbeing of the child versus protection of 'turf' or academic advancement)

- a sense of teamwork and shared control in the evidence-based practice implementation (for instance, scheduling, training, monitoring of performance, adaptation to suit the needs of specific groups of clients)
- perceived reciprocity (that is, 'Do we both get something desirable out of the interaction?')
- frequency of communication with one another.

Increasingly, concerted efforts are being made to provide implementation support to organisations as part of their funding agreements with government organisations. For example, initiatives in the Northern Territory such as the implementation of intensive family support services funded by the Australian Government have included an implementation support role that includes the provision of training, coaching, organisational systems analysis and local and state-wide teaming structures to drive the implementation process in this complex service environment.

■ Conclusion

The chapters of this book have highlighted the ways in which practitioners can use theory and evidence in their practice with vulnerable families in a range of circumstances. The factors that can support or impede the use of evidence-based and promising practices have also been explored. These include the complexity of families' situations, the match between the program or practice and the values and beliefs of practitioners and organisations, and how well organisations support the implementation of the new practice. As we are able to apply our growing knowledge of the factors that support implementation into practice, there is a much greater likelihood of achieving our intended aims of improving the lives of vulnerable families.

REFLECTIVE QUESTIONS
Consider a family situation in which children are vulnerable. What is the existing evidence for possible interventions to reduce this vulnerability?
How could you implement these interventions in your current organisational context?

ACTIVITY
Choose a program from the California Evidence Based Clearinghouse that is relevant to your area of work or study. How has the program been implemented in these different contexts – has it been adapted? Can you identify how the implementation strategy promotes the drivers in Fixsen's model above?

■ Useful websites

Australian Centre for Child Protection: **www.unisa.edu.au/childprotection**

California Evidence-Based Clearinghouse for Child Welfare: **www.cebc4cw.org**

Child, Family, Community, Australia – Research Policy and Practice Information Exchange: **www.aifs.gov.au/cfca**

Child Welfare Information Gateway: **www.childwelfare.gov**

National Implementation Research Network: **http://nirn.fpg.unc.edu**

References

Aarons, G., Sommerfield, D., Hecht, D., Silovsky, J. & Chaffin, M. (2009). 'The impact of evidence-based practice implementation and fidelity monitoring on staff turnover: Evidence for a positive effect'. *Journal of Consulting and Clinical Psychology*, 77(2), 270–281.

Abbott, R.D., O'Donnell, J., Hawkins, J.D., Hill, K.G., Kosterman, R. & Catalano, R.F. (1998). 'Changing teaching practices to promote achievement and bonding to school'. *American Journal of Orthopsychiatry*, 68, 542–552.

ABC. Mission Voices. Retrieved February 2012 from http://www.abc.net.au/missionvoices/general/missions_and_reserves_background/default.htm

Aboriginal and Torres Strait Islander Social Justice Commissioner. (2009). *2008 Social Justice Report*. Sydney: Human Rights and Equal Opportunity Commission.

ABS. (2012). *Year Book Australia, 2012*. Canberra: Australian Bureau of Statistics.

Ackerman, S. & Hilsenroth, M. (2003). 'A review of therapist characteristics and techniques positively impacting the therapeutic alliance.' *Clinical Psychology Review*, 23(1), 1–33.

Ainsworth, M.D.S., Blehar, M., Waters, E. & Wall, S. (1978). *Patterns of Attachment: A Psychological Study of the Strange Situation*. Hillsdale, N.J.: Erblaum.

Ajdukovic, M. & Ajdukovic, D. (1998). 'Impact of displacement on the psychological well-being of refugee children'. *International Review of Psychiatry. Special Issue: Childhood Trauma*, 10(3), 186–195.

Allen, R. & Petr, C. (1998). 'Rethinking family centred practice'. *American Journal of Orthopsychiatry*, 68(1), 4–16.

Allotey, P. (1998). 'Travelling with "excess baggage": Health problems of refugee women in Western Australia'. *Women & Health*, 28(1), 63–81.

Almeida, R.V. & Lockard, J. (2005). 'The Cultural Context Model: A new paradigm for accountability, empowerment, and the development of critical consciousness against domestic violence'. In N.J.Sokoloff (ed.), *Domestic violence at the Margins: Readings on Race, Class, Gender and Culture* (pp. 301–320). New Brunswick: Rutgers University Press.

Altman, J. (2008). 'A study of engagement in neighborhood-based child welfare services'. *Research on Social Work Practice*, 18(6), 555–564.

Ambert, A. (1994). 'An international perspective on parenting: Social change and social constructs'. *Journal of Marriage and the Family*, 56, 529–543.

American Academy of Pediatrics (2002). 'Health care of young children in foster care'. *Pediatrics*, 100 (3), 536–541.

American Humane Association (2008). *Family Group Decision Making in Child Welfare: Purpose, Values and Processes*. American Humane Association.

American Psychiatric Association (1994). *Diagnostic and Statistical Manual of Mental Disorders* (4th edn). Washington DC: American Psychiatric Association.

Anda, R.F., Felitti, V.J., Walker, J., Whitfield, C.L., Bremner, J.D., Perry, B.D. et al. (2006). 'The enduring effects of abuse and related adverse experiences in childhood: A convergence of evidence from neurobiology and epidemiology'. *European Archives of Psychiatry and Clinical Neurosciences*, 56(3), 174–186.

Anderson, S. (2004). 'Men's anti-violence programs also improve parenting'. In R.Fletcher (ed.), *Bringing Fathers In: How to Engage with Men for the Benefit of Everyone in the Family*. Newcastle: University of Newcastle.

Aoun, S., Palmer, M. & Newby, R. (1998). 'Gender issues in psychosocial morbidity in general practice'. *Australian Journal of Social Issues*, 33(4), 335–353.

Arney, F. (2012). Using implementation science as a lens for policy, programs and evaluation in child and family services. Paper presented at the *Outreach and Integration in Family Services: Enhancing the Capacity of the NGO Sector – Colloquium Report*, 2011.

Arney, F., Bowering, K., Chong, A., Healy, V. & Volkmer, B. (2010). 'Sustained nurse home visiting with families of Aboriginal children'. In F.Arney & D.Scott (eds), *Working With Vulnerable Families: A Partnership Approach* (pp. 109–134). Melbourne: Cambridge University Press.

Arney, F., Lewig, K., Bromfield, L. & Holzer, P. (2010). 'Using evidence-informed practice to support vulnerable families'. In F.Arney & D.Scott (eds), *Working With Vulnerable Families: A Partnership Approach* (pp. 247–274). Melbourne: Cambridge University Press.

Arney, F., McGuinness, K. & Robinson, G. (2009). 'In the best interests of the child? Determining the effects of the emergency intervention on child safety and wellbeing'. *Law in Context*, 27(2), 43–57.

Arney, F. & Westby, M. (2012). *Men's Places: Literature Review*. Darwin: Menzies School of Health Research.

Arvidson, J., Kinniburgh, K., Howard, K., Spinazolla, J., Strothers, H., Evans, M. & Blaustein, M.E. (2011). 'Treatment of complex trauma in young children: Developmental and cultural considerations in application of the ARC intervention model'. *Journal of Child and Adolescent Trauma*, 4, 34–51.

Asay, T. & Lambert, M. (1999). 'The empirical case for the common factors in therapy – quantitative findings'. In M.Hubble, B.Duncan & S.Miller (eds), *The Heart* and *Soul of Change: What Works in Therapy* (pp. 33–56). Washington, DC: American Psychological Association.

Ashman, S. & Dawson, G. (2002). *Maternal Depression, Infant Psychobiological Development, and Risk for Depression.* Washington, DC: American Psychological Association.

Atkinson, J., Nelson, J. & Atkinson, C. (2010). 'Trauma, transgenerational transfer and effects on community wellbeing'. In N.Purdie, P.Dudgeon & R.Walker (eds), *Working Together: Aboriginal and Torres Strait Islander Mental Health and Wellbeing Principles and Practice* (pp. 135–144). Canberra: Australian Government Department of Health and Ageing.

Australian Infant Child Adolescent and Family Mental Health Association (2004) *Principles and Actions for Services and People Working with Children of Parents with a Mental Illness.*Sydney.

Australian Institute of Health and Welfare. (2009). *Child Protection Australia 2007–08.* Canberra: Australian Institute of Health and Welfare.

—— (2012a). *Child Protection Australia 2010–2011.* Canberra: Australian Institute of Health and Welfare.

—— (2012b). *The Health and Welfare of Australia's Aboriginal and Torres Strait Islander People.* Canberra: Australian Institute of Health and Welfare.

Australian Museum. Indigenous Australia Timeline – 1901 to 1969. Retrieved February 2012 from australianmuseum.net.au/indigenous-australia-timeline-1901-to-1969

Aviezer, O., Sagi-Schwartz, A. & Koren-Karie, N. (2003). 'Ecological constraints on the formation of infant–mother attachment relations: When maternal sensitivity becomes ineffective.' *Infant Behavior and Development*, 26, 285–299.

Azar, S. & Cote, L. (2002). 'Sociocultural issues in the evaluation of the needs of children in custody decision making: What do our current frameworks for evaluating parenting practices have to offer?' *International Journal of Law and Psychiatry*, 25, 193–217.

Bacon, H. & Richardson, S. (2001). 'Attachment theory and child abuse: An overview of the literature for practitioners'. *Child Abuse Review*, 10(7), 377–397.

Ban, P. (2005). 'Aboriginal child placement principle and family group conferences'. *Australian Social Work*, 58(4), 384–394.

Bancroft, L. & Silverman, J. (2002). *The Batterer as Parent: Addressing the Impact of Family Violence on Family Dynamics.* Thousand Oaks, CA: Sage.

Banks, D., Dutch, N. & Wang, K. (2008). 'Collaborative efforts to improve system response to families who are experiencing child maltreatment and domestic violence'. *Journal of Interpersonal Violence*, 23(7), 876–902.

Barber, J.G. & Delfabbro, P.H. (2004). *Children in Foster Care.* New York: Routledge.

Barber, J.G. & Gilbertson, R. (2001). *Foster Care: The State of the Art*. Adelaide: Australian Centre for Community Services Research.

Barker, C.H., Cook, K.L. & Borrego, J. (2010). 'Addressing cultural variables in parent training programs with Latino families'. *Cognitive and Behavioral Practice*, 17(2), 157–166.

Barnsdale, L. & Walker, M. (2007). *Examining the Use and Impact of Family Group Conferencing*. University of Stirling.

Barth, R.P., Crea, T.M., Thoburn, J.K. & Quinton, D. (2005). 'Beyond attachment theory and therapy: Towards sensitive and evidence-based interventions with foster and adoptive families in distress'. *Child and Family Social Work*, 10, 257–268.

Barwick, M.A., Boydell, K.M., Stasiulis, E., Ferguson, H.B., Blase, K. & Fixsen, D. (2005). *Knowledge Transfer and Evidence-Based Practice in Children's Mental Health*. Ontario, Toronto: Children's Mental Health.

Beilharz, L. (2002). *Building Community: The Shared Action Experience*. Bendigo, Victoria: Solutions Press.

Belt, R.H., Flykt, M., Pajulo, M., Posa, T. & Tamminen, T. (2012). 'Psychotherapy groups and individual support to enhance mental health and early dyadic interaction among drug-abusing mothers'. *Infant Mental Health Journal*, 33, 520–534

Bennett, L. & Williams, O.J. (2003). 'Substance abuse and men who batter: Issues in theory and practice'. *Violence Against Women*, 9(5), 558–575.

Benson, J. & Smith, M. (2007). 'Early health assessment of refugees'. *Australian Family Physician*, 36(1–2), 41–43.

Berk, J. (1998). 'Trauma and resilience during war: A look at the children and humanitarian aid workers of Bosnia'. *Psychoanalytic Review*, 85(4), 640–658.

Berlyn, C., Bromfield, L.M. & Lamont, A. (2011). 'Child protection and Aboriginal and Torres Strait Islander Children'. *National Child Protection Clearinghouse Resource Sheet*, 1–7.

Berry, J.G., Harrison, J.E. & Ryan, P. (2009). 'Hospital admissions of Indigenous and non-Indigenous Australians due to interpersonal violence, July 1999 to June 2004'. *Australian and New Zealand Journal of Public Health*, 33(3), 215–222.

Berry, M., Brandon, M., Chaskin, R., Fernandez, E., Grietens, H., Lightburn, A., McNamara, P.M., Munford, R., Palacio-Quintin, E., Sanders, J., Warren-Adamson, C. & Zeira, A. (2007). 'Identifying sensitive outcomes of interventions in community-based centres'. In M.Berry (ed.), *Identifying Essential Elements of Change: Lessons from International Research in Community Based Family Centres* (pp. 9–17). Leuven: Acco (Academische Coöperatieve Vennootschap cvba).

Berry, M., Charlson, R. & Dawson, K. (2003). 'Promising practices in understanding and treating child neglect'. *Child and Family Social Work*, 8(1), 13–24.

BigFoot, D.S. & Funderburk, B.W. (2011). 'Honoring children, making relatives: The cultural translation of parent–child interaction therapy for American Indian and Alaska Native families'. *Journal of Psychoactive Drugs*, 43(4), 309–318.

Biringen, Z. (2000). 'Emotional availability: Conceptualization and research findings'. *American Journal of Orthopsychiatry*, 70(1), 104–114.

—— (2004). *Raising a Secure Child: Creating Emotional Availability between Parents and Your Children*. New York: The Berkeley Publishing Group.

Boukydis, Z. (2006). 'Ultrasound consultation to reduce risk and increase resilience in pregnancy'. *Annals of the New York Academy of Sciences*, (1094), 268–271.

Bowen, S. & Zwi, A. (2005). 'Pathways to "evidence-informed" policy and practice. A framework for action'. *Policy Forum*, 2(7), 600–605.

Bowlby, J. (1953). *Child Care and the Growth of Love*. London: Penguin.

—— (1969). *Attachment and Loss: Vol I. Attachment*. New York: *Basic Books*.

—— (1979) *The Making and Breaking of Affectional Bonds*. London: Tavistock.

Briggs, H.E. & McBeath, B. (2009). 'Evidence-based management: Origins, challenges and implications for social service administration'. *Administration in Social Work*, 33(3), 242–261.

Brinkman, S., Gialamas, A., Rahman, A., Mittinty, M.N., Gregory, T.A., Silburn, S., Goldfeld, S., Zubrick, S.R., Carr, V., Janus, M., Hertzman, C. & Lynch, J.W. (2012). 'Jurisdictional, socioeconomic and gender inequalities in child health and development: Analysis of a national census of 5-year-olds in Australia'. *BMJ Open* 2012; 2:e001075. doi:10.1136/bmjopen-2012–001075

Bromfield, L.M. & Higgins, D.J. (2005). 'Chronic and isolated maltreatment in a child protection sample'. *Family Matters*, 70(38–45).

Bromfield, L.M., Higgins, J.R., Higgins, D.J. & Richardson, N. (2007). Why is there a shortage of Aboriginal and Torres Strait Islander carers? Promising practices in out-of-home care for Aboriginal and Torres Strait Islander carers and young people: Strengths and barriers. Paper 1. Melbourne: Australian Institute of Family Studies.

Bromfield, L., Lamont, A., Parker, R & Horsfall, B. (2010) Issues for the safety and wellbeing of children in families with multiple and complex problems: The co-occurrence of domestic violence, parental substance misuse and mental health problems. NCPC Issues, 33. Melbourne. Australian Institute of Family Studies. (www.aifs.gov/nch/pubs/issues/issues33).

Bromfield, L.M. & Osborn, A. (2007). '"Getting the big picture": A synopsis and critique of Australian out-of-home care research'. *Child Abuse Prevention Issues*, 26, National Child Protection Clearinghouse, Australian Institute of Family Studies, Melbourne.

Bronfenbrenner, U. (1979). *The Ecology of Human Development: Experiments by Nature and Design*. Cambridge, MA: Harvard University Press.

Brough, M., Gorman, D., Ramirez, E. & Westoby, P. (2003). 'Young refugees talk about well-being: A qualitative analysis of refugee youth mental health from three states'. *Australian Journal of Social Issues*, 38(2), 193–208.

Brown, G. & Harris, T. (1978). *Social Origins of Depression*. London: Tavistock.

Brown, L. (2003). 'Mainstream or margin? The current use of family group conferences in child welfare practice in the UK'. *Child and Family Social Work*, 8(4), 331–340.

—— (2005). Innovation in social work: Family Group Conferencing: A case study. Paper presented at the 2005 European PUBLIN Conference.

Brown, S., Lumley, J., Small, R. & Astbury, J. (1994). *Missing Voices: The Experience of Motherhood*. Melbourne: Oxford University Press.

Bruskas, D. (2008). 'Children in foster care: A vulnerable population at risk'. *Journal of Child and Adolescent Psychiatric Nursing*, 21(2), 70–77.

Burke, K., Ward, J. & Clayton, O. (2007). *ABCD Somali: Translation of the ABCD Parenting Young Adolescents Program for the Somali Community*. Carlton, Victoria: Parenting Research Centre.

Burkhalter, A., Bernardo, K.L. & Charles, V. (1993). 'Development of local circuits in the visual cortex'. *Journal of Neuroscience*, 13(5), 1916–1931.

Burry, C.L. & Wright, L. (2006). 'Facilitating visitation for infants with prenatal substance exposure'. *Child Welfare Journal*, 85, 899–918.

Cameron, M., Elkins, J. & Guterman, N. (2006). 'Assessment of trauma in children and youth'. In N.B.Webb (ed.), *Working with Traumatized Youth in Child Welfare*.

Campbell, J., Glass, N., Sharps, P.W., Laughon, K. & Bloom, T. (2007). 'Intimate partner homicide: Review and implications of research and policy'. *Trauma Violence and Abuse*, 8(3), 246–269.

Campbell, L. (1999). 'Collaboration: Building inter-agency networks for practice partnerships'. In V.Cowling (ed.), *Children of Parents with Mental Illness* (pp. 203–216). Melbourne: Australian Council of Education Research.

Cantos, A.L., Gries, L.T. & Slis, V. (1997). 'Behavioral correlates of parental visiting during family foster care'. *Child Welfare*, 76(2), 309–329.

Cantwell, S. (2004). 'Involving men in a home visit'. In FletcherR (ed.), *Bringing Fathers In: How to Engage with Men for the Benefit of Everyone in the Family*. Newcastle: University of Newcastle.

Carter, B. & McGoldrick, M. (eds). (1999). *The Expanded Family Life Cycle* (3rd edn). Boston: Allyn & Bacon.

Caruana, C. (2006). 'Shared parental responsibility and the reshaping of family law'. *Family Matters*, 74, 56–59.

Cash, S. & Wilke, D. (2003). 'An ecological model of maternal substance abuse and child neglect: Issues, analyses, and recommendations'. *American Journal of Orthopsychiatry*, 73(4), 392–404.

Cashmore, J.A., Higgins, D.J., Bromfield, L.M. & Scott, D.A. (2006). 'Recent Australian child protection and out-of-home care research: What has been done?' *Children Australia*, 31(2), 4–11.

Cashmore, J.A. & Paxman, M. (1996). *Wards Leaving Care: A Longitudinal Study*. Sydney: Department of Community Services.

—— (2007). *A Longitudinal Study of Wards Leaving Care: Four to Five Years On*. Sydney: Department of Community Services.

Caspe, M. & Lopez, M.E. (2006). *Lessons from Family-Strengthening Interventions: Learning from Evidence-Based Practice*. Harvard Family Research Project. Cambridge, MA: Harvard Graduate School of Education.

Caspi, A., Sugden, K., Moffitt, T.E., Taylor, A., Craig, I.W., Harrington, H., McClay, J., Mill, J., Martin, J., Braithwaite, A. & Poulton, R. (2003). 'Influence of life stress on depression: Moderation by a polymorphism in the 5-HTT gene'. *Science*, 301 (5631), 386–389.

Cassidy, J. & Shaver. P (eds). (2008). *Handbook of Attachment: Theory, Research and Clinical Applications* (2nd edn). New York: Guilford.

Catalano, R.F., Gainey, R.R., Fleming, C.B., Haggerty, K.P. & Johnson, N.O. (1999). 'An experimental intervention with families of substance abusers: One-year follow-up of the Focus on Families project'. *Addiction*, 94, 241–254.

Centre for Community Child Health (2004a). *Parenting Information Project. Volume One: Main Report*. Commonwealth of Australia, Canberra.

—— (2004b). *Parenting Information Project. Volume 2: Literature Review*. Canberra: Department of Family and Community Services.

—— (2004c). *Parenting Information Project Volume 3*. Canberra: Australian Government.

Centre for Community Child Health (CCCH) & Telethon Institute for Child Health Research (TICHR). (2009). *A Snapshot of Early Childhood Development in Australia: AEDI National Report 2009*. Canberra: Australian Government.

Centre for Multicultural Youth Issues (2006). 'Family and Community Issues'. Available online at: www.cmy.net.au/FamilyandCommunity.

Chadwick Center. (2004). *Closing the Quality Chasm in Child Abuse Treatment: Identifying and Disseminating Best Practices – The Findings of the Kauffman Best Practices Project to Help Children*. San Diego: Children's Hospital and Health Center for Children and Families.

Chaffin, M. (2004). 'Is it time to rethink Healthy Start/Healthy Families?' *Child Abuse & Neglect*, 28(6), 589–595.

Chamberlain, P., Price, J., Leve, L.D., Laurent, H., Landsverk, J.A. & Reid, J.B. (2008). 'Prevention of behaviour problems for children in foster care: Outcomes and mediation effects'. *Prevention Science*, 9(1), 17–27.

Chapman, L.L. (2000). 'Expectant fathers and labor epidurals'. *The American Journal of Maternal Child Nursing*, 25(3), 133–138.

Chiswick, B.R. & Lee, Y.L. (2006). 'Immigrants' language skills and visa category'. *International Migration Review*, 40(2), 419–450.

Chung, R. (2001). 'Psychosocial adjustment of Cambodian refugee women: Implications for mental health counseling'. *Journal of Mental Health Counseling*, 23(2), 115–126.

Cicchetti, D. & Cohen, D.J. (2006). *Developmental Psychopathology: Theory and Method* (2nd edn). New York: John Wiley and Sons.

Colic-Peisker, V. & Tilbury, F. (2006). 'Employment niches for recent refugees: Segmented labour market in twenty-first century Australia'. *Journal of Refugee Studies*, 19(2), 203–229.

Colic-Peisker, V. & Walker, I. (2003). 'Human capital, acculturation and social identity: Bosnian refugees in Australia'. *Journal of Community and Applied Social Psychology*, 13, 337–360.

Collins, A. & Pancoast, D. (1976). *Natural Helping Networks. A Strategy for Prevention.* Washington, DC: National Association of Social Workers.

Commission for Children and Young People and Child Guardian. (2013). *Queensland Child Guardian Key Outcome Indicators Update: Queensland Child Protection System 2008–2011*. Queensland: Commission for Children and Young People and Child Guardian.

Connell-Carrick, K. (2003). 'A critical review of the empirical literature: Identifying correlates of child neglect'. *Child and Adolescent Social Work Journal*, 20(5), 389–425.

Connolly, M. (2007). 'Family group conferences in child welfare'. *Developing Practice*, 19, 25–33.

—— (2010). 'Engaging family members in decision-making in child welfare contexts'. In F.Arney & D.Scott (eds), *Working with Vulnerable Families: A Partnership Approach* (pp. 209–266). Melbourne: Cambridge University Press.

Connors-Burrow, N.A., Johnson, B. & Whiteside-Mansell, L. (2009). 'Maternal substance abuse and children's exposure to violence'. *Journal of Pediatric Nursing*, 24(5), 360–368.

Coohey, C. (1995). 'Neglectful mothers, their mothers, and partners: The significance of mutual aid'. *Child Abuse & Neglect*, 19(8), 885–895.

Cook, A., Spinazzola, J., Ford, J., Lanktree, C., Blaustein, M., Cloitre, M., DeRosa, R., Hubbard, R., Kagan, R., Liautaud, J., Mallah, K., Olafson, E. & van der Kolk, B. (2005). 'Complex trauma in children and adolescents'. *Psychiatric Annals*, 35(5), 390–399.

Correa-Velez, I., Gifford, S. & Bice, S. (2005). 'Australian health policy on access to medical care for refugees and asylum seekers'. *Australia and New Zealand Health Policy*, 2(1), 23–34.

Council on Community Paediatrics. (2009). 'The role of preschool home-visiting programs in improving children's developmental and health outcomes'. *Paediatrics*, 123, 598–603.

Courtney, M.E., Piliavin, I., Grogan-Kaylor, A. & Nesmith, A. (2001). 'Foster youth transitions to adulthood: A longitudinal view of youth leaving care'. *Child Welfare*, 80, 685–717.

Cowen, E.L., Wyman, P.A., Work, W.C. & Parker, G.R. (1990). 'The Rochester Child Resilience Project: Overview and summary of first year findings'. *Development and Psychopathology*, 2, 193–212.

Cowen, P. (1999). 'Child neglect: Injuries of omission'. *Pediatric Nursing*, 25(4), 401–418.

Cowling, V. (2004). *Children of Parents with a Mental Illness: 2. Personal and Clinical Perspectives*. Melbourne: Australian Council of Educational Research.

Craven, P.A. & Lee, R.E. (2006). 'Therapeutic interventions for foster children: A systemic research synthesis'. *Research on Social Work Practice*, 16, 287–304.

Crittenden, P. (1985). 'Social networks, quality of childrearing and child development'. *Child Development*, 5(56), 1299–1313.

Crittenden, P.M. (2006). 'A dynamic-maturational model of attachment'. *Australian New Zealand Journal of Family Therapy*, 27, 105–115.

Crittenden, P. & Dubowitz, H. (1999). 'Child neglect: causes and contributors'. In Thousand Oaks: Sage Publications.

Cunneen, C. & Libesman, T. (2000). 'Postcolonial trauma: The contemporary removal of Indigenous children and young people from their families in Australia'. *Australian Journal of Social Issues*, 35(2), 99–115.

Curran, G.M., Bauer, M., Mittman, B., Pyne, J.M. & Stetler, C. (2012). 'Effectiveness–implementation hybrid designs: Combining elements of clinical effectiveness and implementation research to enhance public health impact'. *Medical Care*, 50(3), 217–226.

d'Abbs, P. (1982). *Social Support Networks*. Australian Institute of Family Studies, Melbourne.

Daley, M. & Doughty, M. (2006). 'Ethics complaints in social work practice: A rural–urban comparison'. *Journal of Social Work Values and Ethics*. Retrieved 12/2/2007 from http://www.socialworker.com/jswve/content/view/28/44/

Damant, D., Lapierre, S., Lebosse, C., Thibault, S., Lessard, G., Hamelin-Brabant, L., Lavergne, C. & Fortin, A. (2010). 'Women's abuse of their children in the context of domestic violence: Reflection from women's accounts'. *Child and Family Social Work*, 15, 12–21.

Daniel, B. (2004). 'An overview of the Scottish Multidisciplinary Child Protection Review'. *Child and Family Social Work*, 9(3), 247–257.

Daniel, B., Vincent, S., Farrall, E. & Arney, F. (2009). 'How is the concept of resilience operationalised in practice with vulnerable children?' *International Journal of Child and Family Welfare*, 1, 2–21.

Darlington, Y., Feeney, J. & Rixon, K. (2004). 'Complexity, conflict and uncertainty: Issues in collaboration between child protection and mental health services'. *Children and Youth Services Review*, 26, 1175–1192.

Darlington, Y., Healy, K. & Feeney, J.A. (2010). 'Challenges in implementing participatory practice in child protection: A contingency approach'. *Children and Youth Services Review*, 32, 1020–1027.

Daro, D. (1988). *Confronting Child Abuse: Research for Effective Program Design*. New York: The Free Press.

Davis, H., Day, C. & Bidmead, C. (2002). *Working in Partnership with Parents: The Parent Adviser Model*. London: Harcourt Assessment.

Dawe, S., Frye, S., Best, D., Lynch, M., Atkinson, J., Evans, C. & Harnett, P.H. (2007). *Drug Use in the Family: Impacts and Implications for Children*. Canberra: Australian National Council on Drugs.

Dawe, S. & Harnett, P.H. (2007a). 'Improving family functioning in methadone maintained families: Results from a randomised control trial'. *Journal of Substance Abuse Treatment*, 32, 381–390.

—— (2007b). 'Reducing child abuse potential in methadone maintained parents: Results from a randomised controlled trial'. *Journal of Substance Abuse Treatment*, 32, 381–390.

—— (2013). 'Working with parents with substance misuse problems'. In F.Arney & D.Scott (eds), *Working with Vulnerable Families: A Partnership Approach*. Melbourne: Cambridge University Press.

Dawe, S., Harnett, P.H., Rendalls, V. & Staiger, P. (2003). 'Improving family functioning and child outcome in methadone maintained families: The Parents Under Pressure program. *Drug and Alcohol Review*, 22, 299–307.

Dawe, S., Harnett, P.H., Staiger, P. & Dadds, M.R. (2000). 'Parent training skills and methadone maintenance: Clinical opportunities and challenges'. *Drug and Alcohol Dependence*, 60, 1–11.

Day, A., O'Leary, P., Chung, D. & Justo, D. (2009). *Domestic Violence: Working with Men*. Leichhardt, NSW: The Federation Press.

de Boer, C. & Coady, N. (2003). *Good Helping Relationships in Child Welfare: Co-authored Stories of Success*. Partnerships for Children and Families Project. Faculty of Social Work, Wilfrid Laurier University.

—— (2007). 'Good helping relationships in child welfare: Learning from stories of success'. *Child and Family Social Work*, 12, 32–42.

DECS Curriculum Services. Timeline of legislation affecting Aboriginal people. Available online at: http://www.lmrc.sa.edu.au/files/links/Timeline_of_legisation2.pdf

DeKlyen, M. & Greenberg, M. (2008). 'Attachment and psychopathology in childhood'. In J.Cassidy & P.Shaver (eds), *Handbook of Attachment: Theory, Research and Clinical Applications* (2nd edn) (pp. 637–657). New York: Guilford Press.

Delfabbro, P., Borgas, M., Rogers, N., Jeffreys, H. & Wilson, R. (2009). 'The social and family backgrounds of infants in South Australian out-of-home care 2000–2005: Predictors of subsequent abuse notifications'. *Children and Youth Services Review*, 31, 219–226.

Delfabbro, P., Hirte, C., Rogers, N. & Wilson, R. (2010). 'The over-representation of young Aboriginal or Torres Strait Islander people in the South Australian child system: A longitudinal analysis'. *Children and Youth Services Review*, 32(10), 1418–1425.

Delfabbro, P., Kettler, L., McCormick, J. & Fernandez, E. (2012). The nature and predictors of reunification in Australian out-of-home care. Paper presented at the Family Transitions and Trajectories. 12th Australian Institute of Family Studies Conference, Melbourne.

DePanfilis, D. (1996). 'Social isolation of neglectful families: A review of social support assessment and intervention models'. *Child Maltreatment*, 1(1), 37–52.

—— (1999). 'Intervening with families when children are neglected'. In H.Dubowitz (ed.), *Neglected Children: Research, Practice, and Policy* (pp. 211–236). Thousand Oaks: Sage Publications.

Department for Education and Skills. (2006). Children Looked After in England (Including Adoptions and Care Leavers), 2005–2006. National Statistics First Release, SFR244/2006. 16 November 2006.

Department of Families, Housing & Community Services and Indigenous Affairs together with the National Framework Implementation Working Group. (2011). *National Standards for Out-Of-Home Care*, Canberra: Australian Government.

Department of Human Services. (2007). *Aboriginal Family Preservation and Restoration*. Melbourne: Victorian Department of Human Services.

Depew, R.C. (1996). 'Popular justice and Aboriginal communities – Some preliminary considerations. *Journal of Legal Pluralism*, 36, 21–67.

DIAC (2011). Refugee and Humanitarian Issues: Australia's Response. Available online at: http://www.immi.gov.au/media/publications/refugee/ref-hum-issues/ref-hum-issues-june11.htm

—— (2012). Department of Immigration and Citizenship Settlement Database. Available online at: http://www.immi.gov.au/visas/humanitarian/

Diemer, K. (2012). *Victorian Family Violence Trend Analysis Report* 1999–2012, Report No 5. Melbourne: Victorian Government.

DiLeonardi, J. (1993). 'Families in poverty and chronic neglect of children'. *Families in Society: The Journal of Contemporary Human Services*, 74(9), 557–562.

DIMIA (2005). *Australia's Support for Humanitarian Entrants.* Department of Immigration and Multicultural and Indigenous Affairs, Canberra. Available online at: www.scoa.org.au/resources/273696_72752_chapters_1_2.pdf.

Dobash, R.P., Dobash, R.E., Wilson, M. & Daly, M. (1992). 'The myth of sexual symmetry in marital violence'. *Social problems*, 39(1), 71–91.

Dobbins, M., Ciliska, D., Cockeril, R., Barnsley, J. & DiCenso, A. (2002). 'A framework for the dissemination and utilisation of research for health-care policy and practice'. *Online Journal of Knowledge Synthesis for Nursing*, 9, 149–160.

Doel, M. (2010). 'Service user perspectives on relationships'. In G.Ruch, D.Turney & A.Ward (eds), *Relationship Based Social Work: Getting to the Heart of Practice* (pp. 199–213). London: Jessica Kingsley Publishers.

Donovan, R., Paterson, D. & Francas, M. (1999). 'Targeting male perpetrators of intimate partner violence: Western Australia's "Freedom from Fear" campaign'. *Social Marketing Quarterly*, 5(3) 127–144.

Dore, M. & Alexander, L. (1996). 'Preserving families at risk of child abuse and neglect: The role of the helping alliance'. *Child Abuse & Neglect*, 20, 349–361.

Dore, M. & Lee, J. (1999). 'The role of parent training with abusive and neglectful parents'. *Family Relations*, 48, 313–335.

Dozier, M. & Rutter, M. (2008). 'Challenges to the development of attachment relationships faced by young children in foster and adoptive care'. In J.Cassidy & P.Shaver (eds), *Handbook of Attachment: Theory, Research and Clinical Applications* (pp. 698–717). New York: Guilford Press.

Drake, B. (1994). 'Relationship competences in child welfare services'. *Social Work*, 39(5), 595–602.

DuBois, D.L., Holloway, B.E., Valentine, J.C. & Cooper, H. (2002). 'Effectiveness of mentoring programs for youth: A meta-analytic review'. *American Journal of Community Psychology*, 30(2), 157–197.

Dudgeon, P., Wright, M., Paradies, Y., Garvey, D. & Walker, I. (2010). 'The social, cultural and historical context of Aboriginal and Torres Strait Islander Australians'. In N.Purdie, P.Dudgeon & R.Walker (eds), *Working Together: Aboriginal and Torres Strait Islander Mental Health and Wellbeing Principles and Practice*. Canberra: Australian Government Department of Health and Ageing.

Dumbrill, G.C. (2006). 'Parental experience of child protection intervention: A qualitative study'. *Child Abuse & Neglect*, 30(1), 27–37.

Dunn, J. (1993). *Young children's close relationships: Beyond attachment.* Thousand Oaks, CA: Sage Publications.

Dunn, M., Tarter, R., Mezzich, A., Vanyukov, M., Kirisci, L. & Kirillova, G. (2002). 'Origins and consequences of child neglect in substance abuse families'. *Clinical Psychology Review*, 22(7), 1063–1090.

Durlak, J.A. (1998). 'Common risk and protective factors in successful programs'. *American Journal of Orthopsychiatry*, 68(4), 512–520.

Durlak, J. & Du Pre, E. (2008). 'Implementation matters: A review of research on the influence of implementation on program outcomes and the factors affecting implementation'. *American Journal of Community Psychology*, 41, 327–350.

Easterbrooks, M.A. & Biringen, Z. (2005). 'The Emotional Availability Scales: Methodological refinements of the construct and clinical implications related to gender and at-risk interactions'. *Infant Mental Health Journal*, 26, 291–294.

Edgecomb, G., White, S., Marsh, G., Jackson, C., Hanna, B., Newman, S. & Scott, D. (2001). *First Time Parent Group Resource and Facilitation Guide for Maternal and Child Health Nurses*. Melbourne: Victorian Department of Human Services.

Edleson, J. (1999). 'Children witnessing of adult domestic violence'. *Journal of Interpersonal Violence*, 14(4), 839–870.

Edleson, J., Mbilinyi, L., Beeman, S. & Hagemeister, A. (2003). *How Children are Involved in Adult Domestic Violence: Results from a Four City Telephone Survey*. St Paul, Minnesota: University of Minnesota.

Edwards, J. (2004). 'Making the change towards fathers: The example of the Benevolent Society's Early Intervention Program'. In R.Fletcher (ed.), *Bringing Fathers In: How to Engage with Men for the Benefit of Everyone in the Family*. Newcastle: University of Newcastle.

Egeland, B. & Sroufe, L.A (1981). 'Attachment and early maltreatment'. *Child Development*, 52, 49–52.

Ellenbogen, S. & Wekerle, C. (2008). 'Visitation practices in child welfare organisations'. *Ontario Association of Children's Aid Societies Journal*, 52, 18–24.

Ellsberg, M., Jansen, H.A.F.M., Heise, L., Watts, C.H. & García-Moreno, C. (2008). 'Intimate partner violence and women's physical and mental health in the WHO multi-country study on women's health and domestic violence: An observational study'. *The Lancet*, 371(9619), 1165–1172.

Erickson, M. & Egeland, B. (1996). 'Child neglect'. In J.Briere, L.Berliner, J.Bulkley, C.Jenny & T.Reid (eds), *The APSAC Handbook on Child Maltreatment*. Thousand Oaks: Sage Publications.

Evangelou, M., Sylva, K., Edwards, A. & Smith, T. (2008). *Supporting Parents in Promoting Early Learning: The Evaluation of the Early Learning Partnership Project*. Oxford: University of Oxford.

Eyberg, S.M., Nelson, M.M. & Boggs, S.R. (2008). 'Evidence-based psychosocial treatments for children and adolescents with disruptive behaviour'. *Journal of Clinical Child and Adolescent Psychology*, 37(1), 215–237.

Family Violence Protection Act Victoria (2008) http://www.austlii.edu.au/au/legis/vic/consol_act/fvpa2008283/ Retrieved 13.11.2012.

Fanshel, D. (1975). 'Parental visiting of children in foster care: Key to discharge?' *Social Services Review*, 49, 493–514.

Fanshel, D. & Shinn, E.B. (1978). *Children in Foster Care: A Longitudinal Investigation*. New York: Columbia University Press.

Fantuzzo, J.W. & Fusco, R.A. (2007). 'Children's direct exposure to types of domestic violence crime: A population-based investigation'. *Journal of Family Violence*, 22(7), 543–552.

Fazel, M. & Stein, A. (2002). 'The mental health of refugee children'. *Archives of Disease in Childhood*, 87(5), 366–370.

Featherstone, B. & Fraser, C. (2012) 'Working with fathers around domestic violence: Contemporary debates'. *Child Abuse & Neglect*, 21, 255–263.

Feingold, A., Kerr, D.C.R. & Capaldi, D.M. (2008). 'Associations of substance use problems with intimate partner violence for at-risk men in long-term relationships'. *Journal of Family Psychology*, 22(3), 429–438.

Feldman, R. (2003). 'Infant–Mother and Infant–Father synchrony: The coregulation of positive arousal'. *Infant Mental Health Journal*, 24(1), 1–23.

Fernandez, E. (1996). *Significant Harm: Unravelling Child Protection Decisions and Substitute Care Careers of Children*. Aldershot, UK: Ashgate Publishing Limited.

Fernandez, E. & Healy, J. (2007). 'Supporting families and responding to families: Steps on the way to family change'. In M.Berry (ed.), *Identifying Essential Elements of Change: Lessons from International Research in Community Based Family Centres* (pp. 35–50). Leuven: Acco (Academische Coöperatieve Vennootschap cvba).

Finkelhor, D., Ormrod, R.K. & Turner, H.A. (2009). 'Lifetime assessment of poly-victimization in a national sample of children and youth'. *Child Abuse & Neglect*, 33, 403–411.

Fisher, M., Marsh, P., Phillips, D. & Sainsbury, E. (1986). *In and Out of Home Care: The Experiences of Children, Parents and Social Workers*. London: B.T. Batsford Ltd.

Fisher, S. (2011). From Violence to Coercive Control: Renaming Men's Abuse of Women. White Ribbon Research Series: No. 3 http://www.whiteribbon.org.au/uploads/media/449%20White%20Ribbon%20-%20Policy%20Report%20Fisher%20%28web%29%20-%20111220.pdf.

Fixsen, D., Blase, K.A., Naoom, S.F. & Wallace, F. (2009). 'Core implementation components'. *Research on Social Work Practice*, 19(5), 531–540.

Fixsen, D., Naoom, S.F., Blase, K.A., Friedman, R.M. & Wallace, F. (2005). *Implementation Research: A Synthesis of the Literature*. Florida: University of South Florida.

Fleming, L. & Tobin, D. (2005). 'Popular child-rearing books: Where is daddy?' *Psychology of Men & Masculinity*, 6(1), 18–24.

Fletcher, R. (2004). 'Bringing fathers in: How to engage with men for the benefit of everyone in the family'. In R.Fletcher (ed.), *Bringing Fathers In: How to Engage* with *Men for the Benefit of Everyone in the Family*. Newcastle, NSW: University of Newcastle.

—— (2009). 'Brief report: Promoting infant well being in the context of maternal depression by supporting the father'. *Infant Mental Health Journal*, 30(1), 95–102.

Fletcher, R., Matthey, S. & Marley, C. (2006). 'Addressing depression and anxiety among new fathers'. *Medical Journal of Australia*, 185, 461–463.

Fletcher, R., Silberberg, S. & Baxter, R. (2001). *Fathers' Access to Family-Related Services*. University of Newcastle, Newcastle, NSW.

Fletcher, R., Silberberg, S. & Galloway, D. (2004). 'New fathers' post-birth views of antenatal classes: Satisfaction, benefits, and knowledge of family services'. *The Journal of Peri-natal Education*, 13(3), 18–26.

Fletcher, R. & Willoughby, P. (2002). *Fatherhood: Legal, Biological and Social Definitions*. Newcastle, NSW: Family Action Centre, University of Newcastle.

Fluckiger, B., Diamond, P. & Jones, W. (2012) 'Yarning space: Leading literacy through family–school partnerships'. *Australasian Journal of Early Childhood*, 37(3), 53–59.

Fonagy, P. & Target, M. (2004). 'What works for whom? Differential indications for treatment/intervention'. In H.Remschmidt, M.L.Belfer & I.Goodyer (eds), *Facilitating Pathways: Care, Treatment and Prevention in Child and Adolescent Mental Health* (pp. 119–139). Berlin: Springer Medizin Verlag.

Fontes, L. A. (2008). *Interviewing Clients Across Cultures: A Practitioner's Guide*. New York: The Guilford Press.

Ford, J. (2005). 'Treatment implications of altered neurobiology, affect regulation and information processing following child maltreatment'. *Psychiatric Annals*, 35, 410–419.

Ford, J. & Courtois, C. (2009). 'Defining and understanding complex trauma'. In C.Courtois & J.Ford (eds). *Treating Complex Traumatic Stress Disorders: An Evidence-Based Guide* (pp. 13–30). New York: Guilford Press.

Forman, S.G., Olin, S.S., Hoagwood, K.E., Crowe, M. & Saka, N. (2009). 'Evidence-based interventions in schools: Developers' views of implementation barriers and facilitators'. *School Mental Health*, 1, 26–36.

Fox, G. & Benson, M. (2004). 'Violent men, bad dads? Fathering profiles of men involved in intimate partner violence'. In R.Day & M.Lamb (eds), *Conceptualizing and Measuring Father Involvement*. Mahwah, New Jersey: Lawrence Erlbaum Associates Publishers.

Frank, D.A., Brown, J., Johnson, C. & Cabral, H. (2002). 'Forgotten fathers: An exploratory study of mothers' report of drug and alcohol problems among fathers'. *Neurotoxicology and Teratology*, 24(30), 339–347.

Frantzen, D., San Miguel, C. & Kwak, D. (2011). 'Predicting case conviction and domestic violence recidivism'. *Violence and Victims*, 26(4), 395–409.

Friedlander, M., Escudero, V. & Heatherington, L. (2006). *Engagement in the Therapeutic Process*. Washington, DC: American Psychological Association.

Garbarino, J. (1982). *Children and Families in the Social Environment*. New York: Aldine Publishing Co.

—— (1999). *Raising Children in a Socially Toxic Environment*. San Francisco: Jossey-Bass.

Garbarino, J. & Collins, C. (1999). 'Child neglect: The family with a hole in the middle'. In H.Dubowitz (ed.), *Neglected Children: Research, Practice, and Policy*. Thousand Oaks: Sage Publications.

Garland, A.F., Hawley, K.M., Brookman-Frazee, L. & Hurlburt, M.S. (2008). 'Identifying common elements of evidence-based psychosocial treatments for children's disruptive behavior disorders'. *Journal of the American Academy of Child and Adolescent Psychiatry*, 47, 505–514.

Gaudin, J. (1993). 'Effective intervention with neglectful families'. *Criminal Justice and Behaviour*, 20(1), 66–89.

Gaudin, J. & Polansky, N. (1986). 'Social distances and the neglectful family: Sex, race, and social class influences'. *Children and Youth Services Review*, 8, 1–12.

Gaudin, J., Polansky, N., Kilpatrick, A. & Shilton, P. (1996). 'Family functioning in neglectful families'. *Child Abuse & Neglect*, 20(4), 363–377.

Geddes, M. (2006). Evaluating English experience of governments and communities in partnership: The Empire strikes back? Governments and Communities in Partnership Conference. Centre for Public Policy, University of Melbourne.

Gibson, C. & Morphett, K. (2011). 'Creative responses to the needs of homeless children: Promising practice', *Developing Practice*, 28, 23–31.

Ginsberg, L. (1998). 'Introduction: An overview of rural social work'. In L.Ginsberg (ed.), *Social Work in Rural Communities* (3rd edn). Alexandria, VA: Council on Social Work Education.

Girvin, H., DePanfilis, D. & Daining, C. (2007). 'Predicting program completion among families enrolled in a child neglect preventive intervention'. *Research on Social Work Practice*, 17, 674–685.

Gíslason. (2007). *Parental Leave in Iceland. Bringing the Fathers In: Developments in the Wake of New Legislation in 2000*. Akureyri, Iceland: Ministry of Social Affairs and Centre for Gender Equality.

Gockel, A., Russell, M. & Harris, B. (2008). 'Recreating family: Parents identify worker–client relationships as paramount in family preservation programs'. *Child Welfare*, 87(6), 91–113.

Goddard, C. & Bedi, G. (2010). 'Intimate partner violence and child abuse: A child-centred perspective'. *Child Abuse Review*, 19, 5–20.

Goff, S. (2012). 'The participation of fathers in child protection conferences: A practitioner's perspective. *Child Abuse Review*, 21(4), 275–284

Gogtay, N., Giedd, J.N., Lusk, L., Hayashi, K.M., Greenstein, D. & Vaituzis, A.C. (2004). 'Dynamic mapping of human cortical development during childhood through early adulthood'. *Proceedings of the National Academy of Sciences USA*, (101), 8174–8179.

Golding, J.M. (1999). 'Intimate partner violence as a risk factor for mental disorders: A meta analysis'. *Journal of Family Violence*, 14(2), 99–132.

Golding, K. (2006). 'Finding the light at the end of the tunnel: Parenting interventions for adoptive and foster carers'. In K.S.Golding, H.R.Dent., R.Nissim & L.Stott, (eds), *Thinking Psychologically about Children Who are Looked After and Adopted: Space for Reflection* (pp. 195–221). Sussex: John Wiley & Sons.

—— (2008). *Nurturing Attachments: Supporting Children Who are Fostered or Adopted*. London: Jessica Kingsley Publishers.

Gondolf, E.W. (2002). *Batterer Intervention Systems: Issues, Outcomes and Recommendations*. Thousand Oaks, CA: Sage.

Gonsalves, C. (1992). 'Psychological stages of the refugee process: A model for therapeutic interventions'. *Professional Psychology: Research & Practice*, 23(5), 382–389.

Goodfellow, J., Camus, S., Gyorog, D., Watt, M. & Druce, J. (2004). *'It's a Lot Different Now': A Description and Evaluation of an Innovative Family Support Program within Mainstream Early Childhood Services*. Redfern, NSW: SDN Children's Services.

Goodman, R. (2001). 'Psychometric properties of the Strengths and Difficulties Questionnaire'. *Journal of the American Academy of Child and Adolescent Psychiatry*, 40, 1337–1345.

Gottfredson, D.C., Gottfredson, G.D. & Hybl, L.G. (1993). 'Managing adolescent behavior: A multiyear, multischool study'. *American Educational Research Journal*, 30, 179–215.

Gottlieb, B. (1981). *Social Networks and Social Support*. Beverly Hills: Sage.

Gray, A. & Elliott, S. (2001). 'Refugee Resettlement Research Project Literature Review'. Available online at: http://www.dol.govt.nz/research/migration/refugees/refugeevoices/RefugeeVoicesLiteratureReview.pdf

Green, L.W. (2012). Implementation research and practice: If we want more evidence-based practice, we need more practice-based evidence. Paper presented at the First Biennial Australian Conference on Implementation.

Green, R. (2003). 'Social work in rural areas: A personal and professional challenge'. *Australian Social Work*, 56, 209–219.

Green, R., Gregory, R. & Mason, R. (2006). 'Professional distance and social work: Stretching the elastic?' *Australian Social Work*, 59(4), 449–461.

Greenhalgh, T., Robert, G., Bate, P., Macfarlane, F. & Kyriakidou, O. (2005). *Diffusion of Innovations in Health Service Organizations: A Systematic Literature Review*. Malden, MA: Blackwell Publishing.

Greenhalgh, T., Robert, G., Macfarlane, F., Bate, P. & Kyriakidou, O. (2004). 'Diffusion of innovations in health service organisations: Systematic review and recommendations'. *Milbank Quarterly*, 82, 581–629.

Grimshaw, J. & Russell, I. (1993). 'Effect of clinical guidelines on medical practice: A systematic review of rigorous evaluations'. *Lancet*, 342(8883), 1317–1322.

Gruenert, S. & Tsantefski, M. (2012) 'Responding to the needs of children and their parents in families experiencing alcohol and other drug problems'. *Prevention Research Quarterly*, 17, 1–15.

Guerin, B., Guerin, P., Abdi, A. & Diiriye, R. (2003). 'Identity and community: Somali children's adjustments to life in the Western world'. In J.Gao, R.Le Heron & J.Logie (eds), *Windows on a Changing World* (pp. 184–188). Auckland: New Zealand Geographical Society.

Guthridge, S.L., Ryan, P., Condon, J. R,, Bromfield, L.M., Moss, J.R. & Lynch, J.W. (2012). 'Trends in reports of child maltreatment in the Northern Territory, 1999–2010'. *Medical Journal of Australia*, 197(11), 637–641.

Haebich, A. (2000). *Broken Circles: Fragmenting Indigenous Families 1800–2000*. Fremantle, WA: Fremantle Arts Centre Press.

Haggerty, K., Skinner, M., Fleming, C.B., Gainey, R.R. & Catalano, R.F. (2008). 'Long-term effects of focus on families on substance use disorders among children of parents in methadone treatment'. *Addiction*, 103, 2008–2016.

Hague, G, Mullender, A. & Aris, R. (2003). *Is Anyone Listening? Accountability and Women Survivors of Domestic Violence*. London: Routledge.

Haight, W.L., Black, J.E., Mangelsdorf, S., Giorgio, G., Tata, L., Schoppe, S.J. & Szcivczyk, M. (2002). 'Making visits better: The perspectives of parents, foster parents, and child welfare workers'. *Child Welfare*, 81(2), 173–202.

Hallet, C. & Birchall, E. (1992). *Working Together in Child Protection: Report of Phase Two, a Survey of the Experience and Perceptions of Six Key Professions*. Stirling, UK: Department of Applied Social Science, University of Stirling.

Hammond, C., Lester, J., Fletcher, R. & Pascoe, S. (2004). 'Young Aboriginal fathers: The findings and impact of a research project undertaken in the Hunter Valley'. *Aboriginal Islander and Health Worker Journal*, 28(5), 5–8.

Handel, G. & Whitchurch, G. (1994). *The Psychosocial Interior of the Family* (4th edn). New York: Aldine de Gruyter,

Hannon, T. (2007). *Children: Unintended Victims of Legal Process: Action Paper*. Melbourne: Victorian Association for the Care and Resettlement of Offenders.

Hanrahan, C. (2004). *Rethinking Parent Participation: A Process Evaluation of the Parents and Learning Program in Napranum*. Townsville, Queensland: James Cook University.

Hansen, P. & Ainsworth, F. (2008). 'Children in out-of-home care: What drives the increase in admissions and how to make a change'. *Children Australia*, 33(4), 13–20.

Hanson, R. & Spratt, E. (2000). 'Reactive attachment disorder: What we know about the disorder and implications for treatment'. *Child Maltreatment*, 5, 137–145.

Harkness, S. & Super, C.M. (1996). *Parents' Cultural Belief Systems: Their Origins, Expressions and Consequences*. New York: The Guilford Press.

Harne, L. (2011). *Violent Fathering and the Risks to Children: The Need for Change*. Bristol, UK: The Policy Press

Harnett, P.H. (2007). 'A procedure for assessing parents' capacity for change in child protection cases'. *Children and Youth Services Review*, 29, 1179–1188.

Harnett, P.H. & Dawe, S. (2012). 'The contribution of mindfulness-based therapies for children and families and a proposed conceptual integration'. *Child and Adolescent Mental Health*. 17(4), 195–208.

—— (in press). 'Parenting and drug use'. In C.Gerada (ed.), *The Management of Substance Misuse in Primary Care*. London: Royal College of General Practitioners.

Harris, M. & Zwar, N. (2005). 'Refugee health'. *Australian Family Physician*, 34(10), 825–829.

Harris, N. (2008). 'Family group conferencing in Australia 15 years on'. *Child Abuse Prevention Issues*, 27. Melbourne: Australian Institute of Family Studies.

Hawes, D.J. & Dadds, M.R. (2004). 'Australian data and psychometric properties of the Strengths and Difficulties Questionnaire'. *Australian and New Zealand Journal of Psychiatry*, 38, 644–651.

Hayes, A., Gray, M. & Edwards, B. (2008). *Social Inclusion: Origin, Concepts and Key Themes*. Canberra: Department of Prime Minister and Cabinet, Social Inclusion Unit.

Healey, L., Humphreys, C. & Howe, K. (2013, in press). Inclusive domestic violence standards, codes, and guidelines: A strategy for improving service responses to women with disabilities, *Violence and Victims*.

Health Social Services and Public Safety. (2006). Children Order Statistical Bulletin 2006. Retrieved 23rd July 2008, from http://www.dhsspsni.gov.uk/stats-cib-cobulletindec06-2.pdf

Healy, J. & Bell, M. (2005). *Assessing the Risks to Children from Domestic Violence*. Policy and Practice Briefing No. 7. Northern Ireland: Barnardo's.

Heaman, M., Chalmers, K., Woodgate, R. & Brown, J. (2007). 'Relationship work in an early childhood home visiting program'. *Journal of Pediatric Nursing*, 22(4), 319–330.

Heise, L. & Garcia-Moreno, C. (2002). 'Violence by intimate partners'. In E.G.Krug, L.L.Dahlberg, J.A.Mercy, A.Zwi & R.Lozano (eds), *World Report on Violence and Health* (pp. 87–121). Geneva: World Health Organisation.

Hemmelgarn, A.L., Glisson, C. & James, L.R. (2006). 'Organizational culture and climate: Implications for services and interventions research'. *Clinical Psychology: Science and Practice*, 13(1), 73–89.

Henderson, A. & Brouse, A. (1991). 'The experiences of new fathers in the first 3 weeks of life'. *Journal of Advanced Nursing*, 16(3), 293–298.

Henderson, S., Byrne, D. & Duncan-Jones, P. (1981). *Neurosis and the Social Environment*. Sydney: Academic Press.

Herman, J.L. (1992). *Trauma and Recovery*. New York: Basic Books.

Hester, M. & Pearson, C. (1998). *From Periphery to Centre: Domestic Violence in Work with Abused Children*. Bristol: Policy Press.

Hodges, S. & Hernandez, M. (2008). Symposium discussion. Paper presented at the 20th Annual Conference Proceedings – A System of Care for Children's Mental Health: Expanding the Research Base, Tampa.

Hoghughi, M. (1997). 'Parenting at the margins: Some consequences of inequality'. In K.N.Dwivedi (ed.), *Enhancing Parenting Skills: A Guide Book for Professionals Working with Parents* (pp. 21–41). Chichester: Wiley.

Hoghughi, M. & Long, N. (2004). *Handbook of Parenting: Theory and Research for Practice*. London: Sage.

Holden, G., Stein, J., Retchie, K. & Jouriles, E. (1998). 'Parenting behaviours and beliefs of battered women'. In G.Holden, R.Geffner & E.Jouriles (eds), *Children Exposed to Marital Violence: Theory, Research and Applied Issues*, Washington DC: American Psychological Association.

Holder, R. (2007). *Police and Domestic Violence: An Analysis of Domestic Violence Incidents Attended by Police in the ACT and Subsequent Actions*. Research Report. Sydney: Australian Domestic & Family Violence Clearinghouse.

Horrigan, T.J., Schroeder, A.V. & Schaffer, R.M. (2000). 'The triad of substance abuse, violence, and depression are interrelated in pregnancy'. *Journal of Substance Abuse Treatment*. 18, 55–58.

Horvath, A. & Luborsky, L. (1993). 'The role of the therapeutic alliance in psychotherapy'. *Journal of Consulting and Clinical Psychology*, 61(4), 561–573.

Houston, S. (2012). 'Risk assessment: A quick guide'. In K.Griffiths (ed.), *The Social Work Toolkit*. Basingstoke: Palgrave Macmillan.

Howarth, E., Stimpson, L., Barran, D. & Robinson, A.L. (2009). *Safety in Numbers: A Multi-site Evaluation of IDVA Services*. London: The Hestia Fund, The Sigrid Rausing Trust and The Henry Smith Charity.

Howe, D. (1998). 'Relationship-based thinking and practice in social work'. *Journal of Social Work Practice*, 12(1), 45–56.

—— (2010). 'The safety of children and the parent–worker relationship in cases of child abuse and neglect'. *Child Abuse Review*, 19(5), 330–341.

Howe, D., Brandon, M., Hinings, D. & Schofield, G. (1999). *Attachment Theory, Child Maltreatment and Family Support*. Mahwah, NJ: Lawrence Erlbaum Associates.

Howe, D. & Fearnley, S. (2003). 'Disorders of attachment in adopted and fostered children: Recognition and treatment'. *Clinical Child Psychology and Psychiatry*, 8, 369–387.

Howes, C. (1999). 'Attachment relationships in the context of multiple caregivers'. In J. Cassidy & P. Shaver. (eds), *Handbook of attachment: Theory, research and clinical applications,* (pp. 671–687). New York: Guilford Press.

Howes, C., & Spieker, S. (2008). 'Attachment relationships in the context of multiple caregivers'. In J. Cassidy & P. Shaver. (eds), *Handbook of attachment: Theory, research and clinical applications,* (pp. 317–332). New York: Guildford Press.

Hudson, B. (1987). 'Collaboration in social welfare: A framework for analysis'. *Policy and Politics*, 15, 175–183.

Human Rights and Equal Opportunity Commission. (1997). *Bringing them Home: Report of the National Inquiry into the Separation of Aboriginal and Torres Strait Islander Children from Their Families*. Canberra: Human Rights and Equal Opportunity Commission.

Humphreys, C. (2006). *Domestic Violence and Child Protection: Directions in Child Protection*. London: Jessica Kingsley.

—— (2008). 'Problems in the system of mandatory reporting of children living with domestic violence'. *Journal of Family Studies*, 14(2) 228–239.

Humphreys, C. & Harrison, C. (2003). 'Focusing on safety: Family violence and the role of child contact centres', *Child and Family Law Quarterly*, 15(3), 237–253.

Humphreys, C., Holzer, P., Scott, D., Arney, F., Bromfield, L., Higgins, D. & Lewig, K. (2010). 'The planets aligned: Is child protection policy reform good luck or good management'? *Australian Social Work*, 63(2), 145–163.

Humphreys, C., Regan, L., River, D. & Thiara, R.K. (2005). 'Domestic violence and substance use: Tackling complexity'. *British Journal of Social Work*. 35, 1303–1320.

Humphreys, C., Thiara, R.K. & Skamballis, A. (2011). 'Readiness to change: Mother–child relationship and domestic violence intervention'. *British Journal of Social Work*, 41(1) 166–184.

Huntsman, L. (2006). *Family Group Conferencing in a Child Welfare Context*. Sydney: Department of Community Services.

Indermaur, D. (2001). *Young Australians and Domestic Violence. Trends and Issues in Crime and Criminal Justice*, No. 195. Canberra: Australian Institute of Criminology.

Jackson, D. (2011). 'What's really going on? Parents' views of parent support in three supported playgroups'. *Australasian Journal of Early Childhood*, 36(4) retrieved online from http://www.connect.asn.au/info%5CAJEC_Vol36_No4_2011.pdf

Jaffe, P., Lemon, N. & Poisson, S. (2003). *Child Custody and Family Violence: A Call for Safety and Accountability*. California: Sage.

Jaffee, S., Moffitt, T., Caspi, A. & Taylor, A. (2003). 'Life with (or without) father: The benefits of living with the biological parents depend on the father's antisocial behavior'. *Child Development*, 74(1), 109–126.

Javdani, S., Allen, N., Todd, N. & Anderson, C. (2011). 'Examining systems change in the response to domestic violence: Innovative applications of multilevel modelling'. *Violence Against Women*, 17, 359–375.

Jenkins, S. & Norman, E. (1972). *Filial Deprivation and Foster Care*. New York: Columbia University Press.

Jewkes, R. (2002). 'Intimate partner violence: Causes and prevention'. *The Lancet*, 359, 1423–1249.

Jones, H. (1986). *In Her Own Name: Women in South Australian History*. Adelaide: Wakefield Press.

Jordan, B. & Sketchley, R. (2009). *A Stitch in Time Saves Nine: Preventing and Responding to the Abuse and Neglect of Infants (National Child Protection Clearinghouse Issue Paper, No.30)*. Melbourne: Australian Institute of Family Studies.

Jordan, P.L. (1990). 'Laboring for relevance: Expectant and new fatherhood'. *Nursing Research*, 39(1), 11–16.

Jouriles, E.N., McDonald, R., Smith Slep, A.M., Heyman, R.E. & Garrido, E. (2008). 'Child abuse in the context of domestic violence: Prevalence, explanations, and practice implications'. *Violence and Victims*, 23(2), 221–235.

Kagitcibasi, C. (2003). 'Autonomy, embeddedness and adaptability in immigration contexts'. *Human Development*, 46(2–3), 145–150.

Kanfer, F.H. & Schefft, B.K. (1988). *Guiding the Process of Therapeutic Change*. Illinois: Research Press.

Karmarkar, U.R. & Dan, Y. (2006). 'Experience-dependent plasticity in adult visual cortex'. *Neuron*, 52, 577–585.

Katz, L.F., Maliken, A.C. & Stettler, N.M. (2012). 'Parental meta-emotion philosophy: A review of research and theoretical framework'. *Child Development Perspectives*, 6(4), 417–422.

Keel, M.R. & Drew, N.M. (2004). 'The settlement experiences of refugees from the former Yugoslavia'. *Community, Work and Family*, 7(1), 95–115.

Keller, A., Ford, D., Sachs, E., Rosenfeld, B., Trinh-Shevrin, C., Meserve, C., Leviss, J.A., Singer, E., Smith, H., Wilkinson, J., Kim, G., Allden, K. & Rockline, P. (2003). 'The impact of detention on the health of asylum seekers'. *Journal of Ambulatory Care Management*, 26(4), 383–385.

Kelly, L. (1994). 'The interconnectedness of domestic violence and child abuse: Challenges for research, policy and practice'. In A.Mullender & R.Morley (eds), *Children Living With Domestic Violence*. London: Whiting and Birch.

Kenemore, T. (1993). The helping relationship: Getting in touch with the client's experience. Paper presented at the National Center on Child Abuse and Neglect Chronic Neglect Symposium Proceedings, Washington DC.

Kerns, K.A. (2008). 'Attachment in middle childhood'. In J. Cassidy & P. Shaver (eds), *Handbook of attachment: Theory, research and clinical applications* (pp. 366–382). New York: Guilford Press.

Kira, I. (2010). 'Etiology and treatment of post-cumulative traumatic stress disorders in different cultures'. *Traumatology*, 16, 128–141.

Kirkpatrick, S., Barlow, J., Stewart-Brown, S. & Davis, H. (2007). 'Working in partnership: User perceptions of intensive home visiting'. *Child Abuse Review*, 16, 32–46.

Kiro, C. (2006). Child rights, family rights and the family group. Conference: The New Zealand experience. International Conference of the Family Group Conference. Wellington NZ.

Kisely, S., Stevens, M., Hart, B. & Douglas, C. (2002). 'Health issues of asylum seekers and refugees'. *Australian and New Zealand Journal of Public Health*, 26(1), 8–10.

Klapper, S.A., Plummer, N.S. & Harmon, R.J. (2004). 'Diagnostic and treatment issues in cases of childhood trauma'. In J.D.Osofsky (ed.), *Young Children and Trauma: Intervention and Treatment* (pp. 139–154). New York: Guilford Press.

Klein, A. (1996). 'Re-abuse in a population of court restrained male batterers: Why restraining orders don't work'. In E.Buzawa & C.Buzawa (eds), *Do Arrests and Restraining Orders Work?* (pp. 192–213). Thousand Oaks. CA: Sage.

Klostermann, K.C. & Fals-Stewart, W. (2006). 'Intimate partner violence and alcohol use: Exploring the role of drinking in partner violence and its implications for intervention'. *Aggression and Violent Behavior*, 11, 587–597.

Ko, C. (2002). 'Civil restraining orders for domestic violence: The unresolved question of "efficacy"'. *Southern California Interdisciplinary Law Journal*, 11, 361–390

Kobak, R., Rosenthal, N. & Serwik, A. (2005). 'The attachment hierarchy in middle childhood: Conceptual and methodological issues'. In K.A.Kerns & R.A.Richardson (eds), *Attachment in Middle Childhood* (pp. 71–88). New York: Guilford Press.

Kobak, R., Rosenthal, N., Zajac, K. & Madsen, S. (2007). 'Adolescent attachment heirachies and the search for an adult pair bond'. *New Directions in Child and Adolescent Development*, 117, 57–72.

Konrad, E. (1996). 'A multidimensional framework for conceptualising human services integration'. *New Directions for Evaluations*, 69, 5–19.

Kotchik, B. & Forehand, R. (2002). 'Putting parenting in perspective: A discussion of the contextual factors that shape parenting practices'. *Journal of Child and Family Studies*, 11(3), 255–269.

Kovalesky, A. (2001). 'Factors affecting mother–child visiting identified by women with histories of substance abuse and child custody loss'. *Child Welfare*, 80(6), 749–768.

Kroll, B. (2010). 'Only connect … building relationships with hard-to-reach people: Establishing rapport with drug-misusing parents and their children'. In G.Ruch, D.Turney & A.Ward (eds), *Relationship-Based Social Work: Getting to the Heart of Practice*. London: Jessica Kingsley Publishers.

Kroll, B. & Taylor, A. (2000). 'Invisible children? Parental substance abuse and child protection: dilemmas for practice'. *Probation Journal*, 47(2), 91–100.

Kruske, S., Belton, S., Wardaguga, M. & Narjic, C. (2012). 'Growing up our way: The first year of life in remote Aboriginal Australia'. *Qualitative Health Research*, 22(6), 777–787.

Laible, D. (2005). 'Measuring attachment in middle childhood: Challenges and future directions'. *Human Development*, 48, 183–187.

Laing, L. (2000). *Children, Young People and Domestic Violence. Australian Domestic & Family Violence Clearinghouse Issues paper, No. 2*. Sydney: Australian Domestic and Family Violence Clearinghouse.

Lamb, M.E. (2012). 'A wasted opportunity to engage with the literature on the implications of attachment research for family court professionals'. *Family Court Review*, 50(3), 481–485.

Lamberg, L. (1996). 'Nationwide study of health and coping among immigrant children and families'. *Journal of the American Medical Association*, 276(18), 1455–1456.

Lambert, M. (1992a). 'Implications of outcome research for psychotherapy integration'. In J.C.Norcross & M.R.Goldfried (eds), *Handbook of Psychotherapy Integration* (pp. 94–129). New York: Basic Books.

—— (1992b). 'Psychotherapy outcome research: Implications for integrative and eclectic therapists'. In J.Norcross & M.Goldfried (eds), *Handbook of Psychotherapy Integration*. New York: Basic Books.

Lamont, A. (2011). 'Children in care'. *National Child Protection Clearinghouse Resource Sheet*. Retrieved from http://www.aifs.gov.au/nch/pubs/sheets/rs8/rs8.pdf

Lau, A.S. (2006). 'Making the case for selective and directed cultural adaptations of evidence-based treatments: Examples from parent training'. *Clinical Psychology: Science and Practice*, 13(4), 295–310.

Lawder, E.A., Poulin, J.E. & Andrews, R.G. (1986). 'A study of 185 foster children 5 years after placement'. *Child Welfare*, 65, 241–251.

Lee, H.P. & Winterton, G. (2004). 'Australian Constitutional landmarks'. *Queensland University of Technology Law and Justice Journal*, 4(1).

Leung, J. (2003). 'Strengthening families: The restructuring of family services in Hong Kong'. *Journal of Societal and Social Policy*, 2, 51–68.

Lewig, K., Arney, F., Salveron, M., McLaren, H., Gibson, C. & Scott, D. (2010). 'Spreading promising ideas and innovations in child and family services'. In F.Arney & D.Scott (eds), *Working with Vulnerable Families: A Partnership Approach* (pp. 275–296). Melbourne: Cambridge University Press.

Lewig, K., Scott, D., Holzer, P., Arney, F. & Humphreys, C. (2010). 'The role of research in child protection policy reform: A case study of South Australia'. *Evidence & Policy*, 6(4), 461–482.

Libesman, T. (2011). *Cultural Care for Aboriginal and Torres Strait Islander Children in Out of Home Care*. North Fitzroy, Vic.: SNAICC Secretariat of National Aboriginal and Islander Child Care.

Linares, O., Heeren, T., Bronfman, E., Zuckerman, A., Augustyn, M. & Tronick, E. (2001). 'A mediational model for the impact of exposure to community violence on child behaviour problems'. *Child Development*, 72(2), 639–652.

Linqage International (2003). *A.T.S.I. Family Decision Making Program Evaluation: 'Approaching Families Together 2002'*: Rumbalara Aboriginal Cooperative Ltd. and the Department of Human Services – Child Protection.

Littlechild, B. & Bourke, C. (2006). 'Men's use of violence and intimidation against family members and child protection workers'. In C.Humphreys & N.Stanley (eds), *Domestic Violence and Child Protection: Directions for Good Practice* (pp. 203–215). London: Jessica Kingsley.

Littner, N. (1975). 'The importance of natural parents to the child in placement'. *Child Welfare*, 54, 175–181.

Lock, J.A. (1997). *The Aboriginal Child Placement Principle: Research Project No. 7*. Sydney: New South Wales Law Reform Commission.

Locke, E.A. & Latham, G.P. (2002). 'Building a practically useful theory of goal setting and task motivation'. *American Psychologist*, 57, 705–717.

Logan, J. (2010). 'Preparation and planning for face-to-face contact after adoption: The experience of adoptive parents in a UK study'. *Child & Family Social Work*, 15(3), 315–324.

Logan, T.K. & Walker, R. (2009). 'Civil protective order outcomes: Violations and perceptions of effectiveness'. *Journal of Interpersonal Violence*, 24(4), 675–692.

—— (2010). 'Civil protective order effectiveness: Justice or just a piece of paper?' *Violence and Victims*, 25(3), 332–348.

Lovibond, P.F. & Lovibond, S.H. (1995). 'The structure of negative emotional states: Comparison of the Depression Anxiety Stress Scales (DASS) with the Beck Depression and Anxiety Inventories'. *Behaviour Research and Therapy*, 33, 335–343.

Lowe, P., Humphreys, C. & Williams, S. (2007). 'Night terrors: Women's experiences of (not) sleeping where there is domestic violence'. *Violence Against Women*, 13, 549–569.

Luker, M. (2008). 'The half-caste in Australia, New Zealand, and Western Samoa between the Wars: Different problem, different places?' In B.Douglas & C.Ballard (eds), *Foreign Bodies: Oceania and the Science of Race 1750–1940* (pp. 307–335). Canberra: ANU ePress.

Luthar, S.S. & Suchman, N.E. (2000). 'Relational Psychotherapy Mothers' Group: A developmentally informed intervention for at-risk mothers'. *Development and Psychopathology*, 12, 235–253.

Luthar, S.S., Suchman, N.E. & Altomare, M. (2007). 'Relational Psychotherapy Mothers' Group: A randomized clinical trial for substance abusing mothers'. *Development and Psychopathology*, 19, 243–261.

Lynn, R., Thorpe, R., Miles, D., with Cutts, C., Butcher, A. & Ford, L. (1998). *Murri Way: Aborigines and Torres Strait Islanders Reconstruct Social Welfare Practice*. Townsville, Qld: Centre for Social and Welfare Research, James Cook University.

Macaskill, C. (2002). *Safe Contact? Children in Permanent Placement and Contact with their Birth Relatives*. Dorset: Russell House Publishing.

McCaughey, J., Shaver, S. & Ferber, H. (1977). *Who Cares? Family Problems, Community Links and Helping Services*. Melbourne: Sun Books.

McConnell, D. & Llewellyn, G. (2005). 'Social inequality, 'the deviant parent' and child protection practice'. *Australian Journal of Social Issues*, 40(4), 553–566.

McDonald, N. (2011). Fostering children with attachment difficulties: Exploring the experiences of New Zealand carers. Masters thesis. University of Canterbury.

McGowan, P.O., Sasaki, A., D'Alessio, A.C., Dymov, S., Labonté, B., Szyf, M., Turecki, G. & Meaney, M.J. (2009). 'Epigenetic regulation of the glucocorticoid receptor in human brain associates with childhood abuse'. *Nature Neuroscience*, 12(3), 342–348.

MacKinnon, L.K. (1998). *Trust and Betrayal in the Treatment of Child Abuse*. New York: The Guilford Press.

McLaren, H., Gibson, C., Arney, F., Brown, L. & Scott, D. (2008). Sowing the seeds of innovation: Exploring strategies for sustaining the spread of innovative approaches in child and family work. Paper presented at the The History and Future of Social Innovation Conference.

McLean, S., Riggs, D., Kettler, L. & Delfabbro, P. (2012). 'Challenging behaviour in out-of-home care: Use of attachment ideas in practice'. *Child and Family Social Work*, doi:10.1111/j.1365–2206.2012.00825.x

McMahon, A. (1998). *Damned If You Do, Damned If You Don't: Working in Child Welfare.* UK: Ashgate Publishing Ltd.

McMahon, L. (2010). 'Long-term complex relationships'. In G.Ruch, D.Turney & A.Ward (eds), *Relationship-Based Social Work: Getting to the Heart of Practice* (pp. 148–163). London: Jessica Kingsley Publishers.

McMichael, C. & Manderson, L. (2004). 'Somali women and well-being: Social networks and social capital among immigrant women in Australia'. *Human Organization*, 63(1), 88–99.

McPherson, M.D., Delva, J. & Cranford, J.A. (2007). 'A longitudinal investigation of intimate partner violence among mothers with mental illness'. *Psychiatric Services.* 58(5), 675–680.

Maidment, J. (2006). 'The quiet remedy: A dialogue on reshaping professional relationships'. *Families in Society: The Journal of Contemporary Human Services*, 87(1), 115–121.

Main, M. & Solomon, J. (1990). 'Procedures for identifying infants as disorganized/disoriented during the Ainsworth Strange Situation'. In M. Greenberg, D. Cicchetti & M. Cummings (eds), *Attachment in the Preschool Years*, pp. 121–60. Chicago: University of Chicago Press.

Maluccio, A. (1979). *Learning from Clients.* New York: Free Press.

Maluccio, A.N. & Ainsworth, F. (2003). 'Drug use by parents: A challenge for family reunification practice'. *Children and Youth Services Review*, 25(7), 511–533.

Mandell, D. (2008). 'Power, care and vulnerability: Considering use of self in child welfare work'. *Journal of Social Work Practice*, 22(2), 235–248.

Mansell, W. & Carey, T.A. (2009). 'A century of psychology and psychotherapy: Is an understanding of 'control' the missing link between theory, research, and practice?' *Psychology and Psychotherapy: Theory, Research and Practice*, 82, 337–353.

Mapp, S.C. (2002). 'A framework for family visiting for children in long-term foster care'. *Families in Society: The Journal of Contemporary Human Services*, 83(2), 175–182.

Marger, M. (2010). *Social Inequality: Patterns and Processes* (5th edn). Whitby, ON: McGraw Hill Publishing.

Marsh, J.C., Ryan, J.P., Choi, S. & Testa, M.F. (2006). 'Integrated services for families with multiple problems: Obstacles to family reunification'. *Children and Youth Services Review*, 28, 1074–1087.

Martin, A., Ryan, R. & Brooks-Gunn, J. (2007). 'The joint influence of mother and father parenting on child cognitive outcomes at age 5'. *Early Childhood Research Quarterly*, 22, 423–439.

Martin, S.L., Beaumont, J.L. & Kupper, L.L. (2003). 'Substance use before and during pregnancy: Links to intimate partner violence'. *American Journal of Drug and Alcohol Abuse.* 29(3), 599–617.

Martinez-Brawley, E. (1986). 'Beyond cracker-barrel images: The rural social work specialty'. *Social Casework: Journal of Contemporary Social Work*, 101–107.

Mason, J. & Gibson, C. (2004). *The Needs of Children in Care: A Report on a Research Project: Developing a Model of Out-of-Home Care to Meet the Needs of Individual Children, through Participatory Research which Includes Children and Young People.* Social Justice and Social Change Research Centre, University of Western Sydney: Uniting Care Burnside.

Masten, A.S., Morison, P., Pelligrini, D. & Tellegen, A. (1990). 'Competence under stress: Risk and protective factors'. In J.Rolf, A.S.Masten, D.Cicchetti, K.Neuchterlein & S.Weintraub (eds), *Risk and Protective Factors in the Development of Psychopathology* (pp. 236–256). Cambridge: Cambridge University Press.

Mattson, S.N., Crocker, H. & Nguyen, T.T. (2011). 'Fetal alcohol spectrum disorders: Neuropsychological and behavioral features'. *Neuropsychological Review*, 21, 81–101.

Mayes, L.C. & Truman, S.D. (2002). 'Substance abuse and parenting'. In M.Bornstein (ed.), *Handbook of Parenting, Volume 4: Social Conditions and Applied Parenting* (2nd edn) (pp. 329–359). Mahwah, New Jersey: Lawrence Erlbaum Associates.

Meltzer, H., Doos, L., Vostanis, P., Ford, T. & Goodman, R. (2009). 'The mental health of children who witness domestic violence'. *Child and Family Social Work.* 14, 491–501.

Meyers, D., Durlak, J. & Wandersman, A. (2012). 'The Quality Implementation Framework: A synthesis of critical steps in the implementation process'. *American Journal of Community Psychology.* Retrieved from http://www.effectiveservices.org/images/uploads/file/The%20Quality%20Implementation%20Framework_%20A%20Synthesis%20of%20Critical%20Steps%20in%20the%20Implementation%20Process%20.pdf

Middlebrooks, J.S. & Audage, N.C. (2007). *The Effects of Childhood Stress on Health Across the Lifespan.* Centers for Disease Control and Prevention, National Center for Injury Prevention and Control, Atlanta, GA.

Mildon, R. & Polimeni, M. (2012). *Parenting in the Early Years: Effectiveness of Parenting Support Programs for Indigenous Families.* Australian Institute of Family Studies.

Mildon, R. & Shlonsky, A. (2011). 'Bridge over troubled waters: Using implementation science to facilitate effective services in child welfare'. *Child Abuse & Neglect*, 35, 753–756.

Millbank, A., Phillips, J. & Bohm, C. (2006). *Australia's Settlement Services for Refugees and Migrants.* Canberra: Parliamentary Library, Parliament of Australia.

Millham, S., Bullock, R., Hosie, K. & Haak, M. (1986). *Lost in Care: The Problem of Maintaining Links between Children in Care and their Families.* Aldershot, UK: Gower Publishing Company.

Milner, J.S. (2003). 'Social information processing in high-risk and physically abusive parents'. *Child Abuse & Neglect*, 27, 7–20.

Milroy, H. (2008). 'Children are our future: Understanding the needs of Aboriginal children and their families'. In A.S.Williams & V.Cowling (eds), *Infants of Parents with Mental Illness: Developmental, Clinical, Cultural and Personal Perspectives*. Brisbane: Australian Academic Press

Minty, B. & Pattinson, G. (1994). 'The nature of child neglect'. *British Journal of Social Work*, 24(6), 733–747.

Mitchell, G. (1995). *Child Welfare Families: Elaborating an Understanding*. Melbourne: University of Melbourne.

Mitchell, G. & Campbell, L. (2011). 'The social economy of excluded families'. *Child and Family Social Work*, 16, 422–433

Mohammed, M. (2003). 'Woraninta Playgroup'. *Developing Practice*, 5, 61–8.

Momartin, S., Silove, D., Manicavasagar, V. & Steel, Z. (2002). 'Range and dimensions of trauma experienced by Bosnian refugees resettled in Australia'. *Australian Psychologist*, 37(2), 149–155.

Momartin, S., Steel, Z., Coello, M., Aroche, J., Silove, D.M. & Brooks, R. (2006). 'A comparison of the mental health of refugees with temporary versus permanent protection visas'. *Medical Journal of Australia*, 185(7), 357–61.

Morland, L., Duncan, J., Hoebing, J., Kirschke, J. & Schmidt, L. (2005). 'Bridging refugee youth and children's services: A case of cross-service training'. *Child Welfare*, 84(5), 791–812.

Mouzos, J. & Makkai, T. (2004). 'Women's experiences of male violence: Findings from the Australian component of the International Violence Against Women Survey (IVAWS)'. *Research and Public Policy Series, Number 56*. Canberra: Australian Institute of Criminology.

Moyers, S., Farmer, E. & Lipscombe, J. (2006). 'Contact with family members and its impact on adolescents and their foster placements'. *British Journal of Social Work*, 36(4), 541–559.

Mrazek, P.B. & Haggerty, R.J. (eds). (1994). *Reducing Risks for Mental Disorders: Frontiers for Preventive Intervention Research*. Washington: National Academies Press

Mujenovic, Z. (2004). 'Hope to survive'. In S.Dechian, H.Millar & E.Sallis (eds), *Dark Dreams*. Kent Town, SA: Wakefield Press.

Mullender, A. & Morley, R. (1994) *Children Living with Domestic Violence*. London, Whiting and Birch.

Mullender, A., Hague, G., Imam, U., Kelly, L., Malos, E. & Regan, L. (2002). *Children's Perspectives on Domestic Violence*. London: Sage.

Multicultural Perinatal Network (2000). *Attachment Across Cultures*. Toronto: Toronto Public Health.

Murray, S. & Skull, S. (2003). 'Re-visioning refugee health: The Victorian Immigrant Health Programme'. *Health Services Management Research*, 16(3), 141–146.

Nader, K. (2011). 'Trauma in children and adolescents: issues related to age and complex traumatic reactions'. *Journal of Child and Adolescent Trauma*, 4, 161–180.

National Scientific Council on the Developing Child (2007). 'The timing and quality of early experiences combine to shape brain architecture'. Council Working Paper #5. Available online at: developingchild.harvard.edu/library/reports_and_working_papers/wp5/

Neale, A.N., Ngeow, J.Y.Y., Skull, S.A. & Biggs, B. (2007). 'Health services utilisation and barriers for settlers from the Horn of Africa'. *Australian and New Zealand Journal of Public Health*, 31(4), 333–335.

Neil, E. & Howe, D. (2004). *Contact in Adoption and Permanent Foster Care*. London: British Association for Adoption and Fostering.

Nelson, C.A. (2007). 'A neurobiological perspective on early human deprivation'. *Child Development*, 1, 13–18.

Newman, L. & Mares, S. (2007). 'Recent advances in the theories of and interventions with attachment disorders'. *Current Opinion in Psychiatry*, 20, 343–348.

Nexus Management Consulting. (2011). *Evaluation of the Implementation of Triple P in NSW: Department of Family and Community Services*. Sydney: Nexus Management Consulting.

NICE Technology Appraisal Guidance No.102. (2007). Parent-training/education programmes in the management of children with conduct disorders. Retrieved from: www.nice.org.uk/nicemedia/pdf/TA102guidance.pdf

NICHD Early Child Care Research Network (2004). 'Fathers' and mothers' parenting behavior and beliefs as predictors of children's social adjustment in the transition to school'. *Journal of Family Psychology*, 18(4), 628–638.

Nichols, M. (1993). 'Paternal perspectives of the childbirth experience'. *Maternal–Child Nursing Journal*, 21(3), 99–108.

NISATSIC, National Inquiry into the Separation of Aboriginal and Torres Strait Islander Children from Their Families. (1997). *Bringing Them Home: Report of the National Inquiry into the Separation of Aboriginal and Torres Strait Islander Children from Their Families*. Sydney: HREOC.

Nixon, J. & Humphreys, C. (2010). 'Marshalling the evidence: Using intersectionality in the domestic violence frame'. *Social Politics*, 17(2), 137–158.

Northern Territory Government. (2010). *Growing Them Strong, Together: Promoting the Safety and Wellbeing of the Northern Territory's Children, Report of the Board of Inquiry into the Child Protection System in the Northern Territory 2010*. M.Bamblett, H.Bath and R.Roseby. Darwin, NT: Northern Territory Government.

NSW Department of Health (2003). *Policy and Procedures for Identifying and Responding to Domestic Violence*. Sydney: NSW Department of Health.

NSW Family Services Inc. (2009). *The Role of Family Support Services in Keeping NSW Children Safe*. Sydney: NSW Family Services Inc.

Nutt, L. (2006). *The Lives of Foster Carers: Private Sacrifices, Public Restrictions*. London: Routledge.

O'Connell, M.E., Boat, T. & K.E.Warner (eds). (2009). *Preventing Mental, Emotional, and Behavioral Disorders among Young People: Progress and Possibilities*. Washington: National Academies Press.

O'Connor, T.G. & Zeanah, C.H., (2003). 'Attachment disorders: Assessment strategies and treatment approaches. *Attachment and Human Development*, 5, 223–244.

Odyssey Institute of Studies (2004). *The Nobody's Clients Project. Identifying and Addressing the Needs of Children with Substance Dependent Parents*. Melbourne: Odyssey House.

O'Hagan, K. (1999). 'Culture, cultural identity, and cultural sensitivity in child and family social work'. *Child and Family Social Work*, 4(4), 269–281.

Olds, D., Henderson, C., Chamberlin, R. & Tatelbaum, R. (1986). 'Preventing child abuse and neglect: A randomized trial of nurse home visitation'. *Pediatrics*, 78, 65–78.

Olds, D.L., Kitzman, H., Cole, R. & Robinson, J. (1997). 'Theoretical foundations of a program of home visitation for pregnant women and parents of young children'. *Journal of Community Psychology*, 25(1), 9–25.

Olson, S. & Stroud, C. (2012). *Child Maltreatment Research, Policy, and Practice for the Next Decade*. Washington D.C: The National Academies Press.

Osborne, B. (2001). *Teaching, Diversity and Democracy*. Altona, VIC: Common Ground.

Palinkas, L.A., Aarons, G.A., Chorpita, B.F., Hoagwood, K., Landsverk, J. & Weisz, J.R. (2009). 'Cultural exchange and the implementation of evidence-based practices'. *Research on Social Work Practice*, 19(5), 602–612.

Panaretto, K.S., Lee, H.M., Mitchell, M.R., Larkins, S.L., Manessis, V., Buettner, P.G. & Watson, D. (2005). *'Impact of a collaborative shared antenatal care program for urban Indigenous women: A prospective cohort study'*. *Medical Journal of Australia*, 182 (10), 514–519.

Paquette, D. (2004). 'Theorizing the father-child relationship: Mechanisms and developmental outcomes'. *Human Development*, 47(4), 193–219.

Paris, R. & Dubus, N. (2005). 'Staying connected while nurturing an infant: The challenge of new motherhood'. *Family Relations*, 54(1), 72–83.

Pearson, N. (2000). *Our Right to Take Responsibility*. Cairns: Noel Pearson and Associates.

Pense, E. (2004) 'The Duluth inter-agency experience'. *Criminalising Gendered Violence: Local National and International Perspectives*. ESRC Seminar Series. University of Bristol, Bristol.

Perry, B.D. (1997). 'Incubated in terror: Neurodevelopmental factors in the "cycle of violence"'. In J.D.Ofosky (ed.), *Children in a Violent Society* (pp. 124–149). New York: Guilford Press.

Petrosino, A., Turpin-Petrosino, C. & Buehler, J. (2003). 'Scared Straight and other juvenile awareness programs for preventing juvenile delinquency: A systematic review of the randomized experimental evidence'. *The Annals of the American Academy of Political and Social Science*, 589, 41–52.

Pine, B.A. & Drachman, D. (2005). 'Effective child welfare practice with immigrant and refugee children and their families'. *Child Welfare*, 84(5), 537–562.

Plsek, P. (2003). Complexity and the adoption of innovation in health care. Paper presented at the Accelerating Quality Improvement in Health Care: Strategies to Speed the Diffusion of Evidence-Based Innovations Conference.

Polansky, N., Ammons, P. & Gaudin, J. (1985). 'Loneliness and isolation in child neglect'. *Journal of Contemporary Social Work*, 66(1), 38–47.

Polansky, N., Chalmers, M., Buttenwieser, E. & Williams, D. (1981). *Damaged Parents: An Anatomy of Child Neglect*. Chicago: University of Chicago Press.

Polimeni, M., Wade, C. & Mildon, R. (2008). Lessons from Healthy Start, a capacity building initiative: Strategies used to promote training transfer. Paper presented at the ACWA Conference.

Porges, S.W. & Furman, S.A. (2011). 'The early development of the autonomic nervous system provides a neural platform for social behaviour: A polyvagal perspective'. *Infant and Child Development*, 20, 106–118.

Prendergast, M.L., Podusa, D., Chang, E. & Urada, D. (2002). 'The effectiveness of drug abuse treatment: A meta-analysis of comparison group studies'. *Drug and Alcohol Dependence*, 67, 53–72.

Presser, L. & Van Voorhis, P. (2002). 'Values and evaluation: Assessing processes and outcomes of restorative justice programs'. *Crime Delinquency*, 48, 162–188.

Priebe, S. & McCabe, R. (2006). 'The therapeutic relationship in psychiatric settings'. *Acta Psychiatrica Scandinavica*, 113, 69–72.

Procter, N.G. (2005). 'Providing emergency mental health care to asylum seekers at a time when claims for permanent protection have been rejected'. *International Journal of Mental Health Nursing*, 14(1), 2–6.

Pugh, R. (2007). 'Dual relationships: Personal and professional boundaries in rural social work'. *British Journal of Social Work*, 37(8), 1405–1423.

Punamaki, R., Qouta, S. & El Sarraj, E. (1997). 'Models of traumatic experiences and children's psychological adjustment: The roles of perceived parenting and the children's own resources and activity'. *Child Development*, 64(4), 718–728.

Putnam, R.D. (2000). *Bowling Alone*. New York: Simon & Schuster.

Quinton, D., Rushton, A., Dance, C. & Mayes, D. (1997). 'Contact between children placed away from home and their birth parents: Research issues and evidence'. *Clinical Child Psychology and Psychiatry*, 2(3), 393–413.

Quittner, A., Glueckouff, R. & Jackson, D. (1990). 'Chronic parenting stress: Moderating versus mediating effects of social support'. *Journal of Personal Psychology*, 59(6), 1266–1278.

Radford, L. & Hester, M. (2006). *Mothering through Domestic Violence*. London: Jessica Kingsley.

Ramchandani, P., Stein, A., Evans, J. & O'Connor, T. (2005). 'Paternal depression in the postnatal period and child development: A prospective population study'. *Lancet*, 365, 2201–2205.

Reder, P., Duncan, S. & Lucey, C. (2003). 'What principles guide parenting assessments?' In P.Reder, S.Duncan & C.Lucey (eds), *Studies in the Assessment of Parenting* (pp. 3–26). New York: Brunner-Routledge.

Rees, S. & Pease, B. (2007). 'Domestic violence in refugee families in Australia: Rethinking settlement policy and practice'. *Journal of Immigrant & Refugee Studies*, 5(2), 1–19.

Reid, M.J., Webster-Stratton, C. & Baydar, N. (2004). 'Halting the development of conduct problems in Head Start children: The effects of parent training'. *Journal of Clinical Child and Adolescent Psychology*, 33(2), 279–291.

Reimer, E. (2010). Exploring the parent–family worker relationship in rural family support services: 'You build a relationship … and before you know it you start working on the problems that you have got' (PhD). University of South Australia, Adelaide.

Repetti, R.L., Taylor, S.E. & Seeman, T.E. (2002). 'Risky families: Family social environments and the mental and physical health of offspring'. *Psychological Bulletin*, 128(2), 330–366.

Ribner, D. & Knei-Paz, C. (2002). 'Client's view of a successful helping relationship'. *Social Work*, 47(4), 379–387.

Rice, D. & Barone Jr, S. (2000). 'Critical periods of vulnerability for the developing nervous system: Evidence from humans and animal models'. *Environmental Health Perspectives*, 108 (Suppl. 3), 511–533.

Richards, E. (2008). *Destination Australia*. Sydney: University of New South Wales Press.

Richards, K. (2011). 'Children's exposure to domestic violence in Australia'. *Trends & Issues in Crime and Criminal Justice*. Canberra: Australian Institute of Criminology.

Richmond, M. (1899). *Friendly Visiting Among the Poor: A Handbook for Charity Workers* (Reprint 1969 ed.). New Jersey: Patterson Smith.

Riley, S., Brady, A., Goldberg, J., Jacobs, F. & Easterbrooks, M. (2008). 'Once the door closes: Understanding the parent–provider relationship'. *Children and Youth Services Review*, 30, 569–575.

Rivara, F. P., Mueller, B. A., Somes, G., Mendoza, C. T., Rushforth, N. B. & Kellermann, A. L. (1997). 'Alcohol and illicit drug use and the risk of violent death in the home'. *Journal of the American Medical Association*, 278(7), 569–575.

Roberts, V. (1994). 'Conflict and collaboration, managing intergroup relations'. In A.Obholzer & V.Roberts (eds), *The Unconscious at Work: Individual and Organisational Stress in the Human Services* (pp. 187–196). London: Routledge.

Robinson, G. (2005). 'Anthropology, explanation and intervention: Risk and resilience in a parent- and child-focused program. *Anthropological Forum*, 15(1), 3–25.

Robinson, G., Tyler, W., Jones, Y., Silburn, S. & Zubrick, S. (2012). 'Context, diversity and engagement: Early intervention with Australian Aboriginal families in urban and remote contexts'. *Children and Society*, 26(5), 343–355.

Robinson, V. (1930). *A Changing Psychology in Social Case Work*. Chapel Hill: The University of North Carolina Press.

Rogers, E. (2003). *Diffusion of Innovations* (5th edn). New York: Free Press.

Rosenthal, D., Ranieri, N. & Klimidis, S. (1996). 'Vietnamese adolescents in Australia: Relationships between perceptions of self and parental values, intergenerational conflict, and gender dissatisfaction'. *International Journal of Psychology*, 31(2), 81–91.

Ross, S. (1996). 'Risk of physical abuse to children of spouse abusing parents'. *Child Abuse & Neglect*, 20, 589–98.

Rousseau, C., Rufagari, M., Bagilishya, D. & Measham, T. (2004). 'Remaking family life: Strategies for re-establishing continuity among Congolese refugees during the family reunification process'. *Social Science and Medicine*, 59(5), 1095–1108.

Rubin, D.M., O'Reilly, A.L.R., Luan, X. & Locallio, A.R. (2007). 'The impact of placement stability on behavioural well-being for children in foster care'. *Pediatrics*, 119(2), 336–344.

Ruch, G. (2005). 'Relationship-based practice and reflective practice: Holistic approaches to child care social work'. *Child and Family Social Work*, 10, 111–123.

Ruch, G., Turney, D. & Ward, A. (2010). *Relationship-Based Social Work: Getting to the Heart of Practice*. London: Jessica Kingsley Publishers.

Russell, G., Barclay, L., Edgecombe, G., Donovan, J., Habib, G., Callaghan, H. et al. (1999). *Fitting Fathers into Families: Men and the Fatherhood Role in Contemporary Australia*. Canberra: Commonwealth Department of Family and Community Services.

Rutman, D., Strega, S., Callahan, M. & Dominelli, L. (2002). '"Undeserving" mothers? Practitioners' experiences working with young mothers in/from care'. *Child and Family Social Work*, 7 (149–159).

Rutter, M. (2008). 'Implications of attachment theory and research for child care policies'. In J.Cassidy & P. Shaver. (eds), *Handbook of Attachment Theory, Research and Clinical Applications* (2nd edn) (pp. 958–974). New York: Guilford.

Rutter, M. & O'Connor, T.C. (2008).' Implications of attachment theory for child care policies'. In J.Cassidy & P.R.Shaver (eds), *Handbook of Attachment Theory, Research and Clinical Applications* (pp. 823–844). New York: Guilford.

Ryan, F. (2011). 'Kanyirninpa (Holding): A way of nurturing children in Aboriginal Australia', *Australian Social Work*, 64(2), 183–197.

Salisbury, E., Henning, K. & Holdford, R. (2009). 'Fathering by partner-abusive men'. *Child Maltreatment*, 14, 232–242.

Salmon, G. & Rapport, F. (2005). 'Multiagency voices: A thematic analysis of multi-agency working practices within the setting of a child and adolescent mental health service'. *Journal of Interprofessional Care*, 19, 429–443.

Salveron, M. (2012). A journey to a new parent identity: Recovering from identity trauma and negotiating practice in child protection settings. Doctoral dissertation, University of South Australia, Adelaide.

Salveron, M., Arney, F. & Lewig, K. (2010). 'Supporting parents whose children are in out of home care'. In F.Arney & D.Scott (eds), *Working with Vulnerable Families: A Partnership Approach*. Melbourne: Cambridge University Press.

Salveron, M., Arney, F. & Scott, D. (2006). 'Sowing the seeds of innovation: Ideas for child and family services'. *Family Matters*, 73, 39–45.

Sameroff, A. (2010). 'A unified theory of development: A dialectic integration of nature and nurture'. *Child Development*, 81, 6–22.

Sanders, M., Markie-Dadds, C., Tully, L.A. & Bor, W. (2000). 'The Triple P-Positive Parenting Program: A comparison of enhanced, standard and self-directed behavioural family intervention for parents of children with early onset conduct problems'. *Journal of Consulting and Clinical Psychology*, 68, 624–640.

Sanders, M.R., Turner, K.M.T. & Markie-Dadds, C. (2002). 'The development and dissemination of the Triple P – Positive Parenting Program: A multilevel, evidence-based system of parenting and family support. *Prevention Science*, 3(3), 173–189.

Scannapieco, M. & Connell-Carrick, K. (2007). 'Assessment of families who have substance abuse issues: Those who maltreat their infants and toddlers and those who do not. *Substance Use and Misuse*, 42, 1545–1553.

Schofield, G. (1998). Inner and outer worlds: A psychosocial framework for child and family social work. *Child and Family Social Work*, 3, 57–68.

—— (2009). *Parenting While Apart: The Experiences of Birth Parents of Children in Long Term Foster Care: Full Research Report ESRC End of Award Report, RES-000–22–2606*. Swindon: Economic and Social Research Council.

Schofield, G. & Ward, E. (2011). *Understanding and Working with Parents of Children in Long-term Foster Care*. London: Jessica Kingsley Publishers.

Schorr, L. & Marchand, V. (2007). *Pathway to the Prevention of Child Abuse and Neglect*. Washington: Project on Effective Interventions. Pathways Mapping Initiative.

Schweitzer, R., Melville, F., Steel, Z. & Lacherez, P. (2006). 'Trauma, post-migration living difficulties, and social support as predictors of psychological adjustment in resettled Sudanese refugees'. *Australian and New Zealand Journal of Psychiatry*, 40(2), 179–187.

Scott, D. (1992). 'Reaching vulnerable populations: A framework for primary service provider role expansion'. *American Journal of Orthopsychiatry*, 62(3), 332–341.

—— (1997). 'Inter-agency conflict: An ethnographic study'. *Child and Family Social Work*, 22, 4–5.

—— (2005). 'Inter-organisational collaboration: A framework for analysis and action'. *Australian Social Work*, 58(2), 132–141.

—— (2009). '"Think Child, Think Family": How adult specialist services can support children at risk of abuse and neglect'. *Family Matters*, 81, 37–42.

Scott, D., Brady, S. & Glynn, P. (2001). 'New mother groups as a social network intervention: Consumer and maternal and child health nurse perspectives'. *Australian Journal of Advanced Nursing*, 18(4), 23–29.

Scott, D. & Campbell, L. (1994). 'Family-centred practice at the interface between the alcohol and drug field and child welfare'. *Drug and Alcohol Review*, 13(4), 447–454.

Scott, D., Lindsay, J. & Jackson, A. (1995). 'The child protection case conference: Juggling rights, risks and responsibilities'. *Children Australia*, 20, 4–12.

Scott, D., O'Neill, C. & Minge, A. (2005). Contact between children in out-of-home care and their birth families. Retrieved from www.community.nsw.gov.au/docswr/_assets/main/documents/oohc_research.pdf

Scott, D., Salveron, M., Reimer, E., Nichols, S., Sivak, L. & Arney, F. (2007). Positive partnerships with parents of young children. Topical Paper 9: Australian Research Alliance for Children and Youth. Available online at: www.aracy.org.au/publications-resources/command/download_file/id/118/filename/Positive_partnerships_with_parents_of_young_children.PDF

Scott, K. & Crooks, C. (2007). 'Preliminary evaluation of an intervention program for maltreating fathers'. *Brief Treatment and Crisis Intervention*, 7, 224–238.

Scott, S. & Dadds. M. R. (2009). 'Practitioner review: When parent training doesn't work: Theory-driven clinical strategies'. *Journal of Child Psychology and Psychiatry*, 50(12):1441–50.

Scott, T. (2003). *'The Most Enduring of relationships', Engaging Families who have Children in Substitute Care*. Victoria: MacKillop Family Services.

Scottish Government Statistician Group. (2010). Domestic Abuse Recorded by the Police in Scotland, 2009–10. Statistical Bulletin: Crime and Justice Series. Retrieved January 5, 2012, from http://www.scotland.gov.uk/Resource/Doc/330575/0107237.pdf

Scourfield, J. (2006). 'The challenge of engaging fathers in the child protection process'. *Critical Social Policy*, 26(2), 440–449.

Segal, L., Opie, R.S. & Dalziel, K. (2012). 'Theory! The missing link in understanding the performance of neonate/infant home visiting programs for the prevention of child maltreatment: A systematic review'. *Milbank Quarterly*, 90(1), 47–106.

Self-Brown, S., Frederick, K., Binder, S., Whitaker, D., Lutzker, J., Edwards, A. & Blankenship, J. (2011). 'Examining the need for cultural adaptations to an evidence-based parent training program targeting the prevention of child maltreatment'. *Children and Youth Services Review*, 33(7), 1166–1172.

Shand, F.L., Degenhardt, L., Slade, T. & Nelson, E.C. (2011). 'Sex differences amongst dependent heroin users: Histories, clinical characteristics and predictors of other substance dependence'. *Addictive Behaviors*, 36, 27–36.

Sheikh-Mohammed, M., MacIntyre, C.R., Wood, N.J., Leask, J. & Isaacs, D. (2006). 'Barriers to access to health care for newly resettled sub-Saharan refugees in Australia'. *Medical Journal Australia*, 185(11/12), 594–597.

Shonkoff, J. & Phillips, D. (eds). (2000). *From Neurons to Neighbourhoods: The Science of Early Childhood Development*. Washington, DC: National Academy Press.

Siegel, D. (1999). *The Developing Mind: Toward a Neurobiology of Interpersonal Experience*. New York: Guilford Press.

Silburn, S.R., Robinson, G., Arney, F., Johnstone, K. & McGuinness, K. (2011). Early childhood development in the NT: Issues to be addressed. Topical paper commissioned for the public consultations on the Northern Territory Early Childhood Plan. Darwin: Northern Territory Government.

Silburn, S., Zubrick, S., Lawrence, D., Mitrou, F., De Maio, J., Blair, E., Cox, A., Dalby, R., Griffin, J., Pearson, G. & Hayward, C. (2006). 'The intergenerational effects of forced separation on the social and emotional wellbeing of Aboriginal children and young people.' *Family Matters*, 75, 4–9.

Silove, D. & Ekblad, S. (2002). 'How well do refugees adapt after resettlement in Western countries?' *Acta Psychiatrica Scandinavica*, 106(6), 401–402.

Sims, M., Guilfoyle, A., Kulisa, J., Targowska, A. & Teather, S. (2008). *Achieving Outcomes for Children and Families from Culturally and Linguistically Diverse Backgrounds*. Perth: Australian Research Alliance for Children and Youth.

Sinnerbrink, I., Silove, D., Field, A., Steel, Z. & Manicavasagar, V. (1997). 'Compounding of premigration trauma and postmigration stress in asylum seekers'. *Journal of Psychology*, 131(5), 463–470.

Sivak, L., Arney, F. & Lewig, K. (2008). *A Pilot Exploration of a Family Home Visiting Program for Families of Aboriginal and Torres Strait Islander Children*. Adelaide: Australian Centre for Child Protection.

Slade, A. (2005). 'Parental reflective functioning: An introduction'. *Attachment and Human Development*, 7, 269–281.

Smeekens, S., Riksen-Walraven, J.M. & van Bakel, H.J.A. (2007). 'Multiple determinants of externalizing behaviour in 5-year-olds: A longitudinal model'. *Journal of Abnormal Child Psychology*, 35(3), 347–361.

Smith, B. & Mogro-Wilson, C. (2008). 'Inter-agency collaboration: Policy and practice in child welfare and substance abuse treatment'. *Administration in Social Work*, 32(2), 5–24.

Smith, B.D. (2003). 'How parental drug use and drug treatment compliance relate to family reunification'. *Child Welfare*, 82(3), 335–365.

Smith, B.D. & Testa, M.F. (2002). 'The risk of subsequent maltreatment allegations in families with substance-exposed infants'. *Child Abuse & Neglect*, 26, 97–114.

Smith, K., Coleman, K., Eder, S. & Hall, P. (2011). *Homicides, Firearm Offences and Intimate Violence 2009/10. Supplementary Volume 2 to Crime in England and Wales 2009/10* (2nd edn). London: Home Office.

Smith, K., Flatley, J., Coleman, K., Osborne, S., Kaiza, P. & Roe, S. (2010). Homicides, Firearm Offences and Intimate Violence 2008/09: Supplementary Volume 2 to Crime in England and Wales 2008/09. Home Office Statistical Bulletin Retrieved January 5, 2012, from http://webarchive.nationalarchives.gov.uk/20110218135832/rds.homeoffice.gov.uk/rds/pdfs10/hosb0110.pdf

Smith, N. (1999). 'Antenatal classes and the transition to fatherhood: A study of some fathers' views (Part 1)'. *MIDIRS Midwifery Digest*, 9(3), 327–330.

Smith, P., Perrin, S. & Yule, W. (1998). 'Post-traumatic stress disorders'. In P.Graham (ed.), *Cognitive–Behaviour Therapy for Children and Families* (pp. 127–143). Cambridge, UK: Cambridge University Press.

SNAICC. (2012). *Healing in Practice – Promising Practices in Healing Programs*. Melbourne: Secretariat for National Aboriginal and Islander Child Care.

Snyder, C.S., May, J.D., Zulcic, N.N. & Gabbard, W.J. (2005). 'Social work with Bosnian Muslim refugee children and families: A review of the literature'. *Child Welfare*, 84(5), 607–630.

Social Exclusion Taskforce (2008). 'Families at Risk Review'. Available online at: http://www.devon.gov.uk/reachingoutthinkfamily.pdf

Sokoloff, N.J. & Dupont, I. (2005). 'Domestic violence at the intersections of race, class and gender: Challenges and contributions to understanding violence against marginalized women in diverse communities'. *Violence Against Women*, 11(1), 38–64.

Sparta, S.N. (2003). 'Assessment of childhood trauma'. In A.M.Goldstein (ed.), *Handbook of Psychology: Vol 11. Forensic psychology* (pp. 209–231). New York: Wiley.

Spinazzola, J., Ford, J., Zucker, M., van der Kold, B., Silva, S., Smith, S. & Blaustein, M. (2005). 'National survey of complex trauma exposure, outcome and intervention for children and adolescents'. *Psychiatric Annals*, 35(5), 433–439.

Spitzberg, B. (2002). 'The tactical topography of stalking victimization and management'. *Trauma, Violence & Abuse*, 3(4), 261–288.

Sroufe, L.A. (1988). 'The role of infant-caregiver attachments in development'. In J. Belsky & T. Nezworski (eds), *Clinical implications of attachment*, (pp. 18–38). Hillsdale, New Jersey: Lawrence Erlbaum Associates Publishers.

Sroufe, L., Carlson, E., Levy, A. & Egeland, B. (1999). 'Implications of attachment theory for developmental psychopathology'. *Development and Psychopathology*, 11, 1–13.

Stanley, J. & Goddard, C. (2002). *In the Firing Line: Violence and Power in Child Protection Work*. Chichester: Wiley.

Stanley, N., Graham-Kevan, N. & Borthwick, R. (2012). 'Fathers and domestic violence: Motivation to change through perpetrator programs'. *Child Abuse Review* 21, 264–274.

Stanley, N., Miller, P., Richardson-Foster, H. & Thomson, G. (2011). 'Children's experience of domestic violence: Developing an integrated response from police and child protection services'. *Journal of Interpersonal Violence*, 25, 2372–2391.

Steel, Z. & Silove, D. (2001). 'The mental health implications of detaining asylum seekers'. *Medical Journal of Australia*, 175(11–12), 596–599.

Stewart, D., Gossop, M. & Trakada, K. (2007). 'Drug dependent parents: Childcare responsibilities, involvement with treatment services, and treatment outcomes'. *Addictive Behaviors*, 32, 1657–1668.

Stock, C., Mares, S. & Robinson, G. (2012). 'Telling and re-telling stories: The use of narrative and drawing in a group intervention with parents and children in a remote Aboriginal community'. *Australia and New Zealand Journal of Family Therapy*, 33(2), 157–170.

Stone, B. (1998). 'Child neglect: Practitioner's perspectives'. *Child Abuse Review*, 7, 87–96.

Stovall-McClough, K.C. & Dozier, M. (2004). 'Forming attachments in foster care: Infant attachment behaviors during the first 2 months of placement'. *Development and Psychopathology*, 16(2), 253–271.

Strathearn, L., Mamun, A., Najman, J. & O'Callaghan, M. (2009). 'Does breastfeeding protect against substantiated child abuse and neglect? A 15-year cohort study'. *Pediatrics*, 123, 483–493.

Suchman, N., DeCoste, C., McMahon, T., Rounsaville, B. & Mayes, L. (2011). 'The Mothers and Toddlers Program, an attachment-based parenting intervention for substance-using women: Results at 6-week follow up in a randomized clinical pilot'. *Infant Mental Health Journal*, 32, 427–449.

Suchman, N.E. & Luthar, S.S. (2000). 'Maternal addiction, child maladjustment and socio-demographic risks: Implications for parenting behaviors'. *Addiction*, 95, 1417–1428.

Suchman, N.E., McMahon, T.J., Zhang, H., Mayes, L.C. & Luthar, S. (2006). 'Substance-abusing mothers and disruptions in child custody: An attachment perspective'. *Journal of Substance Abuse Treatment*, 30, 197–204.

Sundell, K. & Vinnerljung, B. (2004). 'Outcomes of family group conferencing in Sweden: A 3-year follow-up'. *Child Abuse & Neglect*, 28, 267–287.

Swain, S. (1995). *Single Mothers and their Children: Disposal, Punishment and Survival in Australia*. Melbourne: Cambridge University Press.

Swanson, K., Beckwith, L. & Howard, J. (2000). 'Intrusive caregiving and quality of attachment in prenatally drug-exposed toddlers and their primary caregivers'. *Attachment & Human Development*, 2, 130–148.

Taft, A., Small, R., Humphreys, C. & Hegarty, K. (accepted, September, 2012) 'Enhanced maternal and child health nurse care for women experiencing intimate partner violence: protocol for MOVE, a cluster randomised trial of screening and referral in primary health care'. *BMC Public Health*.

Taggart, A., Short, S. & Barclay, L. (2000). '"She has made me feel human again": An evaluation of a volunteer home-based visiting project for mothers'. *Health and Social Care in the Community*, 8(1), 1–8.

Tanner, K. & Turney, D. (2003). 'What do we know about child neglect? A critical review of the literature and its application to social work practice'. *Child and Family Social Work*, 8(1), 25–34.

Taplin, S. (2005). Is all contact between children in care and their birth parents good contact? Discussion paper. New South Wales Centre for Parenting & Research, Department of Community Services, Ashfield, NSW. Retrieved from www.community.nsw.gov.au/docswr/_assets/main/documents/research_good_contact.pdf

Terr, L.C. (1991). 'Childhood trauma. An outline and overview'. *American Journal of Psychiatry*, 148, 10–20.

Thoburn, J. (2004). 'Post-placement contact between birth parents and older children: The evidence from a longitudinal study of minority ethnic children'. In E.Neil & D.Howe (eds), *Contact in Adoption and Permanent Foster Care* (pp. 184–202). London: British Adoption and Fostering.

Thomson, J. & Thorpe, R. (2003). 'The importance of parents in the lives of children in the care system'. *Children Australia*, 28(2), 25–31.

Thorpe, R. (2007). 'Family inclusion in child protection practice: Building bridges in working with (not against) families'. *Communities, Families and Children*, 3(1), 4–17.

Tilbury, C. (2009). 'The over-representation of Indigenous children in the Australian child welfare system'. *International Journal of Social Welfare*, 18, 57–64.

Tizard, B. & Rees, J. (1975). 'The effect of early institutional rearing on the behavior problems and affectional relationships of four-year-old children'. *Journal of Child Psychology and Psychiatry and Allied Disciplines*, 15, 51–77.

Tobler, N. (1986). 'Meta-analysis of 143 adolescent drug prevention programs: Quantitative outcomes results of program participants compared to a control or comparison group'. *Journal of Drug Issues*, 16(4), 537–567.

Trifonoff, A., Duraisingham, V., Roche, A. & Pidd, K. (2010). *Taking First Steps: What Family Sensitive Practice Means to Alcohol and Other Drug Workers, a Survey Report*. Adelaide: National Centre for Education and Training on Addiction., Flinders University.

Trocme, N., Tourigny, M., MacLaurin, B. & Fallon, B. (2003). 'Major findings from the Canadian incidence study of reported child abuse and neglect'. *Child Abuse & Neglect*, 27(12), 1427–1439.

Trotter, C. (2002). 'Worker skill and client outcome in child protection'. *Child Abuse Review*, 11, 38–50.

—— (2006). *Working with Involuntary Clients: A Guide to Practice*. Sydney: Allen and Unwin.

Tucker, D.J. & MacKenzie, M.J. (2012). 'Attachment theory and change process in foster care'. *Children and Youth Services Review*, 34, 2208–2219,

Turner, K., Richards, M. & Sanders, M. (2007). 'Randomised clinical trial of a group parent education programme for Australian Indigenous families'. *Journal of Paediatrics and Child Health*, 43, 429–437.

Udy, G. (2005). 'SDN's Parent Resource Program: Reflecting our heritage, responding to present needs, reinventing the future for and with struggling families'. *Developing Practice*, 12, 22–30.

UNHCR (2007). *Convention and Protocol Relating to the Status of Refugees*. Geneva: United Nations High Commissioner for Refugees.

—— (2011). *UNHCR Global Trends 2011*. Geneva: United Nations High Commissioner for Refugees.

Van der Kolk, B., Roth, S., Pelcovitz, D., Sunday, S. & Spinazolla, J. (2005). 'Disorders of extreme stress: the empirical foundation of a complex adaptation to trauma'. *Journal of Traumatic Stress*, 18, 389–399.

van Ijzendoorn, M. & De Wolff, M. (1997). 'In search of the absent father – meta-analysis of infant–father attachment: A rejoinder to our discussants'. *Child Development*, 68(4), 604–609.

Victorian Commission of Public Health (1940–1941). '*Report of the Director of Infant Welfare*'. Unpublished.

VicHealth. (2004). *The Health Costs of Violence: Measuring the Burden of Disease Caused by Intimate Partner Violence: A Summary of Findings*. Carlton South, Melbourne: Victorian Health Promotion Foundation.

Videon, T. (2005). 'Parent–child relations and children's psychological well-being: Do dads matter?' *Journal of Family Issues*, 26, 55–78.

Virueda, M. & Payne, J. (2010). *Homicide in Australia: 2007–08 National Homicide Monitoring Program annual report. (Monitoring Report 13)*. Retrieved January 5, 2012, from http://www.aic.gov.au/documents/8/9/D/%7B89DEDC2D-3349-457C-9B3A-9AD9DAFA7256%7Dmr13_004.pdf

Walby, S. & Allen, J. (2004). *Domestic Violence, Sexual Assault and Stalking: Findings from the British Crime Survey. Home Office Research Study 276*. Home Office Research, Development and Statistics Directorate.

Walker, R. & Shepherd, C. (2008). *Strengthening Aboriginal Family Functioning: What Works and Why?* Kulunga Research Network, Telethon Institute for Child Health Research Australian Family Relationships Clearinghouse AFRC Briefing No. 7. Melbourne: Australian Institute of Family Studies.

Walsh, C., MacMillan, H.L. & Jamieson, E. (2003). 'The relationship between parental substance abuse and child maltreatment: Findings from the Ontario Health Supplement'. *Child Abuse & Neglect*, 27, 1409–1425.

Ward, A. (2010). 'The use of self in relationship-based practice'. In G.Ruch, D.Turney & A.Ward (eds), *Relationship-Based Social Work: Getting to the Heart of Practice*. London: Jessica Kingsley Publishers.

Watson, J., White, A., Taplin, S. & Huntsman, L. (2005). *Prevention and Early Intervention Literature Review*. Retrieved 23 August, 2009, from http://www.community.nsw.gov.au/docswr/_assets/main/documents/eip_literature_review.pdf

Webber, R. & Boromeo, D. (2005). 'The sole parent family: Family and support networks'. *Australian Journal of Social Issues*, 40(2), 269–83.

Webster-Stratton, C. (1998). 'Preventing conduct problems in Head Start children: Strengthening parenting competencies'. *Journal of Consulting and Clinical Psychology*, 66(5), 715–730.

Weine, S., Muzurovic, N., Kulauzovic, Y., Besic, S., Lezic, A., Mujagic, A., Muzurovic, J., Spahovic, D., Feetham, S., Ware, N., Knafl, K. & Pavkovic, I. (2004). Family consequences of refugee trauma. *Family Process*, 43(2), 147–160.

Werner-Wilson, R.J. & Davenport, B.R., (2003). 'Distinguishing between conceptualizations of attachment: Clinical applications in marriage and family therapy'. *Contemporary Family Therapy*, 25, 179–193.

Wessells, M. (2006). *Child Soldiers: From Violence to Protection*. Cambridge, MA: Harvard University Press.

Westfall, J., Mold, J. & Fagnan, L. (2007). 'Practice based research – "Blue Highways" on the NIH roadmap'. *Journal of the American Medical Association*, 297(4), 403–406.

Westphal, J.D., Gulati, R. & Shortell, S.M. (1997). 'Customization and conformity? An institutional and network perspective on the content and consequences of TQM adoption'. *Administrative Services Quarterly*, 42(2), 366–394.

White, M. & Winkworth, G. (2012) A Rubric for Building Efective Collaboration. Unpublished manuscript.

Whitebook, M., Phillips, D., Bellm, D. & Almaraz, M. (2004). *Two Years in Early Care and Education: A Community Portrait of Quality and Workforce Stability*. University of California, Berkeley.

Whittaker, J., Kinney, J., Tracy, E. & Booth, C. (1990). *Reaching High-Risk Families: Intensive Family Preservation in Human Services*. New York: Aldine de Gruyter.

Wild, R. & Anderson, P. (2007). *Ampe akelyernemane meke mekarle: 'little children are sacred: Report of the Northern Territory Board of Inquiry into the protection of Aboriginal children from sexual abuse*. Darwin: Northern Territory Government.

Wilk, R. & McCarthy, C. (1986). 'Intervention in child sexual abuse: A survey of attitudes'. *Social Casework*, 67, 20–26.

Wille, A. (2006). *Whakamrama te Huarahi – To Light the Pathways: A strategic Framework for Child and Adolescent Mental Health Workforce Development 2006–2016*. Auckland: The Werry Centre for Child and Adolescent Mental Health Workforce Development.

Williams, N. (2008). 'Refugee participation in South Australian child protection research: Power, voice, and representation'. *Family and Consumer Sciences Research Journal*, 37(2), 191–209.

Willson, P., McFarlane, J., Malecha, A., Watson, K., Lemmey, D., Schultz, P., Gist, J. & Fredland, N. (2000). 'Severity of violence against women by intimate partners and associated use of alcohol and/or illicit drugs by the perpetrator'. *Journal of Interpersonal Violence*. 15(9), 996–1008.

Wilson, D. & Horner, W. (2005). 'Chronic child neglect: Needed developments in theory and practice'. *Families in Society: The Journal of Contemporary Human Services*, 86(4), 471–481.

Wilson, K. & Sinclair, R. (2004). 'Contact in foster care: Some dilemmas and opportunities'. In E.Neil & D.Howe (eds), *Contact in Adoption and Permanent Foster Care* (pp. 165–185). London: British Association for Adoption & Fostering.

Wilson, S., Kuebli, J. & Hughes, H. (2005). 'Patterns of maternal behavior among neglectful families: Implications for research and intervention'. *Child Abuse & Neglect*, 29(9), 985–1001.

Winefield, H. & Barlow, J. (1995). 'Client and worker satisfaction in a child protection agency'. *Child Abuse & Neglect*, 19(8), 897–905.

Winokur, M.A., Crawford, G.A., Longobardi, R.C. & Valentine, D.P. (2008). 'Matched comparison of children in kinship care and foster care on child welfare outcomes'. *Child Welfare and Foster Care*, 89(3), 338–346.

Wise, S., Da Silva, L., Webster, E. & Sanson, A. (2005). *The Efficacy of Early Childhood Interventions. A Report for the Australian Government of Family and Community Services* (AIFS Research Report No. 14). Melbourne: Australian Institute of Family Studies.

Wolcott, I. (1989). *Family Support Services: A Review of the Literature and Selected Annotated Bibliography*. Melbourne: Australian Institute for Family Studies.

Women's Health Policy and Projects Unit (2007). *Guidelines for Responding to Family and Domestic Violence*. Perth: Women and Newborn Health Service.

Woodhouse, D. & Pengelly, P. (1991). *Anxiety and the Dynamics of Collaboration*. Aberdeen: Aberdeen University Press.

Wyatt Kaminski, J., Valle, L.A., Filene, J.H. & Boyle, C.L. (2008). 'A meta-analytic review of components associated with parent training program effectiveness'. *Journal of Abnormal Child Psychology*, 36, 567–589.

Zanoti-Jeronymo, D. (2009). 'Prevalence of physical abuse in childhood and exposure to parental violence in a Brazilian sample'. *Cadernos de Saude Publica*, 25, 2467–2479.

Zeanah, C.H. & Smyke, A.T. (2005). 'Building attachment relationships following maltreatment and severe deprivation'. In L.J.Berlin, Y.Ziv., L.Amaya-Jackson & M.T.Greenberg (eds), *Enhancing Early Attachments: Theory, Research, Intervention and Policy* (pp. 195–216). New York: Guilford Press.

Zeira, A. (2007). 'A case study of one Israeli family in deep distress: Small steps toward a sensitive outcome'. In M.Berry (ed.), *Identifying Essential Elements of Change: Lessons from International Research in Community Based Family Centres* (pp. 103–112). Leuven: Acco (Academische Coöperatieve Vennootschap cvba).

Zhou, A.Z. & Chilvers, M. (2010). 'Infants in Australian out-of-home care'. *British Journal of Social Work*, 40, 26–43.

Zilberstein, K. (2006). 'Clarifying core characteristics of attachment disorder: A review of current research and theory'. *American Journal of Orthopscyhiatry*, 76, 55–64.

Ziv, Y., Aviezer, O., Gini, M., Sagi, A. & Koren-Karie, N. (2000). 'Emotional availability in the mother-infant dyad as related to the quality of infant–mother attachment relationship'. *Attachment and Human Development*, 2, 149–169.

Zubrick, S.R., Silburn, S.R., Lawrence, D.M., Mitrou, F.G., Dalby, R.B., Blair, E.M., Griffin, J., Milroy, H., De Maio, J.A., Cox, A. & Li, J. (2005). *The Western Australian Aboriginal Child Health Survey: The Social and Emotional Wellbeing of Aboriginal Children and Young People*. Perth: Curtin University of Technology and Telethon Institute for Child Health Research.

Zur, O. (2006). 'Therapeutic boundaries and dual relationships in rural practice: Ethical, clinical and standard of care considerations'. *Journal of Rural Community Psychology*E9(1). Retrieved 12 February 2007, from http://muwww-new.marshall.edu/jrcp/9_1_Zur.htm

Index

Aboriginal Australians
    and colonisation, 124
    assimilation and integration policies, 125
    exclusion from Constitution, 124
    genocide, 124
    'Half-caste Acts', 126
    murder, 124
    protection and assimilation policies, 124
    protectionism, 124, 125
    Stolen Generations, 124, 125–6
Aboriginal Child Placement Principle, 128, 249
Aboriginal communities, 19
Aboriginal families
    and child protection systems, 128–30
    and criminal justice system, 127
    culture, 109–10
    demography, 104–5
    evidence-based programs, 110–13
    family decision making, 130–3
    and government policy, 105–7
    over-representation in care and protection
        systems, 105
    parenting and family functioning, 108
    parenting interventions, 108–9
    safety and protection of children, 110
    sexual abuse of children, 106
    transgenerational parenting, 118–19
    vulnerability, 113–19
        adjustment issues, 117–18
        adjustment processes, 114
        community relationships, 114
        coordination and support, 116–17
        sources of, 114, 115
        stressors, 114
    working with Aboriginal families, 119
Aboriginal Protection and Restriction of the Sales of
        Opium Act 1897 (Qld), 124
Aboriginal Protection Board, 125, 126
Aborigines Act 1905 (WA), 124
Aborigines Act 1910 (NT), 124
Aborigines Protection Act 1869 (Vic), 124
Aborigines Protection Act 1909 (NSW), 124
adult mental health services, capacity of, 26
adult-focused services, 26

advertisements, 64
AEDI. See Australian Early Development Index
AIHW. See Australian Institute of Health and
        Welfare
American Humane Association, 131–2
antisocial behaviour, 172
anxiety, 39, 143
attachment theory, 195–200, 204, 211
    application of, 211
    attachment patterns, 196
    child development areas, 197–9
    disinhibited attachment, 197
    early experimental studies, 195–7
    implications of, 9
    inhibited attachment, 197
    limitations, 200–2
    misunderstanding of, 204–5
    primary attachment, 209–11
    reactive attachment disorder, 197
    Strange Situation, 195, 196
attention deficit disorder, assessment, 167
Australia, Refugee and Humanitarian Program,
        79–80
    visa categories, 80
Australian Centre for Child Protection, 27, 86,
        145, 231, 236, 239, 240
Australian Centre for Social Innovation, 15
Australian Early Development Index
        (AEDI), 105
Australian Institute of Health and Welfare
        (AIHW), 213, 216
Australian Nurse–Family Partnership Program
        (ANFPP), 46, 111
Australian Refugee Association, 99
autism, assessment of, 167

babies' homes, 44
baby farming, 44
'bad' dads, 68–70
    antisocial behaviour, 69
    definition of, 69
    domestic violence, 70
    violence behaviour, 69

behaviour problems, 67, 69, 108, 109, 161, 167, 253, 270
bio-psychosocial perspective, 31
brain development, 10–1
'Bringing Them Home' report, 106, 126
Britain, Crime Surveys, 179
Brown, Vera Scantlebury, 43

Caring Dads program, 183
categorical funding, 25
causal relationships, 146
chaotic circumstances, 235
child health centres. See infant welfare centres
child maltreatment
    family violence, 39, 214
    legal requirements, 31
    parental substance misuse, 164
    parenting behaviour, 108
    unrealistic expectations, 169
child neglect-related interventions, 145
child protection intervention, 195, 218, 222, 231, 236
child removal practices, 105
child welfare
    advances in, 43
    ill-judged interventions, 115
childhood adversity, 7
    consequences, 8
children in out-of-home care
    cultural identity, 217
Children of Parents with a Mental Illness, 26
Children's Protection Society, 45
Circle of Security Model, 9
Closing the Gap framework, 107
cognitive and adaptive abilities, assessment, 167
collaborative partnership, 212
colonisation, 105, 126, 132, 178
conflict management, 162
COPMI. See Children of Parents with a Mental Illness
corporal punishment, 91
court-ordered kinship, 118
culturally and linguistically diverse families, 78

depression, 147
    alcohol abuse and, 29
    genetic influences, 8
    maternal, 12, 109
    maternal drug use, 163
    post-natal, 3, 29, 72
    women suffering from, 182
Depression, 1890s, 44
Depression, Great, 43
Depression Anxiety and Stress Scale, 171
deprofessionalism, 158
developmental theory. See attachment theory

developmental trauma disorder, 203
domestic homicide. See domestic violence
domestic violence, 26, 63, 177–72
    and alcohol, 184–5
    assessment of, 186–8
    diversity, 179–81
    and drugs, 184–5
    during pregnancy, 184
    fathers, 183–4
    financial and emotional abuse, 179
    frequency of, 183
    gendered nature of, 178
    identity politics, 180
    impact on children, 27, 183
    Independent Domestic Violence Advisors, 190
    Indigenous women, 180
    intervention, 177, 189
    intimate partner violence, 182, 185
    mental health disorders, 185
    multi-agency advocacy, 190–1
    nonsexual domestic abuse, 179
    policy and legal context, 189–90
    poly-victimisation, 183
    post-partum abuse, 182
    prevalence of, 178–9
    protective strategies, 187
    risk management, 186–8
    risks of exposure, 183
    Safety in Numbers, 190–1
    safety planning, 186–8
    screening for, 187
    substance dependence, 185
    victims, 181–3
    women with disabilities, 180
drug and alcohol abuse, 63
    parents of children in out-of-home care, 215–16
    SDN Children's Services Parent Program, 51
dysregulated stress response system, 10

early school failure, 161
Early Years Education Research Project, 45
ecological model of human development, 13
Emotional Availability Scale, 168
ERGO (empathy, respect, genuineness, optimism), 21
Evian Conference, 79
evidence-based intervention, 236
evidence-based practice, 144, 240, 245

family-based decision making, 237
Family by Family program, 15
family-centred practice, 7, 18–22
family-centred service, 31

Family Group Conferencing, xxv, 130, 131, 132, 133–40, 252
  appropriate model, 133
  funding, 133
  implementation, 134
  key principles, 134–5
  leverage and motivation for parents, 135
  outcomes of, 135
  partnership agreements, 134, 135, 138
  professional inclusion, 139
  program logic, 134
  referrals received, 138
  stages of, 136–8
  use of, 138
Family Home Visiting program, 46
Family Law Amendment (Shared Parental Responsibility) Act 2006 (Cth), 59
Family Partnership Model, 113
Family Partnership training, 21
Family Sensitive Policy and Practice Toolkit, 27
family theory, 12–13
  guiding principles, 12
family violence. *See* domestic violence
Family Violence Protection Act 2008 (Vic), 177
family workers, tasks for, 60
FASD. *See* Fetal Alcohol Spectrum Disorders
fatherhood, 59–60
  artificial conception, 59
  endorsement of value, 58
  equal shared parental responsibility, 59
  father–adolescent relationship, 67
  father–child relationship, 58, 60, 66
  father's role, 58
  in the media, 58
  legal debate, 59
father-inclusive models, 63
fathering. *See* fatherhood
fathers
  barriers for, 60–2
  depression, 68
  impact of, 66–8
  influence on cognitive abilities, 67
  involvement, 58
  risk of embarrassment, 61
Fetal Alcohol Spectrum Disorders, 161
first-time parent groups, 48–50
Focus on Families program, 216
Froebel, Friedrich, 43

gender symmetry debates, 179
Good Beginnings Australia, 231

Healthy Start program, 242
help-seeking pathways, 61
hippocampal NR3C1 gene expression, 8

HIPPY Program (Home Instruction Program for Pre-School Youngsters), 52
home-based outreach program. *See* Pal
homelessness, 25, 26, 27, 145, 215

implementation framework
  drivers, 243
  implementation benefits of, 244
  innovation and adaptation, 243
  practitioner-led implementation, 242
  stages and drivers model, 243
  stages of, 243
  types of, 242–5
    Healthy Start Program, 242
    Positive Parenting Program, 242
Incredible Years, 108
Independent Domestic Violence Advisors, 190
Indigenous kinship relationships, 178
infant welfare centres, 43, 44
integrated framework, 165–72
  attachment, 168
  developmental outcome, 166–8
  emotional availability, 168
  family routine, 170–1
  goals setting, importance, 172–4
  monitoring, 170–1
  parenting skills, 170–1
  parents' state of mind, 171
  social context, 171–2
  values and expectation, 169
intellectual disability, 214
intergenerational issues, 127
intersectionality theory, 179
Invest to Grow initiative, 47

kin relationships, 132
kindergartens, 43, 44
kinship care, 214

Lady Gowrie Pre-School Child Centre, 44
Let's Start program, 113, 114, 115, 116, 117
life expectancy, 127
Long Gully community, 16
Lutheran Community Care, 99

marginalisation, 132
mediation and conciliation, 36
Men's Behaviour Change Program, 184
mental health
  refugees, 84–5
Mental Health Professional Network, 26
Methodist Babies Home, 45
midwifery, 62

migrant families
    services for, 48
Migrant Resource Centre, 99
monotropy, 210
mother–child relationship, 27
Mothers and Toddlers Program, 163
motor and cognitive developmental
        milestones, 40

Napranum community, 52
National Implementation Research Network, 243
National Institute of Child Health and Human
        Development, 66
neonatal withdrawal symptoms, 161
new programs or practices, 240
new social problems, recognition of, 29
nonsexual domestic abuse, 179
Northern Territory Emergency Response
        (NTER), 106

organisational collaboration, 31–9
    funding, 34
    gatekeeping problems, 34
    inter-agency tensions, 34, 36
    inter-organisational level of analysis, 36
    interpersonal level of analysis, 37–8
    inter-professional level of analysis, 36–7
    intra-personal level of analysis, 38–9
    mediation and conciliation, 36
    supervisor role, 38
    team leader role, 38
organisations
    culture or climate of, 241

paediatric nursing, 62
paediatric surveillance, 29, 46
Pal (Parents and Learning), 52
parent–child attachment, 8–9
    importance of, 9
    quality of, 168
    separation anxiety, 9
parent–worker relationship, 146, 148
    collaborative approach, 151–3
    communication, 153
    personalised role, 148
    professional boundaries, 149
    worker characteristics, 153–9
parental behaviour, dimensions, 168
parental substance misuse
    anxiety, 161
    child maltreatment, 163
    drug and alcohol misuse, 161
    intervention, 162–4
        environment enrichment, 162
        maternal reflective functioning, 162

lifestyle problems, 160
    methadone maintenance, 162
    outcomes for children, 161–2
    social isolation, 161
parenting adaptability, 11–2
    components, 11–2
    variable needs, 12
parenting approach, rigidity in, 143
Parents and Learning. See Pal
parents of children in out-of-home care
    characteristics, 215–16
    child removal, 218–20
        domestic violence, 219
        effects of, 222, 223
        financial issues, 219
        mental health issues, 218
        parental identity, 223
        parental resentment, 220, 221
        relationship brokedown, 219
        substance abuse, 218
    involvement of, 216
    negotiation and reconstruction, 218
    parent–child relationships, 217–18
    parental identity, 224–5
    parental resentment, 220–4
    Parents Plus Playgroup, 231–3
    parents' role, 225–8
    parent–worker relationship, 228
    social support and respectful relation,
        230–1
    workers' role, 228–30
Parents Plus Playgroups, 231–3
Parents Under Pressure (PuP) program
    aim, 163
    effectiveness, 163
    home-based intervention, 163
    integrated framework, 165–72
        developmental outcome, 166–8
        emotional availability and
            attachment, 168
        goals setting, importance of, 172–4
        overview, 165–72
        parenting skills, 170–1
        parents' state of mind, 174
        social context, 171–2
        values and expectation, 169
    substantial changes, 164
    use of, 164
Peck, Sister Murie, 43
physical and psychological safety, 231
pilot home visiting service, 72
    attachment-based framework, 72
    outcomes, 72
placement drift, 199, 211
playgroup movement, 45
poly-victimisation of children, 183
poor self esteem, 143
Positive Parenting Program, 109, 242

post-natal depression, 72
poverty
    attachment theory, 199
    child neglect, 144
    domestic violence, 191
    environmental factors, 108
    integrated framework, 172
    parents of children in out-of-home
        care, 215
    poor health and, 127
    refugees and, 79
    relation with homelessness, 25
    social isolation and, 14, 51, 78, 162, 181
prescriptive knowledge, 17–18
Protector of Aborigines Act 1836 (SA), 124
psychosocial treatments, elements of, 109
psychotherapeutically oriented treatment
        group, 163

Racial Discrimination Act 1975 (Cth), 106
Reactive Attachment Disorder (RAD), 197
refugees, 78–9
    ABCD program, 100
    acculturation, 85–6
    and government agencies, 95
    Australian Refugee Association, 99
    cultural challenges, 94
    decision to leave, 82
    effects on children, 87–90, 92–3
    family roles, changes in, 84
    financial independence, 89
    health, 83
    language and communication, 94–5
    laws and cultural norms, 91–2
    parenting challenges, 87–94
    pre-migration experience, 82
    Refugee and Humanitarian Program, 79–80
    refugee experience, 81–6
    religious beliefs, 94
    resettlement, 80–1, 83
    services for, 48
    social support, 93–4
    source countries, 79
    torture, trauma and family separation, 82
    transition experience, 82–3
    trauma and mental health, 84–5
    unemployment, 83–4
    working with, 86–7, 96–100
        interpreters, selection of, 98–9
relationship-based practice, 20–2
resilient children, 172
role performance, analysis of, 30

Safe from the Start program, 27
Safety in Numbers, 190, 191
Scared Straight, 237–8

school drop outs, 161
school truancy, 161
SDN Children's Services Parent Resource
        Program, 50–2
serotonin transmission, 8
service environment, 241–2
service providers, role, 29
sexual assault, 63
social capital, 16–17
social exclusion, forms of, 25
social inclusion, 24, 25
social isolation, 14, 25, 29, 47, 51, 78, 146,
        161, 216
social networks, 14–15
social services, innovation, 44
staff cohesiveness, 241
Stolen Generations, 105, 124, 125–6, 216
Strange Situation, 195, 196, 247
strengths-based practice, 70–1
    drug abusing father, 70
stress, 10
    anxiety and, 83
    cognitive response, 10
    dysregulated response system, 10
    financial stress, 45
    HPA response system, 8
    negative emotions and, 223
    post-traumatic, 83
    stressful life events, 14
    stressors, 157–9
stress response systems, 8
Stronger Futures legislation, 107
Sydney Day Nurseries Association, 44

teachable moments, 45
theory of change, 238–9
therapeutic playgroups, 27
therapeutic relationships, 20
Through the Looking Glass Project, 47
training workshops for early intervention, 65
transgenerational influence, 127
transgenerational parenting, 118–19
trauma
    acculturation, 85–6
    attachment trauma, 109
    classification, 202
    counselling, 83
    refugees, 84–5
    symptoms, 202
    treatment approaches, 203
    type I, 203
    type II, 203
    women suffering from, 182
trauma theory, 212
traumatic childhood experiences, 161
Triple P. *See* Positive Parenting Program
trust, 148

United Nations Convention on the Rights of
the Child, 59, 190
United Nations Convention on the Status of
Refugees, 78, 80
United Nations High Commissioner for
Refugees (UNHCR), 79
Uniting Church, 45
unmarried mothers, 44
urban–rural fringe community, 50

VACCA. *See* Victorian Aboriginal Child
Care Agency
VACRO. *See* Victorian Association for the Care
and Resettlement of Offenders
Victorian Aboriginal Child Care Agency, 129

Victorian Association for the Care and
Resettlement of Offenders, 27, 41
Victorian Cooperative on Children's
Services, 48
Victorian Maternal and Child Health
Service, 48–50
violent and abusive behaviour, program
for, 73–4
fathering approach, 73–4
parenting issues and skills, 73

welfare payments, 106
worker–parent–child relationship, 22
workplace culture, 201
World Health Organisation, 181